D1124061

Writing History

Writing History

A Professor's Life

Michael Bliss

DUNDURN
TORONTO

Project Editor: Michael Carroll
Editor: Cheryl Hawley
Design: Jesse Hooper
Printer: Transcontinental

Library and Archives Canada Cataloguing in Publication

Bliss, Michael, 1941-
    Writing history : a professor's life / by Michael Bliss.

Issued also in electronic formats.
ISBN 978-1-55488-953-2

    1. Bliss, Michael, 1941-. 2. Historians--Canada--Biography.
I. Title.

FC151.B55A3 2011   907.2'02   C2011-901146-8

1   2   3   4   5   15   14   13   12   11

We acknowledge the support of the **Canada Council for the Arts** and the **Ontario Arts Council** for our publishing program. We also acknowledge the financial support of the **Government of Canada** through the **Canada Book Fund** and **Livres Canada Books**, and the **Government of Ontario** through the **Ontario Book Publishing Tax Credit** and the **Ontario Media Development Corporation**.

Printed and bound in Canada.
www.dundurn.com

Dundurn
3 Church Street, Suite 500
Toronto, Ontario, Canada
M5E 1M2

Gazelle Book Services Limited
White Cross Mills
High Town, Lancaster, England
LA1 4XS

Dundurn
2250 Military Road
Tonawanda, NY
U.S.A. 14150

To Kate, Michael, Jasmin, and Joe

Contents

"It's a life's work to see yourself for what you really are and even then you might be wrong."

— Cormac McCarthy, *No Country for Old Men*

"Look," he said ... "I've a whole life behind me that I love and wouldn't want to lose. I'm everything that I've ever been, I'm what's happened to me, not what's happening this instant, not just that."

— Hugh Hood, "Fallings from Us, Vanishings"

"I live in a sort of vacuum, and I suspect that most other writers do too."

— H.L. Mencken, *The Diary of H.L. Mencken*

"the fine quiet of the scholar which is nearest of all things to heavenly peace"

— F. Scott Fitzgerald, *Tender Is the Night*

Introduction

Most of my life has been spent trying to teach and write history. For three years after graduation I taught history to high school students, and then had a thirty-eight-year career as a history professor at the University of Toronto. I taught several thousand students, published a lot of books and articles, including four biographies, and maintained a parallel presence in the wider world as a popularizer and journalist. When I retired from teaching in 2006, with all scholarly projects finished and journalism wound down, it seemed time to look back on my own life as it was lived in a certain period of Canadian and world history. A lot had happened since I was born in a small Canadian town on the shores of Lake Erie during the worst days of the Second World War. As a professional biographer, it was natural to turn from trying to make sense of other people's lives to putting together the pieces of my own.

Not that I have exciting or harrowing war stories to tell. Not that my life was particularly exciting or even colourful — though it's true that lightning struck our house on the day of my retirement. Born into an upper-middle-class family, I was brought up in comparative affluence, had good schooling, made a good marriage, and worked hard and fairly successfully at my profession. We have lived for more than forty years in one of Toronto's most idyllic middle-class suburbs, and we have a summer home in paradise on Prince Edward Island. I was not physically abused as a child, did not experiment with drugs or sex in the sixties, did not crack up in middle age, was blessed with a wonderful family, and was promoted and honoured for my work. My worst health problem was a lifelong struggle with flabbiness. My most serious bouts of depression had a habit of lifting after about six hours. I was not a world traveller — on sabbaticals from the university I simply worked harder — and was not very intimate with the rich and famous.

Why should you bother to keep reading? Because there was enough substance to my life to make it not without interest to readers who wonder about what it was like to be a university professor in North America in the last half of the twentieth century. It's not without interest to a range of people interested in the areas of history that I cultivated — Canada, medicine, biography — and in the process of writing history. Being a public intellectual in Canada had its moments, as did a publishing and speaking career in the history of medicine. Even privileged families have their dark sides, most high-achievers have their doubts and down times. I always thought and wrote a lot about life as I lived it, and am able to root this memoir in heaps of correspondence and diaries. I came to know quite a few people. Several of my books will be taken seriously for a few more years; most have lasted for at least the ten years that Cyril Connolly thought was a mark of literary success.

I worked hard at trying to write well. The highest praise for my books and articles was that they were sometimes hard to put down, despite the apparent dullness of their topic. An artist can do a lot with a few apples and oranges on a table. Almost every life is interesting enough to sustain a book if you know how to write it and if there is one person curious enough to start reading. The default readership is, of course, the grandchildren, but the publisher bets there will be others.

I first thought that any memoir I wrote would be titled *Nothing to Believe In*. As a youth I was deeply religious. For a few years as an undergraduate I planned to study theology with a view to becoming a minister of the United Church of Canada. All those ideas washed away during a long shower one Saturday morning in the autumn of 1961, and for the rest of my life I have been without religious belief. A deep skepticism, both temperamental and methodological, came to shape my approach to writing history and to many aspects of getting on in life. Sometimes it was hard and lonely to do without the assurances and sense of community the church had offered. The prospect that human life is inherently meaningless and very short isn't nearly as comforting as belief in the possibility of personal salvation and eternal life. You go on, you get by as best you can, despite having nothing to believe in — and, while you normally do not talk about these things, you sense that quite a few other people are having the same struggles.

But, of course, you have another set of beliefs that you're acting on every day. Some of your beliefs are provisional and situational, others are imbedded into your genes or bored into your soul by your parents. You realize these beliefs in the way you live, and, if you're a history professor, in the books you write and the way you approach the past. My other books are approaches to the Canadian past, to the search for salvation through medical progress, and to the problems of writing biography. In this book, perhaps reflecting most biographers' eventual return to their favourite subject, I'm approaching my own past. I was made by my family, my town and my country, our then Judaeo-Christian culture, the intellectual climate of the 1950s, and ongoing dollops of good luck. In turn I made books and helped make other historians. This book is an attempt to describe and explain how it all was made.

Nothing is invented or reimagined in these pages. I do not believe in the oxymoronic and now discredited genre of "creative non-fiction." I have tried to make this memoir as honest as I possibly can. I have tried to be self-critical, just as I have been critical of some — by no means all — of my colleagues in a professoriate that too often falls short of its proclaimed standards. While it seems pointless to refight old (and often losing) battles, it is not wrong to indicate the sources of the frustrations and anger and disappointments that sometimes accompanied an energetic life in our times.

In cutting down a longer manuscript — an autobiography written for the family archive as opposed to readers' interests — I have retained some references to the troubled members of my family and to the interaction of family values and private events on professional life. As a biographer I do not believe the public and private sides of life can or should be segregated. At the very least I could not have had the career I describe here without it having been deeply rooted in middle class Canadian values, a great marriage, and a rich family life.

Staying true to the values that gave stability to our personal lives was, in fact, Liz Bliss's and my highest priority. To anticipate, this helps to explain, for example, why we were reluctant to disrupt our family situation in Toronto to go chasing after professional will-o'-the-wisps. More important, it emphasizes that the most important event in the making of my life as a historian, took place on a Saturday night in 1957 when a couple of us decided to skip out of the Sadie Hawkins Day teen dance in Kingsville, Ontario, and go down the road to Harrow. Sadie Hawkins Day ... teen dances ... Kingsville ... Harrow ... 1957. The delight of doing history is that you get used to moving around in time and telling audiences what you remember having seen, what you make of the past — their past and, in this book, my past.

Thanks to Jack Granatstein, Paul Rutherford, and Liz Bliss for good advice after reading early drafts of this memoir, and thanks to Linda McKnight of Westwood Creative Artists for putting me in the good publishing hands of Dundurn Press.

Chapter One

═══════════════

Main Street, Kingsville

I was born on January 18, 1941. We lived in the little Canadian town of Kingsville, Ontario.

Canada had been at war against Germany since September 1939. In January 1941, the Battle of Britain was at its height, as the United Kingdom and the British Empire faced the prospect of German invasion across the English Channel. At the time of my conception the German blitzkrieg had just begun sweeping across the European continent. I don't know whether I was created in a moment of escape from depressing public events, as a statement of hope in the future, as an accident, or as some combination of these.

Except for the men who served and their families, the war was having no visible effect on a tranquil Canadian town thousands of miles from battle. No one in our family joined the military — though dad, who was a doctor, did have to work extra hard because of the doctor shortages caused by war. My only wartime memories are of playing with ration coupons in one of the kitchen drawers, and of being taken to our two Victory Day parades in 1945, first when Germany surrendered, then when Japan collapsed. I was given little flags to wave, but could not see very well through the crowds of big people.

Memories are dim in the fog of infancy. One is of being a silly toddler, rolling around on the floor trying to be the centre of big people's attention. Another, more vivid because it seems to have happened many times, is of crying in my crib in a darkened room. Mother, who I also knew as a warm and comforting presence, seemed to have abandoned me. No amount of sobbing or pleading — desperate, heartfelt, my world seemed to be ending — would bring her back. Sometimes the memory is that she had put me to bed because I had been bad. Sometimes it seems that she put me to bed without my supper, and part of my anguish was physical hunger. Perhaps she had just put me to bed for the night. Whatever the reality, the symbolism — of being deprived, starved, desperately hungry for mother's love — is clear enough.

Kingsville is Canada's most southerly town. It lies on the Lake Erie shore about forty kilometres southeast of Windsor/Detroit. My parents' families, Blisses and Crowes, had lived in Canada for many generations, but they had been border people, moving easily in and out of the United States. Both male lines consisted of white Anglo-Saxon Protestants who had originally settled in the American colonies. The first Bliss, Thomas, a Puritan, came out from Bristol, England, landing in Massachusetts Bay in 1635, fifteen years after the arrival of the Mayflower. My Crowe ancestors were Pennsylvania Dutch ("Deutsch"), who immigrated from Germany in the seventeenth or early eighteenth centuries. Their original surname was Groh, and they were probably members of the Mennonite or Dunker sects.

My ancestors on both sides left for Canada soon after the American Revolution. Johannes Groh settled in Pelham Township on Upper Canada's Niagara Peninsula, in 1788, where he received land grants as a United Empire Loyalist. Samuel Bliss moved a few miles north from Stafford, Vermont, to the settlement of Compton, in the fertile Eastern Townships of Lower Canada (Quebec), in 1810. The Blisses were part of what is sometimes called a "late Loyalist" migration, though by that time loyalty and the search for good farmland were often interchangeable; the Townships had just been opened for settlement.

Many years after "Groh" became "Crow," my mother's brothers objected to being teased as blackbirds and added an "e." The Groh/Crow(e)s farmed and did carpentry in the Niagara region. Mother was born on a farm near the village of Fenwick in 1909. In Quebec, the Blisses did well in cattle for several generations. Father was born on the family farm in 1903, but left it forever when he enrolled as a medical student at Queen's University in Kingston, Ontario. After graduation he began practicing in Chippawa, Ontario, a village on the Niagara River, where Annie Crowe happened to be teaching school. They fell in love, married in Detroit in 1929, and lived for three years in Drayton, Ontario, before dad relocated to Kingsville. My big brother Jim was born in Drayton in 1930, almost exactly nine months after our parents' wedding night at the Statler Hotel in Cleveland.

Kingsville had (and has) two principal streets, Main and Division. Main Street is part of Highway 18, which runs along the Lake Erie shore. Division Street crosses it, and ends about a kilometre south, at the lake. The town developed around the intersection of Main and Division, the "Four Corners," being originally a crossroads hamlet with a fishing harbour.

In the 1890s Kingsville had a growth spurt, becoming a town in 1901 as a result of the odd combination of natural-gas discoveries along the Erie shore and its popularity as a summer resort. Hiram Walker, an American-born, Windsor-based whisky distiller, promoted Kingsville-by-the-Lake as a fresh-air, clean-water playground for the well-to-do. He invested heavily in resort hotels, and backed an electric street railway company that built tracks out from Windsor through the lush Essex County countryside to Kingsville.

Unable to compete with the automobile, the streetcars had stopped running in the Great Depression of the 1930s. After the war, in Kingsville and all across rural Ontario, their tracks were ripped up or paved over. The old rails could still be seen on Main and Division before the first postwar resurfacing. After that, the town's transportation landmark was its only stoplight, a four-sided electric beacon on a concrete and iron stand in the exact centre of the intersection, the exact centre of town. It was the last of its kind in North America, regularly run into by cars and trucks.

Kingsville in the 1940s, population about 2,500, was Mariposa on Lake Erie. It was redolent of Dayton, Ohio, in 1904, Winesburg, Ohio, Gopher Prairie and Lake Wobegon, Minnesota, Robertson Davies's Deptford, and Thornton Wilder's Our Town, and it was exactly on the fringe of Alice Munro country. It was every-small-town North America, a coherent, contained world, where most people knew each other's names and quite a bit about their lives and watched over the little ones. The business area stretched about a block in each direction from the Four Corners. Classic late Victorian red-brick "blocks" lined the south side of Main Street, stores below and apartments above. On the northeast corner of the intersection stood the town's red brick post office. We picked up our mail there, for there was neither home delivery nor street addresses. "Kingsville, Ontario" was all the address needed to reach anyone in town.

Division Street South ran past the Roxy movie theatre and the Carnegie library, then past Epworth United Church and down to the lake past a dozen blocks of elm-shaded homes, Ontario brick and ginger-bread vernacular mixed with standard white frame. Railway tracks looped through the community. Division Street South ended at Lakeshore Park and a government fish hatchery. The town had half a dozen gas stations, seven churches (United, Roman Catholic, Anglican, Baptist, Lutheran, Pentecostal, and Salvation Army), two bandshells, a Lions Club Park, a factory district and Conklin's lumberyard, wharfs for fishing boats and a coal dock in the harbour area, a few secluded and grand mansions, and perhaps twenty residential blocks of unpretentious frame houses. Shady porches girdled most homes. Sidewalks ended about half a mile north, east, and west of the Four Corners. On the fringes of town, houses began to thin, yards became fields, barns appeared, and you were suddenly out in the country.

The centre of my world was our big brick house on a double lot on the north side of Main Street, half a block east of the Four Corners. When I grew old enough to expand my territory by tricycle — like Matt Goderich in Hugh Hood's *The Swing in the Garden* — I would turn right, pass by the Kingsville Fire Department, then Babcock's Restaurant, then a tobacco warehouse in the old Methodist Church, then the Kingsville Hotel, and finally reach the post office at the Four Corners. When I turned left, I passed half a dozen homes with chestnut trees in their front yards, then reached the end of the block at Spruce Street.

On the other side of Main Street — I was not allowed to cross on my own — there was a Cockshutt farm-implement dealership, Cliff William's car dealership and appliance store, and the Kingsville Cold Storage Company. Twice a year the street in front of our house was taken over by men in camouflage outfits carrying guns — hunters bringing their bag of Pelee Island pheasants in to the cold storage before the advent of home freezers.

Now almost a bedroom suburb of Windsor, Kingsville still centres (barely) on its downtown corners, but the streetscape has changed almost beyond recognition. Only the library and the churches seem unchanged. Our old house has gone. It was quite beautiful, built in 1914 of red brick, a two-storey core with single-storey east and west wings, white trim, a vaguely Spanish or Californian red-tile roof, and lawns shaded by birch, maple, poplar, butternut, and willow trees. We also owned a back lot running through to the street behind us. The west wing of the house, which had a separate front entrance, housed my father's offices. A small sign on the lawn announced, "Dr. Q. Bliss, Physician and Surgeon." We had a screened-in back porch, big lawns, and a large vegetable garden in the back lot. The two-car stone garage had been originally conceived as a stable. It was a big, beautiful doctor's house on Main Street.

Kingsville in the 1940s was a quiet Canadian town slumbering in summer sunshine, the children playing in their yards — there's Doc

Bliss's little boy — or playing next door at the fire hall with the kids who lived in its upstairs apartments. The last horses drew the Kingsville Dairy's milk wagons, clopping amiably, knowing every stop on their routes. Milk came in glass pint and quart bottles, the cream sitting three inches thick at the top. The milk man put the fresh bottles on the back step, collected empties and coins, and hopped on as Dobbin trudged on to the next house. Ice wagons and bread wagons had either vanished from the streets or have vanished from my memory, but black Model T and Model A Fords were everywhere. Saturdays, when the farmers came to town, were the busiest days of the week. Dad's Saturday night office hours were particularly busy, and he would often not finish with his last patient until after ten o'clock.

On summer Sunday mornings the hymn-singing from the Pentecostal Church on the back street drifted through our upstairs windows. We walked or drove three blocks to our own church, Epworth United, the largest in town, whose big pipe organ often drowned out its congregation. Epworth was red-brick and dark wood, and had a Sunday School wing and a Memorial Hall, which effectively served as the town's community centre. The first time I remember seeing my name pointed out was on a little paper blue boot on the Sunday School's Cradle Roll. Dad seldom went to church, and mother often seemed too tired to go, but I somehow got there every Sunday, cradled, as it were, by the United Church of Canada.

Mother often took me with her in the car when she drove nine miles east to Leamington, where her parents, Alandes and Minnie Crowe, lived in retirement. Gramma was bedridden with arthritis, and mother was a dutiful daughter. On the way to Leamington, mother might take me down Wigle Lane, where a farmer kept a mangy old black bear in a pit by the side of the road as a kind of local curiosity. Sometimes we would enter Leamington by the road past the H.J. Heinz factory, principally devoted to making ketchup and tomato sauces. When Heinz was cooking, Leamington, the tomato capital of Canada, smelled like ketchup. Most of King's Highway 18 also smelled like tomatoes because so many had fallen from the baskets piled on the wagons and trucks and had been ground to pulp. Tomato blood on the highways.

Toddling and tricycling.

Essex County, the sunny southwestern tip of Ontario, has Canada's most fertile soil and its most temperate climate. In summer it is lush with vegetables and fruit and hundreds of roadside stands. Leamington still has its giant red tomato in the heart of town, and the Heinz plant, a little reduced by free trade, still makes ketchup.

In the 1890s, Canada's first wineries were created on Pelee Island, a few miles out in the lake from the Point Pelee spit, which runs south from the Leamington shore. Driving out on Point Pelee you cross the forty-second parallel, which is also the northern boundary of California. Essex County trivia: twenty-six American states lie wholly or partly north of Canada's "Sun Parlour."

The wineries had disappeared by the 1940s, killed by grape disease and the prohibition experiment (they have since returned). Farmers grew table grapes, peach and apple orchards flourished, fields of sweet corn and tomatoes were everywhere, and greenhouses were beginning to gobble up acreage, despite the effect that summer hailstorms had on panes — then glass, now plastic. Tobacco had been brought to Essex County at the end of the nineteenth century by white share-croppers from the American south and was still an important crop in a decade when everyone still smoked, including my doctor father and his nurse. Our backyard sometimes reeked of tobacco because our neighbour, Archie McLean, had a brick tobacco factory behind his house, one of half a dozen or more in the town. It mostly sat idle, but reopened for a few years in the 1940s to make Macdonald brand cigarettes. The original share-croppers in Essex County did so well in tobacco that they were able to buy out their landlords.

As a farmer's daughter from the almost as lush Niagara Peninsula, mother had a passion for fresh fruits and vegetables, and was always driving into the country to favoured suppliers of newly picked tomatoes, green beans, peas, beets, peaches, cherries, and corn. Some years our own vegetable garden filled almost the whole back lot, and included water-melons, cucumbers, cantaloupe, and flowers grown from seed. My first "work" experiences were helping mother tend the garden. She no longer killed her own chickens — on friends' farms I did see the barnyard start to Sunday dinner — though once dad was given a rooster as payment for his services. Every morning in those years we heard roosters crowing at dawn and later the eight o'clock factory whistles calling people to work.

Essex County summers were hot and sticky, the heat of the night sometimes out of the deep south, with no one able to sleep and voices and curses carrying up the street when the Kingsville Hotel's "beverage room" — the town's beer parlour — emptied at midnight. Some years a species of fish fly plagued the Lake Erie shore. Billions descended on us, seeking light, carpeting our screens and our streets. Street lights were wrapped in red cloth to try to deter them, giving the town an even eerier, vaguely Tennessee Williams-like appearance. The fish flies settled in patches of light on the streets, and were crunched by passing cars. I would lie in bed and through screened windows hear the cars, the drunks from the hotel, and, after Vern Lowes opened a bowling alley across the street from us, the balls rolling and the crash of tenpins. When I was finally allowed to go all the way around the block on my tricycle I would peddle very fast past the pool hall, a hole in the wall of one of the town's oldest brick blocks, whose proprietor, grey and cadaverous, would sometimes be standing on its doorstep, seemingly afraid to come out into a world of breathable air. About 1950, someone opened a teen-friendly, bright, and clean pool room on Main Street; the grey old man on the back street hung himself.

A heat wave would end in spectacular thunderstorms — more of them a year than in any other part of Canada. The sound of rain on the tin roof of our back porch soothed a boy drifting off to sleep. So did the lonely whistle of passing trains. Then I would be jolted awake by the wail of the big siren next door, calling Kingsville's volunteer firefighters to man the trucks and fight a blaze — often caused by lightning. I would be held up to a bedroom window to watch the men come running up, struggle into their fire coats and hats, then roar off in the big red pumper and ladder trucks. "Where's the fire?" "Where's the fire?" everyone would ask Dorothy Bailey, the plump little woman who turned the big wheel that opened the doors of the fire hall. One evening we, and many others, followed the trucks to a spectacular house fire out in the country. The flames lit the night, the family stood huddled and forlorn, the roof collapsed, and the crowd went home.

Kingsville's population doubled in summer. The grand old resort hotels — the Mettawas, the Lakeshore Terrace, the Grovedale House — had closed or shrunk, but cottaging along the Lake Erie shore continued, even as the quality of the lake's water deteriorated. Americans owned many of the summer places west of town at Linden and Cedar beaches. American powerboat "squadrons" from Sandusky and Cleveland, Ohio, made annual visits to the town; we would ogle the chrome and white Chris-Craft yachts, such a contrast to the dumpy fishing boats berthed in our harbour. Nobody in Kingsville owned a power or pleasure boat. Very early on, I heard table talk disapproving of loud, pushy, and gaudily dressed Americans, especially those who demanded immediate medical attention instead of waiting their turn.

On a summer weekend, big new Pontiacs, Buicks, and Cadillacs with Michigan licence plates could be seen parked by creeks and streams out in the county. Newly well-to-do black autoworkers and their families fished and picnicked and perhaps reminisced about summertime and easy living before they had moved north. Dad once told me that on summer nights in the 1930s an outdoor boxing ring was set up at Lakeside Park and good amateur fight cards were held. Joe Louis, he said, once boxed in Kingsville. Dad picked up extra money as ring doctor. He could do nothing the night a fighter swallowed his mouthpiece and died.

Mother took me swimming on summer afternoons, sometimes to a friend's cottage, but usually at the coal dock at the harbour. We walked past coal piles, walked literally over the coals, and then went out on the pier to swim and sun. This seemed healthier than swimming from beaches where shallow waters were brown and gucky and spotted with dead fish floating belly-up (fun to throw at friends, though). Off the coal dock the water seemed cleaner. It was also deeper, over my head in most places. I was starting to learn to swim by age eight or nine, but one day, like a lemming, I followed a group of big kids jumping off the dock, found myself in over my head, and had to be rescued by mother. Back at home we washed off the sand and the coal dust and mom made lemonade or would give me a nickel to take to Babcock's for an ice cream cone.

No one did much birdwatching at Point Pelee National Park in those years (through the 1950s we went to Point Pelee to buy apples, picnic, swim, and take girls), but in the spring and fall everyone gawked at the big "V"s of Canada geese migrating north or south. Because of its southernmost location on a major flyway, Kingsville's other claim to fame was the presence of Jack Miner's bird sanctuary, two miles out of town. Geese could land and feed safely in Miner's fields; some would be trapped and banded to help study migration patterns. Hunters from the Arctic to the Caribbean would mail back aluminum bands to Jack Miner, Kingsville, Ontario, and possibly also read the verse of holy scripture stamped on each band.

"Wild Goose" Jack had built the sanctuary and an international reputation as a great conservationist in the early years of the twentieth century. He was a patient of dad's and I remember being brought into the office and bounced on "Uncle" Jack's knee. When there was nothing else to do in town, the last resort was to go out to Jack Miner's to see the geese in his fields and the peacocks and other exotic birds kept in cages on the sanctuary grounds. Sunday and holiday crowds at Miner's could be huge. These days the sanctuary is run by a foundation, and on a recent visit the old brick buildings and the very few birds seemed woebegone, beyond their time. In most cities, Canada geese are despised as dirty, polluting pests. No longer a threatened species, they are regularly culled. It's the hunters who are now a dying breed, vastly outnumbered by peaceful birders. Hardly anyone serves goose as a holiday delicacy or at any other time of the year, though at the start of this century, Kingsville's best Main Street restaurant was The Vintage Goose.

Even after discounting for childhood memory tricks, winters in the 1940s and 1950s were colder and snowier than they have been recently. Most of Lake Erie froze during several of my boyhood winters. The lake in front of town would become a gleaming winter playground — pleasure skaters and shinny players near the shore, farther out the big ice-boats with sails and heavy iron runners and terrifying speed. Cars and trucks could drive to Pelee Island. I learned to skate at the outdoor rink at the public school, and often skated miles on the lake, but somehow missed being introduced to hockey. There was no indoor rink, no artificial ice in town.

My parents took me to my first movies, the great Disney animated features: *Bambi* (it was no big deal in a hunting town in wartime when Bambi's mother was shot), *Snow White and the Seven Dwarfs*, and *Pinocchio*. From about age five, I managed to get to the Roxy every Saturday afternoon for the matinée double feature. Admission was twelve cents; a box of Super-Pufft popcorn another dime. We started lining up an hour before showtime. Hundreds of us chattered and cheered, ran up and down the aisles, stood on the seats, tossed popcorn. The ushers often had to turn on the lights and stop the show until we calmed down. We chased bad guys with Roy Rogers, Gene Autry, Hopalong Cassidy, and old Tom Mix. We rounded up stampeding cattle, raced across the badlands, robbed stages, fought Indians, shot it out with the gunslingers at high noon. I would gallop home from the theatre, edging my way round doorways, in a kind of western-movie trance.

All the rest of the week we played cowboys and Indians, sometimes cops and robbers. Bang, bang, you're dead. Not just with cocked finger: Kids in the 1940s had arsenals of cap guns — fake six-shooters in holsters on gun belts, and fake rifles with hammer mechanisms that would fire small percussion paper caps, making agreeable gunshot noises, sometimes giving off real sparks and smoke. Adults, who today would be appalled, took our war games as a matter of course. The world had just finished a real war, and most of us would soon learn to handle real guns, either hunting deer, duck, pheasant, and geese or in the high school cadet corps. About 1951, clever marketers created a children's craze for American Civil War hats. Every little boy in Kingsville wore either Union blue or the more popular Confederate grey, as we blasted away at one another, stopping just short of fixing bayonets.

I played with all the kids in our part of town — the Baileys and Beacoms from the fire hall apartments, the Kubises who took over the restaurant from the Babcocks, the kids who lived in the mean, hot apartments over Main Street stores, the garbagemen's kids, the kids to whose parents dad never sent bills and to whom mother sometimes gave our cast-off clothes. Life in a small town was necessarily democratic, and I like to think that aspects of that stayed with me all my life. In later years we never tried to hide ourselves and our children from the real world.

In Kingsville we all looked after Sammy, the mentally handicapped child of our dentist, and often helped him home. "Hello, Mr. Fox," we said respectfully to the straight-backed, formally dressed old man who lived in the big house down the street and came by at exactly 10:15 each morning on his way to the post office (mother told me he had promised a dying fiancée that he would never love another, and he had been a lonely bachelor ever since).

On Hallowe'en we went out with bars of soap to soap windows, but never quite screwed up our courage. Nor were there any outhouses left in town to overturn — lots of them were trashed out in the country.

Mother hated it when I played in the alleys behind Main Street, where we made playgrounds out of lumber piles and orange crates, and she absolutely forbade me from going down to Segar Augustine's creek ("crick") where, remembering the Depression, she thought tramps and hobos still hung out. She tried to confine me to our yard. The trees and bushes were okay for hide-and-seek, but were nowhere near as neat for hideouts as the window wells at the fire hall or the sheds behind the restaurant. Our back lot did make a good battlefield. I dug trenches and foxholes behind the garden and, the Civil War having literally become old hat, we practised our sniping and machine-gunning on the Western front and the beaches of Guadalcanal.

On our front lawns we built great snow forts — the big kids raised the walls way over my head — and then had snowball wars. Hard, icy snowballs hurt a lot. It was more fun for a little boy to throw snow at the high school girls as they marched by at lunch hour and "after four." High school boys were too apt to retaliate, and even some of the girls, losing their cool, would sometimes grab me and wash my face with snow. On perfect winter days there was tobogganing at Conklin's hill. It now seems impossibly small; can it have shrunk? Mother always maintained that it was on a toboggan run with me that she hurt her back, an injury that bothered her for the rest of her life.

Perhaps it was snowballing that gave me the idea to silence brother Jim. He was practising at our piano, playing a Chopin polonaise loudly and endlessly. I got an egg from the fridge, heaved it with perfect accuracy, and was seriously spanked. I never liked the piano, and when it came my turn to take music lessons was a terrible student.

What I really liked to do at home after school and after supper was listen to the radio. Our cabinet-model Philco was the most important piece of furniture in our den, and I spent the last of radio's golden years lying on my stomach in front of it, moving the dial from WXYZ to WJR and WWJ, the Detroit network stations. They carried all the classic shows: *Amos 'n Andy*, *Beulah*, *Jack Benny*, *The Shadow*, *Mr. Keen: Tracer of Lost Persons*, *Gangbusters*, *Inner Sanctum*, *The Lone Ranger*, *Captain Midnight*, *Tom Mix*, *Superman*. Dad made us listen to Lowell Thomas and the evening news, and to Walter Winchell and Drew Pearson on Sundays. When I was home sick from school I listened to some of the great soap operas: *The Romance of Helen Trent*, *Our Gal Sunday*, the rest of the names too interchangeable to remember.

Ninety-five percent of our radio content was American. Windsor's principal station, CKLW, was American-owned and was, in fact, part of the old Mutual Network. When CBC Radio came to Windsor, about 1950, the station was hard to find on the dial and the programming seemed endlessly stuffy. The only exception was *The Happy Gang*, with Eddie Allen and Bert Pearl. There was also a guy with a gravelly voice, apparently named "Rawhide," doing skits that seemed to amuse my brother. He also liked to listen to two Canadian comedians named Wayne and Shuster.

I was about eight or nine when I first saw television. When Cliff Williams, the automobile and appliance dealer across the street, got his first sets to put on display I was invited to come over and watch. I went expecting to see a visual version of the radio program I had been listening to, *Blondie*, and was disappointed that it was just a stupid variety show, with people named Sid Caesar and Imogene Coco. For several years the only television I saw was in appliance dealers' showrooms or windows — a television set playing in a store window would draw a crowd on the coldest night of winter — but then old Mr. Crawford, a neighbour on Main Street, took to inviting me to his house to watch wrestling and boxing matches. He sat in his chair and smoked his big cigars, I sat on the floor and munched popcorn and developed a lifelong fascination with boxing.

There was no daycare, no organized preschool. Big brother Jim was ten years older, so despite my trying constantly to get him to play with me, I was effectively an only child. I started kindergarten later than some of my friends because of my January birthdate. Kingsville Public School was only two blocks away. Our kindergarten classes, taught by Miss Hanna, were in the "little school," a new red-brick building across the street from the old red-brick "big school." Both schools still had separate entrances for girls and boys. The highlight of each half-day at kindergarten would be our milk break, when "Bacy" Beacom, who worked at the Kingsville Dairy, would bring in cases of half-pint bottles of white and chocolate milk. Larry Taggart and I would race to see who could drink his milk the fastest.

Town life was most interesting outside of school. Like when the Planter Company's float, with "Mister Peanut" prancing and scattering samples, drove musically up and down our streets. Or when a barnstorming strong man pulled a bus, when he actually lifted the bus, and did all manner of other feats. Barnstorming ball teams still came to town in the 1940s — the old House of David team from Michigan, an odd product of a failed religious co-operative, whose shtick was their long black beards; Al Schacht, who was either the Clown Prince of Baseball or he was the King with His Court (a catcher and a single outfielder, because he struck out everyone); the hustlers who organized games of Donkey Baseball — the players had to ride around the bases. Soft summer nights — Essex County memories always come back to summer — watching ball games at the Lions Club Park; the wonderful weeks of the Lions Club Carnival and the Kingsville Fair.

All the high school plays were put on in Memorial Hall; so was the town's annual Minstrel Show, its cast a group of young marrieds who sang and danced in blackface and told bad darkie jokes. Bill Brundage, principal of the public school, was always "Mistah Intahlocatah." The church's women raised money by cooking and serving wonderful dinners, including the annual Father-and-Son Banquet, and the annual Sportsman's Dinner. Foster Hewitt, the hockey broadcaster, was the guest of honor at one of these feeds. In 1950, old Connie Mack, legendary manager of the old Philadelphia Athletics, signed my program, with a scrawl that seemed to read "Commie Wack."

I was a normal little boy in almost every way, but notably precocious and almost immediately tagged for acceleration in school. I read early and well, and within a year of getting my first library card had gone through everything on the small children's shelves in the Kingsville Library. My early favourite was Dr. Seuss's first book, *To Think That I Saw it on Mulberry Street*. In grade one about nine of us were singled out to "skip" grade two, taking two years in one.

A rabid dog bit my playmate, Bill Fuller, in our yard one day. I hid out from it in the garage and was never bitten, but my parents felt I had to be immunized against rabies. I have no memory of the long series of painful needles in the stomach that I had to endure, nor of the fact (related in the *Kingsville Reporter* many years later by Bill Fuller's mother) that after the first couple of shots I went into my father's dispensary, found the vials of vaccine, and poured them down his sink, saying I had had enough.

Mother and dad were warm presences to a little boy, mother the more enveloping as dad was so very busy. Mother ran the household, dad was the hard-working doctor, serving his very large practice. He had a special "D" on our car's licence plates to give him exemption from speeding and parking laws, and we had a simple telephone number to give to the operator when you were making a call: "Number 9." The same number for both office and house, and for years there always had to be someone in the house to answer the phone, because what if it were an emergency? Mother seemed to work very hard, too, getting three meals a day for all of us, keeping our big house going, gardening, decorating, seeing her parents in Leamington, supervising our cleaning woman and yard help, ironing my baby brother's diapers, nagging and complaining about shoddy work.

She would spank me when I was naughty, though if I were really naughty I would have to wait till dad came home to give me several whacks with his razor strap. These hurt a lot, and today seem like parental cruelty bordering on child abuse, but corporal punishment of children was absolutely normal and I never for a moment doubted my father's love. The real trouble was that maternal love in our family had a way of being conditional on good behaviour. God, my "Heavenly Father" mother called him, expected me to shape up. One sultry summer night I insisted on rushing right out after supper to get in more play time — it was still light and the cicadas had not yet stopped. Mother told me not to go and I said I was going anyway. "Heavenly Father won't like it," she said. I headed out anyway, and was halfway down our back stairs when a storm began with an enormous clap of thunder. In hysterics, thinking that Heavenly Father was going to kill me, I rushed back into the house, and had to be comforted.

Other times when I was mischievous or disobedient, no more than any normal little boy, mother would withdraw her love and threaten to send me away. I would have to go to the Children's Shelter in Leamington, she would say, and on occasion she would threaten to call up Mr. Brown, who ran the shelter, and have him come and get me. There was apparently a real Mr. Brown, and one day in my father's offices, where I would trespass from time to time, I was told that I had better get out because Mr. Brown was in the waiting room. Again, I fled crying in terror. Gradually the spectre of Mr. Brown — a terrible threat to inflict on a child — was replaced by the threat of being sent to "boarding school" if I did not toe the expected lines, both at home and at school.

The real problem for my parents was what to do with me in the summer months. Aunt Mary was a widowed schoolteacher, a doting aunt who looked on Jim and me as her surrogate children. If she was not visiting us in Kingsville in the summer, serving as a second mother, then we were visiting her in Niagara Falls, and sometimes I would spend weeks there. Aunt Mamie, a warm and personable first-grade teacher, never threatened to send me away. From her home on Armoury Street

I could hear the nearby falls at night; sometimes in the summer I would be taken to see the spectacular displays of coloured lights on the water. I still feel possessively nostalgic about Niagara Falls. I was sent to stay at Aunt Mamie's in June 1950 while mother gave birth to a third son, Robert, almost exactly twenty years younger than my brother Jim. I was now the middle boy.

The summer of 1950 also saw one of the worst polio epidemics in North American history. Like most children, I had gone through the routine childhood infectious diseases — chicken pox, two kinds of measles, mumps — but had escaped the really serious ones — whooping cough, scarlet fever, and the dreaded infantile paralysis. Mother and dad thought that one summer I did suffer a very mild case of polio, but they could not be certain, and they were particularly (and rightly) worried that the polio virus was water-borne. I could not be kept out of the water during a Kingsville summer. Everyone knew that Lake Erie was becoming seriously polluted. There seemed to be more dead fish every summer, and to prove my vulnerability I would begin each swimming season with a case of "pink eye" (conjunctivitis) caught from something in the water. Brother Jim was off to university, and with a new baby at home and dad's health becoming increasingly uncertain, my parents investigated the idea of sending me to a summer camp in northern Ontario.

Another well-to-do Kingsville family told them of the Taylor Statten Camps in Algonquin Park. In the winter of 1950–51 an interesting-looking brochure arrived, and I could not think of any reason not to agree to attend Camp Ahmek for boys in July and August 1951. This was not a children's shelter, not boarding school. It looked like fun.

Later I realized that being able to go to summer camp was valuable to me in many ways, not least in removing me from a family milieu in that small Ontario town that was becoming increasingly troubled.

Chapter Two

Flawed Family

In the 1930s, my father had hired a young White Russian as his nurse-receptionist, a refugee from Communism, named Haidee Fast. Haidee had no formal training as a nurse — this became a well-kept secret — but she was a quick learner and had a good personality. She became indispensable in the office, working very long hours at what was probably very low pay. Haidee was tall and handsome in her white uniform, and seemed to be a good friend of mother's. Every mid-morning and mid-afternoon she would come out of the offices (there was a connecting door) for coffee and a cigarette and gossip with mother about the patients and their ills.

Mother had a sharp temper that seemed to have come from her mother's family, Scanlons, only two generations out from Ireland. She could be quarrelsome with almost anyone, but especially with dad. When my parents had one of their arguments I usually paid little attention to it.

One weekend night, in 1948 or 1949, just as I was going to bed, they began to argue heatedly about something to do with Haidee the nurse. To keep the noise down they took their quarrelling into the farthest room of the offices at the other end of the house. Even so, the sound of mother screaming at dad awakened me in what seemed to be the dead of night. I went downstairs to ask them to stop. "You kissed her! You admit you kissed her!" mother was yelling. "Anne … Anne," father was saying, trying to get a word in. He was literally backed into a corner. I called out to them to stop, was told to go back to bed, and fell asleep again as the berating continued.

Hours later, at perhaps three or four in the morning, I was again awakened by mother, shouting and crying over the upstairs telephone for help. I went into their big bedroom to find that father, still dressed, was lying unconscious on the floor. Something awful had happened. An ambulance arrived and he was rushed to Leamington Hospital in critical condition. It was not evident until late the next day that he would survive. He seemed to have had a heart attack or had perhaps collapsed from total exhaustion. The latter became the official explanation, and the one I always believed, though mother sometimes also said she thought he had had a heart attack.

Overwork as an explanation for father's collapse was perfectly plausible in the sense that everyone in the family, everyone in Kingsville, knew that Doc Bliss had been keeping a tremendous pace for years. Six mornings of each week he would drive off to see patients in hospital — in the early years twenty-five miles to a Windsor hospital, later nine miles to Leamington — and make house calls in the country. His formal office hours were 1:00 to 5:00 in the afternoon and 7:00 to 9:00 in the evening, Monday through Saturday, with a half-holiday on Thursdays. He sometimes squeezed in more house calls over the supper hour and late in the evening. He was on call every hour of the day and night for his obstetrical cases and as our township's coroner. Dad smoked heavily, had no time for exercise, and was significantly overweight.

I don't know whether or not he was addicted to his work. Dad greatly enjoyed his relaxation time. He liked to listen to opera, a taste I never acquired. Most of all, he loved to read and cherished his collection of about 125 historical novels, biographies, and books on current issues, mostly accumulated through years of faithful membership in the mail-order Book-of-the-Month Club. He was also a stamp collector, and would spend hours sorting and mounting stamps of the British Empire.

Father: Quartus Bliss.

Sometimes he would be bitten by a carpentry bug and turn part of the garage into a workshop — building, for example, the curved bookcase that housed his little library in the living room. Every few months he would take out all the books, sort, and reshelf them, delighting in the sensual pleasure of handling them, and fending off my offers to do it all for him. I liked to fondle books too (just as described by the great author, Amos Oz, who writes that he wanted to grow up to be a book). Dad was also a sports fan, who had played rugby at Queen's, and would sometimes take me to baseball games in Detroit. We were there the day that Boston's immortal Ted Williams returned to baseball after serving in the Korean War, and had nine hits, including five home runs, in a double-header.

Dad was respected in Kingsville and throughout the county as a hard-working, clever, and successful doctor. His practice was by far the largest in town. He kept up professionally through meetings of the Essex County Medical Society and annual junkets to conventions in pleasant venues such as Greenbrier Lodge in West Virginia. One year he and mother took a cruise to Alaska, another winter they spent several weeks in the West Indies. I have a vivid memory of being at the Windsor train station late one night to meet mother and dad as a huge black engine, huffing and steaming, pulled in to bring them home from one of their holidays — the glamour of making it in the prosperous 1940s. In Kingsville, aside from being a token member of the Lions Club, dad had little time for other activities outside of medicine. But he was liked by his patients, had a warm bedside manner (a little rough, I thought; I preferred to get needles from Haidee, who was much gentler), and in my eyes did no wrong.

It's not clear whether he did technical wrong in his practice. His office cupboards, in which I innocently snooped, contained grosses of condoms, which he must have distributed to his patients at a time when their sale was still officially illegal in Canada. More significantly, he seemed to carry out a very large number of "D & C"s on female patients, dilation and curettage, a uterine procedure that could have involved aborting a small fetus. I never heard him talk about any of these things, but think he may have felt that it was part of a doctor's job to help troubled patients limit the size of very large families. Conversely, there were the many times when we would hear a baby's first cries through the office door and be told — sometimes shown — that dad had delivered another child. Having been silver medalist of his class at Queen's University in 1928, dad had become a classic small town general-practitioner, Doc Bliss on Main Street. As a result of his upbringing in Quebec he was even bilingual, though I doubt that many of his patients needed doctoring in French.

Like everyone else in Kingsville, I respected my father as a good man doing important work. I completely accepted his authority, appreciated any time he could spare for me, was fascinated by his books and stamps, and, from the time I could talk, would say that I wanted to grow up to be a doctor. I don't remember ever quarrelling or even disagreeing with my father. I knew, and know, almost nothing of his inner life and feelings or of the Bliss family history (dad's father had died of heart disease in his early fifties; his only sister died of the effects of diabetes). I was surprised to learn many years later from my brother Jim and his wife, Mona, that dad had often been unhappy — unhappy with the daily tedium that general practice seemed to be turning into for a man who had once hoped to be a scholar and a researcher; unhappy and trapped and heavily burdened in a small town as he moved into middle age (perhaps he had a slightly depressive personality); and from time to time unhappy in his marriage. I never knew whether or not he had an affair with Haidee Fast, which must have been mother's accusation the night of his first collapse. Probably not, because Haidee stayed on at the office as though nothing had happened. What I did learn, from Jim and Mona, was that father had, in fact, attempted suicide that night by taking an overdose of pills.

———————————

Mother was not easy to live with. Annie Crowe had been the youngest of Minnie and Alandes's five children. She was pretty and smart and was doted on by her mother and her three big brothers. She was the princess of the Crowe family, bound for bigger things than just being a farm girl or finding a man. She topped her class in high school, where she also won prizes for oratory — Anne Crowe always spoke out and spoke up — took a year of teacher training at what was then called Normal School, and hoped to save enough money to go to university and become a lawyer; no mean ambition for a young woman in the 1920s. Then she threw all her plans away to marry handsome "Quart" (Quartus) Bliss, buried herself in small towns, and gradually became deeply frustrated at not having tried to live up to her potential. She cut a little local swath as an elocutionist and was an active member of the wonderfully named Imperial Order of the Daughters of the Empire (IODE). But mostly mother was an almost classic example of a woman sacrificing her aspirations and then failing to fulfill herself in motherhood and housekeeping, despite living well, a Carol Kennicott figure out of Sinclair Lewis's *Main Street*.

Her problems ran deeper. The whole Crowe family was troubled. I do not know much about the personalities of my Victorian-era grandparents, Alandes Crow and Minnie Scanlon, or how they raised their children on their flourishing fruit farm in the Niagara Peninsula. Things began to go wrong for the family as early as the First World War, when the eldest boy, Harry, went through four years of hell in the trenches in France. Harry survived, married, and moved to Detroit in the 1920s. His only child died in infancy, and the big money he thought he had made in the stock market vanished after 1929. By the time I knew him, Uncle Harry was a serious alcoholic, a binge drinker, who in long periods "on the wagon" managed to hold down a job with the U.S. Internal Revenue Service. Harry lived with Aunt Marguerite in a single-room Detroit apartment with a Murphy bed. Mother said he had never been the same after the war.

Their brother Harold had lied about his age to the recruiters and made it all the way to France before he was sent home, humiliated. The smart boy in the family, Harold never quite found himself either. He and his wife also lived in Detroit, were also childless apartment-dwellers, and he too worked for the IRS. Harold had pulled the strings to get Harry hired there when he was down and out. Harold, a pugnacious, aggressive man, was also a hard drinker, and an even harder smoker, two or three packs a day.

The youngest Crowe boy, Art, ran with the Niagara Peninsula sporting crowd in the twenties. He was a pretty good local ballplayer, said to have had a tryout with the Chicago White Sox. He dropped out of school early,

Mother: Anne Crowe Bliss.

worked as a factory hand, maybe rising to bookkeeper, and drank very hard and smoked big cigars.

Mother's school-teaching sister Mary, plain Jane of the family, married one of Art's sporting friends in her late thirties. Her husband, principal of a public school in Niagara Falls, died soon after the Second World War, of an apparently mysterious disease, leaving Mary destitute. She returned to teaching and made it her career, taking great pride in owning and decorating a modest home of her own.

Although Annie, with her doctor in Kingsville, was by far the most prosperous of the family, Mary was arguably the most satisfied and balanced. In her most vicious and irresponsible moods toward the end of her life, my mother was about to tell Mary that her husband's fatal disease had been advanced syphilis, but Jim managed to stop her.

Life did not go well for their parents either. When the children were young, Alandes had built a fruit-canning factory on his farm. It had done well, and was sold, along with the farm, in a merger of canning factories in the mid-1920s. Alandes received stock that would have made him rich, if he had only held on to it. Instead, he played the market and squandered his money in undrilled local oil wells, busted tire companies, and phantom car factories. We still own some of his worthless stock certificates.

Alandes and Minnie lost all their savings in the Depression, and had to leave Niagara. The boys managed to get their father a job as a clerk in a United Cigar store in Detroit, a sad end to generations of farming in the Crow family. By the time I knew granddad, he and his invalid wife were living quietly in their modest rented house in Leamington. I suspect dad helped with their rent. Alandes Crow had apparently been a tough, feisty, bantam of a man in his day. When I came to know him, granddad was mellow and quiet and hard of hearing. When gramma died, about 1952, granddad moved in with us.

Sometimes we would go to Detroit to visit uncles Harry and Harold and their wives — my parents knew Detroit well and loved to shop there — but most often, especially at Christmas and Easter, the American uncles and the rest of the family would gather at our big house in Kingsville. Harry and Marguerite, Harold and Ethel, Art and Gwen, Mary; they were a volatile mix, made explosively rancorous by drink. All the women drank with their men and the two American couples seemed especially brassy and assertive. Everyone drank rye whisky, mixed as "Old Fashioned" or "Manhattan" cocktails or with ginger ale or simply on the rocks. The bottles of Wiser's Deluxe and Canadian Club were kept in the kitchen, never shown anywhere else. Sherry or wine was never served. Late on a Christmas or Easter afternoon in our smoke-filled family room, tongues would loosen, old arguments and resentments and disapprovals start to surface. Someone would have to have a nap upstairs, or decide to leave early, or two relatives would get into a heated conversation, then shouting match, to settle old scores. Sometimes the phone would ring for dad, and he would have to leave the family party, none too sober himself, to drive to the site of a car crash or drowning and declare the victim(s) dead. It was unusual when everyone made it to the dining room table for dinner.

Before the serious drinking there might be time for uncles to spend an hour with me in the back yard playing ball. They were all sports fans, and they wanted to see how I was coming along with my throwing and batting and fielding. I was a bit of a puzzle to them in that I threw with my right hand, even though I was writing with my left hand. I seemed to have a very weak swing batting right-handed, and it was altogether better when they switched me to the left side, but I was never a very powerful hitter. Many years later, a neurologist who noticed my peculiar style of handwriting during a book signing, told me that my brain was a little scrambled, with not all the motor functions controlled on the right side. She told me I was probably ambidextrous in some sports, which was true. My American uncles also seemed to want to make a boxer out of me, and one Christmas gave me a punching bag and several sets of gloves. I bashed away at the bag, and even set up a ring in the back yard for bouts with school chums. I have no idea whether I boxed left- or right-handed. It all ended when someone hit me very hard in the face and I wanted to cry.

Aunt Mary would usually stay with us in Kingsville over the holidays, and after the other relatives had left she and mother would dissect the family: Harry was drinking too much, Harold was smoking too much,

Gwen couldn't handle Art, *etc. etc.* Mother's main complaint, not without a certain amount of justice, was that everyone expected her to always host the family gatherings, no one ever brought anything (other than liquor), and no one helped with the care of granddad. Mother did not drink very much in those days, and only smoked a daily cigarette or two, but had fairly serious back problems and was often in pain. Whatever the reason, she had a nagging, hectoring, vindictive streak that seemed to be getting worse over the years — though much of the time she disguised it with quite extraordinary charm and a quick and lively sense of humour. In both good and bad moods, mother was a clever woman, not to be underestimated.

Mother was obsessed with social mobility. Her boys had to strive to do well in life. Mother was intensely proud of big brother Jim's achievements in school. Jim had always been an outstanding student. He had won Kingsville Public School's Nelson Shield (made with wood from HMS *Victory*) as the outstanding student in grade eight, having skipped a grade. He had topped his class every year in high school, and had achieved nine first-class honour standings in the nine courses he had taken in grade thirteen, then our final year of high school. Jim had also been commanding officer of the school's cadet corps, an outstanding athlete at track and field, an actor in school plays, and county champion at public speaking. He was class valedictorian from high school and won a major scholarship to study Honours Science at the University of Toronto. From there he planned to enter medicine, following in father's footsteps.

Tossed eggs notwithstanding, I worshipped my big brother, usually from afar because of our age difference and occasionally with resentment that he was so perfect and I could never hope to be like him. Mother expected me to match his accomplishments, of which she told me over and over again in every possible way. From the time I entered public school I was to aim at winning the Nelson Shield. I was on the family fast track: skipped a grade, often got perfect marks, one hundred out of one hundred in reading, spelling, and math. In grade five I sailed innocently into the strange world of public-speaking competitions.

There was no choice. Just as everyone had to memorize so many lines of poetry in those years, so everyone in the class had to give a speech. At age ten I had no idea how to begin to write a speech, let alone deliver one. Mother told me not to worry: she would write my speech and she would teach me how to deliver it. Write she did, generating a seven-minute talk on "Canada's Future" that I had to copy in my own hand and then memorize. As for delivery, the former elocutionist who from time to time had been a judge at public-speaking contests in and around town, made certain that I gave my speech with proper inflexion, enunciation, modulation, pacing, posture, grooming, and everything else that judges looked for, along with the originality and good content built into "my" text.

My parents' big bedroom ran along the whole side of our house. Mother would sit at one end of it and have me enter at the other end and say my speech — two or three times a day, day after day, with innumerable false starts and interruptions to correct fidgets, mispronunciations, sing-song rhythms, and every other error that she noticed. I tried to resist, sometimes balking and fighting back, but was cowed by mother's will. Perhaps I was also a little interested in the prospect of winning competitions the way my big brother had.

I did win. In my age category I won our school's competition, the township competition, the Essex County competition. The southwestern Ontario round, to be held in Chatham, posed a serious problem in that we would also have to deliver impromptu or improvised speeches, a response to the suspicion that parents had too big a hand in writing little Suzie's and Michael's highly polished talks. It always troubled me that I seemed to be living a lie in these competitions (mother sloughed off my guilt by saying all parents helped and, in any case, 80 percent of the marks were for delivery), and troubled me even more that I would actually have to think of something to say in the impromptu competition. I didn't want to go to Chatham. Mother and dad bought me off with the promise of a new bicycle if I went and won. I did go, my impromptu talk (on the most recent Hardy Boys book) was well received, and I won the competition. When we arrived home in Kingsville a shiny new two-wheeler, with kickstand and carrier, was waiting in the driveway.

Every win at public speaking generated more rounds of practise sessions, as a determined mother, living vicariously in her sons' accomplishments, drove me toward the speaking perfection to which she had once aspired. Comeuppance came at the provincial championship, held at the Royal York Hotel in Toronto, when I more than met my match before a very large audience, and did not help my cause by giving from memory, and very badly, the same impromptu talk that had served me well in Chatham. In Toronto, I failed to win, show, or place, and, like several of the contestants, was criticized by the judges for delivering content that seemed beyond me. They rightly guessed that I hadn't written my speech.

Immensely relieved that it was all over, and perfectly satisfied with the decision, I could hardly believe how angry mother was at the outcome. Late into the night I could hear her telling Mary, who had come over from the Falls, and dad, who perhaps was not listening, how wrong the judges' decisions had been, how every speech in the contest had been written by parents, how flawed the winners' deliveries had been, how outrageous and unfair it was that I had not won.

We started all over again the next year. It seemed anticlimactic. I won the county competition but had a bout of flu and funked out and disqualified myself in Chatham. Little matter that year, though, as I was one of a group of three students in our school who had been singled out to skip a second grade, and was taking grades six and seven in one year. This certainly impressed mother. In grade eight I rebelled and insisted on writing my own speech, which did not take me far in competition. Worse, at the end of that year Annetta Conklin, whom I usually narrowly bested in public speaking, won the Nelson Shield for academic proficiency. This was not a judges' decision, it was simply a matter of grades, and on my part it was pure and simple failure. I had let the family down.

Mother's determination to mould me into a perfect little speaking prodigy had often been almost unbearable, but had a lifelong impact. I never forgot the lessons of those sessions in the big bedroom and always felt I knew how to deliver a talk. Having been put on the stage at such a young age, I would never be particularly nervous about doing it again. Eventually, I learned to write decent talks, and, using skills acquired as a professional teacher and researcher, came to have a supplementary and very satisfying career as a speaker. Even the content of that first speech mother wrote for me in 1951 stayed with me — it was full of optimism about Canada's resources, its cultural progress, political stability, and boundless future, some of the issues I would mull over for most of a professional lifetime.

In the meantime, brother Jim seemed to be going from triumph to triumph. In Honours Science at the University of Toronto he stood first or second in his class. He was stylishly dressed, popular, a frat man, a biggish man on campus, from everything we heard. Just before going off to university he had begun a romance with a local girl, Mona Hulse, who was pretty and vivacious and would give me extra large scoops of ice cream in her part-time job as server at the Kingsville Dairy. She seemed to me a perfect sister-in-law-to-be.

There was a serious setback in Jim's third year at U of T. Mother and dad had to rush to Toronto after learning, I was told, that Jim had slipped in the shower at his fraternity house and cut himself very badly. For reasons I didn't quite understand, he missed a lot of classes that year and was given aegrotat standing, a pass without writing exams. He married Mona a few months later at a small ceremony in Toronto. (We attended. I was put on a bus early the next morning to visit Aunt Mary in Niagara Falls. Jim and Mona had not said where they were going on their honeymoon, but I assumed it was Niagara Falls, walked from the bus station to the General Brock Hotel and at 10:00 a.m. was knocking on the door of their room. They didn't answer.)

Jim entered medicine at the University of Toronto in 1952, graduated as silver medalist in his class in 1956, and went to McGill to take a doctorate in biochemistry. The weekend he told us of this decision, he explained to me that to go for the degree of a Doctor of Philosophy was to try for the highest possible academic achievement, the ultimate. That seemed impressive, but if anyone could do it Jim could. We saw very little of him in Kingsville, even though Mona's parents also lived in town.

Mother's endless harping on Jim's achievements began to grate on me in high school and I would often lash out resentfully. She had no right to expect me to match his excellence. Mother's general bad temper, her erratic and blackmailing approach to discipline, her habit of withholding approval and love, all bothered me during puberty. There was an almost epiphanous occasion at about age thirteen when I said to myself that I have a mother who is so unfair to me that I don't love her very much. If her love could be cold and conditional so could mine. I didn't know it at the time, but I was already probably scarred by years of her denigration and her denial of affection. If I were to dramatize my life, this moment perhaps was the insight that saved me, for it meant that I would be her match in determination and toughness.

I never redirected my resentment to Jim, and events and maturity gradually drew us closer. Gradually I came to learn astonishing things about the big brother who was held up to me as having been practically perfect. He told me himself, for example, how much he hated Kingsville, and how everyone with any ability got out of little towns like Kingsville as fast as possible. Then I learned how much he resented mother's, and possibly dad's, pressure on him — their endless pressure on him to excel, their deep disappointment whenever he fell short, their determination to mould his life. If it was hard for me to keep up with Jim, it had been harder still being Jim.

I had known nothing of this, or of Jim's more serious problems. Sometime in his university years he was diagnosed as having malignant hypertension, a life-shortening condition for which at that time there was no effective treatment. As a result of some combination of the condition, its prognosis, and the tensions of family life, he was prone to periods of extreme depression. The so-called fall in the shower was in fact an attempt at suicide — he slit his wrists — and the beginning of a serious break-down. For some months he was under psychiatric care, with therapists who concluded that many of his problems were caused by mother. She did nothing to alter this impression, and forever completed her eldest son's estrangement when she told one of his psychiatrists that if he couldn't stand up to the pressures of university it was just too bad and he'd have to quit.

For many years my parents had expected that Jim would return to Kingsville and practice medicine with dad. Father and son, Dr. Quartus Bliss and Dr. James Quartus Bliss. In about 1953, dad became ill with what was diagnosed as a serious heart attack, a "coronary" as they said. To rest his damaged heart he was hospitalized for several weeks, then required to take six weeks of bed rest at home. We now know that the rest treatment probably weakened his damaged heart further. Dad was able to return to practice, though, and, while waiting for Jim to finish his education, took on promising young doctors as assistants.

Mother's nagging and complaining got on my nerves often enough, but otherwise the gothic side of our family's history (by this time, Uncle Art had become a bum on Detroit's skid row) mostly passed me by. Unlike Jim, I did not find Kingsville confining or stifling. School went smoothly, I went to Sunday School every week, joined church groups for boys, read voraciously, made scrapbooks of newspaper clippings about the Korean War, fired away with my Daisy Air Rifle (BB gun) at sparrows and starlings in our back yard, played with my young brother, and had extra time to go around town collecting old newspapers and coat hangers in our groups' fundraising drives.

Mother made me take piano lessons, and here she failed. I hated old Mrs. Coatsworth, balked at practising, was wasting time and money, and never got beyond grade one. By mid-life I would deeply regret not being able to play any kind of musical instrument. The music teacher at Kingsville Public School, Miss Main, was a sour spinster whom we all disliked and tuned out in every way we could. I got out of singing in her school choirs as soon as I could, my apparent tone-deafness being a perfect excuse. Today I can imagine nothing so satisfying as mastering an instrument and singing in a choir, specifically the Summerside Community Choir in Prince Edward Island.

Sending me to Camp Ahmek was one of the best things my parents did for me. Every late June from 1951, I would get on a midnight train in Windsor with a small group of other campers, sleep overnight in a Pullman, and arrive in Toronto's cavernous Union Station early the next morning. It would be full of kids, including beautiful long-legged teenage girls carrying paddles, assembling to board the special Taylor Statten train — like a summer Hogwarts Express — to take us to camp in Algonquin Park. All day on the train we would sing and talk and eat, and at about five o'clock we'd arrive at the Taylor Statten train station and hike our way through an old sandpit to paradise. Nothing gloomy and mediaeval, rather two beautiful summer camps gleaming in the sunshine on Canoe Lake in an emerald parkland that reminded a young reader of the land of Oz.

Taylor Statten had been a leader in the golden era of boys work associated with churches and the Young Men's Christian Association. In the 1920s, he and his wife had founded Camp Ahmek for boys and Camp Wapomeo for girls on Algonquin's Canoe Lake. The Taylor Statten Camps developed a high profile as offering outstanding summer experiences to the children of affluent parents in Toronto, Montreal, Ottawa, and many American cities. For eight weeks in July and August some 500 privileged children, organized by age in sections and cabin groups of six, experienced a Canadian idyll in the heart of a glorious nature reserve.

The air and water were beautiful, the cabins and outhouses were rustically unheated and unlit, the important facilities outstanding. We swam morning, noon, and night. We learned to paddle canoes and ride horses and sail dinghies, we went on nature hikes and canoe trips, we played pirate games on the Pirate Ship and Indian games at Indian

Council Ring ceremonies. Loons and beaver and deer and even black bear and moose lived among us in the Algonquin forest. Cabin groups competed fiercely in swimming and canoeing regattas. Most of us came back summer after summer, building lifelong friendships. Weak kids, sissies, and the introverted either got stronger and tougher or they didn't come back, taking revenge years later in whining memoirs of the horrors of summer camp.

Taylor Statten took the idea of camping as character-building seriously: we sang special graces at every meal, the national anthem at flag raising, and the Ahmek hymn ("Hail to old Ahmek, the maker of men") at flag lowering. We were given morning meditations every day at breakfast. Saturday nights were for amateur theatricals in a beautiful log theatre at the head of Wigwam Bay. On Sunday nights, everyone attended musicales, performed by a staff of outstanding professionals. While I still tried to resist everything connected with good music, enough of the beauty and atmosphere soaked into me to counter the sourness emanating from old Miss Main and poor Mrs. Coatsworth. In our little camp theatre I saw wonderful musicals, *Finian's Rainbow* and a production of *Oklahoma* still talked about at reunions fifty years later. As a senior camper I even sang in the chorus of *Carousel*. Standards were not always high.

We would paddle over to the memorial to Tom Thomson, the great Canadian painter who had died on Canoe Lake in 1917, and be told about his wonderful art and the mysterious circumstances of his death. His ghost was said to haunt the lake; keep your eyes peeled for the lone canoeist late at night or first thing in the morning, gliding silently through the mist. We children lived for days and weeks in our own canoes, tripping through the glorious lakes and over the short portages that make Algonquin Park a canoeists' heaven. Around blazing camp-fires we heard the stories of Bigfoot and the homicidal lunatic escaped from the Huntsville asylum, or of Bigfoot the escaped homicidal lunatic.

Three or four times a summer the whole camps gathered in our Indian Council Ring, a clearing below a great cliff, where Taylor Statten, the "Chief," in full Native regalia, would lead us through prayers to Wakonda and the four winds, light the ceremonial fire and peace pipe, hear rangers' reports, supervise the water-boiling contest and other games, and then tell us of the initiation rites of young Indian braves, alone in the wilderness, who in their fears and troubles, learned to recite the Omaha tribal prayer: "Wakonda-deh-do, Wapodeno, ton-hay." "O great spirit, a needy one stands before you/ I who sing am he." Then old Hiawatha would appear with his braves, explain that it was time for him to go upon his final journey, and fade into the forest, singing softly as he departed.

It took a year or two to get used to camp (though I was never homesick) and begin to learn some skills, but by about age twelve I was completely at home on Canoe Lake. It became my summer home. Camping did build my character, and the summers at Taylor Statten still come back to me in dreams and memory more vividly and often than any other experiences of my life. Sometimes I think it was camp that made me appreciate some of the central characteristics we identify with being Canadian: the north, railroads, nature, canoeing, logging, and the rhythms of summer life in the outdoors. I met no real Indians at camp, but did eventually become friends with boat builders, cooks, and bush workers. Taylor Statten also gave me an introduction to some of Canada's most privileged children, who would not intimidate me when I joined them at college in Toronto, as well as to a particular genus of golden-haired American youth, beautiful, self-assured children of affluence with extroverted personalities and names like Terry and Chip and Wheezie and Ebbie and Chuck and Frostie. On Sunday mornings we all wore white and we sat at chapel in circles on logs on rocky points. Music mingled with the breeze in the pines, the gusts began to ripple the surface of the lake, and we were the luckiest children in the world.

The rest of the year, back in Kingsville, I was often solitary, always reading. The town librarian didn't know what to do with me when I would sign out books in the early afternoon and want to return them in the early evening before she had time to process the day's library cards. By grade eight I was pleading with her to let me borrow books from the adult section of the library because I had gone through everything on the youth shelves. When she stretched a point to allow me to take out the obviously miscatalogued Lone Ranger novels from the adult section, I loitered in the stacks, discovered the writings of Stephen Leacock, some of which were already familiar from our school readers, and persuaded the librarian to stretch a point still further.

Neither mother nor dad was overtly religious — we did not say grace at meals, let alone have family prayers — but my Sunday School and churchgoing was taken for granted. This was never particularly disagreeable, partly because there was nothing much else to do in Kingsville on a Sunday morning. Everything but the churches was closed on Sundays, and the town was literally quiet except for the sounds of church bells and Pentecostal singing. My parents were certainly not sabbatarians, but even they discouraged us from playing noisy games in our front yard on Sundays, though we could do anything we wanted in the back yard. Even the Sunday Detroit paper disappeared from our newsstand when somebody objected to American Sunday papers circulating in Canada.

On Sunday afternoons I usually played games with my father. We started with canasta, a popular card game, but when a Scrabble board appeared in the house dad and I began what became years of titanic Scrabble matches. More often than not I beat him.

Because I was going to be a doctor when I grew up, and because I was good company, and perhaps because he sensed his own frailty, dad began introducing me to his profession. I was his wired guinea pig as he learned to use his brand-new electrocardiograph. I didn't much like going on house calls with him because I had to stay in the car while he examined living patients, so he started taking me on his coroner's rounds to see death. I went to gruesome car crashes out on the county roads and to drownings at Cedar Beach, and found that I could view bodies, even the body of a boy my age, with perfect equanimity. I would have had no trouble in the dissecting room in medical school.

One Sunday afternoon in about my fifteenth year, our Scrabble game was interrupted by the ringing of the office doorbell. The Ontario Provincial Police had broken up a fight and had a bloody drunk in tow who desperately needed medical attention. His face had been slashed.

Dad would have to sew him up, the inside as well as the outside of his cheek, a good test of his surgical skill. He thought I might like to sit quietly and watch.

My training as a historian leads me to discount autobiographical accounts of epiphanous experiences. Truths usually don't come to most people in sudden flashes. Oddly, they have often come to me that way, and I have no doubt of the accuracy of these memories. As I sat and watched my father sew up his patient on that Sunday afternoon in 1955, blood and alcohol fumes everywhere, I thought about how ambidextrously clumsy I was and how awful it would be to have to spend life doing this kind of thing. Medicine was not for me. I would not grow up to be a doctor like my dad.

I don't think we ever talked that over. We played a lot more Scrabble in the next few months. I was vaguely aware of concerns about dad's health, the fear that he might have another heart attack at any time. He had given up smoking after his first coronary, and had lost weight and taken more time off from work, but it did not last. He put the weight back on again and he continued to make himself available to patients all hours of the day and night. I heard mother worry about him, heard her nag him about his eating and his working. Her own health, mental and physical, also seemed to be deteriorating, as she became more irritable with all of us and would take to her bed. One morning she was still in bed when I came down to breakfast and found dad sitting, white-faced and exhausted, at the kitchen table, finishing a meal after a night out delivering a baby. He often became short of breath by then. One day, at a Detroit Tigers baseball game with dad and Uncle Harold, we had to walk up ramps to the second deck of the old Briggs Stadium. Both men became winded and had to stop to rest and pop nitroglycerine. I wondered what I would do if one or both of them had heart attacks on the spot.

On the morning of March 3, 1956, a Sunday, I had some kind of shouting match with mother, which ended with her storming off to bed. Dad had had to go out early that morning to deal with some kind of emergency. He returned for lunch. With mother sulking upstairs I gave him some cereal and toast and we sat down together. Partway through the meal, dad started to say something, half rose from the table, and fell over sideways onto the floor. He tried to suck in air in great gasps. I knew it was another heart attack. I immediately phoned his assistant, George Bruner, who would come as fast as he could. Dr. Bruner told me to go to the fire hall and get someone to bring over their oxygen apparatus. When help came I remember how large my father's stomach was as we turned him over to put on the oxygen mask. He had stopped gasping, and showed no pulse. They tried to resuscitate him on the way to the hospital, but it was no use. Just past his fifty-third birthday, and my fifteenth, father had died on the kitchen floor.

Chapter Three

=====================================

White Leather Jackets

Father's body lay in an open coffin at one end of our big living room. For three days the people of Kingsville came to our front door, were received by our family, and filed by their doctor. He had delivered so many of them and/or their children. The whole of my grade 11A class at Kingsville District High School came to pay their respects. I slept in a back room just around the corner from the corpse, but had no feeling about that. The night of dad's death I had sat up late realizing that nothing could bring him back and life had changed forever. Mother, dressed in black and often veiled, went into screaming hysterics when the coffin was finally closed to be taken to Epworth United for the funeral. The church was full. Following the ceremony we drove in procession to the burial site in Kingsville Cemetery.

I went back to school the next week, and was told that my teachers had chosen me for a special leadership award given annually to outstanding students by the London, Ontario, *Free Press*. Life was a strange roller-coaster.

By then the old town stoplight and most of the Model Ts had disappeared from Kingsville's streets. Automatic transmissions, V-8 engines, chrome trim, and tailfins ruled the roads (and boys who dropped out of high school got well-paying jobs in the auto plants in Windsor and Detroit). The old radio programs were disappearing as everyone bought 17" or 20" black-and-white television sets and pulled in the Detroit stations with rooftop antennae. The literate classes fashionably avoided television for a year or two. We bought our first TV set when dad was bedridden with his 1953 coronary, and took the warnings to protect our eyes seriously by watching it only from a distance and with the lights dimmed.

Dial telephones came into service in Kingsville. Record players had the capacity to handle three speeds: the old 78 rpm, the little yellow 45s with their big hole in the middle, and the amazing 33 rpm long-playing albums. Girls still wore penny loafers and bobby sox and sweaters, boys liked blue jeans and white T-shirts and used Brylcreem to slick their hair, especially the front wave. Both sexes used Clearasil to hide acne. Elizabeth II was the young queen of Canada, and had even come to Windsor on her first Canadian tour, generating a special school holiday throughout Essex County.

There were so many children to cheer the royals because of the effects of the postwar baby boom. But the Progressive-Conservative government of the province of Ontario was keeping up with the times: When the advance vanguard of the boomer generation (1941 made me forever a pre-boomer) were ready for secondary school, we became the first students in the new Kingsville District High School, a sprawling single-storey, yellow-brick building with light and airy classrooms, a machine shop (for boys), home economics room (girls), a real cafeteria, and a big gymnasium. Libraries were not yet standard equipment. Behind the school was a big playing field with a running track. The old two-storey red brick high school was torn down. It had never housed more than about 100 students. There were almost 100 of us in three classes of grade nines in 1953, and about 225 students in the whole school. Most students would not graduate from grade thirteen, because it was still common to enter public school teaching, nursing, accounting, and the banks, let alone the factories, without finishing five years of high school. Only the elite among us were expected to complete "Upper School" and go on to attend university.

No one doubted that I was university-bound. The main question was whether I would stand first or second in my class. In grade nine I took easily to new subjects like algebra, French, and Latin, but was dragged down by low marks in physical education and general shopwork. I was beaten by John Baldwin, who later had a distinguished career with the Canadian Forces. The smart girls, like Annetta Conklin and Sue Hogan, could ace home ec and do well in languages and English, but withered in math and science classes. In grades ten and eleven I brought up my weak subjects — dropping shopwork, at which I was hopeless, for agriculture, where I could memorize the breeds of cows (I had to plant and tend a little garden plot, but it was never graded) and topped the class. I was finally forgiven the humiliation of having not won the Nelson Shield. By these years I had internalized mother's determination that I should be the best in class, and gloried whenever mine would be the only hand raised to answer to a teacher's tough question. I thought well of myself academically; my classmates were tolerant enough not to openly write me off as a conceited prig.

KDHS was mostly blessed with a remarkably good teaching staff, a not uncommon characteristic of Ontario small town schools in those years. A core of veteran teachers (the men likely also to be veterans of the Second World War) who knew their subjects inside-out was supplemented by young professionals just out of teacher training and full of new ideas.

Some of our teachers were making their lives in Kingsville. Others, like Ron Payne, who became an honoured Latin master in Toronto, or Ron Dunkley, later an outstanding math teacher at the University of Waterloo, honed themselves with us for a few years. Our principal, Joseph Creech, was a credit to the profession, a no-nonsense disciplinarian who also taught history with verve and enthusiasm. Mr. Creech imposed his high personal standards on the school and was respected by all of us and throughout the community. Pound for pound, our Kingsville teachers were as good as the staff of any big city school, including those at most of Ontario's private schools. Private schools were known to us as the boarding schools where you were sent if you got into trouble in the public system — or if you were the daughter of well-to-do parents and happened to fall in love with a boy from the lower classes.

A few teachers let us down, and vice-versa. Ron Payne knew his Latin, but his teeth and fingers were stained by nicotine, his mannerisms were effeminate, his breath offensive, and I never bought into the notion that there were any benefits of learning a completely dead language. I never regretted dropping Latin after two years. Madame Wilson, our French teacher, was a nice woman, perfectly fluent and in love with the language and the culture, but hopeless at discipline. Her classes were a cacophony in both languages. With no incentive to be anything but a disruptive smart alec, the real surprise was that I picked up a reasonable reading knowledge of French by the end of high school. It would have been so much better if I had liked French class and spent time learning to speak the language; so narrowing to have finished high school without an appreciation of either music (not offered in Kingsville after public school) or French.

The rock-solid pillars of the teaching staff were Gordon Maclean, the senior maths teacher, and Evelyn Hicks, known as Miss Hicks to everyone in town, including Mr. Creech. Mr. Maclean was a mathematical genius, a quiet, gruff man with a wry smile who seemed to have all of algebra, geometry, and trigonometry in his head, loved to encourage like-minded students, and could barely contain his impatience with the girls who floundered on Euclid, sines and cosines, and equations with two unknowns. Anyone could see how much he hoped that blushing, giggly Carol or Judy would give up and drop math, making his life, and ours, so much more pleasant. Many of them did.

English classes with the formidable Miss Hicks were almost the reverse. The good girls took to English. Few boys, even clever ones like Baldwin and Bliss, had a natural appreciation for poetry or for the principles of composition. Many of my classmates hated English literature and composition, and hated and feared Miss Hicks, a large spinster with a fierce disposition when crossed. They would have liked to drop English and be done with it forever, but it was compulsory. So they sulked through classes, bored and baffled, somehow got through their homework, and eventually scraped through with the passing grades that enabled them to go on to university and have fine professional careers. We had no idea whether Miss Hicks, serious and stone-faced in the best of times, found teaching painful or a pleasure. She had graduated with a degree from the University of Toronto in English Language and Literature many years before, lived with her mother in the nearby town of Essex, and spent summers travelling in Europe.

I found most of her classes painful, but I knew I had to learn her subject. Surprisingly, I found myself half-wanting to learn from Miss Hicks. She had taught Jim ten years earlier and mother had the highest regard for her as mentor of good literary taste and writing skills. Poetry and high-toned literature seemed soppy to a fourteen-year-old boy, whose interests now ran mostly to science fiction and fantasy, but force me to read something and chances were that I would begin to appreciate it. Despite myself, I usually read far ahead in the Dickens and Hardy novels, Shaw plays, and poetry anthologies that were the core of our literature curriculum. I drew the line at leaping ahead with Shakespeare, save for *Macbeth*.

It was even more interesting to learn about writing during English composition classes. What a bother to have to do all those exercises to improve one's style, except that they worked. By drill and determination, Miss Hicks taught us how to use more effective words, how to eliminate unnecessary words, how to vary sentence structures and grammatical forms, how to tell stories with effective introductions and conclusions. By grade thirteen we were writing stories and doing research essays. When Miss Hicks graded these she would note problems, large and small, and we had to correct them. My book of grade thirteen compositions for Miss Hicks is the only artifact I saved from years of high school classes.

Has anyone taught students how to write effective English since the old school curricula were abolished? I had a splendid introduction to the principles of good writing. For almost forty years at the University of Toronto I had to read essays by graduate students in history who had never been taught to eliminate superfluous words or to think about their readers. Thank you, Miss Hicks. I'm trying to apply your rules even as I write these words. Thanks too for the comment when I showed you that published writers were breaking some of your rules, and you said that when I was ready to publish my first book I could break the rules too. But not before.

My lust for reading material was ingrained, obsessive, insatiable. In early public school I went through all the standard children's books, from Doctor Seuss and Thornton W. Burgess through Doctor Doolittle, the adventures of Freddy the Pig, and my special favourites, the books about the land of Oz, of which Baum's *The Wonderful Wizard of Oz* was only the first in a long series. In the 1940s I experienced the delights of serious comic book addiction. Had they not lost their covers, been traded away, or finally thrown out, my collection of the classic Walt Disney, Superman, Batman, and Captain Marvel comics would now be priceless. Classics Illustrated comics were my introduction, and in some cases my only exposure, to great writers ranging from Melville and Dana through Homer and James Fenimore Cooper. Brother Jim passed a few old black-and-white comic books on to me, which I finally understood were Canadian-made comics issued during the war when, because of shortages of dyes and dollars, American full-colour comics were banned. I read Jim's "Canadian whites," but they were of no interest.

In 1951, we collectors switched from comics to bubblegum cards, as the Topps Company issued the first of the modern series of baseball cards. Five full-coloured cards plus a stick of bubble gum for a nickel. I had nearly a complete set of original Topps, including multiple copies of several, such as Mickey Mantle's rookie card, valued today in the thousands of dollars. Most of these disappeared, but not all. In the late 1970s I read an article in a sports magazine about the craze for old baseball cards and suddenly realized that the remnants of my 1951 collection, which I had given to my son Jamie, were upstairs in a shoebox under his bed. A few weeks later we sold my Jackie Robinson and my damaged Willie Mays and a few dozen other cards to something called the Dallas Gold and Silver Exchange for about $1,500. After reinvestment the money eventually covered much of one of Jamie's years at university.

By high school I was haunting the adult section of the Kingsville Public Library, devouring Zane Grey westerns and Richard Halliburton's adventure tales. I came to science fiction through Edgar Rice Burroughs, whose Tarzan books led me to read his Mars adventures, and then I went on to the classics by H.G. Wells. There were no bookstores in Kingsville. My first book buying was on early trips to Toronto, when I found new Oz volumes in the book departments of Eaton's and Simpson's department stores. In Kingsville, I discovered the paperback rack at Burrows' News-stand, and spent quarters to buy the latest Ray Bradbury, L. Sprague de Camp, or science fiction pulp magazine: *Galaxy*, *If*, *The Magazine of Fantasy and Science Fiction*. Then, just as dad had his Book-of-the-Month Club, I became a subscriber to the Doubleday Science Fiction Book Club. I paid $1.10 a volume, plus 20 cents postage and handling, for the monthly hardback selection.

I liked to reorganize and caress my hardback books just like dad with his, and after his death I appropriated some of the more attractive titles from his collection, including Hemingway's *The Old Man and the Sea*, Stevenson's *Dr. Jekyll and Mr. Hyde*, anthologies of the stories of Mark Twain and Edgar Allan Poe, also *The Complete Works of Shakespeare*, *Masterpieces of World Literature in Digest Form*, and *A Subtreasury of American Humor*. After a few false starts, I became intrigued by the contents of a dog-eared paperback Jim had left behind that had the strange title, *Right Ho, Jeeves*. P.G. Wodehouse gradually replaced Leacock as my favourite humourist. The writing of this paragraph was seriously delayed while I ransacked my library to find dad's most useful BOMC Bonus book, our beloved and tattered copy of *The Reader's Encyclopedia: An Encyclopedia of World Literature and the Arts*, edited by William Rose Benet for the Thomas Y. Crowell Company, New York, 1948.

Illustrated histories of the British Navy and Second World War had been boyhood companions. I thought I knew every inch of Korean War battlefields, as I made scrapbook after scrapbook of war clippings. Winston Churchill's memoirs, each volume of which dad devoured, were beyond me, but without realizing it I was being saturated in current affairs by radio. Every night at 6:45 dad insisted on our listening to *Lowell Thomas with the News*, every Sunday night we listened to Walter Winchell's breathless commentary *cum* gossip broadcast. "Dad, dad, President Truman's been elected," I rushed to tell him in 1948, misunderstanding the results of the Democratic national convention, which we had been listening to for hours. "Oh, no son, he's only got the nomination. He's unlikely to be re-elected. Mr. Dewey is the favourite." I knew the names of Truman, Dewey, Eisenhower, and McCarthy before I knew anything about Canadian politics — except that our prime minister, Mr. St. Laurent, had come from the same village in Quebec as my father.

Magazines came to the doctor's office for the waiting room, the subscriptions presumably written off as a business expense. I grew up on the photos in *Life*, the cartoons and "You Be the Judge" in *The Saturday Evening Post*, and, in later years of high school, the Ameri-centric coverage of current events in *Time*. Fanning out from sports pages, I gradually discovered some of the riches of our daily newspapers, especially the *Windsor Star*. The Toronto *Globe and Mail*, which nurse Haidee picked up each day at noon at Statham's drugstore, seemed distant and hard to read, except during the 1956 Canadian pipeline debate. I was a charter subscriber to the glossy new weekly, *Sports Illustrated*, and bought every issue of the vaguely disreputable humour magazine, *Mad*.

I think I came to my interest in history through current affairs and reading tales of exploration and discovery. The ancient history course I took in grade eleven was not very interesting; learning about Napoleon and wars in modern history in grade twelve was quite fun. I knew so much about American politics and culture from my reading and from visiting Detroit and from Lowell Thomas and Walter Winchell that the grade thirteen course in American and Canadian history was a breeze — though the Canadian parts often seemed remote and boring.

The Canada-U.S. border, a minor irritant when we crossed through the Detroit Tunnel or over the Ambassador Bridge, hardly seemed real. Like our magazines, virtually all of our radio and television and music and sports came to us from the United States. I had two American uncles and Detroit, then at its zenith as the great Motor City, was less than an hour away. The nearest big Canadian city, Toronto, was a day-long drive or train ride. In the 1950s I was an avid fan of Bobby Layne, Doak Walker, and the rest of the Detroit Lions. In high school I was surprised to learn that in Canada we play football with only three downs, a strange variation on the real game. We watched hockey from Toronto on Saturday nights and from Detroit on Sundays, but in the 1950s only the last period or so of a game would be shown, apparently for fear of discouraging live attendance.

In Canada, the American relatives bought English woollens and china and Drambuie and Chivas Regal (Wiser's Deluxe and Canadian Club were cheaper on their side of the river). No one played cricket in Essex County, but you only had to look at our flag or our money to know that Canada was a British country. We studied much more British than Canadian history in public school. My grade six/seven teacher, Mrs. Smithendorf, was particularly anglophilic, leading us in rousing renditions of "Rule Britannia" and "There'll Always Be an England," and showing us all the red on world maps. Studying English literature meant just that; no American novelists or poets made it to the Ontario curriculum. The first adventure thrillers dad introduced me to were some of John Buchan's classics — *The Thirty-Nine Steps, Greenmantle, Mr. Standfast* — but I drew a line at his old G.A. Henty empire-building novels, *With Clive in India, With Nelson at Trafalgar*, even *With Wolfe at Quebec*.

I was vaguely aware that Canadian politics was a minor variant from the big league in the United States. I knew nothing about Ottawa and was in my twenties before I first visited our national capital. I knew that dad voted Progressive-Conservative in Canadian elections. Mother was a Liberal, but before 1957 she had never voted because she thought she should not cancel out father's vote. We were told that granddad, who seemed to spend his retirement following Detroit Tigers baseball, had lost interest in Canadian politics after the golden age of someone named Mackenzie King.

I wasn't quite sure who was prime minister of Great Britain, unless it was Winston Churchill, but of course knew of the evil Joe Stalin in Russia and that China had fallen to Communism. We all knew that history had been changed by the invention of the atom bomb. Mushroom clouds were familiar to us from newsreels and then television news. Pundits predicted that World War III could break out at any time and that it might see horrible nuclear devastation. At age eight or nine I went through a period of fearing that the sound of airplanes overhead was a sign that the war had begun and the bombing was about to start.

No one in Kingsville paid any attention to 1950s campaigns for civil defence. But every spring the whole student body of KDHS became the Kingsville High School Cadet Corps. We had several weeks of quasi-military training, marching, and drilling with dummy rifles, and were issued khaki woollen uniforms that must have been surplus from the First World War. The girls paraded in dark skirts and white blouses and blue berets. Everything led up to cadet inspection, an arcane military ceremony featuring a parade through town, a visit from some regular officer of the Canadian Army, and an evening dance. We were affiliated with the Essex Scottish regiment of the Canadian Army, so those of us who made it to officer status wore kilts, and there was the predictable joking.

The itch to write emerged almost imperceptibly in adolescence, not unlike other itches of those years. I liked to write letters. I wrote letters to pen pals, to girls I had met at camp, to my parents from camp. I was proud to work at my very own desk at home, first a little desk and chair during public school, then a good, glass-topped walnut desk in my bedroom. By high school I did not mind the challenge of doing English compositions or even writing my own talks for public speaking competitions. I always came first or second in class speaking, sometimes won for the school, but had no interest in the grind of serious competition — and no opportunity to experience debating contests, which I think I would have liked. Jaded by the grade five experience, I turned down mother's many offers to help me with content and delivery.

Reading and writing were solitary pastimes. I shied from organized activities such as student council or the yearbook. Miss Hicks planted some of my essays and stories in the yearbook though, and one year when I complained about the *Kingsville Reporter*'s failure to print any high school news, I was invited to contribute and wrote two or three articles about school activities, mostly sports. These were my first, and for several years my only, publications.

Sports and games have been almost as important to me as the life of the mind. We played softball and hardball endlessly in our big back yard, hitting balls over the fence, through windows, across the street, and then going inside to swig lemonade and find out how the Tigers were doing. Dad gave me my first football and showed me how to catch and kick it properly. There was no physical education or organized sports in public school, and early in high school I seemed to have a period of physical awkwardness because I was young in my grade and was showing signs of what would be a lifelong tendency to chubbiness. The first time we had to run all the way around the school's quarter-mile track was torture. My mid-term phys ed. mark in grade nine, 50 percent, distressed all of us, especially dad, who had been athletic through college (and a sedentary smoker ever since, about to die of heart disease!).

At Camp Ahmek I learned different games and skills, and excelled in my age group as a canoeist, canoe tripper, and sailor. I learned to pitch horseshoes at camp, and in Kingsville it mightily impressed Jeff Bailey and the other firefighters next door when, after years of watching their evening horseshoe matches, I asked to play and held my own with the men.

I was not allowed to go into either of the town's pool rooms, but just as I entered high school Vern Lowes opened a four-lane bowling alley in Cliff Williams's old store across the street from us. I became an alley-rat, first a good five-pin bowler, then advanced to the serious (American) game, ten-pins. I paid for my bowling by setting up pins, a seriously back-straining job before it became automated and almost unbelievably dangerous by modern standards. Hardwood pins flew every which way.

Other part-time jobs included working around our own yard, working on Gord Maclean's strawberry farm, and pumping gas and washing cars on Saturdays at Jeff Bailey's Cities Service station. Once, when I was very young and had done a bad job raking leaves, dad came out, showed me how to do it right, and made me do it over again before he paid me. Another time, at Maclean's, we were digging holes for some kind of planting and I felt intensely angry at other workers who were doing anything but digging. Mr. Maclean had paid for their time, and I thought they owed it to him to work, not goof off. Idleness on someone else's time seemed something like theft. On canoe trips the whole group was let down by boys who failed to pull their weight. These memories stayed with me, in fact, burned deeper in later years when I thought about work and obligation and the professoriate.

By grade ten I was a fringe player on school soccer and basketball teams. The next year, still in the junior age group, I was school champion in the 100 and 220 yard dash. Running now felt good — at night I would often run half a mile around our block. Years of weekend football at the Lions Park had made several of us pretty good at running, passing, and kicking. In senior grades I was a two-way player, fullback and linebacker, on KDHS's first football team.

Athletic competition always thrilled me. I loved to win and learned to lose more or less gracefully. My best skill was sailing our camp dinghies in Algonquin, where I became one of the better racing sailors on Canoe Lake. I lived and breathed sailing, racing almost every afternoon in qualifiers for our Wilson Trophy race, and was proud beyond measure when I finished third out of thirty boats in the 1955 Wilson. It earned me a special shake of the hand from the Chief, Taylor Statten, before the whole camp, and a special hug and kiss from my counsellor's girlfriend, the poisonously beautiful Julie "DDT" Vanderploeg. In the summer of '56 I was favoured to win the Wilson, was leading the fleet when the wind suddenly changed and it began to rain. I finished a humiliating fifth.

My moment of athletic glory, such as it was, came in bowling. One autumn evening, when I was in grade eleven, someone called from the bowling alley across the street and asked if I would be interested in being a sub for Conklin Lumber in the men's ten-pin league, as they were a bowler short. It would be intimidating to bowl with the men, but what a neat honour. I began my first game with three strikes, and by the seventh or eighth frame the whole alley was watching and applauding as I finished with a score of 242, the best game rolled in the Tuesday night league that year. No matter that I bowled 92 the second game and never again came close to even the 230s. I was asked to join Conklin's and for the next two years in my yellow Conklin shirt with "Mike" embroidered on the pocket and with my custom-drilled 16-pound bowling ball, I anchored Conklin Lumber, leading it to successive last place finishes in the Tuesday night league. My bowling average was in the 140s — not very high, but it would have looked good in, say, a history professors' league.

I always seemed to have crushes on girls, both in Kingsville and at camp. The gym at the new Kingsville High School had a good sound system, teenagers were beginning to assert themselves in the fifties, and no adults objected when senior students formed a Kingsville Teen Club to sponsor Saturday night record hops. Parents were invited as chaperones, an off-duty policeman was paid $5.00 to keep the drinkers and black-leather-jacket types away, pop and chips were available in the cafeteria, and from nine until midnight we fox-trotted and jitterbugged to the big bands (Glenn Miller, Benny Goodman, the Dorseys, Les and Larry Elgart, Duke Ellington), the crooners (Sinatra, Tony Bennett, Kay Starr, Patti Page, Paul Anka), and the early rock and roll and Motown groups (Bill

Haley and the Comets, Elvis, Jerry Lee Lewis, Buddy Holly, the Platters, the Supremes). I dated early and often, and usually had a "steady" date, the girl I was "going" with, at least for a few months before we tired of one another.

We vaguely sensed that sex was on the agenda, but a long way down. It felt good to hold a girl in your arms, to dance cheek-to-cheek, and to kiss her goodnight half a dozen times. In the movies we held hands and at drive-ins there was enough privacy for serious "necking," but most of my crowd were fairly innocent kids, in equal measure scared of and careful with their sexuality. What we mostly did late into the night with our girls was treat them to hamburgers and milkshakes at Mary's Grill on Main Street or the El-Rancho Drive-In on Highway 3 down Leamington way.

Lower class boys often went together with black leather jackets, especially in Leamington and Windsor. The "hoods" and "greasers," with their duck's-ass haircuts usually left us alone. We liked leather jackets too, and found a catalogue that carried white ones. About thirty of us bought these in grade twelve, decorated them with the big green and gold *K*s and bars we earned for athletic achievement, and were instantly recognized as the KDHS hoods.

Ours was a heavily WASPish crowd, already a bit unrepresentative of the changing demography of Essex County. In the late 1940s and early 1950s there was a significant influx of European refugees, the "displaced persons" or "DP"s. A postwar wave of Western Europeans, fed up with rationing and hardship, also came to North America, as did a stream of immigrants from Italy and other Mediterranean countries, looking for a better life. The newcomers worked long hours in the hot fields and greenhouses of Essex County, then somehow scrabbled money together to buy land of their own. The outcome of these Nino Ricci-like family sagas is visible today in the white brick and stone villas that now outnumber redbrick and gingerbread farmhouses in the Essex County landscape. While the towns were still numerically dominated by Anglo-Saxons in the 1950s, hard-working immigrants were literally reshaping the countryside as they made good.

Some of the smartest kids in our school, such as Paul and Gerry Uhrin from Yugoslavia, John and Anna Kinik from somewhere in Russia, Lloyd and Betty Kubis, whose Czech parents had bought Babcock's Restaurant just down from us, were first-generation Canadians. Two Dutch boys, Martin and John Wingerden, who could barely speak English, showed up kicking a soccer ball at the Lions Park and soon joined our football games. John Wingerden and Orest Hyrenowich, whose son would one day play in the NHL, became two of the best male athletes ever to attend KDHS; a Dutch girl, Audrey Pegels, was the best female, and one of the smartest. All of these kids assimilated quickly to the good Canadian life of the 1950s, and many were outstanding athletes and scholars in later life.

The Roman Catholic Church was a block down from our house on Main Street, but in the seventeen years I lived in Kingsville, attending church practically every Sunday, I never entered it once. I knew nothing of Catholic forms of worship and into my teens would have been afraid of what priests might say to me if I went anywhere near the Catholic Church. "Mixed" marriages in our world were marriages between Protestants and Catholics. I was discouraged from going out with Catholic girls and didn't even try to get permission to ask out the one Jewish girl in town. I once overheard my parents discussing a sermon given in our United Church, suggesting that if Catholics were being told to do business only with Catholics, then Protestants should respond accordingly. Roman Catholic kids went to their separate public school, and we never went near it either. The house just across from the Catholic Church was said to be a whorehouse, which somehow added to the stigma, even though its owners were not Catholics.

The church and its culture and beliefs were as natural a part of life as books or radio or sports or girls. At Epworth United, I came up through every level of Sunday school and through boys' groups like Tyros and Trail Rangers, and by high school was a leader in youth activities.

High school boys were asked to be the ushers at Sunday morning service, which seemed a great and solemn privilege. As a thoughtful teenager, I began to take church doctrine seriously. I believed in God, believed in the Christian story of salvation by God's grace and Jesus's death on the Cross. I believed that there was some kind of everlasting life after death and that while hell was probably an exaggeration, we Christians probably had some kind of heavenly destiny. I believed in the Ten Commandments and such United Church addenda as abhorrence of liquor (our communion "wine" was grape juice). I developed a better-than-average working knowledge of the New Testament, and when I first began asking questions about whether biblical events could actually have been true was more than satisfied with explanations about allegory and essential truths. By senior high school, and especially in my loneliness after father's death, I would sometimes go to a second church service on Sunday evenings.

My test for a driver's license, taken a few weeks after I turned sixteen, consisted of driving our car around a residential block in Kingsville. I have not been re-examined since. Nor have I owned a car nearly as powerful as dad's 1954 Oldsmobile. It was a gigantic chariot, seating up to seven people, heavy with chrome, lurid in two tones, green and yellow — coincidently, the colours of KDHS — and powered by a V-8 "Rocket 88" engine. Mother hardly used it, and in my last eighteen months of high school I had the car whenever I wanted it. It used a lot of gas, but at forty cents a gallon (nine cents a litre) a couple of dollars worth could take us as far as we wanted to go on a Saturday night.

I wish I could write otherwise, but I do not remember being bereft at my father's absence. I had the resilience of youth plus a normal teenager's desire to be independent of parental authority. Later, when I needed wise counsel, I missed father horribly. In these years it was not unpleasant to have no one standing in my way. Mother was too occupied with grieving, bill collecting, and raising my young brother, to be much more than a shadowy, albeit often quarrelsome, presence in my life. Many evenings she would give me a dollar to go and eat at one of the town's local restaurants.

The rhythms of a small Canadian town in the 1950s offered no surprises, no special discomforts. Dr. Bruner took over father's practice, renting the offices from mother, who seemed well enough provided for. Our big brick home on Main Street was a quieter and sadder place, but life went on surprisingly agreeably.

I have always been suspicious of nostalgia buffs because they seem to be trying to escape present bleakness by looking backwards. We taught our children what we have always believed, which was that the best year of our lives could be next year, the best week next week, the best day tomorrow. Still, as I play a version of the nostalgia game here, it is hard not to think that the very best year was 1957–58. I was the top student in grade thirteen, captain of the football team, and, at the wheel of my rocket Oldsmobile, king of the road.

Everything came together that year, academically, athletically, and socially. After narrowly losing the academic proficiency award in grade twelve, I settled in to work hard, systematically, and enthusiastically. I did my homework right after school and did it well. We had a good football season, and Coach Dunkley told me he was going to write to the University of Toronto and Western University about me as a prospect for intercollegiate football. At church I was head usher and supervised about seventy-five little boys in our weekly Tyros program. I was so useful that our minister even forgave us when we ushers were caught ducking out of his sermons to go up to the dairy bar for Sunday morning milkshakes. That winter I was a driver for the "No" forces in a local prohibition referendum, taking doddering old folk to the polls to vote against liquor outlets in our town (mother bought her Wiser's in Harrow). Those were innocent times — skipping school on opening day of the baseball season, taking in *My Fair Lady* on a double date in Detroit with one of my teachers. Today he would be fired or worse for going out with a student. In fact, he is a distinguished Member of the Order of Canada.

I never reconsidered the decision to turn my back on medicine. I thought I might become a scientist instead. What better career for a science-fiction buff than astronomy or astrophysics? I was good at math and had taken the grade thirteen physics course as an extra in my grade-twelve year. I also happened to fill out an elaborate aptitude test in our guidance department that year, hundreds of questions such as, "Would you prefer to spend a leisure hour (a) composing a story; (b) watching television; (c) fixing a motorcycle; (d) looking through a telescope?" The test showed I had a strong aptitude for a career in science. But to my surprise I had chosen so many (a)-type answers that the test showed that my strongest aptitude was to become a writer.* Wherever I was going, I seemed to be on top of the world. In my class speech that year I talked a lot about the exploration of space and frontiers, and quoted extensively from Tennyson's "Ulysses," the first poem I had studied and appreciated in my own right. For a young Ulysses, opportunity seemed boundless.

November 19, 1957, was Sadie Hawkins Day at our Teen Club. This institution, now completely forgotten, was the day of the year in Al Capp's popular comic strip *L'il Abner* when the women of Dogpatch literally chased the men, who, if caught, had to agree to be married. There had been headlines across North America the year Daisy Mae captured Abner Yokum. Sadie Hawkins' events were girls' choice and girls' treat. Like Conan Doyle's dogs that did not bark in the night, no girl asked me to our dance this night, nor was there much interest in us wallflower singles on the sidelines, well-dressed, deodorized, and Brylcreemed as we were. The next town, Harrow, eight miles down the road, also had Saturday night teen dances. A few weeks earlier I had watched the Harrow junior girls play basketball in Kingsville and had noticed how many slim and pretty blondes there were on the team. A friend had a car that night, and I suggested to him that we should check out the dance in Harrow.

---

* About this time and without any sense of its significance, I also began feeling compelled to keep a record of my experiences. It started with records of how basketball games and sailing races had gone, and then snippets of diarizing and records of spending. Keeping financial accounts eventually became a lifelong obsession, to the point where I occasionally wondered if my third career aptitude would have been accounting. As a historian and diarist my obsession has been, as Joyce Carol Oates puts it, "To scrupulously record and preserve the very passing of Time."

They were not observing Sadie Hawkins day in Harrow, so boys could ask girls to dance. As I cruised the gym, I noticed a pretty girl in a white blouse and blue cardigan sweater sitting by herself, and on a courageous whim asked her if she wanted to dance. Her name was Elizabeth Haslam, she was fifteen and in grade eleven at Harrow High, and she knew of me because her mother's family had once lived in the Kingsville house my father bought. She was pleasant to talk to, tall and slim and stunningly good-looking, and, in fact, was the star forward on the junior girls basketball team. I felt almost dazed that such a neat girl, who I first thought was much older, would dance with me. We danced every dance and then said goodnight, both of us knowing that I would call and ask her for a date for the next Saturday night. It was another epiphanous experience, pretty close to love at first sight on my part.

We began dating, going to the teen dances, movies in Windsor, house parties, and sports and church events (Liz was an Anglican, a denomination hardly different from the United Church). We had furious ping-pong matches in the basement of her house, and early on I realized that beneath Liz's cheerful, agreeable exterior there was a fierce competitive core. In fact, she was athletically gifted to a remarkable extent, and in those years played on Harrow teams that won county and regional championships in basketball, volleyball, and badminton. One Saturday afternoon we thought it would be fun to go bowling in Kingsville. Liz had never tried ten-pins. "Oh, look, I knocked them all down." By the end of the game everyone in the bowling alley was watching the teenage girl who was a natural bowler at a time when the few girls who went into bowling alleys almost all played 5-pins. Liz could have played for Conklin Lumber.

Liz was not so sure she cared all that much for the talkative Kingsville boy who seemed even more self-centred than normal seventeen-year old males. The road we started on that Sadie Hawkins night in 1957 had bumps and curves and detours, especially in the early years, but we would eventually realize that we wanted to take the journeys of our lives together, and we have — bowling along together, as it were. As teenagers we put a lot of miles on the big Oldsmobile, and over time Liz sat closer and closer to me as we drove the county highways and up and down Main Street on steaming Saturday nights in the 1950s.

If it was right out of movies like *American Graffiti* to cruise the fifties in Essex County with a pretty girl in a green and gold Oldsmobile, it was Canadian magic to paddle other pretty girls across Canoe Lake in Algonquin Park. I had graduated from camper to staff at Taylor Statten. We had staff dances with the Wapomeo girls every week in the big Ahmek dining hall, and, if you were having a romance after the dance you paddled your girl back to Wap under the amazing canopy of stars, or, best of all, by the light of the moon. On clear August nights you saw showers of shooting stars. Sometimes the mist would be rising from the water. Singling home from Wapomeo in the small hours of the morning stimulated thoughts of Tom Thomson, Canoe Lake's immortal artist. Sometimes a paddler could get completely lost in the mist, or be mistaken for Tom Thomson.

The grade thirteen or "Upper School" final examinations in June were set by the Ontario Ministry of Education for the whole province and were graded on an anonymous basis by moonlighting teachers in big arenas in Toronto. These marks were used as entrance criteria by the universities, and as standards for awarding scholarships. The whole of a high school career hinged on the Upper School finals. In May and June 1957 I studied religiously for my exams, and breezed through most of them. English comp was particularly easy because one of the optional topics for the major essay was "New Moon" and, guessing it might be a topic, I had memorized an essay I had written on the significance of the first satellite, the little Russian gizmo named Sputnik. After exams I took the train to camp. For my second year on staff I had lucked into the amazing job of assistant sailing instructor at Wapomeo. I would spend my summer on the docks of a girl's camp, teaching them how to sail.

The Upper School results were released toward the end of July. On a sunny, breezy Saturday afternoon several of us, male guides and female counsellors, paddled to Ahmek to phone home to get the news on which our school futures depended. My marks were outstanding: 90s in all the math subjects, 86 in English composition, a near-perfect 99 in history. In an era before grade inflation, marks above 75 were first-class honours and not awarded generously; I had nine Firsts and one Second. My average, about 85, put me in the top tier of students in the province. Like brother Jim, I had won a major scholarship to the University of Toronto. The paddle back across the lake, into a stiff headwind, was exhilarating.

Sailing instructor, Camp Wapomeo, 1959.

Chapter Four

Varsity Blues

I was home from camp long enough to outfit for university, helped by Jim. In Windsor we bought a Harris Tweed sports jacket for $35 and a pair of grey flannel slacks. I wore my new outfit, with white shirt and tie, on the train to Toronto to begin life as a college student in the autumn of 1958.

I went a week early because I had been invited to try out for the University of Toronto's intermediate football team, the "Baby Blues." I was able to get into my room in University College's Sir Daniel Wilson Residence, built on the site where Jim had lived ten years earlier. I was registered in the Honours Mathematics, Physics, and Chemistry program, and, also like Jim, had been awarded a $1,500 scholarship that would cover tuition ($335 annually) for my four years, provided that I maintained first-class standing. I had also won one of the $500 Edward Blake scholarships for proficiency in a mix of subjects. Mine was for the highest combined Ontario standing in algebra, geometry, history, and English. There had never been any doubt that I would choose to attend the University of Toronto, which in our view ranked far above all other universities in Canada.

Football was my first priority, as it also was that autumn for a University of Toronto law student who had played briefly with the Toronto

Argonauts and was picking up a few dollars running a college team. Coach John Sopinka was a no-nonsense guy who would go on from sports to a distinguished career in the law and a seat on the Supreme Court of Canada. The competition to make his team was brutal, involving some of the best high school football players in Ontario. I was strong and fast and determined, if a little small, and survived cut after cut, finally making the team's taxi squad — I might get into a few games later in the season as injuries took their toll. Probably in a year or two I would move up to the senior team, the Varsity Blues, which that year was the best college football team in Canada. One day in late September, during a scrimmage with the big Blues, I hurt my back and had to miss a couple of weeks of practice. Sopinka then cut me, suggesting that I'd have no trouble making the team the next year. When I healed I dropped down to our interfaculty league, still good calibre football. With other things on my plate I never again tried out for a university team.

The first problem was to make it as a student in Honours Math, Physics, and Chemistry, MPC, one of the more demanding and competitive of the thirty or forty highly structured four-year honours programs offered in the Faculty of Arts and Sciences. The 135 students in MPC were the cream of the crop, nationally as well as from Ontario. Andy Adler, for example, who also lived in Sir Dan's, had won the Prince of Wales Medal as the top student in Ontario, with an average well over 90 percent. He later became a professor of mathematics at the University of British Columbia. In fact, there were several dozen truly brilliant students in the MPC course. I realized this when John Coleman, our calculus professor, began asking the class questions. Coleman, the best of our teachers, learned who everyone was and taught these large classes Socratically, asking students by name to give answers. John Scott, our physics professor, never knew anyone's name, but famously told us to look to our right, then to our left, and reflect on the fact that one in three of us would fail to finish first year.

I was never in danger of failing, but as our first few weekly assignments of maths and physics problems proved surprisingly difficult, I began to realize that this was very serious business. What if I wasn't as smart as I had thought?

Much of the time I sublimated academic worries in the happy rhythms of college life. The main campus of the University of Toronto, Ontario's oldest and largest, is set in the heart of the city, snug by Queen's Park and the Ontario Legislature. In 1958, some 30,000 students attended classes in the multi-faculty, multi-college institution, the most privileged being out-of-towners, like myself, who lived in campus residences. Even to get to a university was still comparatively unusual — only about 7 percent of high school students went on to higher education. Just being there made us part of an elite. Claude Bissell, an English scholar who had just become U of T's youngest president, told us in his welcoming address in Convocation Hall that we should be "angular," an invitation to be vaguely non-conformist. We were not very: during my undergraduate years most men in Arts and Science wore jackets and ties to class, most women wore skirts, and we all looked down on the scruffy engineering students with their "Skule" jackets and their raucous manners.

Society still thought that universities stood *in loco parentis* to their students, which translated into prohibition of the possession of alcohol in our residence rooms and strictly enforced hours when women could visit. Issues involving drugs other than alcohol were so remote on campus as to be practically invisible. While women were welcome in all the courses the university offered, very few could be found in medicine, engineering, law, or dentistry, let alone forestry. Women were not allowed to be members of Hart House, the university's athletic, dining, and cultural centre.

The twenty-two of us in Taylor House of Sir Daniel Wilson wore academic gowns and jackets and ties at evening dinner. After meals we would gather in our common room to read newspapers and discuss important things before drifting off to study in our single rooms. The house still had an initiation ritual — mostly blindfolded silliness culminating in freshmen being dowsed with buckets of water — balanced against a proud record of very high academic achievement. The year before I arrived some half dozen men of Taylor House men had stood

I-1, first in the first-class honours cohort in their respective honours programs, in other words top of their class. Our house's don in residence, Bill Macomber, a Californian, was taking his doctorate in philosophy. On Saturday and Sunday nights, actually any night of the week, he served tea and biscuits and good, intense conversation in his suite.

I never felt particularly at home in the broader life of University College, the university's original and secular college, which had been federated with various church-founded colleges since the 1880s. I chose UC over, say, the United Church's Victoria College, because it had a reputation for academic excellence and because my brother had gone there. During my years at UC the dominant group, both intellectually and socially, was Jewish, the products of the coming of age of the Toronto Jewish community and the golden years of schools like Harbord and Forest Hill collegiates. UC's Junior Common Room was nicknamed the Jewish Common Room, and while there was never any obvious cultural friction in the college — actually the reverse — it was not surprising that a church-going Protestant would be attracted to the campus-wide Student Christian Movement. The SCM offered study groups, social activities, counselling, and an annual Agnostics Weekend for open-minded non-believers.

Greek-letter fraternities still dominated the broader social scene on campus, their big houses lining St. George Street from Bloor Street down to College Street. Jim had joined a fraternity, but I couldn't see the point of the extra cost, since residence and the SCM offered more than adequate fellowship. I had no taste for drinking or for the rowdy partying that enveloped all of St. George Street on Saturday nights after football games. The Blues went undefeated in the season of 1958–59, and for some of their games all 25,000 seats in Varsity Stadium were filled. Whenever they scored we all stood and were led in the U of T song ("Toronto is our University/Shout oh shout men of every faculty") by the Blue and White Marching Band. We danced to live orchestras at Blue and White dances in Hart House, including the locally famous big bands of Benny Louis and Ellis McClintock. Early in first year I thought I might like to try writing for the campus newspaper, *The Varsity*, but when I went to its office to volunteer the odour of in-group exclusivity drove me right back out.

From visits to Jim and Mona during his Toronto medical years (at the time he was finishing his doctorate at McGill, then he spent a post-doctoral year in England with Nobel laureate Peter Medawar, and then took an appointment in the Physiology Department at McGill), I was fairly familiar with downtown Toronto, especially its movie houses and its Murray's and Honey Dew chain of restaurants. I had been to the Canadian National Exhibition and had taken camp girls to dances at the phantasmagoric Casa Loma. Now, instead of going to frat parties on Saturday nights, I would get together with two or three other KDHS grads and buy $1.50 standing-room admission to Toronto Maple Leafs games at Maple Leaf Gardens. We were those kids in white leather jackets on the rail behind the blue seats, just below the band shell. On Sundays, by myself, I sampled the preaching at Bloor Street United, Trinity-St. Paul's, Knox Presbyterian, and even the old People's Church, not far from the intersection of Yonge and Bloor. In addition to my scholarships I had a decent allowance from mother, saved a few dollars from working at Wapomeo (where I had been promoted to head of sailing, absolute summer heaven), and never had to take a serious part-time job.

It would have been a college idyll of the late fifties, even better than high school, except for the growing realization that I had lost my way intellectually.

I wasn't cut out to be a mathematician, a physicist, a chemist, or an astronomer. I didn't like most of my classes. Our chemistry and physics professors were distinguished enough in their specialties, but commonplace and often boring teachers. Aside from Coleman, whose interrogations scared me almost speechless, our maths masters were incomprehensible. The old codgers who taught us a compulsory course in actuarial science, Shepherd and Bailey, rank in memory as the two worst lecturers I ever heard, a very tough competition. Physics and chemistry labs were three-hour ordeals of fumbling with archaic equipment and being badgered by fuddy-duddy instructors with schoolmarmish ideas about writing up lab books.

About the only course that interested me was a two-lecture-a-week option I was taking in English Literature, in which we studied short stories, poetry, and novels, and had to write four 1,500-word essays. It was said that the MPC students, because of the clarity of their minds, wrote better English essays than the English language and literature majors. I sent Miss Hicks a copy of a term paper I did on T.S. Eliot, which earned me an A.

I did not think I was going to get A or perhaps even B grades in my required courses. As I wrestled with advanced problems in maths or physics, or tried to understand G. de B. Robinson's arcane lectures in multi-dimensional geometry, I realized that I did not have the sharpness of intellect or the commitment required to excel at this level. Suddenly, the prospect of a life in science seemed uninteresting, unlikely. Having been a big fish in a small pond in Kingsville, I was sometimes out of my depth and floundering in the big world of U of T. It was a frightening, deeply upsetting experience. Falling back on the comfort of my religious upbringing, I prayed a lot.

Although my self-confidence was being shattered, and I was distinctly short on self-understanding, I always had a core of conventional rationality or practicality, more inner stability than anyone else in the family, that kept me from rushing over cliffs. I did not know that my brother's college crisis, ten years earlier, had been a suicide attempt, nor did I understand how common it is for young people to have everything thrown into question when they find themselves alone and at sea. I was not homesick, not clinically depressed or in need of anything more than basic guidance counselling, maybe simply a father's good advice. Instead, I chose to seek comfort in the church. Late in November of first year I decided to abandon math, physics, and chemistry and become a United Church minister. As preparation to enter theology, I would start over the next year in the Honours Philosophy course.

Should I drop out of school right away? That would be a humiliating public display of the failings already haunting me in class. I learned that if I did reasonably adequate work in my MPC course I could transfer into virtually any second-year honours program in the humanities (a street down which no one ever went the other way). Over Christmas I told my family of my intentions and that they should not expect me to have good enough standing to maintain my scholarship. The pressure having lifted, and with much help on my assignments from a brilliant residence-mate, Robin Armstrong — later Dean of Arts at U of T and president of the University of New Brunswick — I got through the second term of MPC, studied hard for final exams, and came out of what I thought would be a lost year with a very high B average, standing II-4, about twenty-ninth in the class (and losing my scholarship). My A grades in calculus and actuarial science were comforting souvenirs of having been a decent math student.

So I was going to be a minister. The family could not understand what had come over me, and most of my non-church friends thought I was more than a little peculiar. My rationale for choosing a future in the church was that if the claims of Christianity were true then spreading the Christian gospel was the highest possible calling. I thought I had a calling. If the religious mission was valid, then I had a calling. If it wasn't valid and I didn't have a calling, then life would surely be meaningless. Lose your bearings, your ethical grounding, and anything a person could get away with would be permitted. A person might just as well rob banks for a living.

Increasingly desperate variations of these propositions would keep me headed for theology for the next three years. In Kingsville I was enthusiastically welcomed as a United Church "candidate" for the ministry, a great credit to Epworth United. The little old ladies and good Christian gentleman who made up my home congregation were very proud of their favourite son.

Now I had to finish undergraduate training. The route through philosophy to theology was a fairly well-beaten path that I set out on as a second year student in September 1959, though still at the "godless" University College and still keen on football and dancing and sailing. I had also decided to leaven my philosophy major with an optional minor in history. Somebody had suggested that I should get to know a fellow UC student named Jim Spence, who was said to be interested in becoming a Presbyterian minister and was probably heading toward the same course. I knew the name from his campaign to be elected freshman rep on the UC Literary and Athletic Society — the college had been plastered with signs reading "Don't Be Dense, Vote Jim Spence." Jim was a Toronto boy who had graduated from the elite high school run by the university, University of Toronto Schools. We became classmates and intellectual kindred spirits, forging a good and lasting friendship. When dotage overtakes us, Judge Spence and Professor Bliss will still find time over dinner and drinks to babble happily about the splendid undergraduate training we had in philosophy.

Honours Philosophy (History or English option) was a highly structured and rigorous program, not unlike MPC in its unusually high standards, designed to introduce us to major philosophers and their ideas. We began with the Greeks and finished in fourth year with courses on existentialism, linguistic philosophy, and modern metaphysics. Our professors were a mixed bag of young and old eccentrics and geniuses, brilliant teachers, and semi-competents spinning in strange intellectual worlds. Naively assuming that all philosophers were wise men, I was deferential to all my teachers — pompous old Fulton Anderson, who gave us all copies of his 1935 non-selling book on Plato; young, earnest Charles Hanley, who took over the Plato course when Anderson got sick and who flushed beet red and stuttered whenever anyone asked him a question; David Gauthier and David Gallup and David Savan, who ably led us through British and continental philosophy and the early metaphysicians; old James Dryer, our Kant man, only slightly less incomprehensible than Kant himself; and, of course, our star teacher, Rabbi Emil Fackenheim, a metaphysician who later moved to Israel and became a world-renowned philosopher of Jewish exceptionalism. I do not remember how Fackenheim resolved the paradox of how an omnipotent God could be constrained from making a square circle, but I do remember how important he judged the question.

The thirty-five of us in our course were about as mixed a bag as our instructors — a handful of would-be theologs like Spence and myself; two or three mysterious women inclined to wear black and smoke a lot; a few cheerful girls from North Toronto who would leave U of T with a line on potential husbands; some central Europeans with thick accents and a passion for Fichte and Hegel; Rae Gaouette from Timmins, who quarterbacked our faculty football team; Wayne Sumner, the quiet but very bright classmate who eventually became chair of the U of T's Philosophy Department and a University Professor; and Danny Goldstick, president of the U of T Communist Club.

Goldstick's public adherence to Communism in our first year at U of T generated national press attention in an era when most Communists still seemed to be security risks. Danny was, in fact, a friendly, cerebral fellow, following his father in the family's political faith, and about as serious a threat to national security as a church organist. We got to know him in spite of our misgivings about probably getting into RCMP reports, and we appreciated his extreme intelligence, oblique style, and off-beat sense of humour. Danny vied with Sumner for top standing in the Philosophy stream, later did his graduate work with A.J. Ayer at Oxford (we wondered what Ayer meant when he was said to have remarked: "There is nothing more I can teach you Mr. Goldstick"), and also had a long career at U of T. More than thirty years after his under-graduate coming-out, Professor Goldstick could still be found manning the Communist Party information desk in the University of Toronto's arts building. His faith outlived the Soviet Union itself.

I never fancied myself as a real or potential philosopher, and was taking the program only as preparation for theology. Most courses came to interest me in their own right. Some were dense and very hard to comprehend; none, with the possible exceptions of symbolic logic and whatever was taught by the food-stained British visitor, Spilsbury, was worthless. I often felt over my head and inarticulate when talking with my professors or the *philosophes* among my classmates — Spence, very much a true philosopher, was always the exception — but I paid intellectual dues to philosophy and, almost to my surprise, found that it was contributing to my personal development. Basic philosophic and basic scientific methods seemed to me to have in common insistent, uncompromising skepticism. Absolutely everything was to be questioned, nothing was to be taken for granted, there had to be evidence for or a means of verifying or falsifying any true or serious proposition. Radical Cartesian doubt seemed to rule philosophy, and came increasingly to rule my own outlook, as it has to a substantial degree ever since.

I tried to compartmentalize my views by exempting my Christian faith from either scientific or philosophic scrutiny. Faith was almost by definition beyond reason. True, there were some historical, factual claims made about the life and mission of Jesus Christ, and many of these could not stand up to serious scrutiny, but were they really the essence of Christianity? Through Spence and other friends at the SCM, I was introduced to modern theological currents — Paul Tillich's notion that Christianity was about being ultimately concerned, the Barthian injunction that God commanded us to believe no matter how irrational belief seemed, Buber's concept of faith as "I-thou" fellowship, and more. Christian existentialism — don't think too much about Christianity, just be one — seemed one possible reconciliation, or at least led to some of the interesting writings of Kierkegaard and Sartre and Camus and notions of commitment and authenticity. We were searchers after truth, and most truths were provisional. Certainly nothing could be settled until after final exams.

I had to take one or two history courses a year as part of my honours program, and through third year took elective courses in English literature. My first university history course, a second year survey of British history, was deadly dull in both presentation and content. In third year I chose to take American rather than Canadian history because the United States was historically a more important country than Canada. It was a happy choice because one of the lecturers in that course,

Professor Kenneth McNaught, proved to be stimulating, controversial, and inspiring. I signed up for his specialized course in fourth year, and also balloted for and was accepted into the senior undergraduate history seminar most in demand, "Liberty versus Authority: The Nineteenth Century Tradition," taught by a young hotshot professor, John Cairns.

"I'd so much like to be a top student again," I wrote Liz while studying for second year exams. I had done all my assignments, handed in essays on time, and organized myself fairly well to handle a heavy workload. In third year I wrote sixteen essays ranging in length from 1,500 to 3,500 words. My handwriting had always been very hard to read — students would later tell me that even my question marks on their essays were unintelligible — so in Toronto I had bought a typewriter and learned to touch type, eventually becoming very fast. On occasions when I got deeply interested in a subject, such as a third-year course on Spinoza, who can be read as an attractive pantheist, my papers were given straight As. It happened more often in history, and I was particularly proud of the long paper on Karl Marx and Michael Bakunin that I presented in Cairns's seminar, which was enthusiastically received and given an A+. My argument was that while neither thinker was intellectually sound, Bakunin's anarchism at least saved him from advocating the subjugation and/or elimination of everyone who disagreed with him. Anarchists didn't accept authority lightly. I took considerable interest in Marx and Marxism in several of my fourth-year courses, concluding that Marx's writings and their popularization were mostly intellectual gobbledygook that had nonetheless become historically important because of their appeal as a surrogate religion. Thus the resurgence of Marxism as radical intellectual chic in the 1960s and 1970s left me coldly skeptical, just as the fashionable postmodernist relativism of the 1980s and 1990s seemed to me to be based on fallacies we had covered in week two of second year ethics. Under serious critical analysis, most social theorizing, which historians often took as gospel, seemed to collapse into trivia, bunkum, or meaninglessness.

There was no authority directing us undergraduates to attend classes, leading to experiments with the joyful anarchism of student life. For one reason or another I missed a significant percentage of all my classes, a high percentage of the 9:00 and 10:00 a.m. classes. Spence, who was far more diligent, agreeably covered for me by making carbon copies of his lecture notes, some of which I still have. I wanted to beat him in the final standings at the end of the year, but he had actually been to the meals that I could reconstruct only from his doggy bags. I could never match Jim's commitment to and understanding of philosophy, and always ranked behind him. He was one of the three or four in the class who always got Firsts while I bounced around at the top of the Second Class group, standing II-1, II-2, and II-4 in my three years of philosophy and history. I was not a top student, did not regain my scholarship, and by graduation was not confident that I had the capacity ever to do much academically. I seemed to have one of the best second-rate minds in my class — and would always feel, as the writer Raymond Chandler put it, that "I have the type of mind that can become a pretty good second-rate anything, and without much effort."

Or perhaps I had spread myself too thinly, and still had not found my way. Campus and residence life offered so much more than courses, which is why I often cut classes. I would be sleeping in after late-night talk fests, often enough about metaphysics in don Macomber's suite with Spence, who seemed to thrive on conversation and sleeplessness. One year, Taylor House went wild for bridge, the then-popular card game, with sessions sometimes lasting thirty hours. One of our brightest freshmen failed his year as a result, then turned up a few years later as a member of Canada's national bridge team. Sometimes I would cut class because I had been reading Camus or Dostoyevsky into the morning hours. Or I would disappear for a long weekend in Essex County, sometimes hitchhiking to save a few dollars.

I played football every autumn, house league basketball every winter, and made a few dollars refereeing basketball at Hart House. Taking advantage of being in Toronto, I saw live ballet for the first time and was dazzled. I took in plays at the old Crest Theatre, notably Dinah Christie and Tom Kneebone in the annual "Spring Thaw" reviews. Hart House theatre was in its late golden age, and the productions were thoroughly professional except that Robert Gill's penchant for reviving obscure Bernard Shaw plays was theatrically disastrous. One of our former Taylor House members, David Helwig, trumped all of Gill's work one year as the writer and lyricist for a brilliant, haunting musical, *Katy Cruel*. Helwig was to have a long and prolific career in Canadian letters, finishing as poet laureate of Prince Edward Island.

In the first two years in Toronto I sometimes dated girls I had known at camp or in residence. Nothing came of this, not even casual sex, for I was chaste more or less on principle. I didn't drink either in those years, but gradually took up cigarette smoking. I had been given my first cigarette as a fifteen-year-old camper after we were drenched in a thunderstorm on a canoe trip in Algonquin, and in university saw nothing objectionable in a habit practised by almost everyone.

My interest back home was in seeing Liz Haslam. Liz was beautiful, popular, and a good student. She was chosen as her school's representative to meet Queen Elizabeth in Windsor during a royal visit and also Harrow's representative in the Tomato Queen competition at Leamington's annual Tomato Festival. She was not chosen tomato queen, but for years would blush bright-red whenever I got out the Festival brochure to show our friends. We danced to the new Glenn Miller Orchestra, directed by Ray McKinley, at one year's festival in Leamington, danced at school proms in Harrow and Kingsville, danced one summer under the stars when the outdoor pavilion at the old Lakeshore Terrace Hotel was reopened. After Liz registered at the University of Toronto in September 1960, a year of dances and movies and plays and residence parties convinced us that we were very much in love and would probably get married.

One day in the 1980s, when I was wandering around a vacant lot on the Kingsville shore, I stubbed my toe on what seemed to be a strange rock formation. Looking at it closely, I realized it was part of the ruins of the Lakeshore Terrace's old marble dance floor.

Splendid summers as head of sailing at Camp Wapomeo gradually gave way to a need to move on. In my last summer there, 1960, I wrote my longest piece of prose to that time, a little manual about how to sail the Aykroyd dinghy. It was mimeographed and sold to the campers. In spare hours I read *The Brothers Karamazov* and Walt Whitman's *Leaves of Grass*, and tried to think deep thoughts.

Knowing I was a student minister, the staff asked me to give regular talks at camp chapel services. Several times I was invited to give sermons at Epworth United in Kingsville. As an SCMer I also participated in morning services at Hart House and the occasional Toronto church. Speaking continued to come easily, but I often felt socially shy, especially with the Toronto private-school crowd, who seemed more sophisticated, relaxed, and articulate than my Kingsville, and even my camp, friends. I did not have the courage to participate in an SCM program of soap-box evangelism on campus, or in debating competitions. I was not invited to join the elite University of Toronto History Club, whose members were invited for meetings at some of the city's most exclusive homes. If I had been, I might have been too daunted. When Jim Spence wondered if I was interested in being rushed for membership in his very good fraternity, Kappa Alpha, I said I would rather not.

The year I was president of Taylor House I tried to be clever and witty in my toast to the don at our annual dinner, and was neither. I presided over another year in the house's steady decline into academic mediocrity. Instead of Firsts we led the residence in failures. We became briefly notorious beyond the campus when one of our freshmen ran blindfolded into a brick wall during initiation ceremonies and had to be hospitalized. That was the end of initiations at University College, and my first lesson in the power of the media to distort and embarrass. "It could have happened to anyone," was my debut quote in the *Toronto Star*. "Just like falling down stairs."

I had casually watched John Diefenbaker and Lester Pearson on television during the 1957 and 1958 election campaigns, but had no views of any kind about Canadian politics when I entered university. In second year I attended a talk on campus given by Member of Parliament Stanley

Knowles, one of the leaders of Canada's Cooperative Commonwealth Federation, or CCF Party. Knowles was an ordained United Church minister and looked exactly like Liz's father. By the time he had finished speaking, mostly about the need to create the Kingdom of Heaven on earth, I was a committed CCF socialist.

Committed only for talking purposes; I did not become involved in Model Parliament or any other campus political activities, and I did not join the party. The varieties of politics at U of T seemed remote from real life, the province of glad-handers, nerds, and glad-handing nerds. There was interesting common-room chatter about the social changes beginning to happen in Quebec, and at a memorable dean's evening in 1962 the distinguished journalist Blair Fraser commented that he did not think talk of Quebec independence would amount to anything unless the minister of natural resources in the Lesage government, René Lévesque, decided to opt for separatism. I did try to stand up and walk around for my beliefs by demonstrating on several occasions for nuclear disarmament. One of our Easter marches took us past Sir Daniel Wilson residence, where we were bombed with water balloons.

We, of course, cheered on the civil rights movement in the United States. One day in the summer of 1962, Liz and I were appalled to come across a private beach on Lake Erie outside of Harrow which had a sign, PLEASE, NO COLORED. I wrote an angry letter to the *Windsor Star* about the beach, which eventually was integrated by blacks from Detroit. On the other hand, reticence about social activism surfaced in SCM debates, where I spoke strongly against endorsing the Campaign for Nuclear Disarmament on the ground that taking political positions was not the mandate of a Christian organization. The SCM went political anyway. Not unlike the United Church, it soon came to bend with every passing ideological breeze. Many years later the remnants of the Student Christian Movement were expelled from their offices in Hart House, having become just a Maoist front group.

Candidates for the United Church ministry were required to spend two summers of their student years serving on Canadian mission fields, usually as summer substitute preachers in rural areas. Jim Spence went to Barvas, Saskatchewan, for Presbyterian mission field service after second year. His time there ministering to kindly but dour farm folk was sometimes lonely and hard — he also had to conduct a funeral — but he recommended the experience as personally rewarding. Having finally outgrown camp, I applied to go on a United Church field in the summer of 1961. Anxious to see more of Canada, I asked to travel as far from Toronto as possible.

The dirt road ran 378 miles north from Peace River, Alberta, to Hay River, Northwest Territories, on the south shore of Great Slave Lake. After twenty-four hours on the bus I was covered in dust. When my trunk arrived a day or two later, everything in it was covered with dust. Hay River was not quite the end of the road — you could drive another 300 miles to Yellowknife — but it was close enough. It was a distribution hub for the Mackenzie River system, a struggling community of about 2,000 people, with unpaved, unlit streets and everything built on pilings driven into the permafrost. There was nothing exotic or adventurous about a town whose main industries were transportation and government. People had a lot of guns, but mostly for shooting rabbits.

I was to be the summer minister for the United Church congregation, about thirty-five mostly middle-class families, who had just distinguished themselves by erecting their first church, a little A-frame wooden house of worship. They had no winter minister, only summer students. After a month of services in the local high school we had a grand dedication of this second United Church building in Canada's Northwest Territories. I moved from my billet with a local family into a log manse next to the church — two rooms, an oil stove, electricity, no running water, outhouse.

It was not an arduous mission field, only the one congregation, one or two services to conduct on Sundays, and a lot of routine visiting. My twenty-minute Sunday sermons were homilies on the need to be

Christian and to be moral, and because I could deliver them well and seemed conscientious I was well received. Every second week I gave morning meditations on the town's radio station, CFHR, "Voice of the Arctic." It was a CBC affiliate, playing mostly tapes of old broadcasts shipped from the south (the Christmas programs would air in February). The station manager asked me to sub for him while he went on holidays, so I was briefly producer, researcher, and host of the other live show, the fifteen-minute nightly *Talk of the Town* (baseball scores, weather report, hospital report, interview with a local politician). The station manager also edited the town's weekly paper, *The News of the North*, so I became its lead reporter and editorial writer. I played some softball, coached a team in the women's league, got to know some of the young teachers rotating through the north, and learned to bake bread on my little oven. "I can't really become thoroughly dedicated to my studies or my ministry…" I wrote Liz, "perhaps because there are so many other things that I'm interested in … sports, newspaper work, etc. etc."

I soon realized that it hardly mattered if I was dedicated to my ministry, because no one expected or wanted me to do more than go through the motions with reasonable intelligence and earnestness. Churchgoing to most of my congregation was just a pleasant ritual. When I slept-in and missed giving my morning radio meditation, no one seemed to notice. "The Good News falls like a lead balloon on the people…" I told Liz. "I could probably stand up and read *The Wizard of Oz* and they'd still politely say they 'enjoyed' the service." Toward the end of the summer I decided to speak out on the town's overwhelming social problem, drink, with no result except raised eyebrows at a prudish outsider daring to suggest that the new curling rink be dry. There was intense religiosity in Hay River, but when I saw the almost orgiastic ecstasy of members of the Pentecostal sect at their summer camp meeting, I was appalled and almost frightened. My personal self-improvement project that summer was to stop smoking, at which I failed.

At summer's end I spent a week in Yellowknife, where I preached to the local congregation, toured the Giant Yellowknife gold mine, and was told by many good folk that the huge residential school for Natives was a mistake because there was absolutely nothing the children could do with their education when they went back to their reserves. Early in September I flew out from Yellowknife to Edmonton, escorting an Eskimo boy who needed special medical treatment. I was so anxious to get home to Liz that I spent most of my summer earnings on air fare back across the country rather than take the train. Two years later, most of the old town of Hay River was destroyed in a flood, maybe related to immorality at the curling rink. Eventually the United Church group merged with the local Anglican congregation.

As Jim Spence reflected on his mission field experience, on the philosophic issues our courses posed about the existence of God, and on the occasional problems he was having with his girlfriend's Presbyterian parents, he became increasingly doubtful of his calling, and shared his doubts with me in long, wonderfully articulate letters. By the time I returned from Hay River, Spence had decided he was a practical atheist and had suspended his candidacy for the ministry.

I soldiered on in the autumn of 1961, no longer with illusions about changing the world through pastoral work, but puzzled about life's meaning or purpose without faith in something transcendent. It gradually dawned on me that Jim and most of my other friends were doing just fine without faith. More important, the Chinese wall I had erected to protect my religious ideas from my skepticism began to crumble. A fourth-year course in British analytic philosophy led me to wonder about the meaning of the words we used in religion and metaphysics. God could not square a circle because the concept of a square circle is meaningless, nonsensical. And what about God Himself? What about the concept of an omnipotent personal being who could never be seen, touched, or heard?

I had been asked to give a sermon at Epworth United that autumn and Liz and I took the train down to Essex County for the weekend. During a long Saturday morning shower, my mullings about the future, the meaning of life, and the United Church resolved themselves in another epiphany, a flash of insight. It wasn't true. None of it was true. God was a superstitious invention, Christianity just another supernatural religion that at best comforted people with hope of an afterlife. As I would soon write in an essay for analytic philosophy, the very idea of a life after death, an incorporeal personal existence, was probably logically untenable. It was not only possible to live a good human life in an absurd universe — you lived, did your best, got as much fulfillment as you could out of life (Spence was talking a lot about self-actualization), then died. It was both possible and probably desirable to dispense with organized religion. I had no calling to be a United Church minister, no interest in being one. Time to get on with life.

I was committed to give the sermon the next day at Epworth. Fortunately my announced title was "What Think Ye of Christ?" and I found I could rewrite the sermon to leave everything ambiguous. People should make up their minds about Christianity, one way or the other. My undeclared subtext was that I had just made up my mind the other way. A few weeks after this homecoming I let it be known that I had changed my mind about going into the ministry.

My family were delighted. I had finally gotten over the hang-ups that had been leading me, they believed, down a road taken mostly by wimps and losers. On the other hand, every United Church minister who talked to me about my decision urged me to stay with the church because I was surely just going through a phase. Doubts were normal and didn't matter; the church had latitude for differing views. I soon came to realize that many of these ministers were themselves racked by doubt and/or worn down by the grind of church work. Every tough-minded candidate for the ministry I knew eventually got out.

Desperately, possibly dishonestly, trying to stave off decline by letting anyone believe anything, the United Church and most mainstream Protestant churches began a very long period of shrinkage, the end of which is not yet in sight. Recently, at Epworth United in Kingsville, the worshippers were old and few, the youth program pathetic, and there were no ushers. The minister, a former evangelical who had come to Canada from the United States, told the congregation how after much prayer he had decided that God was calling him to put his hat in the ring as a candidate for moderator of the United Church of Canada.

Now what? Having abandoned science, which at least offered many career paths, I was about to get a degree in philosophy that seemed to lead nowhere. The top students in the class were going on to graduate work, a prospect that did not interest me even if my grades could suddenly become good enough. I had neither aptitude for nor interest in becoming a professional philosopher. Some friends had already gone into law, which could be entered after second year, and mother offered to finance me through that three-year course. I did not know any lawyers, thought their work was probably deadly dull, did not want to remain dependent on mother, and never took the option seriously.

Journalism seemed a more interesting possibility. Beyond high school, my only experience was in Hay River, but a friend was pyramiding summer work at a Toronto newspaper into a permanent job and perhaps I could too. I applied for one of the summer reporting positions offered by the *Toronto Star*. Mark Harrison, a distinguished journalist, interviewed me, and advised me to begin with an apprenticeship on some smaller paper, such as the *Kitchener–Waterloo Record*. The pay would be small, something like $35 a week, but if I were good I could move up. I thanked Harrison and never gave that route into journalism another thought.

Fellow apostate Spence had the same career dilemma, though he would have been a better prospect for graduate school and he knew much more about careers in law. Both of us had been nothing but students since age five. We both wanted to get out into the world, make some money, and marry our girlfriends. In the *ancien régime* still dominating our cultural mores, the idea of couples cohabiting or casually copulating outside of marriage was not respectable. The average age of marriage was much lower than it is now.

High school teaching was a respectable, well-paying profession that seemed have something to do with the life of the mind. A beginning teacher could earn $4,500 to $5,500 a year with long summer breaks.

Every Ontario school board was hiring frantically to cope with enormous pressure from the teenage baby boomers. The Ontario Department of Education did not recognize that philosophy courses had special value, but we could obtain type-B teaching certificates in history after only two summer courses, and could be teaching in September after our first eight weeks at the College of Education.

History now seemed more relevant than life on the ethereal and nearly incomprehensible frontiers of philosophy (in these regards not unlike mathematics and physics), a position underlined for me at virtually every lecture Kenneth McNaught gave in his course on the progressive tradition in America. The clichés about charismatic teachers were mostly true of McNaught: he made history come alive, he inspired us with a passion to study history, he convinced us that history was the key to understanding our world, he challenged us to vigorously attack conventional wisdom, including his own idiosyncratic socialism. McNaught was the most influential of my undergraduate teachers. I began to think that if I had any future in an intellectual pursuit it would be in history.

Every April 1st the *Globe and Mail* blossomed with half-a-dozen pages of advertisements for secondary school teachers. Every school board in Ontario took rooms at the Park Plaza Hotel on Bloor Street, and at nine in the morning a great hiring fair began. I applied for positions with various boards, was most valued by a recruiter for the Hamilton Board of Education, and by five o'clock had finished the only job search of my life. In September I would be a history teacher in Hamilton at the good starting salary of $5,500. Jim Spence would teach history in Toronto.

It had been an undistinguished and sometimes unhappy, if not unproductive, undergraduate experience. For years I would be embarrassed whenever someone recalled that odd religious infatuation, and would dismiss it as juvenile foolishness. It both was and was not. Had I been less lonely and/or had better advice I might never have considered a clerical vocation. But there was nothing foolish about wanting to understand the human condition. To have begun that quest by receiving a splendid introduction to philosophy, culminating in a realization that my real intellectual path would wind through history, actually laid a good foundation.

The University College class of 6T2 held its graduation banquet in the college. The speaker was James Coyne, recently resigned as governor of the Bank of Canada after a public fight with the Diefenbaker government. Something of a folk hero in liberal and Liberal circles, Mr. Coyne was actually a lugubrious, pessimistic man, who spent his allotted time and more telling us of the grim economic outlook for Canada. We would all have to tighten our belts if we were to survive the hardships in store for us, Mr. Coyne told us as we prepared to make our way in the world.

He was exactly wrong. The recession of the late 1950s and early 1960s, which we privileged students had never actually noticed, was lifting even as Coyne spoke. Canada was about to enter the longest sustained period of growth it had yet experienced.

Chapter Five

Apprenticeship

Central Collegiate Institute in downtown Hamilton was a red-brick educational factory. Its 2,500 students were said to make it the largest high school in the British Commonwealth. In September 1962, I began teaching history to some 270 of these students, nine classes of grades nine and ten. My eight-week teacher training course at College of Education in Toronto had been moderately useful, not nearly as unpleasant as a full year there would have been. Teaching young people came easily and naturally — except for the day I had to tell a kid to put his switchblade away. The hard part of the job was adjusting from the late-night rhythms of college life to be at work on time.

The established teachers at Central tended to be grey and tired. Most of us young newcomers were feeling our way in teaching and mostly looking forward to weekends. I taught a night-school class to pick up extra money, and, surprisingly, when a colleague took sick found myself also teaching a night course in English Literature. Friday afternoons I sped down the Queen Elizabeth Way in my blue and white Vauxhall Cresta, my first car and the last British-made car I would own, to see Liz in Toronto. Except for Tiger-Cat football games, Hamilton was of no interest. No one who worked at Central Collegiate seemed to care about the school, which has long since disappeared.

Majoring in English, Liz would graduate from her three-year General Arts program in 1963. She too was drifting toward teaching. In March a friend called about a vacancy just developing at Lawrence Park Collegiate in Toronto, for which it was somehow permissible to hire before the April-Fool's-Day starting gun. I phoned the school and was immediately called in for an interview. A history teacher had just become pregnant in only her second year at the school and would not be returning in September. The purpose of the interview seemed mainly to confirm that I would not become pregnant. I assured Lawrence Park that I was interested in teaching as a career and could not conceive, and was offered the job. I told the vice-principal at Central that I would not be coming back the next year, and the day after that came down with infectious mononucleosis and was off work for six weeks. In September I started at Lawrence Park, where I taught happily for two years before returning to graduate school, pregnant with the ambition to become a real historian.

Graduate, get married. Everyone was doing it. Jim Spence was headed back to law school after a rocky teaching experience — he was much too intellectual and civilized for the classroom — but not before marrying his sweetheart from our SCM-theolog days, Kathie Andrews. Jim's family had a large social circle in Toronto, and for Liz and me the various receptions and parties were an introduction to a mostly unfamiliar, vaguely intimidating world. When a north Toronto matron joined our group at one party and asked what someone in the group had meant by using the word Camus, Jim gave her a splendid review of the Camus Restaurant in Quebec City and its cuisine. She told us it was on her list for her next visit.

The Spence wedding and reception were at Knox College, a beautiful setting, and the first occasion I wore formal dress. It was a dry wedding, of course, but in the interval before the reception we groomsmen retired to the college board room to pass around a flask of gin supplied by the best man, the affable Chris Armstrong.

Two weeks later the Spences and a few other college friends came down to Essex Country for our wedding on June 29, 1963, in St. Andrew's Anglican Church, Harrow. It was a smallish gathering on a beautiful summer day, and after the service we all walked across the street to the Haslam home for a reception in their large back garden. This, too, was

Liz and Michael and Olds '88, June 29, 1963.

dry, but later that night one of my mother's well-to-do American friends held what we were told was a memorable champagne afterglow party for the out-of-town guests.

We spent our wedding night at the Kent Motel, outside of Chatham. The next day we finished the drive to Toronto and moved into an apartment in one of the newish buildings in the Thorncliffe Park development in the suburb of Leaside. For $135 a month we had a large two-bedroom apartment with balcony. Our honeymoon had been the long Dominion Day weekend. On Tuesday we went downtown to begin our summer courses, Liz's first, my second, at College of Education.

Liz was hired to teach English at East York Collegiate, a big school in a largely blue-collar suburb. My students at Lawrence Park, which served one of the most desirable residential areas of North Toronto, were spectacularly good. The average level of intelligence in some of my classes at Lawrence Park was higher than in most of the courses I later taught at the University of Toronto, and the students, not having become inhibited or otherwise distracted, were more fun to teach. My colleagues were outstandingly good, if somewhat hidebound. I ran the school's United Nations (current affairs) Club, founded a Philosophy Club, and one winter coached the junior boys' basketball team to a record of about three wins and very many losses.

Life settled into a pleasant routine of teaching, bridge evenings, golf (a game that brought out the worst in me and I soon abandoned), summer weekends at friends' cottages in Muskoka or Haliburton, movies, theatres, and house-parties in Toronto. We took our real honeymoon over Easter in 1964, spending the better part of a week in Quebec City. On the way home we visited the village in the Eastern Townships, Compton, where my father had grown up. The more prominent native of Compton had been Louis St. Laurent, prime minister of Canada from 1949 to 1957. The St. Laurent family had known the Blisses. One of the St. Laurent brothers still kept the family general store in Compton. When Liz and I walked in and before we could say a word, Mr. St. Laurent, just recovered from a stroke, exclaimed, "You're a Bliss." We never did find the old family farm, but enjoyed tea with the St. Laurents and paid our respects to generations of my forebears in the local cemetery.

With time on my hands after teaching, I enrolled at both the University of Toronto and York University to take history courses. I would need more credits in history if I were ever to return to university for graduate work, an idea that floated vaguely in the back of my mind. I took my first university course in Canadian history in the beautiful summer of 1964 at the U of T's downtown campus. I was especially inspired by a young Ph.D. named Barbara Fraser, who seemed about to make a name for herself in a male-dominated academic world, but was killed in a car-train collision on her way home to Alberta that autumn.

In November 1963, I was just finishing a day of teaching at Lawrence Park when a student came in with the news that president Kennedy had been shot. I had to discuss the event with all of my classes the next day. Thanks to my father, Lowell Thomas, Mr. Creech, Stanley Knowles, Ken McNaught, and the needs of my students, I was now intensely interested in current issues. The hardest day's teaching had been a year earlier when I had to explain to the students why a nuclear war could break out in the next few days or hours as American naval forces prepared to confront missile-carrying Soviet ships en route to Cuba. Politically I considered myself an NDP supporter, cast my first votes for the NDP, and several times wrote Prime Minister Pearson urging him to take a tougher public stand against the Vietnam War. During the election campaign of 1962, I met Mr. Pearson, very briefly, as he and his entourage poured out of their campaign bus literally to go mainstreeting in Kingsville. Early in 1965 I took my Lawrence Park UN Club students on a civics junket to Ottawa. We stayed in the Chateau Laurier, toured Parliament Hill and the Mint and the National Gallery, and, like many thousands of Canadians then and since, were appalled by the juvenile conduct of members of Parliament during question period in the House of Commons. The one speaker who completely silenced the rude cacophony, we noticed, was the Leader of the Opposition, John Diefenbaker.

By the winter of my second year at Lawrence Park I was beginning to become professionally restless. It was often said that many high school teachers began to vegetate intellectually after three or four years, and even at this excellent school the staff room was often as dense with apathy, bitching, and inertia as it was with tobacco smoke. Whatever life had in store for me, I did not want to become a vegetable.

In February 1965, having tired of sharing our dining room table for lesson preparation, we spent $164 to buy a handsome, single-pedestal, teak desk. The weekend it came I was so keen to use it that I used my new knowledge of Canadian history to draft an essay about how little anyone seemed to understand the centennial Canada was preparing to celebrate in 1967. Confederation, I pointed out with grumpy contrariness, was not the achievement of Canadian independence, but merely an administrative reorganization of British North America done without significant input from the people. On a whim I sent the essay to *Maclean's* magazine as a submission to its back page "For the Sake of Argument" feature.

I could hardly contain my excitement when it was accepted for publication and with payment of $500. Nothing I had done since leaving high school did more to boost my confidence. Within a week I had made up my mind to leave Lawrence Park and go back to university the next year to see how far I could go with graduate studies. I wrote a second article, on the good reasons for Canada's history being dull, which was also accepted by *Maclean's*. Forty-five years, more than two million published words, several Smith-Corona typewriters, and a bin full of Apple computers later, my writing is still done on the talismanic teak desk.

On a roll that spring, I screwed up courage to contact a publisher about an idea to fill a void I had noticed during my Canadian history course. There was no good single-volume compendium of basic documents in Canadian history. It would surely be relatively easy to compile excerpts from Lord Durham's *Report*, the British North America Act, the Statute of Westminster, great political speeches, *et cetera*, write introductory passages, and aim the book for senior high school and college courses. Knowing nothing about publishing, I approached the Ryerson Press because it was owned by the United Church of Canada and presumably would not cheat authors. The editor there, Gary Lovett, was cautiously encouraging, and introduced me to a wonderful technological innovation, the photocopy machine. I spent the summer of 1965 copying and editing documents, had a final manuscript ready that autumn, and in my first year as a graduate student published what could reasonably be called a book, *Canadian History in Documents, 1763–1966*, edited by J.M. Bliss. (It at first seemed authorially dignified to call myself "J.M." Bliss. Soon, however, I decided it was snooty to use my initials and became simply "Michael." Confusion in my use of my names — my parents named me John William Michael, but always called me Michael — started to become serious in the 1990s as computers became confused about whether I was John, Michael, John Michael, or simply non-existent. The family occasionally added to the confusion by telling callers asking for "John Bliss" that they must have the wrong number.)

I had enough history credits and good-enough grades to be admitted to the Master of Arts program in history at Toronto. Really first-class students usually took advanced degrees at other, ideally more prestigious, universities than they had attended as undergraduates. Although I had A grades in my make-up history courses, I was not technically a first-class honours student, and had no hope, for example, of winning a big Woodrow Wilson or Canada Council scholarship. Liz and I were not interested in leaving Toronto and, in any case, did not think we had the resources to finance work at any university outside of Canada, if one would have wanted me. Toronto was clearly the best university inside Canada, I was at least changing disciplines from my undergraduate specialty, and I was still unsure of my ability to do a doctorate. If the master's worked it would be on to the Ph.D. program. If not, it would be back to the high schools.

Liz's teaching salary would cover most of our costs. The Ontario government, keen to encourage the production of university professors to teach the baby boomers, had recently established a program of $1,500 graduate scholarships that were awarded almost automatically to new admits. John Cairns and Ken McNaught wrote the letters of recommendation that helped win me my OGS. I thought I would specialize in the history of Canada because Barbara Fraser's course and my documents project had stimulated me, and because Canadian history was one of the strengths of the University of Toronto.

At twenty-four, and after three years of high school teaching, I had regained much of the self-confidence that had been lost during undergraduate years and had vastly improved my work habits. Although I smoked heavily, played no organized sports after university, and kept up with friends over after-school drinks, I had very good health and what now seems like boundless energy. About this time, brother Jim, who seemed to be on top of the world as a brilliant professor of physiology at McGill, told me of his malignant hypertension, his need for powerful drugs to ward off some of its effects, and of the likelihood that the condition would seriously shorten his life. Back in Kingsville there was worrying evidence that our mother had become reliant on alcohol to relieve stress and loneliness. My three uncles had died of the effects of their addictions, two of alcoholism, one from emphysema. Exceptionally, my maternal grandfather, Alandes Crow, carried on as a mellow, gentlemanly soul, living quietly with his memories (he had once heard Sir John A. Macdonald speak) and his baseball games and his devotional literature, finally to die of old age in 1966 in his ninety-eighth year. I hoped that along with granddad's fine head of hair I had inherited his longevity genes.

To register in the U of T History Department in September 1965 we had to confirm our courses with the graduate secretary, Professor William H. Nelson. I joined a long lineup outside his office at 10:00 a.m., and it moved agonizingly slowly. Two hours later, as I was finally near the front of the line, Nelson announced that it was lunchtime and he would resume interviews at two o'clock. The one compensation in this infuriating return to student status was that I struck up a conversation with the fellow in front of me, a genial Manitoban named Gerry Friesen, who also planned to do Canadian history. Gerry later wrote an acclaimed history of the Canadian prairies as the capstone of a long career at the University of Manitoba.

The U of T History Department was almost overwhelmed with ambitious graduate students, particularly in Canadian history. My classmates came to include Paul Rutherford, David Bercuson, Jim Miller, Mary Vipond, Susan Houston, John Eagle, David Hall, Angus Gilbert, Colin Reed, Paul Stevens, Bill Acheson, Chris Armstrong, Viv Nelles, Ken Dewar, Michiel Horn, Irving Abella, Keith Cassidy, and many others, most of whom would eventually hold senior chairs at Canadian universities. The department was still a vaguely musty and authoritarian and casual academic sort of place in the mid-sixties, but it glittered with its critical mass of bright students.

It also had the dean of Canadian historians, Donald Creighton, highly acclaimed biographer of Sir John A. Macdonald and former head of the department, whose seminar was so popular with students that he gave it in two crowded sections. In my section, about fourteen of us met weekly with Professor Creighton in his office to discuss the high points of Canadian political history in the age of Macdonald and Sir Wilfrid Laurier, mostly the age of Macdonald. Creighton was in his mid-sixties, thin and visibly dour, soft-spoken but very opinionated and intimidating. He did have a sweet smile, flashed most often when a student offered judgments that supported his views, which were mostly to the effect that Macdonald was always right and Liberals were always wrong.

Professor Creighton was always formal, addressing us by our last names. He didn't keep ashtrays out and none of us wanted to be the first to smoke in an office without ashtrays, but after someone, usually one of his favourites, had lit up, Creighton would reluctantly produce an ashtray and by the end of class would be smoking himself. Like most of his generation, he understood Stephen Leacock's notion of higher education as consisting mostly of tutors and students smoking at each other. Some classmates were cowed and sycophantic in their seminar presentations, a few of us would respectfully disagree with Creighton on occasion, almost everyone found the seminars intense, stimulating, and memorable. They were an excellent training in the fundamentals of Canadian constitutional and political history.

I also took a seminar on twentieth-century British history from Trevor Lloyd, young, very English, very learned, and so completely absorbed in his subject that most students found him difficult to understand as he conducted what appeared to be monologues with himself. Both Trevor and his subject seemed fascinating and intellectually exciting, a relaxed, undogmatic contrast to Creighton's classes. My third seminar, in Canadian political science from a professor in the Department of Political Economy, was a complete waste of time, the genesis of an opinion I never changed to the effect that standards of teaching and learning in the discipline of history at Toronto tended to be higher than in most of the other humanities and social science departments, philosophy excepted. I always felt that "political science" was a misnamed pseudo-discipline — the idea of a "science" of politics defies comment — and mostly fraudulent.

With regular work habits, a superior undergraduate education in philosophy, years of teaching under my belt, and a happy marriage but as yet no children, I had no trouble with graduate studies. I often went straight from a seminar to the library to begin preparing for next week's class, read carefully and widely, gave model presentations, and was always active in discussion. My grades were always first class and I would easily qualify for the doctoral program.

The department had recently dropped its requirement for a master's thesis in favour of a research essay. I did mine under Creighton's supervision, and, still mired in my United Church background, decided to study the social and political ideas of one of its components, the old Methodist Church of Canada, during the First World War. I wet my feet as a serious researcher in the United Church Archives, located handily at Victoria College, and was so intimidated by Professor Creighton that I took as law his suggestion that we hand in our work by the middle of June. After three years of lesson planning and school bells I met deadlines without realizing how hard it is for many students to organize their time and estimate the effort required to produce punctually. While other classmates struggled with their research papers into the summer of 1966, my essay, "Ploughshares Into Swords: The Methodist Church in World

War I," was on Creighton's desk and Liz and I were off to Europe for a summer of touring.

We flew into Paris and spent nine weeks abroad in the summer of 1966, roaming from city to city on a Eurail pass. The dreariest passages in memoirs tend to be descriptions of the author's travels. Our European wanderings, from Paris through Copenhagen, Munich, Innsbruck, Florence, Rome, and on to London and Edinburgh, were unexceptional and mostly predictable. In 1966, European cities were still soot-blackened and smelly; North Americans were advised not to drink the tap water in France and Italy. War scars had not disappeared, and we took a side trip from Munich to see the concentration camp at Dachau, a macabre visit on a beautiful summer day. One of us got puking drunk at Munich's Hofbräuhaus; both of us sat in drenching rain through a band tattoo at the Edinburgh Festival; we found we loved West End theatre in London, saw our first opera in Rome's Baths of Caracalla, and visited many art galleries and museums. The summer tour, which cost us $1,500 (our basic guide book was Arthur Frommer's *Europe on $5.00 a Day*), was the closest we could come to the "year off" that a later generation would consider an entitlement of youth.

In my second year of graduate studies — first in the doctoral program — I took seminars in American history from Kenneth McNaught and from one of the younger Canadian historians, Ramsay Cook, who everybody recommended as a coming scholar, and found time to audit the seminar offered by yet another of the young Canadian historians, Robert Craig Brown. These courses were interesting to the point of genuine intellectual excitement, first-rate professors and mostly first-rate classmates engaged week after week in the best kind of academic discussion.

Ramsay Cook's seminar on Canada in the age of Laurier and J.W. Dafoe was simply outstanding. Cook, a short, fiery, but friendly redheaded historian from Manitoba who had mastered the literature on Quebec and Canadian nationalism, was a particularly inspiring teacher and scholar. If Creighton had taught us the nuts and bolts of Canadian political history, Cook was on the cutting edge of intellectual history — except that in seminars he had trouble getting a word in edgewise, as our group generated extraordinarily intense energy without him. I had a lot to say every week, but so did David Bercuson, an aggressive left-wing product of Montreal's Jewish community; so did Oleg Soroko, a visiting professor of Canadian studies from Moscow and an orthodox Communist; so did the extroverted and very witty Chris Armstrong, a U of T graduate back from doing master's degrees at Oxford and Harvard; so did Susan Houston and Mary Vipond and half a dozen other members of the seminar, when they summoned up the courage to interject. Here was the frontier of Canadian scholarship and it was very stimulating. Rather than study under the old master, Creighton, I decided I wanted to work with Cook, probably to do my thesis on the social and political thought of the Methodist Church.

There was a palpable sense in the mid-sixties, which may seem hard to recover now, that the future of the writing of Canadian history was in the hands of the young professors and their students at the University of Toronto. Our graduate history society brought in distinguished visiting professors, including the iconic F.H. Underhill — who delivered a blistering, almost embarrassing attack on Creighton's view of Canadian history — and after their talks we would argue over beer at the Arbor Room in Hart House about what needed to be done in Canadian history and how we were going to do it. Our professors were also activists, often found commenting on current affairs and Canadian issues in the newspapers and on radio and television, and this too seemed to go with the expertise. Having already tasted publication in *Maclean's*, and having rejected the idea of starting at the bottom of the journalism ladder, I hoped to follow in the footsteps of Cook, McNaught, Cairns, and other academics and enter the media, at the top as it were, on the strength of my learning — when I had some to display.

In the meantime, I started building a personal library by subscribing to McClelland & Stewart's new Canadian Centenary Series, a multi-volume history of Canada. The pledge to purchase seventeen books at $6 each seemed like a major commitment. My own documents book was published and Ramsay Cook had suggested I submit a short version of my M.A. paper as an article for the *Canadian Historical Review*, which he edited. In the Canadian history industry, patronage and power were even more concentrated than in the normally small cubicles of ivy towers.

I was too busy learning Canadian and American and British history to become involved in many other aspects of graduate student life. High school teaching skills were readily transferable, so I did not feel the need to apprentice as a teaching assistant. We enjoyed the social company of other graduate students and their wives and were glad that Liz's income gave us a relatively high standard of living — no garret apartments, no humid basements, unusually fancy brick and board bookshelves in our living room.

I again voted NDP in the 1965 election, but my politics began changing on the weekend in 1967 when I attended a NDP educational conference at the invitation of Trevor Lloyd. As I listened to men and women of the left discuss how to use the power of the state to create formal equality — say, by forbidding anyone from educating their children privately — I decided that these were the voices of ideologues and nascent totalitarians with whom I had little in common. Ken McNaught's presentation of American history from a socialist standpoint also aroused contrarian objections. It had been stimulating at the undergraduate level, and Ken would always be an engaging, delightful person, but now it was clear that neither American history nor the world could be fitted into the simple intellectual straightjacket he seemed to offer. The years of studying philosophy predisposed me to question all ideologies and ideologues.

Most of us planned to spend the summer of 1967 reading to prepare for written and oral comprehensive examinations the next autumn, the final hurdle before tackling a doctoral thesis. In March, Ramsay Cook called me into his office, told me I was well-enough prepared to take my comps that spring and advised me to get on with it. These examinations were and are a hugely intimidating, often terrifying barrier for graduate students in history. Just the prospect of them has driven students to nervous breakdown. My first reaction to Cook's suggestion was to reject it. But McNaught and Trevor Lloyd, who supervised my minor fields of American and British history, seemed to agree with Cook that I was ready, and Craig Brown, who I turned to for disinterested advice, summed it up nicely: "If they think you're ready, and if you take the exams because they urged you to, do you really think they could fail you?" Alone among my classmates I registered for the spring comps, six weeks away.

I dove into the stacks of the library, took out forty-two books (sign-out forms for each book had to be filled out by hand), lugged them home, told Liz to leave me alone for the duration, and began reading. Without skimming I could go through two books a day in those years, some 500 to 800 pages. It was fashionable on campus to try to increase one's reading capacity by taking highly hyped courses in speed reading; it was invariably found that more speed meant less comprehension, so I was never a customer of Ms. Evelyn Wood, self-advertising patroness of a magical skill.

The exams went smoothly. The dreaded oral exam was an almost pleasant seminar, marred only by what I later understood as McNaught's favourite ploys with graduate students — to ask about classic books no longer read by anyone, in this case Bryce's *American Commonwealth*, and about the most obscure topics that he had happened to have read obscure literature about, on this day the presidency of Grover Cleveland. I stuttered and dodged and faked my way through answers, was invited to leave the room while my examiners deliberated, and was soon brought back in, congratulated, and taken to the Faculty Club for drinks. Suddenly I had a whole summer ahead of me with nothing to do but begin to think about my thesis.

Good times: That spring I learned that I had won a Canada Council Doctoral Scholarship, worth $2,500, and a University of Toronto scholarship for another $2,000. I was invited to attend a Centennial Seminar in Victoria, BC, one of a series sponsored by the federal government at which selected professors and graduate students would discuss Canadian issues. It was my first trip west, a splendid experience intellectually and socially. The senior scholar and chair of our seminar was another grand old man of Canadian history, William L. Morton. After long days of discussion and socializing, we would gather over beer, Morton with his bottle of Hudson Bay scotch, and we would talk still more Canadian history.

Better times: The day after my oral exam, Professor McNaught asked me if I would be interested in preparing a bibliography for U of T President Claude Bissell to use in a course about Canada he was to teach the next year at Harvard University. Originally a specialist in Canadian literature, Bissell had decided to take a sabbatical from his presidency by going to Harvard as that institution's inaugural William Lyon Mackenzie King Professor of Canadian Studies. McNaught had been asked to find a student to draw up a reading list.

The best of times: As I worked on Bissell's bibliography that June I wondered if I would be paid for the effort. Nothing had been said about payment — I would have done it without any — but a week after I submitted my thirty pages of annotated recommendations, getting to chat with the president for about five minutes in his impressive office in Simcoe Hall, a cheque for $500 arrived for me from the University of Toronto. Two weeks later I received a message to please come and see the president. Was there something wrong with my bibliography? Would I be asked to give the money back? Not at all. At our meeting on July 4, 1967, Bissell told me that Harvard had a problem finding teaching assistants qualified to handle tutorial groups in a course about Canada. They had suggested that he bring a graduate student down from Toronto with him to do the job. Would I like to go to Harvard for the 1967–68 academic year?

Another day of jubilant celebration. A kind of personal independence day, because here was the opportunity for advanced seasoning outside of my home university, so obviously lacking on my Torontocentric *curriculum vitae*, that I thought had slipped away. Far more: it was an opportunity to spend a year at America's greatest university working at close quarters with the president of Canada's national university. I had no idea exactly what doors might open as a result of the experience, but every reason to believe that nothing but good could come of it. All following from Ramsay Cook's advice to get on with my comps. Less than two years after returning to Toronto as another in the herd of B-plus students, just a face in the crowd outside Nelson's office, I had caught the brass ring, was on my way up the greasy academic pole, had become the fair-haired boy of my class of historians-in-training.

Professor Cook hinted broadly that I was a front-runner for the next Canadian history job at Toronto. Recording this in a snippet of diarizing that summer, I added: "The old feeling has returned of being able to accomplish everything in the reasonable limits of my ambition. These limits being to be a successful university teacher and a competent historian. With a great deal of luck and application I sometimes think I could leave my mark as an historian."

On July 1, I had attended a ceremony in honour of Canada's centennial on the grounds of the Ontario Legislature. I noticed Professor Creighton in the crowd and struck up a conversation with him. I asked if there was any special recognition in this year of his biography of our first prime minister or his recent book, *The Road to Confederation*. In the longest talk he ever had with me, mostly a bitter monologue, Creighton said that he could not expect any recognition from the Liberal government in Ottawa and had not received any from the Conservative government of Ontario. He had been particularly snubbed in Ottawa, he told me, when John Diefenbaker had been prime minister and had crudely pretended to be a Sir John A. buff. Not a happy man, Donald Creighton would later write about how he would have much preferred to do French history.

Like millions of Canadians, we took in Expo '67 in Montreal that centennial summer, but our real excitement was getting settled in the Boston area and preparing to teach Canadian history for the first time at the university level. While maintaining my student status at Toronto (and my Canada Council scholarship), I was appointed a teaching fellow at Harvard. We rented a shabby but comfortable flat over a convenience store at 94 Oxford Street in Cambridge, a few blocks north of Harvard

Yard. Liz scouted the possibilities of teaching. After doing substitute teaching in Boston's bedroom suburbs, she got a job in November at Needham High School, an excellent all-American school set on a hill overlooking a beautiful upper-middle class community.

My work at Harvard was to give weekly tutorials to two sections of about eighteen students each in Social Sciences 12, an introduction to the study of Canada, taught by C.T. Bissell. Harvard found a Canadian graduate student in its faculty of education to teach the other two sections in what had proven a surprisingly popular course. Most of our students were freshmen. Many were of Canadian background or involved with the hockey team, or both. Almost all were woefully ignorant of Canada. "Canadian Studies at Harvard is largely a farce," I wrote home. "One insignificant lower level course full of freshmen and Canadians going along for the ride."

Teaching the Harvardians was easy and pleasant — they were bright and polite, too independent and too busy with other activities to be very demanding. I attended Bissell's lectures, which were delivered a bit rustily but with splendid dry wit, and met occasionally with him on course business. After a meeting early in the term he took me to the Harvard Faculty Club, where a Harvard professor joined us at the club table.

"I'm Claude Bissell, visiting this year from the University of Toronto."

"Oh, and what do you do there?"

"Well, actually I'm the president."

Bissell's personal diaries, now in the University of Toronto Archives, show that he was annoyed that Harvard took no interest in him or his chair other than to milk his appointment for whatever publicity it was worth. "Still boiling about the lack of Harvard concern," he wrote early in October. "No introduction to my first lecture, no library display re Canada; no office; no secretary." He did not find the return to the classroom easy, and thought the students were neither sympathetic nor responsive to his first lecture. He took comfort in a comment by the chairman of the English Department that a class of Harvard freshmen was "the meanest audience in the world."

115

Claude and Christine Bissell and their poodle, Zephyr, had a visitors' suite in Quincy House and were generous about inviting us to appropriate social events and giving us symphony tickets they couldn't use. One day I met Bissell crossing a street in Harvard Square and he introduced me to his companion, another Toronto faculty member, Marshall McLuhan. McLuhan was at the height of his fame that year and had taken a sabbatical at Fordham. Bissell told me how determined he was to make sure that McLuhan, an old friend, returned to Toronto.

Despite its start-up problems, the Harvard year was a delight and a relief to the Bissells after almost a decade of administrative service in Toronto. There are references in his diaries to a Harvard interest in his returning on a permanent basis after the end of his Toronto presidency. An affable, Stephen Leacockish sort of man, also with Leacock's shrewdness, Bissell told me that the Harvard life was too seductive — if he stayed he would spend all his life in common rooms and drinking.

Liz and I spent our free time enjoying the Boston area and New England, which I told a friend was "as close to a perfect environment as I've ever seen: an ideal mix of the pastoral, urban, and intellectual." We joined the Harvard Yacht Club to sail dinghies on the Charles River on glorious autumn days. We picnicked on salami and champagne at Walden Pond; saw the American Revolution's beginnings on the green at Lexington, the little bridge at Concord, and Bunker Hill; followed Freedom Trail around the historic sites of downtown Boston and the Common; and saw *Waiting for Lefty* and *All My Sons* and *Waiting for Godot* at the Charles Playhouse.

Ticket holders at Harvard football games had stepped from the pages of fashion magazines. The Wellesley University campus was the most beautiful college setting we had ever seen. We explored the Massachusetts coastline from Gloucester and Salem in the north to Cape Cod in the south, and spent Memorial Day weekend on Nantucket Island. On a tour of Hyannis Port harbour we saw young Senator Edward Kennedy out sailing with one of his children, and he waved at us. One snowy day in January some Harvard friends invited us to go skiing. They had assumed that all Canadians skied. We never had, but after a day of falling down the hills decided we liked the sport and spent spring break taking lessons at a New Hampshire resort.

Because I was not a Harvard student we thought we might have trouble meeting people. Somehow invitations issued, with mixed results:

> We were at a party last Wednesday night with four Rhodes Scholars, two Commonwealth fellows, and a Fulbright scholar. At least two of the fellows and two of their wives were the worst kind of snobs. When I was asked "And what are you here for?" I felt it was a suggestion that I should quietly sneak out the back door. The two I was at ease with and could identify with and found it easy to talk to were from Saskatchewan and Iowa.

Early that fall a Harvard doctoral student in history who had been a Toronto undergraduate introduced himself. He was Bob Bothwell, class of 6T6, now in his second year of doing diplomatic history at Harvard, and a bit lonely and down-at-the heels in Boston. That, it turned out, was the chronic condition of most of the Harvard graduate students we met through Bothwell. They were all very bright ("coherent Danny Goldsticks" I told Spence), but found Harvard and its history department both cold and competitive. They were less-well funded than students at Toronto, and yet the Americans dared not drop out for fear of being drafted and sent to Vietnam.

Bothwell and I became good friends and spent much time together that year. He had, and has, one of the most flashingly brilliant minds I have ever known, and had read more history than anyone I had ever met. He had recently broken up with his Toronto girlfriend, history student

Margaret MacMillan, and was having an on-again off-again romance with a Georgetown University grad who wore raincoats and her hair very long and liked to tell us about her former part-time job as some kind of clerk at CIA headquarters outside of Washington. It was actually a very boring job, she said, the CIA folk only getting high on their work during the Cuban Missile Crisis.

With Bothwell, I could talk Canadian history and compare notes on our respective thesis projects. I had abandoned the idea of working on the Methodist Church after realizing how little interested I was in religious history. Trying to figure out what to do instead — the custom in history was for a student to choose his own thesis topic, not to have a project assigned by a supervisor — I thought back to reading I had done for McNaught's classes, particularly a little book, *Dream and Thought in the American Business Community*, by the business historian E.C. Kirkland. Kirkland's aim was to show that American businessmen had more complex ideas about life and society than was allowed by the left's one-dimensional characterization of captains of industry as greedy robber barons. Creighton had once casually asked our seminar if we knew of any work in the history of Canadian business. No one did, partly because apart from studies of the fur trade and the cod fishery very little serious Canadian business history had been written. Combining these thoughts, intrigued by the idea of working on a subject about which I knew almost nothing, I had persuaded Professor Cook to let me switch from Methodist social thought to studying business social thought during the late-nineteenth and early twentieth centuries.

I began research in my spare time at Harvard, using the good Canadiana collection at the Widener Library, a particularly user-friendly place in those days in that it allowed smoking in its principal reading rooms (like many smokers I was so heavily addicted that serious work in non-smoking areas had became uncomfortable). Progress was slow and confused, as I had little idea where I wanted to go with the topic, but I worked hard and went through masses of material. My major discovery was four thousand pages of testimony given to a Royal Commission on the Relations of Capital and Labor that the John A. Macdonald government had set up in the late 1880s to study Canada's nascent industrial system. No Canadian historian had mined this lode of high-grade data about factories, unions, child labour, business attitudes, and much more. I slogged excitedly through the testimony — "slogged excitedly" is not an oxymoron, but an exact description of my experience with archival research.

Where I would be working the next year was soon settled. Canadian universities were frantically expanding to serve the baby boomers and it was not uncommon to give faculty appointments to graduate students with unfinished theses. Early in December I had a telephone call from A.P. Thornton, chairman of Toronto's History Department, asking me to accept a full-time, ongoing appointment as a lecturer in history at a salary of $9,000. He agreed that I could take a leave of absence in my second year to finish my thesis. The opening had developed so early in the year because Ramsay Cook had just been asked to succeed Bissell at Harvard for 1968–69. I was exultant, as was Bob Bothwell, who knew he would likely be hired as Cook's teaching assistant that year. We had a liquid celebration at the old Wursthaus in Harvard Square, which ended many hours later with Bothwell being sick in our bathtub.

More often than not our conversations were about the gathering crisis in American life. The Vietnam War and the Lyndon Johnson administration had become deeply unpopular, black Americans were rioting in major cities, and student unrest was spreading from Berkeley to other campuses. Harvard was as yet comparatively unaffected, though that autumn I attended a large public lecture by the celebrated economist, John Kenneth Galbraith, who seemed like the prophet Jeremiah with a sense of humour as he delivered a passionate attack on the conduct of the war. To attend a James Dickey poetry reading, we had to pick our way through a crowd demonstrating against the Dow Chemical Company, makers of napalm, which was recruiting on campus. "Dow Shall Not Kill" they chanted. The night Martin Luther King was assassinated, April 4, 1968, we thought it best to stay inside. There were still hardly any black students at Harvard, but Cambridge had a large black population and from the streets we heard occasional shouts of "Kill Whitey." "Will they now shoot Robert Kennedy?" I wondered in my diary. I was deeply opposed to the Vietnam War, and had come to believe that the United States was both destroying an Asian civilization and jeopardizing its own.

We had a window on epic events in American politics — President Johnson's decision not to run again, Eugene McCarthy's crusade for the Democratic nomination, Bobby Kennedy's entry into the race, and then the incredible second assassination, when he was shot by Sirhan Sirhan the night he won the California primary. As Kennedy lay dying through the next day we were glued to the radio, and on the news of his death we could not help but weep for the promise of America.

Canada looked wonderfully attractive that spring. As our Harvard course drifted to completion — in February, at Bissell's invitation, I gave my first two university-level lectures; he thought I did well, but displayed an edge of radical cynicism — we were all anxious to come home. The political news from Canada was of the contest to succeed Lester Pearson as leader of the Liberal Party. It was astonishing to hear of the rise of the dark-horse minister of justice, the urbane intellectual, Pierre Trudeau, and also to hear of the role that Ramsay Cook had in furthering Trudeau's campaign among intellectuals in English Canada. Here was the historian engaging in the best kind of political activism on behalf of the best kind of candidate. When the Spences visited us that winter, Jim and I shared moments of early Trudeaumania, such a contrast to the mess of American politics. Trudeau seemed be an amazing cross between John F. Kennedy and the young Wilfrid Laurier.

Back home, in June, we went with the Spences and Chris Armstrong to a Trudeau election rally at a shopping centre in Oshawa. Public Trudeaumania: the crowd was vast, the prime minister descended from the heavens by helicopter, he delivered a moving plea for help in building a just society in Canada, and rose again into the air and disappeared. We had come home too late to be enumerated and so lost the opportunity to vote for Pierre Trudeau in 1968. During my Harvard year I had become increasingly disaffected with ideologues of all stripes, both the anti-Communist crusaders who were destroy-ing Vietnam, and the simple-minded and vulgar protesters who called themselves the New Left. I told Trevor Lloyd that I had become not only a Pierre Trudeau Liberal but probably even a Mackenzie King Liberal.

The inauguration of Canadian studies at one of the world's great universities went mostly unnoticed at that university. By the end of our course Bissell himself was tired of teaching and worried about the gathering North American student protest movement. After dropping in briefly during the final exam, Bisell wrote in his diary that the students "were largely a faceless lot, and my general distaste for them returned." Still, what we had done was of some news value in Canada. With Bissell's consent, the other teaching assistant and I wrote a wrap-up article about our academic experience that year, which was immediately accepted for publication in the *Globe and Mail*'s Saturday *Magazine* under the heading "Closing Harvard's Canada Gap." We took modest satisfaction in having taught the students to appreciate a country much like theirs, but subtly different, and in that year of terrible strain on the United States noted how often the students commented on the promise of Canada, "because their own society seems to have fallen short of its ideals." "In the abstract," we concluded, "this is good for Canada. In fact it is a tragedy for us all."

Chapter Six

Lecturing

I do not remember her name. She was a freshman student, enrolled in one of the Canadian history tutorial groups I led as part of my teaching responsibilities in my first year, 1968–69. She was a beautiful, milk-fed, shy girl, fresh from her family's farm in Saskatchewan, who had come to the University of Toronto because it was Canada's best school. She seemed intimidated by her classmates, but as she started contributing to the weekly discussions it was evident that she had been brought up to believe in social justice and righting the wrongs of history. A good mind and a lovely personality seemed to lie just below a fragile surface.

As the term went on her attendance became sporadic and then stopped. One of her classmates told me that she lived in Rochdale College and was having trouble. I saw her only one more time, walking across the campus. She looked white, gaunt, and ill, and brushed by me without acknowledging my greeting. I never learned what finally happened to her. Every year a percentage of our students would just drop out and disappear.

Rochdale College had opened that year. It was a featureless high-rise concrete apartment building on Bloor Street just west of St. George, built by a campus housing co-operative as a kind of residence for U of T students, but also with pretentions, partly tax-driven, to become a centre of counter-cultural, unstructured, but "relevant" education. Volunteers offered "courses" at Rochdale — no grades, no exams, just meaningful discussion.

Some of my left-wing students persuaded me to attend a session of Rochdale's "course" in Canadian history that winter. It was led by Stanley Ryerson, an old man of Canadian Communism, who had written a dogmatic, almost cartoonish history of Canada as the product of endless class struggle. In a grungy suite at Rochdale about a dozen of us rapped for a couple of hours about Canadian history without any meeting of minds. No one knew anything about my student. On the way out I noticed the elevators stank of urine. I never went into Rochdale again.

About that time I was dismayed by a column in *Saturday Night* magazine in which a former Anglican minister recommended that the young live life to the fullest by not being afraid to experiment with mind-expanding drugs. I thought it one of the most irresponsible pieces of advice I had ever read. For the first time that year I began to wonder what was happening in a Canadian world whose basic values I had mostly taken for granted. More so the day on the plaza outside our arts building, Sidney Smith Hall, when I watched the president of the University of Toronto's Student Administrative Council, Steven Langdon, preside over a "mass meeting" of students. The issue seemed to be whether/when the crowd, about one to two hundred strong, would take direct action and occupy a building in the interest of forcing someone to listen to their demands. A few years earlier the biggest crowds on St. George Street had been partying fraternity types after Saturday football games. Now as I watched the blond-haired, strikingly handsome Langdon, bullhorn in hand, harangue chanting students, it aroused dark thoughts about Germany in the 1930s.

I used to joke that if Canadian student radicals adopted the tactics of the Sons of Freedom sect of the Doukhobors and demonstrated in the nude then we'd be able to see their problems more clearly. As we struggled to understand the counterculture, it became evident that these students were not so much rebels against their parents' generation, or against the 1950s, as they were the naïve children of postwar affluence. In the 1950s their parents and their culture had raised them to be individualists, to believe in expressing themselves, to search for beliefs and then fight for them, to try to change society but also to expect better lives for everyone, including themselves, than previous generations had experienced.* The very large numbers of baby boom kids were getting ready to take over the world. Most were quietly and traditionally going along trying to get educated, though almost everyone was beginning to wonder whether all the old rules still had to be followed. A largish handful of students was testing every guideline. Some were advocating revolution now, revolution in manners, morals, and in higher education. Welcome to the sixties. Welcome to a time of moral disorder.

Neither Liz nor I was affected by these new times. Like most of our friends we were moderate and monogamous, anxious to get on with careers and building families. In my lifetime I had one drag on a marijuana cigarette one night at a summer cottage. The effects of drinking too much alcohol, a more common misadventure, were so unpleasant — my mind was too important to me to let it become blurred and fuzzy — that the family propensity to alcoholism was never a serious threat. It's true that in the 1950s and 1960s virtually everyone, Liz Bliss excepted, was addicted to tobacco. We worked and lived in clouds of cigarette smoke, our sense of smell anaesthetized to what now seems intolerable stink. I smoked in tutorials, seminars, and while I lectured, also early in the morning, late at night, and at my typewriter, thirty or more cigarettes a day. At about $4 for a carton of two hundred smokes, nicotine was as cheap as it was ubiquitous.

Most of the political activism of the sixties passed me by, at first. Steven Langdon and his lieutenants in the "student power" movement seemed a minor problem for the university's administration to handle. On the front lines of learning there were few signs of unrest, none affecting the seminars I took as a graduate student. In 1965–67 the University of Toronto was able to contain and channel early signs of student interest

---

* I was very impressed by the interpretations in a classic analysis, *The New Individualists: The Generation After the Organization Man*, by Paul Leinberger and Bruce Tucker (New York, 1991).

in change by holding massive but well-organized "teach-ins" on Vietnam and other current subjects. Busy learning my trade, I paid no attention to these. When I began teaching in 1968 as a full-time lecturer in history, working out of a windowless, telephone-free interior office in the second floor of Sidney Smith Hall, little more than student dress and hairstyles seemed to have changed since my own freshman year. I usually wore a jacket and tie to class and was short-haired, clean-shaven, even sideburn free. Most of the students were still deferential.

A happy constant at Toronto was that most of our students were among the cream of the crop — Ontario's best, often Canada's best — men and women with good minds and a deep interest in expanding them in the best ways. Many of them in these years asked more questions and raised more challenges than students had before or would afterward. Some of the most intellectually radical students were open to critical discussion of all possible ideas. I deeply believed that a university was a place to confront ideas as freely and openly and fully as possible; sharp disagreements would be common and natural. Only bad manners or incivility should be avoided in intellectual give-and-take. Even the rude and closed-minded students should be treated courteously and given a hearing. I lost patience with students on a few occasions over many years, but never lost my temper.

I was privileged to have landed a teaching job in Canada's largest and best history department. Since the 1890s the modern history staff at the University of Toronto had contributed to the education of every level of student, from three-year General Arts graduates to Honours History specialists, and now to hordes of graduate students. Prime ministers, premiers, diplomats, many teachers, and even a surprising number of business leaders had mostly good memories of taking history courses at Toronto from such luminaries as George Wrong (founder of the department), Frank Underhill, Chester Martin, Bertie Wilkinson, the sightless but well read-to and famous lecturer Donald MacDougall, Donald Creighton, J.M.S. Careless, and Ramsay Cook.

By 1968, the result of a decade of unprecedented expansion in the department was that large numbers of undergraduates also took courses from relatively young scholars, some of them American, a few female. In my entry year so many of us had the same first name — Michael Marrus, Michael Dafoe, Michael Finlayson, Michael Cross, Michael Bliss — that it seemed as though a desperate chairman had invented a new criterion for making appointments. The underlying nub of truth was that most teaching positions were still not advertised, nor were there formal search committees. Hiring was often by the grapevine, as I had been contacted, and as Paul Rutherford and Bob Bothwell would soon also be hired. As with me, many new appointees had yet to finish theses. Intake was still mostly male — no Michelles were hired in my year.

Toronto had expanded from its strong base in British and Canadian history. My forty-five colleagues now included specialists in American, European, Mediaeval, and Russian history, even Latin American, Japanese, and the history of India. The department did not yet teach African history, nor — with one outstanding exception — was it interested in thematic approaches to history. In the early 1970s, Jill Conway and Natalie Davis, respectively an Americanist and a historian of early modern Europe, launched what became a famous, pioneering course in the history of women. Both would go on to spectacular careers in academe, Jill as president of Smith College and a bestselling memoirist, Natalie at Princeton as the biographer of Martin Guerre.

The chairman of the department in 1968 was A.P.T. "Archie" Thornton, a ruddy Englishman who had been a tank commander in the North African campaign and then a well-known historian and defender of the British Empire with his book *The Imperial Idea and Its Enemies*. Thornton and Donald Creighton, the latter in his final year of teaching, both followed tradition and referred to juniors like me as "Bliss," actually a term of familiarity in that the formal "Mister," used to address students, was dropped. Neither Thornton nor Creighton ever took me to lunch or otherwise noticed me. Virtually everyone in the department agreed that Thornton was an incompetent chairman, completely lacking administrative skill and finesse. He probably would have agreed. In her Toronto memoir, *True North*, Jill Conway also savages him as a chauvinist and womanizer. Bill Nelson used to claim, totally maliciously, that on D-Day plus three, Archie had attacked Canadian tanks by mistake.

The Canadian "area" in the department was large, talented, productive, and influential. After Creighton retired our grand old man of Canadian history was Colonel C.P. Stacey, back in Toronto after many years in Ottawa as official historian of the Canadian Army in the Second World War. Known as a stern martinet, Stacey had recently had a positive personality change, apparently as a result of a happy second marriage. Bald and bubbly, impish and happy, Charles made a point of getting to know us juniors. He liked lunchtime company, and every day led a pack of us to the Faculty Club where he gloried in the exchange of professional gossip and lore. Bill Eccles, our dapper and totally francophile historian of New France, sometimes joined us at table, despite his professed disgust at the Faculty Club's inadequate, i.e., non-French, cuisine. J.M.S. Careless, back in the ranks after service as chairman before Thornton, tended to go his own way and spend as little time in the department as possible. But Maurice was always affable and, on rare occasions when he chose to socialize, a wonderful raconteur.

Craig Brown, Carl Berger, and Graeme Patterson were all relative newcomers. Craig and Carl were hard-working professionals, the former writing a major biography of Sir Robert Borden, the latter having just published a seminal book in Canadian intellectual history. Patterson published little, being content to lead an Oxbridge-like don's life in his quarters at Trinity College, where he liberally dispensed good scotch and dry sherry. Ken McNaught, our Cadillac-driving Rosedale Red, taught mostly American history but published on Canadian subjects — he had written the standard biography of J.S. Woodsworth, founder of the CCF. McNaught lunched in his office by himself, but more than made up for that by inviting young and old to dinner parties and receptions in his beautiful home, where his wife, Beverley, was a perfect hostess.

The History Department's ancient habit of gathering for afternoon tea had fallen victim to space constraints and the slightly increased pace of academic life. But the tradition of entertaining colleagues at one's home was still intact, in fact, it was sanctified at the highest level by the constant socializing Claude and Christine Bissell did in the university's presidential mansion at 93 Highland Avenue in Rosedale. Our first visit to 93 Highland came when the Bissells threw a lavish welcome-back party for Marshall McLuhan in September 1968, the agenda being to help keep McLuhan in Canada.

We gradually overcame social jitters on occasions big and small, and began doing our share of entertaining. Professor Creighton even came to our house for the party celebrating Paul Rutherford's completion of his thesis, telling me as he was leaving that my wife's pre-Raphaelite profile was strikingly beautiful. Pre-Raph or not, Liz enjoyed the functions put on by the University of Toronto Faculty Wives Association, including the annual tea at 93 Highland. The notion that we lived and worked in real communities of scholars (and their wives) still survived, as did some bonds with our students. In the Oxbridge tradition, some professors would hold their seminars and tutorials in their digs. Most years, Liz and I would host the final session of my seminar over chili and beer in our home.

No one lived far from campus in the Toronto of the first half of the century. Many colleagues were renovating Victorian houses in the Annex or Cabbagetown; others, including McNaught and Eccles, had somehow raised the $25,000 or so it took to buy a rundown but very large Rosedale house in the 1950s. In our apartment in distant Leaside, a long haul by bus, subway, and streetcar, we felt rather outside the professorial loop. We wondered how long the good, genteel life in Toronto would continue in the teeth of the city's growth. Would the urban core, including the area around the university, go the way of many American cities in the 1960s and become unlivable? Some of the buildings thrown up on campus to meet the needs of the new university population were unpromising harbingers. Sidney Smith Hall in particular was a concrete and cinder block monstrosity, a cold, characterless building not even imposing enough to be considered Stalinist. It was just a bleak educational warehouse.

Other aspects of the old university were on their way out. A few years before I was hired the History Department staged a bitter, painful debate about curricular change in the honours program, a disagreement that divided the old guard from young reformers. Then, just as I joined the department, the university decided to go whole hog and abolish the distinction between honours and general courses in the Faculty of Arts and Science. Toronto's honours courses had been thought by many to be the foundation of its reputation. They had produced generations of solidly educated graduates, many of whom had gone on to illustrious careers. I cherished the intellectual experience I had had in Honours Philosophy, History option. An honours degree from Toronto was as good as any degree from any American university, and our elite graduates did very well in competitions for Woodrow Wilson and other international scholarships.

To meet growing student demand, Toronto was developing "satellite" campuses in the far suburbs. Claude Bissell's hope was that the new campuses in Mississauga and Scarborough would offer good General Arts degrees to large numbers of students, while the downtown, or St. George, campus evolved into a home for honours undergraduates and a flourishing graduate school. We would combine the best features of the great American state universities and their private ones, educating both the masses and the elite. There was talk of the downtown campus becoming "Harvard North."

Now in a climate of rampaging ersatz egalitarianism, the honours courses were suddenly deemed to be unacceptably elitist, the basis of what today might be called two-tier education at Toronto. A blue-ribbon committee of the faculty, headed by the neo-Marxist political scientist C.B. Macpherson, concluded that all courses should be freely available to all students. The university went along. In a three-year phase-out, Toronto's core and historic approach to undergraduate education was liquidated. Under the New Program departments offered a huge smorgasbord of courses that students could sample virtually at will. Fifteen courses would give Joey or Suzie a three-year BA, twenty courses a four-year degree. They could specialize as much or as little as they wanted to. The word and concept "honours" disappeared from our lexicon. The piously optimistic hope, naive from the beginning, was that the quality of our offerings would level up, rather than down.

Quality went down. The good change was that when planning their program, students could now study published evaluations of courses and their instructors. Course evaluations, first produced by the students as "anti-calendars," then standardized in co-operation with the faculty, were an innovation that almost overnight elevated the quality of teaching in Toronto, which in the old regime had been fitful, autocratic, and unaccountable. On the other hand the course evaluations supported a form of teaching that sometimes pandered to the lowest common denominator, and the rules now allowed virtually unlimited freedom of course choice. Some students gorged themselves at our academic buffet on deserts only; others nibbled at salad. The New Program interacted with academic faddism to spawn such dubious intellectual offspring as cinema studies and introductions to the problem of God in science fiction. The next fifteen years or so were spent in efforts to restore a semblance of structure and discipline to the Toronto curriculum.

My supervisor and mentor, Ramsay Cook, had been a member of the committee that recommended abolishing the honours program. Then in the winter of 1967–68 he suddenly jumped ship, announcing that he would not return to U of T after his year as Bissell's successor at Harvard. Instead he accepted an offer from the fledgling York University, which had just emerged from a chrysalis period on our campus into full-blown independence on two campuses north and northeast of downtown.

Cook's defection to York shocked most of us in Canadian history. We were told he was leaving mainly because of overwork. Tagged as a coming superstar, Cook was said to have found himself supervising nineteen doctoral students at a time when graduate supervision earned no worksheet credit. There was probably much more to the story of his exit, but I never learned the details. When he visited Harvard in 1968, just after announcing that he was leaving U of T, Cook was appropriately close-mouthed, but also obviously bitter. He commented to me that professors had too much freedom to be idle, that someone should check every office at 9:00 a.m. to see who was at work and who was not. Cook himself would continue to do some work at U of T, supervising the cream of his doctoral students, including me.

Cook was joining his good friend and former colleague, Jack Saywell, at York, and in the next few years that ambitious institution rapidly expanded its history department by hiring a number of excellent young scholars, including such classmates and friends as Chris Armstrong, Viv Nelles, Bob Cuff, Irving Abella, and Jack Granatstein. York's history department hoped to equal and surpass ours as Canada's largest and best. Over the years institutional rivalry would have many repercussions at higher administrative and provincial levels. To us the Yorkies' natural chippiness at being the new players on the university scene seemed magnified several times over by their sensitivity about the ghastly wasteland of their main campus and the relatively low calibre of many of their students. "You have to be good to get here," I would reassure anxious students at each year's first class on our campus. "If you weren't good you'd be at some other Toronto university." (Toronto's eventual third university, Ryerson, was then still a technical institute to which nobody at U of T paid any attention).

Of course we were collegial with our York counterparts. Travelling between the universities was so bothersome that hardly any students took advantage of possibilities for joint study — or faculty for joint appointments — but we saw York friends constantly on social and professional occasions. In about 1972 I suggested to Craig Brown that we get together with the York Canadianists for the occasional dinner and work-in-progress presentation. Craig spoke about his work on Sir Robert Borden at the first of these affairs, held at our Faculty Club. Colonel Stacey fell sound asleep during the talk, as he did at most of the presentations. Our York-U of T colloquium in Canadian history flourished through the 1970s, perambulating politically among the campuses until we settled on the comforts of Trinity College. When Maurice Careless presented a particularly tedious paper on local history, previously a talk to the Kamloops Historical Society, Chris Armstrong decreed that the colloquium was now the Kamloops Society. Meetings were well-attended and the discussions both well-lubricated and high-powered.

The standard teaching load in the department in 1968 was nine hours a week of class-contact over our two thirteen-week terms. In early years I lectured for one term to about three hundred students in one of the big Canadian history survey courses, lectured for one term to about sixty students in a course on Canadian economic development, gave year-long tutorials to several groups in each of these courses, and conducted a senior undergraduate seminar on the Canadian and American response to industrialism. The burden was not as heavy as colleagues had carried in the past, nor did I have to teach outside my specialty. Still, like most beginning teachers, I had to work frantically writing the fifty-two fifty-minute lectures I gave that first year. My course enrollments and grading responsibilities were much higher than the departmental average.

On the other hand, I had no stage fright, no worries about teaching technique, and there were no major crises. I wrote on April 11, 1969,

> I gave my last lecture in History 300 this morning and was told by four or five students afterward that these were the best lectures they'd had in their three years of University. That was surely the ultimate compliment. As I remember the year I put an immense amount of work into the lecture preparation. All year long I felt that I was constantly flirting on the edge of disaster, and was never really confident for more than one or two weeks that I could pull off everything successfully. I've still not lost the habit of looking in the want ads for other jobs that I might take.

I never believed that undergraduates were informed and critical enough to pass reliable judgment in course evaluations, but their very high ratings of my courses were, of course, entirely warranted. I told the students in my small seminars that the success of these small, intense, student-led discussions was almost entirely a function of the mix of students and their effort. My first seminar group was one of the best I would ever have at Toronto, generating several lifelong friendships — though not with the one student who later became a mob hit man and wound up jailed for life.

———

I liked to use marathoning as a metaphor for the experience of writing a thesis or book. An academic's first marathon, the doctoral thesis, is almost always the hardest. You not only have to finish an enormous endurance test, but to break the thesis tape you have to convince a committee of judges that your form and pace are of good quality. You have no experience pacing yourself, no experience coping with the effects of hitting a wall of exhaustion and despair. Worse, trying to write a thesis while teaching at an advanced level is like having to stop every few hundred yards during a marathon to have a discussion with members of the crowd and then get going again. The drop-out rate is very high.

We needed income after returning to Toronto. To a full teaching load I usually added an extra night course, and in the year I had off to finish my thesis I still taught part-time — and did not finish. I plugged along with my investigations of Canadian business thought as recorded in the crumbling pages of eighty-year-old copies of *Industrial Canada, The Canadian Manufacturer, The Monetary Times, The Canada Lumberman, The Canadian Grocer,* and other obscure trade journals. An early by-product of my industry was that I persuaded the Maclean-Hunter publishing company to donate its priceless runs of its early business journals to our university's Rare Book Library. This good work on behalf of our library proved counter-productive, as I found it more difficult to get access to the material after it was transferred from Maclean-Hunter to the university that employed me. I complained angrily and loudly about our librarians' distrust of readers.

My first visits to the Public Archives of Canada, in Ottawa, were more pleasant (except for the day when somebody — a thrill-seeking archivist? — stole my car from the parking lot and took it for a joyride). The main reading room of the then new archives building on Wellington Street was open twenty-four hours a day, the staff were helpful and efficient, not even blanching at my order for hundreds of pages of photocopies (later they established limits and raised prices), and it was fascinating to leaf through the original correspondence of Macdonald, Laurier, Borden, and other leading Canadian politicians. Early days in the archives introduced me to the thrill of discovering important documents. For example, no one previously had noticed a letter from George Stephen, president of the Canadian Pacific Railway, to Sir John A. Macdonald, mentioning that in the 1880s Stephen had contributed $1,000,000 to the Conservative Party, a sum so astonishingly large that it calls into question the integrity of Canadian elections in that decade and would have utterly destroyed the prime minister had it been known.

Even coffee breaks at the archives were interesting, as researchers chattered noisily about our work and about the profession. I noticed that I had different habits from most archives users: I would limit my breaks to ten minutes worth of caffeine, nicotine, and talk, while many other researchers and staff would stretch their cafeteria time, sometimes to half an hour or longer, as though reluctant to go back to their work. I wanted to get on with it, to get as much done in a day as I possibly could and to minimize time away from home. These habits were becoming ingrained and essential to my productivity. After a full day's work in the archives I would take an hour off for dinner, then go back to the reading room until ten or twelve at night.

In the middle of my thesis marathon, and never wedded to the idea of making business history a career specialty, I went seriously off course. One day when we were talking about the dullness of Canadian history, Graeme Patterson said it was too bad we couldn't find some sex in the subject. I started gathering material for a lighthearted lecture on sex in Canadian history. At first it was a few minutes of not very good jokes — the west getting screwed, Ontario on top, Canada as Kipling's frigid

"Our Lady of the Snows," and John Kenneth Galbraith's story in his memoir, *The Scotch in Canada*, about watching a bull service a heifer while chatting with the beautiful neighbouring farm girl. "That looks like fun," young Galbraith said to the girl, "I'd like to try that." "Go ahead, John," she replied. "It's your cow."

Then, while browsing in a 1915 publication for Canadian social service workers, I came across an ad entitled, "Pure Books on Avoided Subjects." It was for "The Self and Sex Series," books published in the United States and Canada with titles such as *What a Young Boy Ought to Know*, *What a Young Man Ought to Know*, *What a Young Husband Ought to Know*, *What a Man of 45 Ought to Know*, with parallel titles for women. Using the interlibrary loan network that had recently developed, I was able to track down copies. They were pre-Freudian sex manuals, carefully phrased attempts to introduce Christian men and women to the perils and pleasures of their sexuality. Mostly perils, because the authors were mainly concerned that people should not squander their vital energy — concentrated as semen in the male, somewhat nebulous in the female — through self-abuse or onanism or any other kind of sexual excess.

I had stumbled upon a rich vein of purity literature from the nineteenth century, a body of thought and advice that revealed interesting nineteenth-century physiological and sexual assumptions about to be turned upside down in the twentieth century. My reading took me to American characters like Sylvester Graham and Harvey Kellogg, food faddists who preached vegetarianism to help dampen animal passions while inventing graham crackers, peanut butter, and corn flakes, and to the first sex education in Canadian schools, talks given by a professional purity worker named Arthur Beall. In the first thirty years of the twentieth century, Beall toured Ontario trying to terrify grade eight boys about the effects of masturbation. In the climax of his visit he would have the boys all chant after him: "The more the penis muscle is used the weaker it gets. The less the penis muscle is used the stronger it gets."

What fun for my lecture on sex in Canadian history, sometimes known as "Sex with Bliss." There was also raw material for serious study of the history of sexual ideas, in those years still a largely virginal field. Where did these ideas come from? How important were they? Did anyone listen to the purity workers? (A boy who heard Arthur Beall later told me the talk got him interested in masturbation.) Perhaps I should switch my research interest away from tedious Canadian businessmen and plunge into this exotic field of social history, the bounds of which were not confined to Canada. In a few weeks I did an immense amount of work, which I presented to Ramsay Cook with a view to changing my thesis topic.

Cook was not impressed at the way I seemed to have gone off half-cocked. He told me my papers on sex were shallow, he had no special interest in that field, and that if I wanted to pursue this line of work I would need a new supervisor. On reflection, I realized that Cook was probably right, swallowed my disappointment, and went back to my dreary partnership with desiccated Canadian bankers and grocers.

The purity material was too good not to use, and so the first presentation I gave at an annual meeting of the Canadian Historical Association, in Winnipeg in 1970, was entitled: "'Pure Books on Avoided Subjects': Pre-Freudian Sexual Ideas in Canada." It was delivered to a packed house and I was introduced by Maurice Careless, who noted that this was a session about what might be called "Careless Bliss." In both the oral and the published paper I offered serious arguments about the location of these sexual ideas in the vitalist school of physiology and the empirical fact that the first people to observe uncontrolled masturbation were the staff of lunatic asylums, who were taken in by the *post hoc propter hoc* fallacy. Until it was reversed by the Freudians, the dominant paradigm of sexual thought in the English-speaking world seemed to be the idea of "creative sexual repression."

My article would be reprinted several times and frequently cited, although its obscure publication in Canada meant that it was largely ignored by the American and British scholars who soon moved into this field. The subject had taken me far from any previous work and had a lasting effect: as I pursued nineteenth-century medical views on sexuality I came across books and journals dealing with the history of medicine, which seemed to me to be a fascinating area of study. A year or two later I worked up a lecture on the role of medicine in Canadian history, seeing it as a kind of homage to the family business.

There was also welcome interest in this work outside of the university, creating opportunities not often available to young scholars. I had a round of radio interviews, including a very good one with the host of the CBC's show *As It Happens*, Barbara Frum, as well as invitations to give talks to audiences ranging from psychiatrists at the Toronto Academy of Medicine through the congregation of Toronto's First Unitarian Church. "That was all very interesting, Professor Bliss," a Unitarian said to me after I had given a very strange Sunday morning sermon. "But could you please tell me how you cure impotence?" Peter C. Newman, then editor of *Maclean's*, insisted that a popular version of my article should indicate what was particularly Canadian about these sexual ideas. He fell for my absurd suggestion that Arthur Beall was advocating a distinctively Canadian approach to masturbation.

The study of Canadian businessmen taught me foundational lessons about the role of market forces, interest groups, tactics of special pleading, the usefulness of being able to identify a cause with the national interest, and the interplay of collectivist and individualist views of society. As my thesis took shape, I spun out working papers and chapters as scholarly articles and presentations at conferences. My insight into how business interests manipulated nationalism to justify a "National Policy" of tariff protection in the nineteenth century led to reflections on how others, including the producers of culture, especially academics, do the same. I became suspicious of everyone who tries to get subsidies and protective legislation from governments, though I was also aware of how hard it is for most people to have to function in highly competitive marketplaces where they are apt to become the victim of capitalism's penchant for creative destruction. Just as workers tried to take collective action to earn "a living wage," so small businessmen had tried to do the same so they could secure "a living profit," a phrase that would become the title of my thesis and the book based on it.

The surge of Canadian nationalism in the 1960s seemed to me little more than a new round of protectionism and anti-Americanism promoted by politicians like Walter Gordon, as well as a clamour for jobs and subsidies on the part of professors, graduate students, and other cultural producers. There were also disturbing signs, highlighted in articles about Quebec by both Pierre Trudeau and Ramsay Cook, of a resurgence of nineteenth-century integral or ethnic nationalism, a kind of neo-tribalism that had ugly overtones. Even in the History Department there were disgusting currents of resentment at some of our American-born colleagues as carpet-bagging foreigners. When as a young Canadianist I was approached to contribute to a couple of anthologies reflecting the new nationalism, *Close the 49th Parallel, Etc.*, and *The New Romans*. I submitted pieces that were sharply opposed to the anti-American, statist views of most of the authors.

The closest I came to a personal manifesto was a rebuttal to an older Canadian historian, L.F.S. Upton, who had called for a return to an older tradition of Canadian history as fulfilling a comforting role, telling us about our national identity. In "Searching for Canadian History," published in the *Queen's Quarterly* in 1968, I warmly argued that our only responsibility was to try to tell the truth about history. Some of us were nationalists because Canada happened to stand for values we believed in, but it was entirely possible that North American societies might change. I suggested, for example, that it was not inconceivable that Canadians might come to repeat Goldwin Smith's argument in his classic 1891 book, *Canada and the Canadian Question*, in favour of "a wider, more fulfilling English-speaking community in North America."

I thought I was trying to write Canadian social history, not the outdated nationalist and constitutional history the old guys had churned out and that seemed to have turned the mainstream of Canadian history into a bit of a backwater. Many of us were influenced by an explosion of new approaches to history in the United States, and we wanted to emulate them here. But what could we and our students read as sources for Canadian social history? Most books relevant to Canadian labour or business or urban or immigrant history had long been out of print. With *Canadian History in Documents* selling well (it got adopted in British Columbia high schools, which bought 25,000 copies, elevating the Blisses briefly into the Volvo-owning academic stratum), I tried to interest publishers in reprinting certain works, such as *Canada and the Canadian Question* or the testimony given to the Royal Commission on the Relations of Capital and Labor, that were effectively documents in Canadian social history. The University of Toronto Press was interested in an idea introduced to me by Linda Grayson, one of our doctoral students, to republish letters written in the 1930s from desperately poor Canadians to Prime Minister R.B. Bennett.

As we worked on this project and I talked about other possibilities, the Press's lead Canadian editor, R.I.K. Davidson, suggested that UTP should issue a series of reprints and document collections in Canadian social history with myself as general editor. We went to work vigorously, and in 1971 the first four books in the Social History of Canada series were published: *The Wretched of Canada, Canada and the Canadian Question*, J.S. Woodsworth's *My Neighbour*, and E.W. Bradwin's *The Bunkhouse Man* (still the best book ever written about Canadian workers). We had many more titles in the works. It was easy to secure the rights to books not in copyright. For each title, UTP paid me a $250 advance against 2.5% royalties on sales. Nellie McClung's early feminist tract, *In Times Like These*, became far and away our bestseller, still in print more than thirty-five years later. The few cents I received every time someone bought a copy of McClung and the other titles was satisfying testimony to our foresight in sensing and helping to foster a growing interest in Canadian social history.

Liz returned to teaching at East York Collegiate when we came back from Harvard. We thought it time to have a family; she became pregnant, and resigned her job to raise our children. Maternity or paternity leave did not yet exist. In 1969, we paid what seemed like the enormous sum of $33,000 to buy a small three-bedroom house on a quiet street in south Leaside. On October 19, Liz gave birth to our son, James Robert Quartus. She was still in hospital with the baby on the night of October 23, when I had a call from my sister-in-law, Mona, saying that my brother Jim had been found dead in his laboratory at McGill. Jim was thirty-nine. We had been very close the last few years, and I still idolized him. My last conversation with him had been to tell him that he had a namesake. He probably died of a heart attack or stroke brought on by years of hypertension, but it was decided not to do an autopsy to avoid the possibility of finding suicide. For all his brilliance and promise, Jim's was a life that had not worked very well.

Jamie was an easy and happy child, a good starter baby. We were keen to have another, and on April 13, 1971, Laura Elizabeth came into the world. She was born early in the morning on a day when I was scheduled to give the final lecture in my big Canadian history survey course. Dead tired, on the way from Woman's College Hospital to the university I bought ten dozen roses and ten dozen cigars. I told my students that I was cancelling the class to honour our newborn flower child, and gave out roses to the women, cigars to the men. The first time I saw baby Laura she seemed transcendently beautiful.

All of this busy-ness slowed progress on my thesis. But I learned to concentrate with babies literally at my feet, and by the winter of 1971–72 had a first draft of my doctoral thesis ready. Friends and colleagues gave me critical feedback, and in a final, exhausting sprint to the finish I revised and polished it early that spring. I wrote that April, in what was becoming regular diarizing,

> The months since February have been hard, perhaps harder than any before. The thesis went on and on as did the teaching. Reading week was 10 straight 12 hour days of revision, with no rest. At least a dozen people

have told me how exhausted I looked during March, probably looked ashen and gray. Finally the thesis was handed in last Wednesday and there's no point now in regrets or second thoughts. Have not felt any sense of relief — though by all rational considerations I should.

My thesis examination that May, in a hot upper room at the School of Graduate Studies, was completely routine. I remember almost nothing about the final test, not even the names of most of my examiners, other than Cook and Craig Brown. Carl Berger used to tell students after thesis exams of Stephen Leacock's quip that with the Ph.D. you are now pronounced full and need never have another idea. I felt drained, as though I had no ideas. It was considerable compensation that my colleague, Michael Cross, told me he wanted to publish a revised version of the thesis in a social history series he had just been commissioned to edit for Canada's leading publisher, McClelland & Stewart.

We took the summer off, sort of, spending it in Fredericton, where I taught a course at the University of New Brunswick. Before and after the course we had our first tours of Atlantic Canada, including a visit to Liz's father's birthplace on Prince Edward Island. We stayed with her two aunts at the family's "Hazeldean Farm," a beautiful spot in the exact heart of the island. Aunts Doris and Muriel might have been characters in any of the works of Lucy Maud Montgomery — in fact, they had known her — and Hazeldean farmhouse could have been a model for "Green Gables."

It said something about New Brunswickers' interests that only fifty students took my course in the history of Canada since Confederation, as opposed to about two hundred who registered for an utterly tedious course on the Maritimes from 1713 to 1848 (I sat in on some of the lectures). My students were a notch or two below the Toronto norm, as symbolized by a public school principal from Doaktown, NB, who submitted a 2,000 word essay with 139 spelling errors. Afterward he apologized, saying that if his secretary had not been on holiday she would have cleaned it up for him.

Having had to work fairly hard at my teaching, not feeling at all rested, I vowed never to give another summer course.

═══════════════

On January 21, 1971, I wrote in my journal:

> The Student Power movement at U of T appears to be entering its final paroxysm. The Faculty Council today defeated the principle of [faculty-student] parity by a wide margin at a meeting in Convocation Hall. There were various student attempts to intimidate us, such as the publication of an "Action Plan" in yesterday's *Varsity*, giving students instruction in how to seal the exits. The crowd was menacing, characterized by noise and tom-toms both at the beginning and end. The hall smelled of incense …
>
> When the vote was announced there was fairly considerable silence. Then a student leader announced that students were leaving the Faculty Council and would not return until their demands were met, that we were not a legitimate body and that they would not recognize any of our proceedings. There were shouts of "Burn the Fucking University Down," "Let's Bomb the Place," "Go to Hell All of You."

Jan. 22:

> They were occupying the foyer of Sidney Smith today, having brought furniture down from the lounge and blaring rock music … Faculty were simply ignoring them … A leaflet was passed out calling us "cretins," "anachronisms," "senile."

In Canada we suffered nothing like the agonies of race riots, presidential assassinations, the Vietnam War. Toronto was a good city to live in, the university was an intellectual gourmet supermarket, and most of the students were good kids. Still, the late sixties and early seventies were a time of unprecedented turmoil, in classrooms and across the campus. The mix of countercultural values, the rise of the New Left, and demands for student power, led to a seemingly endless series of disturbances, demands, marches, mass meetings, ultimata, sit-ins, threats, and more threats. At the highest levels of the administration Claude Bissell and his advisers, men who had flown bombers over Germany and landed in Normandy on D-Day, seemed utterly baffled about how to deal with a few hundred student radicals posing as revolutionaries. Time and again the administration seemed to bow to student demands; time and again the demands escalated, the atmosphere deteriorated, and insiders and outsiders began to wonder whether the rule of law was being upheld on the campus of the University of Toronto.

Bissell's problems were partly of his own making. He had become convinced that the university's governing structure, a board of governors appointed by our owner, the province of Ontario, with academic policy set by a faculty-dominated senate, ought to be reformed. His decision to launch a reconsideration of university governance in 1968 was like calling the Estates-General just as the Jacobin movement began to gather strength. Bissell found himself harassed by student demands at every turn, and often had lukewarm faculty support. The last chapters of his bittersweet memoir of his years as president, *Halfway Up Parnassus*, are a sad chronicle of confrontations with Langdon's legions and other rude and obstructive student groups.

Bissell was several times on the verge of calling in Toronto police to keep order or clear occupied buildings. He always pulled back, partly out of a sense that student silliness would eventually subside, partly out of fear that serious violence could break out, as it had at several American universities, and in Canada at Sir George Williams University in Montreal (now Concordia) when protesting students burned down the computer centre. What a commentary on a sick time in our history that the president of the University of Toronto felt he had to cancel his traditional opening address to the students for fear of being the victim of "some wild drug-sustained fling."

As a junior faculty member, I was only an onlooker at most of the confrontations. Privately and publicly I found almost everything about the counterculture, the New Left, and the student movement appalling, and I do not find some of the self-serving apologias offered up as histories of the era convincing. The values of the counterculture were narcissistic, nihilistic, or absurdly utopian. It was no surprise that within a year of its opening, Rochdale College had abandoned all of its founders' dreams and decayed into a filthy, drug-riddled haven for lost souls and criminals. The intellectual pretentions of the New Left, trying to filter the absurdities of Marxism through the sophistries of Herbert Marcuse, with slogans by Mao Zedong, ought to have been far beneath serious consideration. Students who claimed that they possessed the wisdom and maturity to run the university at every level seemed like spoiled or precocious children at best, ugly totalitarians at worst.

The History Department, along with Political Economy and Sociology, hosted a disproportionate share of radical student politicians. At that time, I did not know Bob Rae, a brilliant history undergraduate who would go on to become NDP Premier of Ontario and temporary leader of the Liberal Party of Canada. Despite being seen as a "moderate" student leader on our campus, Rae was prominently loud and arrogant, outwardly full of himself, apparently a pretentious pup. Many people paid a heavy price to give Bob Rae an education and a maturity that he might have developed in the 1960s had he paid serious attention to the study of history.

One of the most menacing and blustering of the student radicals was a history major from St. Michael's College, Gregory Kealey. Greg took the course that Michael Cross and I taught on strategies of Canadian economic development, as did a number of student radicals, in part drawn to Cross. Michael was a bright and personable colleague with very left-wing views, a kind of role model of academic radicalism in a restrained Canadian way (his first wife was a granddaughter of William

Lyon Mackenzie King). Kealey was interested in labour history, he contained his arrogance and rudeness just short of direct confrontation, and he was willing to learn about subjects that interested him. I hired him one summer to assist me in editing the documents generated by the Royal Commission on the Relations of Labor and Capital. Our planning meeting had to be held in the Don jail, where Greg was serving a two week sentence for having thrown a clod of dirt at a mounted policeman during a demonstration outside the American consulate on University Avenue. Kealey eventually wrote and facilitated a lot of leftist labour history and became a vice-president of the University of New Brunswick.

From time to time we worried that crazed students would cross the line into serious violence. These were the years of separatist bombings and kidnappings in Quebec, culminating in the crisis of October 1970, when Trudeau imposed the War Measures Act on Canada. I defended the government's actions in a student-sponsored debate before a large audience. One of the ideologues of the radical student left defended separatist-terrorism, stopping just short of endorsing murder. Evil times. After listening to a rabid demagogue haranguing sympathizers in the foyer of Sidney Smith Hall one day, several of us took our more valuable books home from our office. The university had stated it would not insure us against their loss.

In lectures and tutorials the atmosphere was often heady and not without intellectual excitement. I could hardly say my name without someone putting up his hand to challenge me. All views seemed open to question, no assumptions could go unexamined. Many of my students, including my first two doctoral candidates, Veronica Strong-Boag and Jim Struthers, and the leading campus journalists Linda McQuaig and Tom Walkom, had reasonable, flexible minds, and we could argue about virtually anything and then agree to disagree. The new approaches to our country's history some of us were trying to pioneer were, by comparison with my own days as an undergraduate, breaths of fresh air, only to be polluted by gusts of simplistic, stale Marxist and Maoist posturing. For two years I participated in an experimental, multi-disciplinary course, "The Search for Community," taught by a team that also included a political economist, a sociologist, and a law professor. Like many sixties experiments it was exciting at first and then fizzled into the worst of all academic conditions, tedium. It did give me the opportunity to read good books outside my field.

The silliness of the age only occasionally infected my classroom. One radical student, also later a professor, argued to me that when the Toronto *Globe* published a poem by Keats in 1895, it was evidence of a desire to reach out to a working-class audience. One year my lectures were punctuated by ignorant interjections from a Maoist student named Jules. "That's all horseshit, Professor!" Jules would say when I recognized his constantly waving hand, and he would ramble on in a counter-lecture until the other students became fed up and told him to sit down and be quiet.

There were occasional ugly confrontations in other classes, and some very bright lecturers gave up and left the university in disgust at being subjected to what would now be considered unacceptable verbal harassment, usually to excel in what we always called the real world. Under the best of circumstances, teaching at the university level is stressful and exhausting for those who try to do it well. My journals, which are the principal source for most of the rest of this memoir, show that I sometimes found the grind of lecturing, tutoring, grading, and troubleshooting depressing, and wondered whether to enter a different profession. At other times, usually after an exciting class, I thought I had the best job in the world.

After shepherding through a major reform in university governance, Claude Bissell retired from Toronto's presidency in 1971, taking satisfaction, he wrote, "in mere survival." During and after his Harvard sabbatical, the great good place that this gentle scholar and fine human being had served so well for so long seemed to have been polluted, stained. I always thought that the student leaders, Langdon, Kealey, Rae, and others, had been arrogant and childish in the damage they caused to the lives of Claude and Christine Bissell. Still, the university would carry on, and while much of our sense of community had collapsed, there were still pockets of greatness and glimmers of goodness in its uncivil hallways and classrooms.

The summer of 1973 brought welcome relief from years of heavy teaching. Liz was pregnant again, and in June we moved into a four-bedroom home on Bessborough Drive in north Leaside, with a large lawn that would be the kids' playing field. In an overheating housing market we got into an auction, displayed our cute children to impress the aged owners with our wholesomeness, offered several hundred dollars more than the asking price, and got the house for $66,000. We sold our south Leaside house for $49,000, a 50% gain in about four years.

Sally, Michael, Jamie, Liz, Laura, 1986.

I had launched a new project, to write a biography of the millionaire philanthropist and pork packer Sir Joseph Flavelle, and threw myself into fascinating, productive research. I revised my doctoral thesis for publication in little more than a week, rewriting a chapter a day. At the beginning of September I handed in that manuscript, and our son Jamie had his first day at school. The next day, September 4, Liz went into Woman's College Hospital — I was at the university; she drove herself down and gave birth to our third child. Sara Ann Kathleen Bliss, a very nice little bundle, completed our family. By then, fathers were often allowed into delivery rooms — they had not been in 1969 — but because Sally was a breech baby I again missed the opportunity to see the moment of birth.

I never found out what happened to that girl from Saskatchewan. I hope she was okay. I wish I had tried to help her. The drug culture was, and is, a crime against the human spirit.

Chapter Seven

Governing

The "Ban Banfield" posters began appearing several weeks before Professor Edward Banfield, a distinguished American urbanologist, was scheduled to give a seminar and two lectures on our campus. A remnant cell of student radicals who styled themselves the Toronto chapter of the American organization, Students for a Democratic Society, was urging that Banfield be prevented from speaking. They made the utterly spurious claim that he was a racist.

We could all see trouble brewing. A week before Banfield's visit I witnessed a confrontation in the History Department hallway between Bill Nelson, who had become the president of the Faculty Association, and Jill Conway, his colleague in American history who had become vice-president for Internal Affairs and was responsible for maintaining order on the campus (historians were over-represented in the broader life of the university). Bill bluntly told Jill that the administration had a record of failing to anticipate trouble, that it was absolutely certain trouble was coming in this case, and that if the administration did not act to preserve free speech on campus, using police if necessary, the Faculty Association would have a lot to say.

The administration's only response to this and other warnings, we learned later, was to try to get Banfield's visit postponed or cancelled.

When that did not happen, Simcoe Hall was completely unprepared for the ugly scenes that developed. On March 12, 1974, Banfield's attempt to give a seminar was shouted down by a handful of radicals. Later that afternoon he managed to deliver a public lecture (a very academic analysis of the limits of social science) to a raucous crowd, but as it ended the SDS group, shouting "Smash Racism" and "Banfield Go to Hell," formed a menacing circle around him at the podium. A dozen or so faculty, myself included, formed a cordon and, amidst noise and jostling, got him out of the room. Three uniformed members of the university's security force stood by, doing nothing.

That night there were many calls to senior members of the administration from faculty who were concerned that free speech at the University of Toronto was not being defended. My contribution was to phone our provost (the university's chief academic officer), Donald Forster, whom I had known since he had been a don in residence, and complain bitterly about the failure of our new president, John Evans, to do or say anything in defence of the right to speak freely. Forster agreed that feelings like mine were widespread.

When Banfield entered the West Hall of University College the next afternoon to give a second public lecture to an audience of several hundred people, the podium had already been seized by about fifteen SDS activists. They said that Banfield would not be allowed to speak. Campus police made no attempt to clear the podium or in any way interfere with the law-breakers. The atmosphere was electric and menacing. Banfield and his sponsors had to leave the room, and the meeting was adjourned.

It is a sobering experience to see a university professor — or anyone else — denied the right to speak, and students denied the right to hear, by a gang of impassioned thugs. I stayed in my seat, reflecting on our sad situation, and only learned of the immediate aftermath a few hours later. After Banfield was prevented from speaking a delegation of about twenty-five faculty members, led by Nelson and other members of the History Department, went directly to see President Evans in his office at Simcoe Hall, told him what had happened, and demanded that he take action. Bob Spencer, our mild-mannered professor of German history, politely told the president of the University of Toronto that perhaps he should familiarize himself with what had happened to German universities in the 1930s.

When Evans showed the group a letter he had written to Banfield apologizing for the previous day's disruptions, Nelson told him that he had better make it a form letter because he'd have to use it again and again. When Provost Forster suggested that the delegation leave Simcoe Hall by a rear door, because students were now congregating at the front door, one of my former philosophy professors, David Gauthier, said he'd be goddamned if he'd leave by the back door, and was going out the front. "Dr. Evans," Nelson said, "you get down here and make sure that your own faculty can leave by the front door. Why don't you start acting like a president and go and speak to your students?" Evans said, "That's exactly what I had in mind." He spoke briefly to a group of students outside Simcoe Hall and went back inside and the doors were locked.

Naturally, the *Globe and Mail* published the lecture Banfield had been prevented from giving, generating comments that it was offensive only in being so dull and opaque. But for the next two weeks the campus was in turmoil over Banfield and the free-speech issue. The administration explained that it knew the university's police force was inadequate to keep order, but it did not believe the university community would support the use of Metropolitan Toronto Police on the campus. Many faculty members, especially in the History and Political Economy Departments, found this position outrageous and untenable. The Faculty Association passed strong resolutions amounting to ultimata to the administration: if appropriate steps were not taken it would demand resignations.

I was still an insignificant assistant professor, but had never been so angry about a matter of principle. Quoting liberally from John Stuart Mill's *On Liberty*, I drew up a statement protesting the administration's refusal to defend free speech and cancelled a couple of my classes in protest. I told a reporter for the *Star* that if the current president would not protect free speech at our university then we ought to find one who would. The comment appeared on the front page. I suddenly had disproportionate media access and felt that on such an issue one should not keep quiet. I spoke in favour of free speech at a number of campus events and in the broadcast media, garnering enough attention in an ugly time to cause some members of my family to worry — unnecessarily, I thought, although SDS was threatening various colleagues — about the safety of Liz and the children.

Doctor John Evans, whom I eventually came to know and like very much, had made his reputation as a medical administrator, the founding dean of the McMaster University Medical School. The rest of his career would go far more smoothly than these strange days of almost inconceivable academic disorder. His strength lay in administration and in his knowledge of our professional faculties. He had few contacts with the Faculty of Arts and virtually no experience with the waves of student radicalism that had buffeted us for several years. He relied on Jill Conway to handle these issues (for all his faults, Claude Bissell, we felt, would have made an appearance at Banfield's lectures), and Jill did not believe in being tough with radical students. An idealist, and in those days fashionably radical herself (it did not last; she eventually finished her career as a director of the old Merrill Lynch brokerage firm at the height of its wild financial frenzies), Jill still believed in the old concept of a university as a place set apart, where privileged students and privileged professors would reason together. The thought of inviting tough Metro policemen on campus to manhandle rowdy students was more than she could stomach. So she dithered. Colleagues had warned Simcoe Hall that putting Jill in charge of discipline was like asking hard-drinking Archie Thornton to look after the liquor cabinet.

The seriousness of the university's predicament was brought home at the highest level when the Governing Council, our new governing body, held its monthly meeting. The Banfield affair and its consequences would be high on the agenda. I had a precious admission ticket. The governors of Canada's largest and most important university convened to chants from SDS demonstrators outside on the front campus, egged on by someone with a bullhorn. Nervous administrators scuttled in and out of the meeting, and peeped out the windows. Half an hour into an already disputatious meeting — student members of Governing Council were unhelpful at the best of times — we heard loud crashes and suddenly the bullhorn was inside the building. Evans announced that demonstrators had broken into Simcoe Hall just as a yelling crowd of them burst through the closed doors of the Governing Council chamber. They filled whatever seats they could find and many sat on the floor.

After a few minutes of total confusion, someone moved that council adjourn. The last word came from one of the SDS storm troopers, a woman who filled the void of silence as the meeting ended by yelling "Chickenshit." A few minutes later I was standing near President Evans and Vice-President Conway as they surveyed some of the damage to the building. I resisted the urge to comment that their chickens had come home to roost. The next day council resumed its meeting under heavy police protection, and there were no further incidents. The use of police on our campus to protect order and freedom was long overdue. For several years, basic human rights had been repeatedly jeopardized to appease spoiled and dangerous children.

The Banfield affair fizzled that spring and summer in a nearly farcical hearing of the university's archaic disciplinary body, Caput. The SDS leaders turned the proceedings into televised guerilla theatre before finally being convicted of discipline breaches and suspended for several years. The university was too timid to bring charges of criminal trespass and assault against the students, but the SDS members went to court to charge my colleague Bob Bothwell with assault during the first melee, when we had escorted Banfield out of West Hall. That case dragged on for months before a judge finally threw it out. I testified on Bob's behalf. These were the final death-throes both of serious student radicalism and the old, impossible idea of the university campus as a sheltered, self-governing haven where people would behave rationally and politely.

Desperately tired, in the summer of 1974 I was fortunate to be at the beginning of my first experience with one of the great perks of academic life, a sabbatical from undergraduate teaching. Time off to recharge one's batteries or carry out a special research project was mutating from a special privilege to something like a guaranteed right in most Canada universities. About every seventh year one could give up a certain percentage of salary and go on sabbatical. The Canada Council had a program of Leave Fellowships that made up most of the shortfall. There were, and are, almost no restrictions on how sabbaticals can be spent, leading to much recharging and "research" in the south of France. Part of the cost of spending most of a career in Canadian history was that I would never have a sabbatical outside the country.

The beginning of my year off, June 1974, coincided with the publication of my first scholarly book, *A Living Profit: Studies in the Social History of Canadian Business, 1883–1911*, one of the first two titles in McClelland & Stewart's Canadian Social History Series. A pleasant wine and cheese party at Hart House launched the book and the series during that year's Toronto conference of the Canadian Historical Association. The downside of the launch was a mess McClelland & Stewart was in for having neglected to include in these books an acknowledgement of financial support from the new Social Sciences Research Council of Canada. A lowly editor stayed up very late the night before the party stamping the firm's thanks into every copy. I was unhappy because I had hoped to publish a book that would not require a subsidy, but would be financially viable on its merits. I was taken by surprise when M&S, a commercial firm, sought a government subsidy. Subsidized publication struck me as being just a step away from vanity publishing. How little I knew about the special problems of being an author in Canada. As well, at the time of publication and celebration McClelland & Stewart had not yet sent any books to bookstores or for review. It somewhat diluted the thrill of authorship.

Eventually, *A Living Profit* was reasonably widely reviewed, sold out its first edition, and was reissued before falling out of print in the 1980s (and being erased, Soviet-style, by a new Marxist editor from every list of the Canadian Social History Series' titles; Bliss on business was not fit to be considered social history). It did not make a great splash, nor had I expected one. It was a 150-page academic monograph, a little paperback on a narrow topic, as were most of its companions in that series. I saw it only as a first effort, a warm-up for better to come. The day I delivered the final manuscript, October 24, 1973, I noted in my journal, "Perhaps it's an important achievement, but I'm not especially moved at the thought, still feeling that there's something wrong, that I've skillfully tailored a suit of clothes that won't fit anyone. I can't see how my book is going to change many people's ideas about Canadian history or any particular theme of Canadian history." I wanted to do better than this. I wanted to publish at least one big and important hardback book before I retired.

During thesis research I had come across the papers of Sir Joseph Flavelle, an Ontario-born businessman who, in the late nineteenth century, had become a millionaire meat packer, public servant, and philanthropist, the Canadian equivalent of a John D. Rockefeller or Andrew Carnegie. Flavelle, a prominent Methodist churchman, had also been at the centre of a storm of accusations of shameless profiteering during the First World War, when he was also czar of the Canadian munitions industry. Was he "Holy Joe" or "Old Black Joe" or a bit of both? He had died in 1939, but his legacy was still all over Toronto, from the Canada Packers (now Maple Leaf) food conglomerate through the Flavelle wing of the Toronto General Hospital to Flavelle House, his mansion, at the University of Toronto. I had taken my first history tutorials in Flavelle House (my tutor's office had been a former linen closet), which had then become the home of our law school. Thanks to the lack of enterprise of our university librarians — still mostly concerned with protecting their collections from users — Flavelle's personal papers had been donated to Queen's University in Kingston, where I first saw them. It was instantly clear that Flavelle was a thoughtful, fascinating person and businessman who had left an extremely rich paper trail. An obituarist had mentioned that in one way or another Flavelle had touched the lives of Canadians at more points than any man of his time.

My thesis had been an amorphous, open-ended tour of the ideas advanced by many Canadian businessmen. Now I was attracted by the notion of settling down with one key figure and learning everything

I could about him. A biography, I thought, would be easy to organize — you follow your subject from his birth to his death. Assuming the sources are good, in biography it might be possible to be thorough to the point of being definitive. The objectivity issue, an old methodological saw, did not particularly worry me. As I had concluded during an undergraduate course in the philosophy of history, most problems involving epistemology, bias, and method in the writing of history tend to clear up when subjected to a poultice of professionalism, skepticism, and elementary regard for evidence. Too few historians understand this, possibly because of their lack of grounding in either science or philosophy. I trusted myself to try to be impartial, as all professional people must in their work.

Not long after finishing my thesis, I told my friends I was going to do a biography of Flavelle. I contacted his descendents, told them of my interest, said I intended to do it as an independent project and would not ask for or take financial support from them, but hoped they would be interested in the project and help wherever possible.

Flavelle's grandchildren were as accommodating as I had hoped they would be, especially June and Flavelle Barrett, first cousins who had come together in second marriages. They supplied me with many contacts who had known Sir Joe, and eventually loaned me all the private family correspondence they had withheld from Queen's. Early one evening I brought home a large cardboard box full of Flavelle's letters to his wife and children, and stayed up all night excitedly reading and taking notes.

Most of the institutions Flavelle had been connected with cooperated by giving me access to their records. The paper chase involved lavish luncheons in the executive dining room of the Canadian Imperial Bank of Commerce, where I explained to not unfriendly bankers my need to see the bank's minutes; and it included clambering around a dark, dirty warehouse at Canada Packers' old William Davies factory on the hottest day of summer, searching for more corporate records. To work on the minutes of the Board of Toronto General Hospital, I was given a room opening from a main corridor. One day the door opened and an aged patient, intravenous hook-up in tow, shambled in. "I just had to come in," he said. "I heard your typing. I was the Canadian junior typing champion in 1936, and ever since then I've loved to hear good typists at work."

Much of the drudgery of going through the Flavelle Papers at Queen's, an eighty-box collection, was obviated by a deal I worked out with the archivist, Ian Wilson, to borrow ten boxes at a time and take them to Toronto for perusal and safekeeping in the United Church Archives, then on our campus. I shuttled the boxes back and forth myself, usually making the exchange on a Friday and arriving back in Toronto only after the UCA had closed. I would then work furiously on the boxes in the smoky comfort of my study all weekend, dropping them off at the United Church Archives on Monday with most of the work done. The staff there paid no attention to me and allowed me to do all the photocopying I wanted for a token charge.

Flavelle made his millions as a pork packer in the 1890s. The half million pigs a year that flowed down the Don River Valley on the Grand Trunk Railway to the William Davies factory were probably responsible, I realized, for Toronto getting its derisory nickname in the rest of Canada, "Hogtown." To understand the economics and science of meat packing, I met with top executives of Canada Packers, with retired hog buyers, and with expert bacon curers. My best day's work was a guided tour of a Canada Packers "dis-assembly" line. We followed live hogs up the ramps to the killing pens at the top of the factory, watched their reaction as they realized their fate, and then accompanied the carcasses down the line, as they were scalded, scraped, decapitated, disembowelled, inspected, dis-membered, pickled, packaged, and shipped to the world as Maple Leaf bacon and ham. It was a messy, bloody business, but it generated the best passage in the biography: "The pig's last sound is a deep-throated shriek of terror, as unsettling as any human scream...." And after seeing it all, I still had no qualms about eating the final product.

Back in the 1890s Flavelle's Canadian bacon had risen to prominence in Britain mostly because of the energy of his agent there, John Wheeler Bennett, who was nicknamed "the Bismarck of the Bacon Trade." Bennett was long dead, but his only son, Jack Wheeler-Bennett, was not only very much alive, but a distinguished historian and biographer, knighted for his authorized biography of King George VI. I contacted Sir John, who was delighted by my project, and for three years we had Easter luncheons in Manhattan as he passed through on his way home from wintering in Arizona. Sipping straight vodka in the leather and oak ambience of the Century Club, Sir John regaled me with stories of his father, Flavelle, prime ministers, and statesmen he had known. It seemed remarkable to talk to a man who had met both Kaiser Wilhelm II and Adolf Hitler. Very much his father's son, Wheeler-Bennett was among the last historians to believe that British imperialism had been an almost unqualified success.

As head of the Canadian munitions industry during the First World War, Flavelle had hired a University of Toronto scientist, Horace Speakman, to turn Toronto's Gooderham distillery into an acetone factory. Later, he had made Speakman the first director of the Ontario Research Foundation. When I found my way to Speakman in Toronto in 1973, he was a wizened little man, vaguely resembling Bertrand Russell, who began in a whispery voice, "Professor Bliss, I want you to know that I have not been just a scientist. Please go into my dining room and look carefully around you." The walls of his dining room were covered with paintings by members of the Group of Seven. "Now, Professor Bliss, please take a good look at the titles behind the glass in this bookcase." He had what appeared to be a complete set of first editions of the work of D.H. Lawrence, including a copy of *Lady Chatterly's Lover* with a thank-you letter Lawrence had written him for buying a copy. Lawrence hoped he would not judge the book obscene. At the end of a stimulating interview, Dr. Speakman gave me a pewter Chinese urn that Flavelle had given to him.

Speakman died not long after I met him. A year or so later I was called by a lawyer for the university, who told me that Speakman's bequest of his estate, including his paintings and books, to Trinity College was being contested by his children. They claimed their father was of unsound mind when he had revised his will not long before his death. I was one of the last non-family members to talk to him, and could I testify that he had been rational? I was happy to do this, using the notes I had made of the interview in my journal, and was only mildly embarrassed when my reflections on my own philistinism were read out in court. The suit was finally settled privately.

The cost of researching the Flavelle project was not high — hiring a student to do newspaper research, gas for the Kingston trips, airfare to New York. When I wrote President Evans, inquiring about support from the university's research funds, he replied enthusiastically that Flavelle was so important in the history of the university that I should name my sum. I thought about $7,000 would do the trick, an almost embarrassingly small figure at a time when the average grant in, say, the biomedical sciences, was already around $60,000. What we in the humanities always needed most, however, was not money but time. We needed grants that would release us from the need to teach.

Other than leave fellowships, the only major released-time program was the Canada Council's I.W. Killam Awards, which compensated universities for releasing faculty for up to two years to work on worthy projects. It seemed that the Killams were for well-established, senior scholars. But young historians were agog when a classmate and good friend of ours (he had married Liz's college roommate), Bob Cuff, taking up a position at York University after study and teaching in the United States, received a Killam only a couple of years after finishing his doctorate in American history. If Cuff could get a Killam, perhaps we too had a shot. I was thrilled when my Killam application earned me an interview in the final round of adjudication, and then only mildly disappointed to be turned down. It was explained to me that the Cuff precedent had sparked a deluge of applications from bright young scholars like myself; everyone knew I would get a Killam eventually. In any case I had my full sabbatical year to break the back of the project.

Well into the research, I began writing the first draft of the Flavelle biography in July 1974. I composed on my typewriter, usually worked during normal business hours, and, while words would come fairly easily on a good writing day, still would occasionally waste time staring at a blank piece of paper. Often, I would find my research inadequate and have to go back to the libraries and archives. The further I got into Flavelle's life, the more I realized how varied and complex and wide-ranging his business and philanthropic activities had been. Long hours of wrestling with bacon curing and hog marketing paid a priceless dividend in giving me the confidence to approach exotic topics, a hallmark of my later work. Meanwhile, the pile of drafts and redrafts of chapters mounted. I knew I was totally engaged in the project when Flavelle began appearing in my dreams, usually as inaccessible and disapproving.

There were distracting obligations. By then I was supervising graduate students, a job that was supposed to continue during sabbaticals, although many supervisors just disappeared and a fair number of colleagues did not have any students to supervise. I was also interested in trying to advance my career in every reasonable way, and had always hoped to become involved in the world of publishing and punditry. My university salary did not seem sufficient to support our family at the standard of living we would have enjoyed if I had gone into medicine or law. Throughout the 1970s I was making considerably less at the university than I would have earned by staying in high school teaching. I was both unhappy with my salary and eager to supplement it with royalties, speaking or consulting fees, and other kinds of outside income.

Universities traditionally have given faculty almost unlimited leeway to pick up extra income from writing, consulting, *et cetera*. Although we were salaried employees, unlike law or accounting firms the university did not feel it had a claim on how we used our expertise after a day's work on campus. So long as a professor showed up for class, held office hours for student consultation, and did his marking, no one was particularly concerned about what else he did. Early in my career there was still no policing of professors' moonlight activities, leading, of course, to significant abuse by a few. By the 1980s faculty members at most universities had to file annual reports on their significant outside activities, as well as account for their university time. I never cancelled a class to go moonlighting, never had a problem reporting my activities.

Promotion hinged largely on publication, so that academics who did nothing but moonlight, or simply did nothing, were held back. My appointment was as a lecturer until I finished my thesis, then as an assistant professor. With the publication of *A Living Profit* I was promoted to associate professor and given tenure, assurance that the university would not terminate my appointment unless I gave it cause by being demonstrably incompetent or committing acts of moral turpitude. I always knew I could pass any employment review, and did not consider getting tenure particularly important. The main threat to my free speech came from howling radicals and hesitant administrators. It was not obvious to me that tenure was good for the university or even in the best interests of professors. If the aim of your team is excellence, would you give the players tenure?

At the University of Toronto Press, R.I.K. Davidson gave me almost *carte blanche* to grow the Social History of Canada series of reprints. Scholars pelted me with suggestions of important books to reprint and ideas for new anthologies. I was unusually businesslike by academic standards in holding colleagues to deadlines for producing their introductions. From 1972 to 1975 we issued a new book in the Social History of Canada series every six weeks. The mandarins of the press then became alarmed at the size of their investment in the series. Complaining that I had proven the most energetic outside editor they had ever worked with (only in academia is energy and speed apt to be a mark against a person), they reigned in Davidson and me, slowing us to a crawl. With this window closing, and content with having given colleagues, students, and libraries access to twenty-nine important works of Canadian social history, I moved on. A few more books were published before the series petered out. Some of the titles I resurrected in the 1970s are still for sale by UTP.

I critiqued manuscripts for publishers, began getting books to review for scholarly journals and newspapers such as the *Financial Post*, was available to talk about Canadian history with reporters and on radio and television, and wrote occasional opinion pieces about business or politics for the *Post* or the *Toronto Star*. Publicizing — popularizing — history by reaching out to a wider audience, which all of my mentors had done, seemed part of a professor's job. It also generated interest in my work, and, as dribs and drabs of piecework payment added up, a welcome, if minor, source of extra income. In 1974, I took a few days to dash off a short and simple history of Confederation for an educational publisher aiming at the junior-high school market. *Confederation* remained in print for many years and seemed to be particularly popular at the CBC as their researchers' main source for facts on the birth of the country.

Canada's most prominent journalist, Pierre Berton, had decided to write a history of the building of the Canadian Pacific Railway. While he had a national reputation as a columnist and polemicist, he had little experience writing history. When I first read of his CPR project I thought Berton, some of whose recent books had been little more than opinionated trash, was almost certain to make a terrible hash of it. To my surprise, one day in 1970 I was asked if I would serve as his academic adviser on his railway project, reading his manuscripts for accuracy and for a fee. I agreed to do it mainly for the money — a then-high reading fee of $10 an hour. I expected the content would be very weak.

To my near amazement, Berton's two volume history (*The National Dream* and *Towards the Last Spike*) was thoroughly researched, well-written, and generally accurate. My reports on his manuscripts were highly positive, with only routine corrections of factual errors and a few sharp queries about interpretations. I knew Berton had a good researcher, but ten minutes with him on the phone convinced me that he also had a detailed knowledge of his subject and was his own author. It was clear that the project could be a great success.

Berton responded well to my criticisms. Although his biographer gives me too much credit for the success of Berton's railway books, I was pleased to be associated with excellent works of popular history that became record-breaking national bestsellers. The experience cured me of the snobbery toward journalists or "amateurs" that infects people who earn doctorates and get professorial appointments. As Berton once pointed out, he was the real professional, actually earning his living with his pen as opposed to professors with their multiple subsidies.

Contact with Berton paid a further dividend in the summer of 1975, when he asked me to be the historical consultant on a popular history project he and Jack McClelland were launching. Natural Science of Canada Limited, intended to produce series of books for mail-order sale on the model of Time-Life Books in the United States. NSL had published a number of slim volumes during the centennial boom in Canadiana in the late 1960s, had gone into limbo for a few years, and now had financing for a multi-volume series, Canada's Illustrated Heritage. Buyers would sign up to receive a book every month or two, always with the option of rejection. The sixteen or seventeen volumes were to be written by veteran journalists. Berton and McClelland were assembling a lean team of editors and consultants to produce the series. My job would be to make sure the manuscripts were historically balanced and accurate. My fee would be $2,000 a volume, way beyond $10 an hour. It seemed like handsome outside income now that the Social History of Canada series was winding down.

In my junior years I dutifully attended and spoke up at department meetings and accepted committee and other responsibilities, including service on a major university task force on academic appointments. I had come to know many of the senior faculty members most involved in university politics, and during the Banfield affair had been constantly active. As my sabbatical waned, I was approached by Charles Hanley, a faculty representative on the university's Governing Council and one of my former philosophy teachers, who asked if I would stand for election as his replacement. Chuck assured me that I would have the support of senior faculty who were concerned that there should be representation on Governing Council by the non-radical younger professors.

Flattered, but also daunted, I consulted widely, got assurance from my chairman of a reduction in teaching load to compensate for GC duties, and agreed to let my name stand. I was elected by acclamation. This was not so much a testimony to the strength of my candidacy as a sign of faculty disinterest in the university's new unicameral system of government.

The Governing Council was a single governing body composed of representatives of faculty, students, alumni, and the community. It did not work smoothly. The meetings I had observed during the Banfield affair had been depressing debacles, and the first one I observed as a governor-elect, in March 1975, was no better. "Jesus Christ," I ranted in my diary. "These people are supposed to be running a great university and the weight of intelligence brought to bear on its problems wouldn't make a hole in a damp Kleenex."

I did not have to worry about being a governor until my sabbatical ended. By the summer of 1975 I had broken the back of the Flavelle project by drafting good chapters that covered more than half of his career. I knew I could finish the book in another summer or two, leaving the winters free for teaching, governing, consulting, and whatever turned up. Life seems busier in the retelling that it actually was. When everything is written down, a lot happens to all of us in a single day. Think about the level of detail in *Ulysses* or *In Search of Lost Time*.

I served a three-year term on Governing Council, from 1975 to 1978. It seemed important service at the time, and opened many doors and introduced me to many interesting people outside the History Department. I made new friends, saw the workings of the university at the highest level, learned the nuts and bolts of administration, and, helped by others' sound judgment, decided that my forte and future should be as a scholar, not an administrator.

Student radicalism had virtually disappeared, leaving the Governing Council system as part of its legacy. The fifty-person council, with absolute power to run the university, was unsure how to carry out its mandate, fraught with tensions and animosities between members of its various "estates," and unpopular with the faculty. Faculty members resented the shrinkage of their influence and power that came the abolition of the old senate, which they had dominated. Student governors, while not quite equal to faculty in numbers, were on all committees and were often ignorant, disruptive, or both. Their one-year terms severely limited their effectiveness and learning capacity. (The most articulate — I was going to write "smartest," but he was not — student governor during my term was probably Michael Sabia, who went on to a glittering if uneven career in Canadian business. His Governing Council performance was extravagant and uneven.) The idealistic "reinvention" of university governance at Toronto, meant to be a model for the English-speaking world, was not being noticed anywhere, except perhaps as an experiment to avoid.

Doctor John Evans and his handful of senior administrators were struggling to keep a ship on course that often seemed pilotless and rudderless. The educational climate was worsening, as the expansion of the system had ended and the provincial government started to hold the line on grants to the universities while requiring them to cap tuition fees. Evans's administration had to put in place processes and policies suitable to a modern bureaucratic institution, even as it struggled to clean up layers of the barnacles and sludge that universities accumulate. By virtue of his remarkable fluency, good humour, and personal charisma, President Evans had a strong hold on the alumni and government-appointed members of council. To faculty members, especially the core of historians and political scientists who ran the Faculty Association and had been involved in the Banfield affair, he seemed aloof, impersonal, and uncaring. He seemed to think of the faculty as just another "estate" of the university, no more important or useful than the student estate. In the spring of 1976, Evans urged council to reject a proposal for increased faculty representation on its key committees. The result was an angry backlash, as the Faculty Association threatened to hold a vote on becoming a certified union unless the administration agreed to bargain collectively with it. We had the makings of a nasty confrontation between the University of Toronto and its faculty.

As a faculty member of council, caught between the Faculty Association and the administration, I found I had little influence with anyone, just one vote and one voice. I tried to be conscientious, mastering the minutiae of policies the administration was bringing forward, speaking as helpfully as I could in debate. I could not be particularly helpful to the administration, though, because I had serious doubts about the viability of the Governing Council system and also resented the administration's determination to treat council like the bothersome obstacle it often was. The administration did not help its case by frequently being harried and uninformed and bringing poorly thought out policies to council.* I talked a lot at council and committees ("It's hard to avoid talking when so little of good sense is said by others," I noted. "The appointees sit there like dummies in the President's pocket"), but little I talked about is worth remembering.

In the spring of 1977 the chair of council, Marnie Paikin, a smart, public-spirited woman from Hamilton, sounded me out about chairing our Academic Affairs Committee the next year. She said the only concern they had in approaching me was whether I believed enough in the system to honestly try to make it work (she was probably influenced by a quixotic attempt I had just made to undermine student activism by questioning the university's legal basis for collecting fees on behalf of student societies; had I succeeded they would all have folded up). I said that I would do my duty. As Chair of Academic Affairs in 1977–78 I invested enormous amounts of time in making the committee work more smoothly and with better relations with the university's divisions and their administrators. Otherwise, none of the matters we dealt with proved memorable. Sydney Hermant, a great businessman alumnus of the university, told me every time I saw him that year that I was the most powerful academic in Canada. I would laugh hollowly. My informed attempts to warn our presidential search committee that the dean of Graduate Studies, Jim Ham, would be a disastrous successor to

---

* The administrators seemed particularly hard-pressed during budget discussions, usually about cuts, which brought out every faculty and divisional interest group in full voice. The most remarkable voices were those of the entrepreneurial deans of Law and Business, Marty Friedland and Max Clarkson, both of whom managed to get extra funding for their faculties out of Simcoe Hall and the Governing Council at a time when the hapless, badly led Faculty of Arts and Science seemed to be receiving blow upon blow. Friedland, in particular, pleaded his case as though he were a counsel advocating elementary justice to a starving widow and her children. In his memoirs, *My Life in Crime and Other Academic Adventures*, Friedland remarks on how much support his Faculty received from president Evans, how its budget kept increasing at a time of general contraction, and what a fine president Evans was.

John Evans, had no influence either. Ham was appointed and proved a disaster.*

Governing was not hard work. The pabulum of committee meetings was much easier to ingest than classroom stew or research smorgasbords, and sometimes in those years I thought administration would be a less demanding career path. Governing Council experience was qualifying me for an administrative position even as I decided not to run for a second term. A wise colleague, Tom Langan, had remarked that our obligation as scholars was to do our duty's worth of administrative service and then go back to our studies.

My last meetings as a governor, in June 1978, featured more complicated rounds of controversy about the role of faculty and librarians in the university, and left me feeling drained and annoyed, a kind of kept gadfly of Governing Council. At the end-of-year reception a graduate student member told me how much he would miss my "shrill voice" having so much to say on so many issues. According to my diary, "I commented that for all the good I had done my place might as well have been filled by a corpse." On reflection, I wrote bitterly that two or three of us had perhaps played a decisive role "in maintaining the credibility of this stupid, inefficient, and incompetent system of university government. We did as much as anyone, more than most, to make it keep working. Perhaps we shouldn't have helped it maintain its legitimacy this long." As official thanks for my service to the university, Provost Donald Chant presented me with an inscribed chairman's gavel. It seemed a perfect symbol of our institution's malaise that the gavel was inscribed to "Proffessor Michael Bliss."

The good news was that the Governing Council and the Faculty Association reached a memorandum of understanding that both staved off unionization and protected faculty from the vagaries of an estates-dominated council. Within a few more years, council finally

---

* We could see the disaster in the making when Ham made presentations to Academic Affairs. Listening closely revealed that the engineer/dean's sentences often did not parse, nor did his words exactly make sense. Vague comparisons with Sarah Palin come to mind, though Jim was probably a gentleman of the moderate left. I thought the best candidate to succeed Evans was Marty Friedland, the dean of law. I do not know whether he was taken seriously as a contender. As late as the 1970s it seemed likely that there would be old Toronto WASPs who would consider his being Jewish a significant problem.

reformed itself, restoring faculty dominance in academic matters, restoring effective bicameralism, and settling down as a mostly rubber-stamp body seldom noticed on campus. In the end, the University of Toronto's great experiment in university governance did not amount to much. The institution kept going, with the Governing Council doing little harm.

My last meetings of Governing Council coincided with the publication of *A Canadian Millionaire: The Life and Business Times of Sir Joseph Flavelle, 1859–1939.* I had finished the book by working long days in summers and during holiday weeks and on weekends during the winters. My biggest problem with the manuscript was length — first drafts were far longer than my publisher, Macmillan of Canada, would accept. Foregoing the option of producing a two-volume biography that no one would read, I cut, hacked, pruned, clipped, trimmed, eventually condensing on a phrase-by-phrase basis (though leaving in one of the war chapters a cameo appearance by a beagle in a flying helmet). The exercise proved invaluable in teaching me how to write to length — I never had a problem like that again, until I came to write this memoir, not an easy genre — but the book still came in at over 500 pages. Macmillan was the leading Canadian publisher of serious works of history; my editor, Ken McVey, had heard about my project from Ramsay Cook and been an early enthusiast.

The labour that went into the final revision of *Millionaire* was concentrated on trying to make the prose flow and sparkle. I wanted my books to be accessible to all intelligent readers, from high school students to doctors of philosophy and anyone in between. In writing I aimed at clarity and precision, with a few basic literary flourishes, allusions, and jokes. Later reviewers were wrong in suggesting that I had been influenced by Donald Creighton, whose style I considered purplishly contrived. My writing mentors were: (1) Miss Hicks, my high school English teacher; (2) A.J.P. Taylor, the British historian, whose prose was clear, punchy, and often unorthodox in thought and construction; (3) Edward Gibbon, whose rolling, periodic sentences in *The Decline and Fall of the Roman Empire* seemed a useful contrast to Taylorian brusqueness; (4) All the novelists and poets who made me conscious of the uses of metaphor and simile.

On *Millionaire's* official publication day I rushed out to get the newspapers and read the reviews. There were none. "What if they published a book and no one reviewed it?" I wondered in my diary. A few days later, however, Macmillan threw a lovely launch party in Flavelle's old house, "Holwood," by then the law school. History friends, Governing Council friends (including Marnie Paikin, who had graciously forgiven me for telling a reporter that the council was a "laughingstock"), and many Flavelles turned out, the grandchildren happily pointing out the banisters they had slid down as children and the locations of the old toy cupboards. Marty Friedland, dean of law, told me it was disconcerting to read in the book that Flavelle had been casually anti-Semitic, but consoled himself with the thought that a pork packer would not have a lot of Jewish acquaintances. While waiting for reviews to come in, I was mollified by its having already tipped in the scales in favour of my promotion to full professor.

Not everyone who had started out to set the academic world afire in the late 1960s had reached senior professorial rank ten years later. Analogies between long-distance running and academic careers work on several levels. The late 1960s had been like the start of a great race for the generation of ambitious intellectuals hired to fuel university expansion. A decade later some of the casualties and drop-outs were evident. In our department, for example, neither of the two young Latin American historians hired in my year was able to finish a thesis on time, and both were dismissed. So was the Japanese historian whose claim to have finished his thesis proved false. A few of our high profile historians, such as Natalie Davis, were lured away by great American universities. Some whom we had hired on the basis of immense promise, proved to have been sprinters, fast starters who were already running out of energy and sinking into academic lassitude. Some of our most senior scholars, the dons of high promise of my undergraduate years, had slowed to a walk and were never going to publish the great book expected of them, probably not any book. Marriages were also breaking up, more or less independently of scholarly success or failure, some with echoes of the popular play *Who's Afraid of Virginia Woolf?*

With the heady days of expansion long passed, we had few appointments to make in the department. The positions that did come open were hotly contested. Edward "Ned" Shorter, a prolific Europeanist, and Bill Eccles, probably a misogynist, did not think much of the scholarship of Sylvia Van Kirk, whose thesis on the role of women in the fur trade would soon be published to great acclaim. At the crucial meeting of our search committee to consider Sylvia's candidacy for a job, Ned, a free spirit, sauntered in dressed in his working professor's garb — jeans and a denim shirt opened to the middle of his chest. "Hiya, Motherfuckers," he announced, and then launched into his objections to Sylvia, mostly to the effect that her approach to history was antiquarian. We eventually hired Sylvia, and she served the department long and well despite being shabbily treated by the remnants of patriarchy, including her first husband.

Whether or not Norman Cantor is accurate in calling the 1970s and 80s "the great academic depression," universities were now steeping in the brine that has made the professorial life so ripe for caricature by writers from David Lodge through Richard Russo. Feeling the pinch of inflation and government retrenchment in the 1970s, but with the acute sense of entitlement that comes to those used to standing first in their class, professors at many universities decided they should become certified unionists. Leftist colleagues liked to think of themselves as members of an oppressed intellectual proletariat, and unionization came naturally. Jack Granatstein, then a man of the moderate left and always a ruthless pursuer of a better academic life, was a main organizer of what became the faculty union at York. Unionization was on everyone's lips one night in 1976, as Percy the waiter passed gourmet hors d'oeuvres and took our drink orders at Chris Armstrong's party to celebrate Ramsay Cook's having won the Tyrrell Medal of the Royal Society of Canada. Sipping scotch and sherry and wine in a beautiful home in Lawrence

Park, the professoriate, in their elbow-patched corduroy sports jackets and button-down shirts, argued organizational tactics and whether or not it was feasible to go on strike.

Bob Cuff's academic entrepreneurialism in winning a Killam Fellowship at a young age had been impressive, but it was gradually becoming noticed that he did not have much in the way of new publications to show for his two Killam years. His first book turned out to be his last, which is about average for history and the humanities. Sadly, this very popular scholar, whose failure to publish puzzled all of us, died at a relatively young age, as did his wife. Still, if academic success was measured by the ability to pull in grant money, Cuff had done well for York.

Despite provincial retrenchment, in the 1970s the federal government increased its funding to granting agencies, triggering the kinds of opportunities Bob had seized and that others soon latched on to. The Canada Council had given a sociologist a million-dollar grant, its first, to investigate the Canadian identity. Nothing resulted. A team of historians and others from the University of New Brunswick wanted more than a million to study United Empire Loyalists. A group of geographers at U of T were cooking up a multi-million-dollar project for a multi-volume historical atlas of Canada. An enterprising American social historian at the Ontario Institute for Studies in Education, where standards were notoriously suspect, went through more than $100,000 in grant money to show there was a lot of mobility in mid-nineteenth-century Hamilton, Ontario — expensive verification of what many of us thought was obvious.

Almost without exception the academic entrepreneurs assumed their entitlement to large sums of taxpayers' money. It was simply taken for granted that the creation of new knowledge, however obvious or obscure and trivial or long in the making, was worth whatever it cost. I never believed this. My studies of the almost infinite capacity of business and other interest groups to wrap their requests for other people's money in flags of patriotism and public good, combined with my own values, made me highly critical of people and projects that consumed tax dollars without significant results. Some senior colleagues scandalously frittered away their time on Killams. Supplicants for grants in business history asked for huge sums to generate knowledge that would be of no interest or use to anyone, if it could ever be compiled. The Canada Council was treated as the Canada Cow, a public tit to be sucked — sucked innocently perhaps, but also shamelessly and endlessly. As I brought in a major biography at a total cost in research grants of less than $20,000 — I finished this and later projects with unspent grant money, which I returned — it was hard not to be angry at colleagues' boondoggling. At times my journal became a compendium of complaints about the ethical blindness of academia, the subsidy mongering, the squandering of public money, the hypocrisy. People to whom the ordinary taxpayers of Canada were giving enormous privileges were behaving like self-righteous parasites. Sometimes I wondered if I wanted to continue to be part of a system fueled by profound unconscious hypocrisy.

The everyday centre of my life was our home and family in Leaside. Liz's perspective on both university events and her husband's crotchets was always sane: don't take any of it very seriously. My other crutch was my journal, which I now kept regularly and used as an outlet for frustrations, ambition, insecurities, and anger. Writing in it became a kind of private biographical and therapeutical exercise. I needed several kinds of exercise, because I too often responded to stress by putting on weight, leading to a contrapuntal series of crash diets and workout programs. But with the writing on the wall about smoking — Liz and the children hated my cigarette habit, and I had developed a smoker's cough — I decided to quit. At Christmas 1976 I armed myself with nicotine pills and sugar-free chewing gum, had my last cigarette at a dinner party at Carl Berger's, and got up the next morning a non-smoker. It was very difficult, the hardest test coming when I went back to writing in the new year. It took me a further twelve months to break my addiction to gum.

We visited our families in Harrow and Kingsville two or three times a year. Mother finally seemed to be mellowing a bit, as her father had in his old age, though she had also become a recluse — a little old lady in a big, cold house with a couple of cats — and she could not get through a day without her Wiser's. Mother died in September 1977, apparently from the effects of a fall, possibly from an overdose of medication. She was sixty-nine, had been a widow for twenty-four years, and when we opened her safety-deposit box we realized that she was down to her last $20,000 in savings. In the eulogy I gave at a family service I talked about the wonderful natural ability Annie Crowe had, the price she paid when she gave up the possibility of a career to marry Quartus Bliss, and how the frustrations of her life seemed to have eased a bit in her final years as our children's grammy.

That fall I sold our big house on Main Street to John Kubis, the town's most prominent realtor, who I had first seen flipping hamburgers in the restaurant just down the street when his family had come to Canada. For John, buying the Bliss house seemed to be another sign of his success in his adopted country. As part of the cleaning out of the house I destroyed father's medical records, what I later came to realize was an act of archival desecration. On our final trip from Kingsville we had father's old operating table strapped upside down on the roof rack of our car. Arriving in Toronto about midnight, dead tired, I was brought up short by the crash as the table hit the top of the garage. It survived to serve as a handsome diaper-change table for grandchildren, and then their kitchen table.

Kubis could not find a use for mother's house. For a time it was derelict. Eventually it was sold for redevelopment. The town's historical society could not stop its demolition. Jim's widow sent me the picture in the *Kingsville Reporter* of the wrecker's ball hitting our old Ontario house. A drugstore and doughnut shop took its place. I was never able to drive into Kingsville again without feeling pangs of sadness at the destruction of my home on Main Street.

American historian Arthur Schlesinger Jr. observes in his autobiography that we learn best from those with more experience than we have. Schlesinger never felt satisfied working in university settings because, he wrote, "teaching less experienced students would, I feared, only encourage parochialism and complacency." Perhaps this is just another way of rephrasing the old saw, "Those who can do, those who can't teach."

Teaching had its compensations: most students were pleasant, bright people, the cream of the crop, often a delight and a privilege to work with. Fun, too: I sometimes was involved in Hart House debates, which were usually of high quality, and had good informal experiences — such as a student evening at Devonshire House, a residence mostly for engineers, which ended with much beer and a loud round of "Here's to Mike/Here's to Mike/Here's to Mike/He's a Horse's Ass." On the other hand, as I crept up on forty, and with a sense of having achieved my academic goals, I began to wonder how committed I was to year after year of seminars, lectures, marking essays, marking exams, sitting on committees, and sitting around common rooms gossiping and complaining.

My late night reading had always been good fiction — favourites include Conrad, P.G. Wodehouse, John O'Hara, Anthony Powell, Hugh Hood, Joyce Carol Oates, and Penelope Lively. I often thought about trying to write novels or stories, only to realize that I had no literary imagination and no experience at, or obvious flair for, creative writing. The best I could muster was to devise a canonically and historically accurate plot for a Sherlock Holmes adventure set in Canada. Knowing I would have trouble fleshing it out, I approached Jack Batten, a good freelance writer, and we collaborated to produce "The Adventure of the Annexationist Conspiracy," my only published work of fiction. We sold it to a weekend rotogravure magazine; it has since been anthologized in a collection of classic Canadian crime fiction.

Batten was one of the stable of journalists Pierre Berton and Jack McClelland had signed up for the Canada's Illustrated Heritage series. Working on the project I got to know all the authors — from old pros like Bob Collins, William Stephenson, Max Braithwaite, and June Callwood, through moonlighting novelists like Harold Horwood and Joy Carroll — and, of all people, Margaret Atwood. June Callwood, by then a veteran journalist, was one of the worst writers of popular history I ever dealt with, but was gracious and willing to learn, and determined to make something out of her dreadful manuscript on the 1890s. Ms. Atwood wanted to try her hand at writing popular social history, partly because of her interest in the pioneer writer, Susannah Moodie.

Already world famous, Atwood also already had a reputation as a dragon lady. I met her in April 1976 to discuss her project over lunch at the trendy Courtyard Café in the old Windsor Arms Hotel. I was so intimidated that I accepted her recommendation and ordered a dish I normally loathed and that almost made me ill. In conversation I found that she was charming, smart, knowledgeable, keen to write history, and in almost no way like her image. Her book, *Days of the Rebels: 1815/1840*, was easily the best-written in the series, full of lively observations about the mistreatment of the poor, the problem of body odour, and how hard everyone worked. In later years I liked to remind her that I was one of the few people who knew of her one foray into writing unembellished history. I noticed in our discussions how closely she identified with Susannah Moodie's love-hate relationship with the Canadian wilderness as against the easy-going acceptance of it by Susannah's sister, Catherine Parr Traill. I tended to identify with Traill.

Sandy Ross, who did our book on the 1950s, had accepted my first journalism for *Maclean's* in the mid-1960s. He had gone on to become a popular columnist and editor-in-chief of *Canadian Business* magazine. In the 1970s, Sandy commissioned my first significant magazine pieces, annual reviews of the most important business books. *Canadian Business* prospered so much that his assistant, Margaret Wente (destined to become one of the best columnists in the history of Canadian journalism), would call me with the unheard-of request to *add* words to my articles because they needed more filler between their advertisements. One of my earliest pieces for *Canadian Business* was a scathing review of *Bronfman Dynasty* by Peter C. Newman, all of whose books, then and since, I found unreadable, inaccurate, and smarmy. Newman's ham-fisted feel for Canadian history, combined with his absurdly baroque prose, made June Callwood look like a smooth professional.

There was no comparison between Newman and Berton as popular historians. Pierre, whom I came to like very much for his no-nonsense professionalism and the remarkable amount of knowledge he had filed away over many years, was easy to work with on the Illustrated Heritage series, and would often chat with me about other projects he was considering. I recommended backup research assistants to him, read several of his books in manuscript out of camaraderie, and saved him from the occasional howler. My other favourite popular historian was James H. Gray, author of *The Winter Years*, *Red Lights on the Prairies*, *Booze*, and half-a-dozen other books about life in Western Canada. I never worked with Jimmy Gray, but brought him to the University of Toronto in our history speakers' series, a gesture of recognition by the academy that he remembered warmly. His talks were well attended, and late into the night the crusty Calgarian held court in our living room to students and professors sitting literally at his feet.

The prominent young tycoon Conrad Black also wanted academic approval for his first foray into history, the major and controversial biography of Maurice Duplessis that he published in 1976. I experienced his yearning for recognition when CBC Radio asked me to interview him about the book for their Sunday morning show. It was another case of image being misleading, as the already notorious Black was obviously both able and amiable — except that he was still livid about a scathing review Ramsay Cook had written of his book in the *Globe and Mail*. Black and I went out for drinks after our session, he gave me the Palm Beach phone number of Bud McDougald, the grand old man of Argus Corporation and Canadian business generally (who answered his phone when I called and gave me a good interview about Flavelle), and suggested that we have lunch together. We didn't at that time, but our paths would cross again. My defence of Black's biography at a social gathering led to a tongue-lashing from Cook.

Pierre Berton and Jack McClelland had more enthusiasm than business acumen. Canada's Illustrated Heritage series was an editorial success — we produced well-written and beautifully illustrated books of popular history — but a publishing disaster. When forecast sales proved wildly optimistic, it was decided to cut back by using cheaper everything. The project became a nightmare for editor-in-chief Toivo

Kiil and his hard-driven staff, and there was no satisfaction, only relief, when the final volume, covering the 1960s, was published. NSL never reprinted the books, lost its shirt, and folded.

More work came my way just as NSL was winding down. A lawyer at the downtown firm of Borden Elliott, Ross Murray, hired me in the summer of 1977 to help him make the case that some fifty-five acres of land in downtown Toronto (the territory lying roughly between Spadina Avenue and Bathurst Street, Front Street and the Gardiner Expressway), belonged to Canadian National Railways, rather than to the government of Canada, the province of Ontario, or the city of Toronto. Nobody could produce title to the fabulously valuable acreage, the ownership of which had been in dispute since the 1840s. This round of the CN lands case had been simmering for several years, and Murray's researchers had compiled some twenty thick volumes of pertinent documents plus a superb collection of old Toronto maps.

Ross Murray was an extroverted gnome king of a man who liked to brag about not having lost a case in twenty years. When I told him I was worried about getting involved in something this complex, he said that it would be the kind of experience that separates men from boys. Billing at the lawyer-like, professorially amazing rate of $55 an hour, I read all of Murray's volumes, told him that his research was inadequate, and made several trips to Ottawa gathering more material.

As I prepared our case, the only way I could make it coherent was to write the history of those fifty-five acres, beginning with their cession to the Crown by the Mississauga Indians in 1808. Much of the land had been part of the Fort York military reserve during and after the War of 1812, but then the reserve had fallen into gross neglect. The Great Western Railway, ancestor to the CNR, laid its tracks into the city of Toronto in the 1840s straight across the reserve, ignoring protests from the remnants of the military. All the threads seemed to come together in the machinations of a long-dead lawyer named Philpotts, who seemed to have acted simultaneously on behalf of all of the quarrelling parties — the Great Western, the British military, and the city of Toronto. My manuscript history of the fifty-five acres had just reached a stage in which

Philpotts, negotiating with himself, was making critical decisions in the interests of his several clients, when Murray phoned me to say there had been an out-of-court settlement. Please stop the meter. I did no further work except to bill Murray and the CNR for $25,000. It is my best unfinished and unpublishable manuscript. I never decided who had the best claim to the CN lands.

The more Canadian history I taught, the more I became interested in current Canadian affairs, especially national politics. My enthusiasm for Pierre Trudeau gradually faded in the 1970s, as his governments drifted first to the left, then into what appeared to be cynical opportunism combined with simple fatigue. Ottawa's elaborate experiments in controls — first of energy prices, then of all wages and prices — seemed to me to combine economic illiteracy with a Central Canadian determination to keep the west in perpetual fiefdom. I began considering myself a Progressive-Conservative supporter, and wrote occasional letters offering gratuitous advice — no doubt worth what it cost — to the party leader, Robert Stanfield, and my member of Parliament, Jim Gillies. I always had reservations about Stanfield, who seemed slow and ponderous and completely over-matched against Trudeau. Even though Joe Clark was young and untested, I thought his advent to the PC leadership in 1976 was probably a step forward.

Toying with thoughts of some kind of broader involvement in politics, I wrote more op-ed pieces about the Conservatives, usually for the *Toronto Star*, and then persuaded Sandy Ross to have me do a profile on Clark for *Canadian Business*. In December 1978, Mr. Clark gave me an hour-long interview. I found him articulate, able, and impressive, and wrote a positive though not sycophantic profile. Chatting after the formal interview, I hazarded the opinion that the prospects for the Conservatives were looking very good, but perhaps they were too hopeful about what they could achieve in office. Clark said I might be right.

At exactly this time I was asked by our provost, with whom I had worked closely the year of the Academic Affairs Committee, if I would become a vice-provost of U of T with responsibility for the Faculty of Arts and Science. I suddenly stood at a fork in the road. To go into full-time administration would be to choose a career path that might lead to a university presidency, while putting writing and scholarship on hold. I weighed the options, balancing the opportunity to escape from the classroom with a significant raise in pay against what I knew of the boredom and trivia of most administrative work. Friends seemed to think I should seize the opportunity, for I could always come back to writing. Then Liz made the telling comment: for three years I'd never seemed happy with Governing Council work, and had mostly come home angry and complaining. Did I really have a taste for more of the same? Could I stand it?

With many misgivings, I decided to turn the offer down. I told my journal that if the best happened it would be better to finish a career as a Donald Creighton or Maurice Careless than a Claude Bissell. I never again was challenged to think seriously about administration at Toronto, and that was just as well for both my mental and physical health. Liz was right, as usual.

Chapter Eight

The Discovery of Insulin

The critical reaction to *A Canadian Millionaire* could hardly have been better. I cherished a reviewer's comment that Bliss writes so well one would hardly know he was a professor. I had succeeded in reaching beyond the academic market to tap a community of intelligent readers interested in serious Canadiana, especially the history of Canadian business. The book sold out its first printing in the autumn of 1978. It won several awards, including the recently established John A. Macdonald Prize offered by the Canadian Historical Association for the best book of the year. At that time the award involved several thousand dollars, supplied by Manufacturers Life Insurance, plus a medal inscribed to the author of the biography of Sir Joseph "Flavalle." It nicely complements my Governing Council gavel.

I was now in demand as a speaker in and around Toronto, notably making the list to give one of the venerable Royal Canadian Institute's Saturday night lectures in Convocation Hall. My talk on "The Peterboro Methodist Mafia and the Renaissance of Toronto" was well received, except for the two members of the audience who had to be taken out while I was talking, one with an epileptic fit, the other with a heart attack. Liz complimented me on really knocking them dead.

Surprised at the sales of *Flavelle*, the Macmillan editors first told me there would be enough copies for the Christmas book-buying season, then said there would be no remaining demand by Christmas, then decided to reprint the book to meet the Christmas demand, then found they had placed their order too late. The book was out of print and unavailable in December. My anger at Macmillan's ineptitude became intense — phrases like "incredibly incompetent bastards" dot my diary entries that autumn — but my protests were dismissed as normal authorial short-term bitching. In fact, Macmillan also let its authors down in the long-term. In the 1970s the firm used a glue for binding its books that became brittle with age. Like John Diefenbaker's memoirs and most other books Macmillan published during that decade, copies of *A Canadian Millionaire* do not stand the test of time. Open a hardback edition of the book without extreme care and it falls apart. The words, of course, are imperishable.

Short lists of finalists for the Governor-General's literary awards were not announced in those years. My colleague and friend, Carl Berger, was one of the judges in that year's non-fiction category. He later told me that the panel of three judges had decided that two books were tied and they had wanted to honour both, one being *Millionaire*. When told that there could only be one winner, they spent several hours deliberating before finally giving the 1978 award to an ex-convict and former bank robber, Roger Caron, for his memoir *Go-Boy*. When I read *Go-Boy* I thought it was pretty good, and certainly Caron needed both the money and the recognition more than I did. Ironically, his career was being promoted by Pierre Berton, who was having a not uncommon writer's fantasy about the act of writing transforming convicts into honest citizens. Caron, who had benefited from skillful editing, had his fifteen minutes of fame, wrote one more book, a flop, then returned to bank robbing and then prison, before dying without further literary honours.

A professorial acquaintance paid me a kind of ultimate backhanded academic compliment by suggesting that after Flavelle I wouldn't need to publish another word for the rest of my career. I felt I still had a few more words in me, and thought it was time to range widely and put together all the work I had done, plus more, in a two-volume social and economic history of Canada. I assumed I would be a shoe-in for one of the precious Killam fellowships this time round, and that was a consideration in turning down the offer of the vice-provostship at U of T.

I did not even reach the Killam interview stage with this project — I did worse in the competition than five years previously. It was a traumatic rejection. The appraisers, academic conservatives to a fault, had judged my project to be too sweeping and too ambitious. Probably, I had not written a good application — I was too impatient and sure of myself to do these well — but all I thought was that years of hard productive work had gotten me less than nowhere in major grant competitions. Bitterly disappointed, I briefly considered quitting academia altogether and trying to make my living with my pen. "That doesn't seem economically very sensible," I told myself in the spring of 1979. I licked my wounds, noting Sir John A. Macdonald's aphorism that when Dame Fortune empties her chamber pot on your head you should simply remark on the pleasant spring shower. I vowed never to apply for a Killam again and to stay as far from the probably corrupt, certainly corrupting, public trough as I could.

Writing commissioned history was a possibility. I had an offer to do a biography of Garfield Weston, founder of the bakery-supermarket dynasty. There were other straws in the wind, including a centennial history of the Maclean-Hunter publishing empire. But I was chary about becoming someone else's kept historian, a form of work inviting its own kinds of corruption, and I was not sure whether I wanted to write any more business history. Instead, I decided to take a good look at another project that had been sometimes on my mind for many years, the idea of writing the history of the discovery of insulin.

Every Canadian schoolboy knew that insulin as a therapy for diabetes had been discovered in Toronto in the early 1920s. Most knew the names of Frederick Banting and Charles Best — Banting and Best

— as the discoverers of insulin. At the university we had research buildings named the Banting Institute and the Best Institute. Outside our Medical Sciences Building the province of Ontario had erected a historic plaque to the discovery of insulin.

While we were at Harvard in 1968, brother Jim wrote me a letter containing this paragraph:

> When we see each other, I want to discuss the possibility of a collaborative effort on a book. This is very confidential, but the Medical Research Council has a secret file of documents concerning the events surrounding the discovery of insulin — these to be released to historians when the last man involved dies — and Charlie Best is in poor health and is the last man. The true story is sure-fire for a popular but accurate book, not just for its scientific interest but for the violent clashes of personalities that accompanied the discovery. The combination of an historian and a physiologist would seem to be the ideal team for the story....

I later realized that Jim had been chatting with the chairman of physiology at McGill, F.C. McIntosh, who had become interested in the insulin events while trying to write an obituary of James B. Collip, a distinguished endocrinologist who had died in 1965 and had played some kind of murky role in the insulin story. McIntosh knew of at least one explosive document that had been suppressed for many years.

I dipped into the existing literature on the discovery of insulin and realized it was inadequate to the point of incoherence, not least in being unable to explain the odd fact that the Nobel Prize for the discovery of insulin had been awarded not to Banting and Best, but rather to Banting and someone named J.J.R. Macleod. Intrigued, I responded favourably to my brother's suggestion. But he was too sick to follow it up and Best was in no hurry to die. Instead, Jim died in 1969. As Best lived on through the 1970s I would occasionally walk by the plaque on our campus, reflect on what a great thing it had been to give insulin to the world, and, remembering Jim's letter, wonder when someone would write the definitive account of the great discovery. My work and my training were in other areas of history. I had to get on with my thesis and then the Flavelle biography.

I had enjoyed giving my annual lecture on the history of medicine in Canada in my Canadian history survey course, and from time to time toyed with the thought of moving more seriously into medical history if opportunities developed. In the mid-1970s many opportunities did open in Canada when one of the old private health insurance companies, Associated Medical Services, which had been legislated out of its primary business by the advent of universal state health insurance, decided to use its leftover funds to support teaching and research in the history of medicine. AMS's Hannah Institute began to fund chairs in medical history connected with each of Ontario's medical schools. At a Governing Council social occasion, John Evans suggested that I might want to become our medical school's first Hannah professor. I did not take him seriously — it was a serious matter to claim competence to teach any subject at a university level, let alone the history of medicine to medical students. As professors often feel but seldom admit, I was uncomfortable enough posing as an expert in mainstream Canadian history.

Charles Best died in 1978, just as I was wondering what to do after Flavelle. I idly considered a book on insulin, but thought it too difficult to do well. It might work on the popular level — when Pierre Berton asked for my advice on what he should do next, I urged him to think about insulin. The next spring, when the Killam rejection killed my project for a sweeping social and economic history of Canada, I wrote in my journal, "Among the consolations was the thought that I could turn to the book on Insulin that I had long thought needed writing." Berton had no interest in the idea, nor, I found out, did our first Hannah professor of the History of Medicine, Pauline Mazumdar.

One of the coincidences that helped rekindle my interest in insulin was a casual reading of a 1973 book on polar exploration, *Peary at the*

Pole: Fact or Fiction? by Dennis Rawlins. Working from Peary's note-books, Rawlins, a scientist turned history buff, was able to recreate Peary's explorations day by day, showing exactly what he had done and where he must have been, and how his own documents showed that he almost certainly had not reached the North Pole. It was fascinating to see how notebooks could be used to reconstruct events in minute detail many decades after the fact.

The staff at our Thomas Fisher Rare Book Library told me that the Frederick Banting Papers, containing original notebooks, were about to be made available for research. Banting's widow had recently died. They also told me that I had better see parts of the collection that would not be immediately opened, particularly two accounts of the discovery of insulin that Banting had written in 1922 and 1940, which had never been published.

I wrote in my journal on May 30, 1979,

> So, I became the first historian to read Banting's own account of the discovery of insulin — about a 15-page 1922 account and then 80 pages from 1940 — which is notable principally for his attack on other people — on Macleod, above all, as arrogant, cowardly, and almost all other derogatory adjectives B. could think of; on Collip, as having refused to tell B&B his original recipe for preparing insulin. On other doctors who cut him out of developments to the point where in March 1922 he was drinking himself to sleep every night, sometimes on alcohol stolen from the labs. Rich details about encounters with various people, about conditions in the labs, and so on. Marvellous source.

I had thought these were the secret documents Jim had referred to in 1968. A few months later I discovered that Banting's first biographer, Dr. Lloyd Stevenson, had just published an account of the discovery of insulin that Banting's supervisor and fellow Nobel laureate, J.J.R. Macleod, had written back in 1922. In the University of Toronto Archives I found correspondence from the 1950s between Charles Best and our then-president, Sidney Smith, who, quite improperly, forbade Stevenson from making use of the document. Stevenson had arranged for its publication immediately on learning of Best's death. Hank McIntosh had probably seen a version of this document, which I now realized was just the tip of an iceberg.

The director of our Institute for the History and Philosophy of Science and Technology liked the idea of a book on insulin, suggesting that I apply for "big money" (hundreds of thousands of dollars) from the Hannah Institute and assemble a board of advisors to give me credibility on the medical side. I found out how little credibility I had when I phoned the director of the Hannah Institute, G.R. "Pat" Paterson, told him of my interest in an insulin project, and was told very coldly that there were a number of other people interested in something similar. Paterson did not want to talk further, and gave me absolutely no encouragement.

Friends had not been very encouraging either. Carl Berger thought I was too influenced by wanting to become another Pierre Berton. Paul Rutherford thought that at best there was a scholarly article in the insulin story. I weighed the pros and cons fairly carefully and decided that an insulin project would be too risky. In any case, I was being distracted by new opportunities appearing almost daily that were tempting me to reconsider the ease and perks of becoming an administrator. I chose not to put my hat in the ring to become principal of one of our new colleges — privately I thought it should be closed. I did allow my name to go forward in the search for a new president for Peterborough, Ontario's, fledgling Trent University, and was eventually interviewed. Peterborough had been Flavelle's hometown; the chair of the search committee was a local businessman cut from Flavellian cloth and an admirer of *A Canadian Millionaire*.

No sooner had that job gone to someone else than I had a morning phone call from Wilbert Hopper, head of the Calgary oil company, Petro-Canada, who wanted me in Calgary right away to discuss writing the history of one of the firms they were taking over, Pacific Petroleum. Its former CEO, an Oklahoma-born oilman named Kelly Gibson, was also a fan of *Millionaire*. By evening I was in Calgary, and spent the next ten days interviewing Gibson and other old-timers in the oil patch, including the legendary Frank McMahon. I was given tours of oil fields, visited the first Syncrude plant in the tar sands, and went on to Vancouver for more interviews. I was well paid for my time, everything was first class, and it all contrasted with both the Hannah Institute's reluctance even to talk to me about insulin and, as I noted in my diary, "the insufferable shittiness of the Canada Council." I drafted a prospectus for a Pacific Pete history, and awaited a final decision to go ahead.

I had one more year to teach before being entitled to another sabbatical. As classes began and with still no word from the west, I began considering doing an independent history of Timothy Eaton and his department store — Eaton's was still a legendary and flourishing Canadian business — as a way of marking time. Walking across the campus on September 20, 1979, however, I happened to meet Richard Landon, head of the Fisher Library, who asked me when I'd be coming in again to start work on insulin. I told Richard I thought the project was not for me. He said that would be too bad because the Banting Papers were so rich and the idea of using them so good.

The encounter caused me to reconsider. As we chatted at a Toronto Blue Jays game, Jack Granatstein told me it was a terrific project. Maybe it was worth taking a risk. I realized that I would not need big Hannah money or a fancy advisory board. All I would need was my sabbatical and a few thousands of research dollars. I could probably beat out any of the competitors Paterson seemed to have been referring to, but even if the project did not succeed there would have been little harm in having spent a sabbatical on an interesting flyer.

That fall I began telling people of my plan, made some contacts on the medical side of the campus, and arranged interviews with interested old-timers. Lloyd Stevenson, who I feared might want to do more work now that documents were open, indicated from retirement that he was not interested. In fact, there was no competition to write the history of the discovery of insulin. The more I read about discoveries, though, including the coming of penicillin, the more interested I became. "Positively excited at what a good book *Insulin* can — will — be," I wrote. "For the first time that intense feeling of wanting to get on with it, get into it, drop all the outside work, etc., as peripheral and trivial, use up my savings if necessary as I bring this project home as a really great book." I was nothing if not an enthusiast for my projects. When the Pacific Pete project fizzled — partly because the western oilmen decided an eastern professor wouldn't know enough about the business — and when teaching ended in the spring of 1980, I plunged completely into insulin. It became a wonderful research adventure that changed my life.

It began very badly, as I got into a bitter, probably foolish struggle on a point of principle with the bureaucrats in our recently created Office of Research Administration. During Governing Council days I had found its leadership suspect, especially on the occasion when ORA proposed that the university appropriate faculty members' copyright on their publications. We put a quick end to that. Now ORA was trying to implement guidelines governing the ethical review of grant applications. During, and immediately after, my council service, I argued that tenured professors had been judged by the university to be fully professional and should not need to be second-guessed about how they went about their research. Anyone thought to require ongoing ethical review never should have been given tenure in the first place.

This sensible view was swept aside by bureaucratic and scientists' fears that researchers would abuse their subjects. Nazi doctors' treatment of Jews was the horrible example that we must never repeat, however unlikely that seemed in contemporary Canada. Tenure was evidently not a stamp of trust. If you were going to use human subjects in research, you would have to pass ethical review. Were human subjects going to be used in my research into the discovery of insulin? Of course they were — unless I reasoned that dead people were not human subjects. I was not willing to resort to this diplomatic untruth, reliance upon which soon became historians' standard way of avoiding ethical review. So I was called in for an ethical review of my project.

As a full professor, a former chair of Academic Affairs, a member of our Honourary Degrees Committee, a candidate for various positions in university administration, and author of a prize-winning biography, I was an angry and hostile reviewee before a group of colleagues for whom I showed little but contempt. In my opening statement I said it was not clear whether the meeting was being scripted by Kingsley Amis or Franz Kafka. The committee members had next to no idea what they were doing or why they were doing it, knew nothing about the ethical dilemmas I would face with the project, and seemed faintly sheepish throughout the whole exercise, an academic ritual of going through the motions. Of course approval of my plans was virtually automatic. In those years I was anything but mellow; temperamentally inclined to be a good hater, I neither forgot nor forgave, and from then on went out of my way to avoid the Office of Research Administration. Later, I seemed to be on the verge of patching up relations with a new director (her predecessor had finally been fired) when, sitting at her desk in a handsome office, she refused to take an application to be mailed to Ottawa without my supplying a thirty-cent stamp. I could not believe the pettiness of bureaucracy.

By the formal beginning of my sabbatical, July 1, 1980, I had already put in six weeks of highly intense and productive research. The next six months were even more productive, and by January 1, 1981, I was ready to start writing the first of what I now realized would be two books. The manuscript of *The Discovery of Insulin* went to the publisher in November 1981, the manuscript of *Banting: A Biography* some eighteen months later.

The research problem was to find every scrap of paper that would shed light on the discovery of insulin and interview every person with memories that had not been written down. Then I had to sort it all out and write it up intelligibly. The main theme of the book, I first thought, would be to explore the conflict over credit for the discovery of insulin. If insulin had been discovered by Banting and Best, as most people assumed — their names were everywhere at Toronto and they had become Canadian icons — why had the 1923 Nobel Prize been awarded to Banting and Macleod? When Banting divided his prize money equally with Best, why had Macleod done the same with J.B. Collip, a biochemist who had briefly been part of the research team? Why did Banting so fiercely hate Macleod, and, at least in 1922–23, also hate Collip? Who had done what?

All of the principal players were dead. Banting's papers, handily available at our Fisher Library, were a wonderfully rich collection. Banting and his assistants seemed to have saved almost everything. I was given access to everything in the Banting collection, including super-sensitive material not open to the public, but which would be available to any other qualified scholars — except that no other qualified scholars were interested. Charles Best's widow, Margaret Mahon Best, told me that she had a large collection of his papers. Would I like to come and see her in their family home in north Toronto? "I've had a wonderful life," were the first words that Mrs. Best, still a beautiful woman in her late seventies, said to me as she thanked me for a copy of *A Canadian Millionaire* and showed me artifacts in her large, gloomy living room. We spent quite a few hours together as she pulled out documents and read them to me, one at a time, painfully slowly.

It happened that Margaret Best's sister, Linda Mahon, had been employed as Charles Best's secretary at the university. Linda still presided over Best's empty office at the Best Institute. As I interviewed her about her boss, I noticed that the glass-enclosed bookcase beside me contained file boxes labelled, "Discovery of Insulin." Neither of the friendly but cagey Mahon sisters was in any hurry to stop talking and let the young historian go fishing in documents. Margaret Best was particularly tantalizing in the references she made to personal diaries, which she clearly was not ready to let me see.

As with all of my projects before this memoir, I told everyone what I was doing. People are normally helpful to historians and the more people who knew about my projects the more likely it was that others with knowledge or documents or contacts might seek me out. Early on, for example, I had a call from a Doctor Robert Cleghorn, who said he had known everyone on the discovery team and would like to have lunch with me. Bob Cleghorn had just retired to Toronto after a distinguished career in endocrinology and psychiatry at McGill. Over several lunches he reminisced in detail about having worked in the 1930s and 1940s with Macleod and Collip, and also Banting and Best. Cleghorn was one of a group of old-timers who thought that Banting and Best had appropriated excessive credit for the insulin research from their collaborators. After our first lunch he promised to send me an article that would tell me all I needed to know about Best. It turned out to be a study of megalomania.

Another old Toronto researcher who sought me out was Bernard Leibel, a former worker at the Banting Institute during Banting's lifetime, and a hard-boiled type in his speech and mannerisms. Leibel wanted to impress upon me that no one should raise any significant questions about Banting and Best's versions of the discovery of insulin. Whole careers in Toronto, he argued, hinged on belief in the fundamental truth underlying what Leibel agreed was probably "a beautiful fairy tale." Banting had personally told the story of insulin to Leibel before his death in 1941, and Leibel, whose own career had rested on Banting's coattails, saw himself as its guardian. He also argued that I should not write or do anything that might upset those sweet old ladies, the Mahon sisters.

I told Leibel and everyone else that I wanted to write the fullest, most accurate account of the discovery of insulin possible, that as a professional historian and an outsider to the medical community I had no axes to grind, no personal involvement with anyone. I gave away many copies of *A Canadian Millionaire* as evidence of my *bona fides*. The Best family remained a little wary — though Charles and Margaret's surviving son, Henry, had a doctorate in Canadian history and to his credit felt professionally obliged not to stand in my way, Leibel's advice to him to the contrary. Linda Mahon's refusal to show me documents in Best's office was finally overcome when she had to close it and deliver all Best's files to the University Archives, where, of course, I was waiting for them. To my great surprise the four or five boxes of "Discovery of Insulin" material had nothing to do with Best, but rather contained insulin-related correspondence by J.J.R. Macleod, who had been Professor of Physiology in the 1920s and whose files Best had taken over when he was given the chair after Macleod left Toronto.

Margaret Best never did let me go exploring in the family papers or her diaries. That did not matter, however, because I got a call one day from the president of the Canadian Diabetes Association, Doctor Ken Gorman, who had heard about my project and thought I might know what should be done with several boxes of papers they had just received from the family of a W.R. Feasby, recently deceased. Feasby had been a close associate of Charley Best. Gorman delivered the Feasby papers to my home. They were a gold mine.

In the 1950s Best had asked Feasby, a half-blind supernumerary in the Physiology Department who fancied himself a medical historian, to ghostwrite his (Best's) biography. He gave Feasby all his important documents, was interviewed by Feasby, and then made extensive comments on draft biographical chapters that Feasby submitted to him. He also had a typescript made of his wife's diaries, which he gave to Feasby. Suddenly I had in my hands all of this biographical data and, unbeknownst to her, all of Margaret Best's diaries. Unfortunately, or perhaps just as well from the ethical perspective, the diaries were almost useless for my purposes, little more than a gushy name-dropping account of travels and social events.

But the rest of the Feasby material was explosive. The papers contained damning evidence of Charles Best's determination to rewrite history to his advantage. He had given Feasby his own confidential 1922 account of the discovery of insulin and other contemporary documents, and then expected Feasby to "spin" the documents entirely to his greater glory and to the denigration of Collip and Macleod. Example: Best had written Macleod on August 9, 1921, describing his and Banting's first interesting test of a pancreatic extract on a diabetic dog. "We followed your instructions in preparing the extract," Best wrote Macleod. Thirty-five years later, Best suggested that Feasby publish the letter without the paragraph containing that sentence. When Feasby presented Best with a draft of a biography, Best went through it and made several hundred changes in his own hand. Virtually every change was to the greater glory of Charles Best.

My instinctive anger at this astonishing, clumsy attempt to rig the historical record, was soon tempered by the realization that it was deeply pathetic. Both the written sources and contacts with Cleghorn and others alerted me to the fact, finally confirmed in the biography published by Henry Best in 2003, that in the 1950s and 1960s Charles Best had suffered from periods of severe, debilitating depression, possibly an inherited disposition. Part of Best's coping with his melancholy involved obsessively magnifying his role in the insulin story — which had been arguably marginal — to the point where the retelling became nearly a parody. Best, in effect, told the story of how Charley Best had discovered insulin with the help of Fred Banting.

Thanks to Margaret Best, who had a certain sense of fair-mindedness, I managed to locate Banting's former associate/secretary/administrator, Sadie Gairns, another little old lady who lived alone in a small flat in Toronto. Gairns had been hired by Banting in 1923 to replace Best as his research assistant and then had become the organizer of all his projects and eventually the administrator of the university's Banting and Best Department of Medical Research, which he chaired. After some cajoling and another copy of *A Canadian Millionaire*, Miss Gairns agreed to talk to me off the record.

We had several very long sessions that were immensely revealing, both of Banting's character and of the tensions between Banting and Best. Miss Gairns felt that Best had contributed little to the discovery of insulin, and had then disqualified himself from whatever glory he deserved by pestering Banting in every possible way to give him more power and influence in the university. In February 1941, Sadie Gairns told me, it was Charles Best who was scheduled to be the next Canadian medical researcher to go to England for liaison purposes. Banting only decided to go when Best suddenly backed out of the trip. Thus, Banting had gone to his death in the crash of the Hudson bomber on which he was a passenger. When Best appeared in the department a few days after Banting's funeral, seeking help writing an obituary of Banting, Miss Gairns had said to him: "Dr. Best, if you had done your duty, you would not be writing Dr. Banting's obituary." When Best was given Banting's position as head of the Banting and Best Department, Sadie Gairns resigned immediately and never worked again. She had never married.

The Banting papers confirmed Fred's intense dislike of Charley, and much more. Banting had been an intermittent diarist. In 1939, he began keeping a more detailed and intimate diary — his "war diaries" — which on first reading I found breathtaking. The detailed account of his last flight, including an accusation that Best was "yellow," ends with speculation just before the final take-off from Gander, Newfoundland, on how easy it would be to sabotage his plane. The plane did crash, the diary was found on his body, and, of course, a story grew up that the great Dr. Banting's plane had been sabotaged. Earlier passages in the diaries reflected Banting's fascination with chemical-bacterial warfare, of which he became the Canadian founding father in 1940.

His experience of real fatherhood, as well as marriage, had been extremely messy. His first wife, Marion, had borne one son, Bill, three years before a bitter divorce in 1932. His second marriage, to Henrietta Ball in 1939, was not going particularly well either, his diaries revealed. It had been evident to me from meeting Sadie Gairns that she had deeply loved Banting, and in his papers I found an agonized letter from her indicating that he had seduced her at the Canadian Medical Association's meeting in Calgary in 1936. In later meetings with Miss Gairns, a very proper woman, I never had the nerve to raise this issue. How could I ask a sweet old lady what it had been like to have sex with Fred Banting?

That problem recurred some months later when I interviewed Dr. Priscilla White, a paediatric diabetes specialist who had worked in Boston at the noted Joslin Clinic. After his divorce from Marion, Banting had some kind of affair with her. I found Dr. White very late in her life and suffering from the almost complete short-term memory loss of classic Alzheimer's disease. She still had excellent recall of past events, including knowing Banting. Wrestling with ways of framing my question, I did not ask "Did he seduce you?" but rather "How would you describe your relationship with Dr. Banting? Was it purely platonic?" "Yes," she replied, explaining that it developed no further in large part because Dr. Elliott Joslin disapproved of her seeing a divorced, immoral man, however much good the man had done for children with diabetes.

Veteran Canadian journalist Isabel LeBourdais had few scruples about people sleeping around, and got in touch with me to tell me the full story of her late husband's role as co-respondent in the 1932 Banting divorce. One winter night, Donat LeBourdais, a friend of Banting's at Toronto's Arts and Letters Club, had been in Marion Banting's apartment going over some kind of script with her. Fred and Marion were effectively living apart. Suddenly, a fist smashed the glass beside Marion's door and forced it open. Banting and two burly private detectives rushed in and announced they had found the couple in a compromising position. "Jesus Christ, Fred. Why didn't you knock?" LeBourdais said.

As I listened to the LeBourdais story I kept saying to myself, "All I'm trying to do is write about the discovery of insulin." What did I care about the Banting divorce? Or the details of his death? Or the fact that in his war diary he recorded his doubt that Bill Banting was really his son?

But it was all too interesting — the troubled later life of Canada's only Nobel laureate in medicine. The most famous man in the country during his lifetime. A man Sadie Gairns told me would have been happier if he had been a country doctor and never been involved with insulin. I decided that as soon as I finished my book on the discovery of insulin I would write a new biography of Banting. Research would proceed simultaneously for both books.

At first I could not find significant collections of Collip papers. The search led me through storage closets in the Biochemistry Department at the University of Western Ontario, where Collip had finished his career, in which we discovered forgotten boxes of correspondence as well as the cut-down garbage cans in which Collip had mixed hormonal concoctions during his last research projects. Acquaintances also put me in touch with his family. His daughter, Barbara, a McGill graduate in medicine, had moved to the United States with her husband, and was delighted to learn of my interest in her father. I spent several days in Barbara and Jackson Wyatt's beautiful home in the deep southern city of Rome, Georgia, going through the Wyatt collection of Collip family papers. In the next room, Collip's widow was eking out her final moments, comprehending nothing.

The search for more Macleod papers and a more thorough understanding of British involvement in the insulin story led me to England and Scotland for three weeks in the autumn of 1980. Macleod had ended his career in his native Scotland as Regius Professor at the University of Aberdeen. No one ever located Macleod papers in Scotland, but former students and colleagues of Macleod's were generous with time and hospitality — not least because they were Scots nationalists, who believed that their man had never been properly recognized by the Canadian and British cheerleaders for Banting and Best. Over long, mellow dinners, I learned of the history of British discrimination against Scots in United Kingdom medical research, and in language and education. In a picture-perfect cottage in a village that could have been named Brigadoon I was treated to a recitation by the last poetess of the Buchan dialect. Like Brigadoon itself, these good people who were so kind to a visiting Canadian have since vanished into the mists of history.

In London I thought I should check with the British Medical Research Council, to which Toronto had given authority for the introduction of insulin in the United Kingdom, on the off-chance that they had kept a few documents. They had piles of documents in their archives, every scrap of paper relating to the early years of insulin in the U.K., every telegram and letter that had passed between London and Toronto and Eli Lilly and Company. Lilly had become involved fairly early in the insulin story, when production problems in Toronto had caused the university to enter a joint venture, pooling all knowledge and patents to facilitate insulin manufacture. I had also gone to Indianapolis to see the Lilly archive, but it was initially fairly unrewarding. The company's historian, a friendly Hoosier named Gene McCormick, showed me the references to insulin in the manuscript history of the firm that he had prepared, and treated me to one of the best dinners I have ever had in the unlikely venue of Indianapolis's Airport Holiday Inn. But I was not given permission to go fishing in the company's archives.

Nor, at first, could I find the University of Toronto's own records of its handling of the insulin discovery. An Insulin Committee of our Board of Governors had been formed to deal with the discoverers (who transferred their basic patent to the university for one dollar), with Lilly, the MRC, and all other insulin licensees. No one knew where its records might be. Someone finally suggested that the last secretary of the Insulin Committee, a former employee of the university's Connaught Laboratories, either had the records or knew where they were. So I landed on the north Toronto doorstep of Dr. Albert Fisher, a stiff and suspicious martinet, who told me that he did have some records of the Insulin Committee, that he was writing its history, and I could see the records after he was finished.

But I need to see them now, I pleaded, suspecting correctly that Fisher would never finish his project. "Here's a copy of my most recent book." "Well, I'll go through the documents and see if there's anything that would be useful to you, but it's not likely." "Well, perhaps it would be easier for you if I went through them myself..." And so on through several more visits and phone calls until Fisher relented and took me into his basement. There I found five filing cabinets containing the records of the University of Toronto's correspondence about the intro-duction of insulin throughout the world. When I told Fisher that I would have to live in his basement for a month going through these files, he gave up and let me borrow whatever I wanted. I filled my car's trunk with files and read them in my study, carefully brushing mouse droppings out of each file before using it. When I returned the files to Fisher I suggested that he either make sure they were fully insured or consider returning them to the university because they were almost priceless. He gave me the usual brush-off, saying he would finish his history first.

A few months later, when I began collating documents from the various collections, I realized that some items in the three-way correspondence between Toronto, Lilly, and London, could only be found in the MRC archives, not in Toronto where copies ought to have been. Fisher, I concluded, had destroyed some documents. This was the last straw. I wrote the university archivist that Dr. Fisher had in his possession a number of invaluable files that belonged to the university, and that for security's sake the university ought to insist upon their return. I copied the letter to Fisher. The next day the Insulin Committee records were delivered to the University of Toronto Archives. Albert Fisher did not speak to me again.

It was well-known that the award of the 1923 Nobel Prize for the discovery of insulin was highly controversial. In the view of some old-timers, including a former secretary of Stockholm's Caroline Institute, which awards the Nobels in physiology or medicine, a great mistake had been made in not giving the prize to Banting and Best, or perhaps to Banting, Macleod, and Best. I doubted that I could sort out this part of the story. Everyone knew the Nobel deliberations were secret and if they had an archive it must be closed. Still, for completeness's sake I should get a formal denial of access from the Caroline Institute.

To my complete surprise, they replied that they had recently changed their archive policy, that researchers could now apply for access to documents more than fifty years old, and that the insulin records would be available to me if I visited. When I said that I would fly over as soon as I could, they asked if I realized that most of the relevant documents were in Swedish. I called the Canadian embassy in Stockholm about hiring a translator, and was told the going rate in Sweden was $600 a day, much more than I could afford. What to do? An obliging secretary at the embassy called back a few days later to tell me that her daughter, a fluently bilingual schoolteacher, would be on holiday about the time I proposed to come, and could do my translation work for $100 a day, cash. The only loser in the transaction would be Sweden's tax collectors.

I had just enough research money left for the trip. When I took the subway out to the Karolinska Institute in a Stockholm suburb in June 1981, I assumed that I would find a palatial establishment at one of the world's meccas of medical research. Instead, there were a few modest red-brick buildings, set in parkland, and one secretary in charge of a small archive on the fourth floor of the administrative building.

The secretary invited me to browse in the stacks of the archive where the boxes of documents were neatly filed and dated — "Nominations 1923," "Reports 1923," "Deliberations 1923," and so on, each year included an unusually thick box labelled "Self-Nominations." I could see any documents I wanted (one day I looked in the self-nomination boxes, which seemed mostly to consist of letters by pedlars of cancer cures and other patent medicines nominating themselves for their great contributions to humanity). Many of the nominations were in English. My translator was very fluent, also very beautiful, and was able to read to me the gist of the Swedish documents while we worked. When the staff of the archives went out to lunch, earlier than we wanted to go, they gave me the key to the stacks — literally the key to the Nobel archive. At four o'clock we would join these pleasant people for coffee and cakes.

The archive contained a complete, richly detailed documentary record of the decision, controversial even as it was being made, to give the 1923 Nobel Prize to Banting and Macleod. The committee was strongly influenced by the key nomination, which had come from the Danish Nobel laureate, August Krogh, who had visited Toronto late in 1922 and then begun Scandinavian insulin manufacture. Krogh argued that Banting could never have made it to insulin without the direction of Macleod. He considered Best a student assistant and, with some qualms, did not see the point of honouring Collip, who had left Toronto by the time of his visit and whom he never met.

This was the perfect icing on my research cake. I found time to interview Rolf Luft, the veteran member of the Nobel committee who had been championing Best's claim, and found that he had never consulted the documents, had been peddling hearsay evidence traceable back to Best's distortions of history, and that he had nothing to contribute.

At the end of my week in Stockholm, I could be seen outside of my fairly seedy tourist hotel giving a beautiful blond Swedish woman large amounts of cash. I imagined writing a story about the obvious inference that could be made and the improbability of the claim that she had merely been translating the records of a Nobel Prize committee for me.

The research unfolded amazingly well, in small doses and large. It was frustrating that Banting's original notebook could not be found anywhere in his papers — the joint Banting and Best notebooks in the collection seemed to pick up the research several weeks after it had started. Then someone mentioned that the library of the Toronto Academy of Medicine was rumoured to have a Banting notebook. The librarian said she thought they did, though no one had ever looked at it. When she brought it out, there was the page on which, on the night of October 31, 1920, Banting had written down the idea that resulted in the discovery of insulin. I was amused to see that he spelled the disease "Diabetus," amazed to realize that his actual idea was worded differently from the idea he later remembered having recorded. Banting had always quoted himself from memory, and done it inaccurately. No one else knew this. All other writing about the discovery of insulin, including Banting's, misquoted the original idea. Turning the pages of this notebook, I realized it also contained a complete record of the first six weeks of the insulin research, a period no one had known anything about.

A box in the Banting papers labelled "Student Notebooks" was probably not worth bothering with, but had to be checked, just in case. A thick file of index cards in this box was not from Banting's student days at all, but contained more of Banting and Best's notes from the summer and autumn of 1921. Medical historians had recently drawn attention to very good articles on pancreatic research that a Romanian physiologist, Nicolae Paulesco, had published a few months before Banting and Best began their research. A slighting reference to Paulesco's work in one of Banting and Best's early articles was clearly incorrect. Could it have been a deliberate denigration of a competitor, potentially a scientific scandal? Well, in my hand was the index card containing Charles Best's 1921 précis of the key Paulesco article, which had been published in French. There on the card was Best's obvious translation error, mistaking the words "non plus" as meaning no good.

Here was another index card, Fred's note on Banting and Best's first trial of their extract on a human diabetic:

Clinical Use
Dec. 20. Phoned Joe Gilchrist —
gave him extract that we knew to
be potent. — by mouth — empty stomach
Dec. 21 — no beneficial result.

In the privacy of my carrel in the depths of the Fisher Library, I would quietly exclaim "Eureka," then share my excitement with Katharine Martyn, the librarian in charge of the collections, then take my stories home to Liz. This is a great project, I would tell her, and if it doesn't become a great book I'll have no one to blame but myself.

A dear old chemist, nonagenarian Peter Moloney, told me on his deathbed of the time in 1922 when they almost blew up the university's medical building trying to make insulin. J.J.R. Macleod's former secretary, Maynard Grange, blind and keeping the furnace on in her north Toronto apartment in the dead of summer, told me of Banting coming in to get a book Macleod had recommended in 1921 and commenting, "The goddamn little son of a bitch knows absolutely everything about this subject." Almost all the secretaries had survived to give me their stories. "Fred Banting, you're acting like a fifteen-year old," the professor of medicine's secretary had told him one day. "When are you going to grow up?" Over fine single malt scotch, another remembered Banting showing her the seven cents that was all the money he claimed to have left in the world.

The interviews went on and on, my files becoming stunningly rich. Many of the old-timers who had started out as researchers at the Banting Institute in the 1930s had vivid memories — of drinking

parties, sing-songs, bothersome reporters, and designing women, experiments to cure cancer, revive the victims of drowning, discover the secret
of royal jelly. "The world never understood Banting…" exclaimed crusty
old Bill Franks, inventor of the Franks anti-gravity flying suit and one
of Canada's most honoured scientists. "The world should pull up its
socks." On the patio of his lovely home in Rosedale, Alan Walters, dean
of Toronto psychiatrists, finally leaped to his feet in exasperation and
exclaimed: "They were just children … Banting and Best … just children
… they never grew up."

"Next person who calls me Sir Frederick," Banting told his gang
after receiving a knighthood in 1935, "will get his ass kicked."

I had thought a book on the discovery of insulin would centre on the
theme of controversy over credit — the friction among the researchers
that had erupted, incredibly, in a fight in the lab between Banting and
Collip at the moment of discovery, a moment that arguably belonged
more to Collip than to Banting. Then it began to dawn on me that credit
was secondary. The real insulin story was of the breathtaking impact that
the introduction of insulin had on the starved, dying diabetic children
who first received it. Here was high and inspiring medical drama, inter-
laced by the problems that the discovery team had in producing more
than dribs and drabs of impure insulin in the early months of 1922. The
true primary focus of the book, I realized, should be the patients and
what insulin did for them, not the scientists and what may or may not
have been their childishness. I eventually concluded that the discoverers
were more like Canadian hockey players, reacting childishly to stress by
dropping the gloves.

The Banting papers contained several boxes of patient records.
Some files were disappointingly thin. The first patient to be given
effective insulin, sixteen-year-old Leonard Thompson, had been a charity case about whom little was ever known. The resident who did the
autopsy on Thompson when he died in Toronto in 1935 was still alive
and full of good stories, talking about how as he removed the pancreas
his assistants joked that it should be hung over the door of the Banting
Institute. He thought Thompson's pancreas had been preserved. The

next day I told Liz I was going to the university on a pancreas hunt. After about ninety minutes I found Leonard Thompson's preserved pancreas in our Pathology Department's collection of specimens. It is still occasionally put on display at the university on special occasions, always tastefully.

Banting's scrapbook contained a photo of a beautiful teenage girl, Elsie Needham, with an annotation in his handwriting about her being the first child to have been brought out of diabetic coma by the use of insulin. Wondering what happened to her, I was able to trace her through her Toronto hospital records for another twenty-four years before she disappeared. Everywhere I give lectures on these events I speculate that Elsie Needham might have moved to that locality and hope someone will come up afterward and tell me about their Aunt Elsie.

We had better luck tracing the first patient in the United States to receive insulin, Jim Havens, son of an Eastman Kodak executive in Rochester. The secret of my historical detection was a call to telephone information in Rochester to ask if there were any Havens listed in their directory. Within a few minutes I was talking to James Havens Junior.

The most remarkable of the early Toronto stories appeared to be that of Elizabeth Hughes, the teenage daughter of a distinguished American statesman and jurist, Charles Evans Hughes. Elizabeth, diabetic since 1918, was initially refused treatment in Toronto because the supply of insulin was so limited. When she was finally brought to the city from Washington (her father was serving as Secretary of State) in August 1922 and examined by Banting, Elizabeth was fifteen years old, five feet tall, and reduced to forty-five pounds (twenty kilograms) from her diabetes. She was within days of death from starvation. Insulin gave her an astonishing reprieve. The last item in her file in Banting's papers was a 1929 engagement photo of a beautiful young woman about to marry a handsome young lawyer.

In another Holmesian feat, I looked up the husband's name in the most recent *Who's Who in America*, found him listed, and wrote him a letter asking about the later course of Elizabeth's disease and the circumstances surrounding her death. "Dear Professor Bliss," the answering letter began, "Your letter addressed to my husband was read with interest by both of us. Yes, I am very much alive ..." In the summer of 1980, Elizabeth Evans Hughes Gossett was just short of her seventy-third birthday, living with her husband in Grosse Pointe, Michigan, taking her insulin, and still in such good health that she could not see me because they were about to leave for six weeks in China.

When they returned I was on the doorstep. Having always assumed she was dead — my life as an historian was doing post-mortems on dead people — to be greeted by Elizabeth Hughes in person was like seeing someone resurrected. A thin, graceful woman, with some of the wrinkles of age and perhaps a facelift (I'm told she was moderately offended that I referred to her as wizened), she was very friendly, giving me the better part of a day of her time, lending me all her correspondence with her mother both before and after being saved by insulin in Toronto. "However, Professor Bliss, now I must beg you to respect my privacy. I cannot bear publicity. My life as a diabetic before receiving insulin was a nightmare. When I awakened from it I determined to live a normal life, and, as completely as possible, I did that, telling hardly anyone of my condition. I could not bear the publicity your book would give me. Perhaps after my death it will not matter."

We went round and round the issue. This was at a time when legislative protection of patient records and privacy was still practically non-existent. Over lunch, Elizabeth talked about how all her friends would stare at her if they knew she had diabetes — I did not know how to avoid seeming to stare at her. We finally agreed that I would disguise her identity with a pseudonym and other inventions. In the first draft of my manuscript she became "Kathleen Lonsdale," the daughter of a prominent American political figure. Just as I was finishing the book in the spring of 1981, Liz Bliss's mother happened to hear on a Detroit radio station of the death of Mrs. Gossett. Her husband confirmed that I could use her real name and quote from her letters.

It was a great loss to history that Elizabeth's voice and her memories of coming to Toronto to get insulin were not recorded. I doubt that she would have talked to me at all, however, had I come with a tape recorder. I did not make tapes of any interviews, partly because transcribing tapes is time-consuming and expensive, mainly because I judged that most of my subjects would clam up if they thought they were speaking for some kind of official record. Neither then, nor later, did I ever use consent forms in my interviews, a favourite device now often required of researchers by the ubiquitous ethics review boards. Like any journalist, I was an adult talking to adults. My professional standing was a guarantee of my discretion and a commitment to treat sources fairly. No one I interviewed for any project later complained that I had misused or misquoted their remarks. By the time we issued a twenty-fifth anniversary edition of *The Discovery of Insulin* in 2007, sixty-six of the sixty-eight subjects were dead, the sixty-seventh died a few months later. My interview files are available in the insulin collections at the Fisher Library.

Did I know what I was doing with this insulin material? Lacking any significant training in science or medicine, beginning with no knowledge about diabetes — no one I knew was touched by it — I was proposing to write an authoritative account of a complicated and highly controversial discovery made sixty years earlier. Doubts about my capacity to do more than vulgarly popularize the discovery of insulin were fairly held, and no one was more worried about this problem than I was. I knew I had to get an education in diabetes, I had to have help, I must not publish a sentence that could not withstand critical scrutiny.

In the medical section at the university bookstore I found the most current edition of *Joslin's Diabetic Manual*, a guide for patients. I also bought a good medical dictionary. Then I turned to the literature on the history of diabetes. I hired my most brilliant student to spend a summer doing a background paper on the history of diabetes before the coming of insulin. At first glance, Banting's and Best's notebooks seemed Greek to me. I had to get them in usable form anyway, and thought that making a full typescript of all the notes might help. By the time I finished it, I realized that I understood about 90 percent of what was going on. A phone call to our Department of Physiology put me in touch with the husband and wife team of Anna and Otto Sirek, both diabetes researchers who had originally come to Toronto to work under Charles Best. They were delighted to let me draw on them, virtually at will, for technical help. Everyone in the medical world responded generously to requests for help — except Bernard Leibel, who kept grumbling about the damage I would do to the sacred story of Fred Banting and Charley Best's heroic struggles.

When I needed explanations of technical points in the insulin notebooks, Otto Sirek supplied them. When I needed to know what it was like for Banting to do pancreatectomies on laboratory dogs, Anna, who was still using dogs in her research, decided to show me. She took me into the animal operating room in the bowels of our medical building and had me observe her working in the abdomen of several research animals. The doctor's son, who had once seen his brother do similar surgery at McGill, and had watched hog slaughtering at Canada Packers, was not queasy. Reassured, Anna had me don operating garb, scrub properly, put on gloves, and assist her as she took out a dog's pancreas, the basic procedure Banting conducted at the beginning of the work in 1921. Having me examine and touch the pancreatic ducts, showing me how easy it would be to miss small portions of the pancreas while trying to remove it — as crucially happened to Banting, probably with several dogs — Anna was literally giving me a feel for my subject.

In both teaching and research I always realized that the best way to deal with lack of knowledge is to admit it. My first presentations about my project were entitled "The Discovery of Insulin: Some Questions," and were hesitant, unpresuming talks about the evolution of the controversy over credit and where I thought research could take me. I always concluded with a plea for help, and would afterward quietly ask friends if I had made any egregious technical or interpretive errors. It was terrifying to give talks to high-powered doctors and researchers, especially my first presentation to a packed house at our Physiology Department. I felt better when Otto Sirek said that so far as he could tell my only mistake had been to mispronounce the word "glycogen."

The work went on during my 1980–81 sabbatical, with my relatively small research costs covered by a grant from the U of T's Connaught Fund (the money we had received from selling the Connaught Laboratories a few years earlier). When I realized that I could not finish the book in a single year, and needed time to write the Banting sequel, I swallowed my principles and decided to apply, yet again, for one of the two-year Killam fellowships. Yet again, I was turned down. On hearing the news I went for a long walk in nearby Mount Hope Cemetery, then went back to work. I knew I could fall back on the Connaught Fund — it had a special senior fellowship program that I had founded during my term on Governing Council — for at least one more year of released time. I learned by the grapevine that the Killam Committee had rejected me this time because they did not think I could handle the medical issues surrounding the discovery of insulin. My diaries for this period ooze determination to show the unprintable, unprintable bastards that they were wrong again.

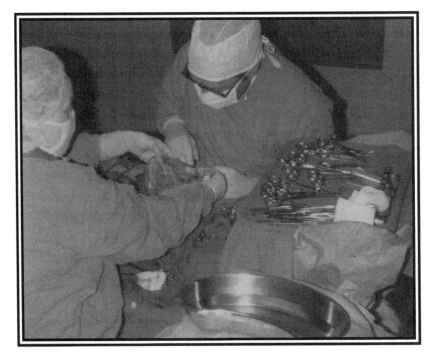

Becoming a medical historian.

January 4, 1981:

Have just finished making a memo on the original plan of work in the insulin experiments. Yesterday A.M. I sat down formally to begin "writing" — which is actually the putting together of the notes and the beginning of putting it on paper. Very slow and frustrating progress, but in fact this is exactly what I know from experience to expect. And by the end of the day I'd made the amazing discovery of the importance of grafting in the original plan of work. Something no living person knows anything about or could discover — and that probably Banting, Best, and Macleod had forgotten all about. A pleasing piece of work for an historian.

Writing *The Discovery of Insulin* was extremely difficult because the landscape was so strange, the issues so complicated, and the importance of getting the story right so great. From undergraduate days I had composed on a typewriter; now I reverted to writing by hand, deliberately slowing down to manage the problem of complexity. I wanted to feel, to massage the words as they were put to paper. I had thought my research assistant's good study of diabetes before insulin would be the basis of my first chapter, but found again and again that I was redoing her work. My approach was different enough that I had to go back through all the documents to absorb them myself. After this experience I almost never used research assistants, except for scut work. It seemed like employing a stand-in to do one's sexual foreplay. When you took over you weren't prepared, and if the assistant had done a good job then the assistant should go all the way.

At age forty, and at peak energy levels, I was able to generate long hours of concentration at my desk and with the documents. On normal projects I liked to stop a day's work at four or five o'clock; with *Insulin* and *Banting* I would often wander into my study after dinner, get caught up in the documents, and work into the night. Even using a fountain pen, even traversing this difficult terrain, the words came quickly and exactly. My productivity was very high, often 2,000–4,000 good words a day, generated from the documents. I thought I was writing about three times as quickly as most academic historians, those who write anything at all. In memory, the delights of that project seem like the thrills of an athlete's championship season, or perhaps the perfect marathon.

On reflection, I was more marathoner than team player, doing virtually all of the research and writing in solitude. I cherished long days of writing without the telephone ringing or any interruption except from the family (I never felt I had to leave our noisy house and retreat into complete solitude). The work was arduous and exhausting, the satisfactions were intense. Experiencing something like a literary equivalent of the "runner's high" — periods when the activity seems absolutely effortless and can go on forever — I gloried in the opportunity to be a writer, wanted to do more writing, wanted never to have to return to teaching. I went through a period of reading Hemingway's letters and stories, admiring him for his absolute commitment to writing life as honestly as possible. Honesty, however, dictates that Hicks was more influential in shaping my prose than Hemingway. One day, as I drew on memories from first year science courses, I commented to Liz that my whole life seemed to have been a preparation for writing this book.

I read as much fiction as history, and with at least as much pleasure and profit. It had intrigued me when a Canadian writer known mainly for his short stories, Hugh Hood, announced his plan to produce a twelve-volume novel, *The New Age/Le Nouveau Siècle*, about the Canadian experience. I was very impressed by Hood's first volume, *The Swing in the Garden*, published in 1975, even more by volume two, *A New Athens* (1977), and when I put down volume three, *Reservoir Ravine*, in 1979, I wrote Mr. Hood an unabashed fan letter — only the second time in my life I had done that, the first being many years earlier to Gordie Howe, who never answered. Hugh Hood did reply, we began a correspondence, we met for lunch on one of his trips to Toronto, I had dinner with Hugh and Noreen Hood at their home in Montreal, and we kept up a friendship, both literary and personal, for many years. The only literary "criticism" I have written is an essay arguing that of the six greatest Canadian novels, three are by Hugh Hood.

Hugh was an eccentric genius — one of his eccentricities was that he would be the first to tell people of his genius — and superficially we seemed to have little in common. He was a devout Roman Catholic, whereas I had not wavered from the practical atheism that had descended upon me in the shower in Kingsville in 1961. We had in common an intense sense that the only way to understand events was through studying their unfolding in history (for Hugh history was divine revelation) and in all their bewildering complexity (for Hugh the beauty of creation). I admired Hugh and Noreen's total devotion to life in the arts, and often felt like a philistine in their company — except when Hugh and I talked baseball, as he was a great fan of the old Montreal Expos.

Occasionally I had bouts of melancholy, despair, depression — probably just biorhythmic lows, certainly nothing verging on a clinical condition — when the meaninglessness of life and the absence of God, the absence of the comforts of simple religious faith, seemed oppressive. "I don't believe in God, but I miss Him," Julian Barnes begins his meditation on death, *Nothing to Be Frightened of*. I had turned away from many joys when I abandoned Christian belief. On the other hand, I had been so steeped in Christianity that religious language and symbolism, as in Hugh Hood's writings, were perfectly comprehensible. I don't think it was the Hood influence so much as this general predisposition, but early in the insulin research I noted how often some of the patients, and their physicians, fell back on their spiritual heritage for images and metaphors to describe the wonder of the coming of this medical breakthrough. Words like "salvation," "resurrection," "miracle," were used to describe insulin's effects; the scientists were engaged in a struggle for "immortality"; and so on.

Just as novelists like Hood were dealing with big issues, eternal questions, I realized that the narrative of the discovery of insulin also addressed fundamental questions. Novelists and historians, Christian as well as secular, were witnesses to the human struggle to transcend. I did not believe in supernatural salvation or immortality, but I was writing a book about secular salvation and about scientific immortality. I made this explicit in the first and last paragraphs of my introduction and in certain images, especially the concluding sentence of my penultimate paragraph: "With insulin, the stone was rolled away, and diabetes became a matter of life, not death."

The most explicit reference was a comment that the great American diabetologist, Elliott Joslin, made about the events of 1922. "By Christmas of 1922," Joslin wrote, "I had witnessed so many near resurrections that I realized I was seeing enacted before my very eyes Ezekial's vision of the valley of dry bones." I looked up the text in the Book of Ezekial, chapter 37, and found Joslin's beautiful and moving metaphor for the coming of insulin:

… and behold, there were very many in the open valley; and, lo, they were very dry.

And he said unto me, Son of Man, can these bones live?

And … lo, the sinews and the flesh came upon them and the skin covered them above: but there was no breath in them.

Then said He unto me, Prophesy unto the wind, prophesy, Son of Man, and say to the wind," Thus saith the Lord God: "Come from the four winds, O breath, and breathe upon these slain, that they may live.

So I prophesied as he commanded me, and the breath came into them, and they lived, and stood up upon their feet, an exceeding great army.

Turning to the biography of Fred Banting, I shifted focus to see him as a product of his time and his country, "An honest, unpretentious son of rural Ontario, wrestling with a reputation and position he had never expected to have, dealing with people and responsibilities that constantly threatened to overwhelm him." I compared him with Lindbergh, compared him (at Hugh Hood's suggestion) to a character from *The Great Gatsby*, and argued that he fulfilled Joan Didion's definition of a great literary character as "so ambiguous and driven and revealing of his time and place that his gravestone might well contain only his name and nationality."

My points of reference for Banting were not the lives of other researchers or Nobel laureates, but books about Canada and Canadians written by Stephen Leacock, Donald Jack (his Bartholomew Bandy books), and Hugh Hood. I made the biography as rigorously objective as possible — as long as Sadie Gairns and Bill Banting were alive I was not going to mention the seduction or the parenthood issues — but also made clear my view that the biographer's job is not so much to write a case history as it is to re-create a life. It was not casual that my favourite quote about the biographer came from Walt Whitman, writing about the poet as resurrectionist: He "drags the dead out of their coffins and stands them again on their feet ... He says to the past, Rise and walk before me that I may realize you."

***

After days or weeks of intense effort on insulin I would turn to other projects for variety. I turned down offers to do major books, including a biography of George Drew and the concluding volume in McClelland & Stewart's Canadian Centennial series, but for a handsome fee did run through my typewriter a flawed manuscript biography of former Ontario Premier John Robarts. The final product was still flawed, causing me to resolve never again to be involved in ghostwriting or collaborations. My main literary dalliance was with magazine journalism, particularly a relationship that developed with the old *Saturday Night* magazine, then enjoying a kind of golden age (of critical esteem, not profitability) under the editorship of Robert Fulford and Bernadette Sulgit. In 1981–83, I wrote five feature articles for *Saturday Night*, two of which won National Magazine Awards.

The most interesting *SN* assignment was a profile of the Canadian-born economist, John Kenneth Galbraith, then in his early seventies and a grand old man of leftish economics. I read or reread all his principal books and, in November 1980, spent several days following Galbraith around as he lectured to students at Yale, then interviewed him at length on the train from New Haven to Boston. Galbraith's intellectual root-edness in the Canadian tradition of agrarian protest was striking — his father had been an organizer for the United Farmers of Ontario around the time of his birth, and my first title for my article was "The Last Member of the United Farmers of Ontario." This connection still is not understood by Galbraith biographers. Nor had others noticed his eye for journalistic devices, like the deliberate creation of catchy phrases or titles: "conventional wisdom," "the affluent society," "the new industrial state." He talked to the students about literary productivity; if you can write only a thousand publishable words a day, Galbraith would remark, you can turn out a very hefty book every year. All his talks ended with an exhortation to students to learn to speak and write well. "These are wonderful weapons. If you can speak and write, the content doesn't matter very much, for you can get away with all sorts of foolishness ... as my career attests." I identified with that.

My other profiles were of Jack Gallagher, the word-spinning pro-moter of Dome Petroleum, which in the early eighties became one of the great corporate failures in Canadian history; Brian Peckford, Conservative premier of Newfoundland, who had not yet become a figure of ridicule for financing a hydroponic cucumber plant; and the ski area of Whistler, British Columbia. The Whistler assignment was much the most pleasant, as Liz and I spent two weeks skiing the spectacular slopes of Whistler and Blackcomb Mountains, dining out every night at *Saturday Night*'s expense to review the local cuisine. I had first skied Whistler after guest lecturing in Vancouver in the late 1970s, when the community consisted of little more than a few plywood motels and a Husky Oil station. If I had had the good sense to borrow every cent I could and invest it in a valley bisected by the River of Golden Dreams, I could have become very rich. We all have our real estate regrets.

I submitted occasional op-ed pieces to the *Toronto Star* and the *Globe and Mail*, usually writing about national politics, usually from a moderately conservative point of view. An early piece I wrote attacking liberal abortion got me tagged as more socially conservative than I normally was. Radio and television interviewers liked to use me to provide historical background for current events, not least because I had given considerable thought to their mediums — to the need to simplify complex issues, to develop quotable sound-bite phrases, not to hog airtime on panels. I made myself as available as possible to both print and broadcast journalists, always answering calls, always trying to be helpful.

By 1979, I had become a card-carrying Conservative. I thought that Mr. Trudeau had shot his bolt and that the country desperately needed change. Joe Clark's minority government seemed ready to restore economic discipline to the country. It never occurred to me that the new government would be defeated in the House of Commons in only a few months. When that prospected loomed, in December 1979, I thought the Conservatives should call the Liberals' bluff, because even if it did come to an election they would surely win. I did not think it possible that on such short notice Mr. Trudeau could be resurrected.

My misjudgments continued through the constitutional struggles of 1981–82, as I tended to side with conservatives who worried that Mr. Trudeau was doing serious harm in proposing to bull ahead with his reform proposals, whatever the provinces felt. His draft Charter of Rights and Freedoms seemed to me a rejection of our British tradition of parliamentary sovereignty in favour of an American-style constitutionalizing of rights that would deliver immense power to the courts. I noticed how the legal/judicial community's support for the charter blended with their usually undeclared self-interest. I also thought that

Mr. Trudeau's plan to ask Britain to implement constitutional recommendations without significant provincial support would have landed Canada in a constitutional crisis. Governor-General Ed Schreyer would have had to refuse to transmit a request to Westminster that the Supreme Court had ruled legal but unconstitutional, and this would have precipitated another election.

It never came to that, as a compromise settlement that satisfied every province but Quebec was finally reached. Mr. Trudeau later told me that the main pressure on him to compromise came not from the governor-general but from within his cabinet and from his chief provincial allies, the Davis Conservatives in Ontario. It did not particularly bother me that René Lévesque, the separatist premier of Quebec, either accidently or deliberately mishandled the final negotiations and wound up isolated and angry. Trudeau's manoeuvres had been both legal and constitutional, had the support of federal members of Parliament from Quebec, and at least had the merit of having settled our outstanding constitutional issues. Soon I also realized that Canadians' human rights were much better protected by the constitutionalized Charter than they had been when left to provincial legislatures and Parliament.

Chapter Nine

Toward 1984

The more I cultivated my writing life, the less I felt I had in common with many academic friends. I had done much of what I aspired to in a university setting. Insofar as I could compare salaries, my efforts had earned almost derisory recognition. The more I learned about salary profiles at the University of Toronto — data released only reluctantly and in anonymous aggregations — the more disconcerted I was to realize that historians were paid largely by seniority and not nearly as well as, say, the staff of the over-funded Ontario Institute for Studies in Education. I had carried one of the heaviest undergraduate and graduate teaching loads in the department, been given extremely high teaching ratings, done at least a full share of committee service, not to mention Governing Council service, and was writing good books. And I was one of the lowest paid full professors in the University of Toronto.

Looking ahead at mid-life, the prospect of another quarter century of lectures on Laurier's naval policy, arguments with graduate students, grading essays and exams, History Department politics, and the unspeakable dreariness of the corridors of Sidney Smith Hall, seemed soul destroying. I wanted to stay away, perhaps escape completely from the academic mouse race. My second year on the insulin-Banting project,

1981–82, was financed with a Connaught Senior Fellowship. How could I stay away for a third year? Stay away forever?

A possible angel appeared in the summer of 1981, in the unlikely form of blue-suited public relations personnel from the Manufacturers Life Insurance Company, now Manulife, Canada's largest insurance company. Manulife had funded, through the Canadian Historical Association, the John A. Macdonald Prize, which I had won for the Flavelle biography. Sir John A. had been their first president, heading the firm on its founding in 1887 while also serving as prime minister (in those days no one thought it a conflict of interest that sitting politicians would earn extra income by helping to guarantee the bona fides of companies whose most visible beneficiaries were women and children). The Manulife people had been particularly pleased that a book of business history had won their prize, and now wondered if I could advise them on a possible project for their firm's centenary. They did not think anyone would be interested in reading a history of their firm. What other history could they support?

I responded that the history of business in Canada had never been written. What would you require to write it? they asked. Two full years, or three years on two-thirds time, I estimated. The Manulifers seemed agreeable, and we began negotiating the details of a contract. In January 1982, I told my chairman of my plan to be a part-timer for the next three years, and he responded generously. If he had not, I had resolved simply to resign, work full-time on the Manulife project, and let the future take care of itself.

Negotiations with Manulife suddenly floundered that spring when they went on an internal austerity kick and the project fell apart. Not being able to face crawling back to the History Department, having built a nest egg from journalism, I decided on a third year away from teaching. I would just go on leave without pay in 1982–83. Whereas some men's response to mid-life angst is to walk away from their wives, mine was a trial separation from the university.

Other irons glowed in the fire. I had a call from a fellow Canadian historian, Dick Clippingdale, who was on leave from Carleton University to serve as senior policy adviser to Joe Clark. Now that constitutional change was effectively completed, Clippingdale told me, the Progressive-Conservatives were interested in having someone write an authoritative history of their contribution to the process. Would I be interested? They would give me complete access to Clark, anyone else I wanted to interview, and all the files. Of course I was interested, and soon I was in Ottawa meeting with Clippingdale and Clark.

In the summer of 1981, I had signed contracts for the publication of *The Discovery of Insulin* and its sequel, the Banting biography. It was not yet common in Canada to use agents, so I staged a small auction, submitting the manuscript simultaneously to the four houses I had worked with: McGraw-Hill-Ryerson, McClelland & Stewart, the University of Toronto Press, and Macmillan. All four wanted to do the book. Three offered me a $5,000 advance against royalties. McClelland & Stewart offered me a $25,000 advance and the same again when *Banting* was ready.

I wondered if the flamboyant Jack McClelland, whose enthusiasm for publishing books often outran his business sense, could be trusted to carry out his commitments, respect the scholarly *sine qua non* of my books, and not try to turn me into an imitation Pierre Berton. Jack was personable and persuasive. He was offering me more money than anyone else because he seemed to know how to sell more books. Maybe he would sell tons of them. Liz thought that if I didn't sign with McClelland I'd always have a lingering regret at what might have been. The final negotiation with Jack went so well, I recorded in my journal, "that I came away wondering what I'd missed; how have I been screwed?" "Not to worry," I added, "but go on and submit the most nearly perfect manuscript they've ever seen in that house."

The final polishing of the manuscript was unusually thorough. Obsessed by the need to have mastered the medicine and science, I had it read by ten experts, including several old-timers. The most helpful was Sir Frank Young, a British researcher in endocrinology who had visited Toronto in the 1930s and in the 1950s became the founding master of Darwin College, Oxford. On the way back from Stockholm in 1981 I stayed with the Youngs in Oxford, and spent two days at Sir Frank's living room table where we went over the manuscript line by line. We not only argued points of science and evidence, but also my approaches to spelling, punctuation, grammar, and syntax. "Bliss," he would say, "this book will be read by Fiji Islanders and Nobel laureates. You have to get it right."

Eugene McCormick, Eli Lilly and Company's historian, made a special trip to Toronto after reading the relevant chapters and finding to his surprise that I had many more documents than he had been able to obtain from the Lilly archive. He also brought me the remaining documents I had not seen. My most demanding critic reader was Diane Mew, one of the best freelance editors in Canada, an Englishwoman with both high standards and a fine dry sense of humour. We had worked together so successfully on Flavelle that I had her participation written into my next several contracts.

While the manuscript was in press I gave several anticipatory lectures, including one entitled "The Discovery of Insulin: Some Answers." From my first sight of riveting before-and-after photos of some of the early insulin patients I knew I must have slides made of these and other pictures, with a view to illustrating my talks. In the medical world, I noticed, speakers almost always used slides — probably, I liked to joke, because of doctors' short attention span. My lectures gradually became spectacular slide shows, often ending with the before and afters flashing on the screen while I read Joslin's comment about Ezekial and the dry bones. In June 1982, I spoke at the Canadian Diabetes Association's national meeting in Moncton, the first time I had attended a diabetes meeting. The reception by these workers, activists, and patients was far better than I had anticipated. "Good applause when I stopped the formal speaking, then some interesting questions, then a good thanking of me — then as I left the podium a standing ovation, the first I've ever had for anything in my life. Remarkable."

On the evening of September 7, 1982, an editor from McClelland & Stewart brought to the house my first copy of *The Discovery of Insulin*. For the first several days it was seldom out of my sight; I cuddled the book as though it were a new baby. A few weeks later I wrote in it George

Chapman's comment on finishing his translation of Homer: "The work that I was born to do is done."

—————————————

The New York Times scooped all reviewers by publishing a 2,800-word article by Larry Altman on *The Discovery of Insulin* in its science section on September 14, 1982. The next morning I had calls from both the Massachusetts Institute of Technology and Yale asking me to come down and talk about my work. The Canadian press paid no attention to Altman's story. CBC News did, but then called back to say they were having to postpone coverage because of the assassination of the president of Lebanon. I had no calls from anyone at any Canadian university.

At MIT, I was a guest lecturer in one of Carl Kaysen's courses. At lunch afterward we discussed James Watson's *The Double Helix*. Kaysen had been one of the publisher's readers of the original manuscript. MIT's professor of the history of medicine told me my lecture was the best presentation of the history of a discovery he'd ever heard.

The Canadian media, for whom science/medicine was a low priority, eventually caught up. The book had good coverage and reviews. As a McClelland & Stewart author I was sent on a national promotional tour, doing radio, television, and newspaper interviews from Halifax to Vancouver. My first interview in Ottawa was on a daytime television show hosted by Margaret Trudeau, former wife of the prime minister. My publisher's representative told me that Ms. Trudeau was a hopeless lightweight; I should ignore her and make what I considered my important points. Margaret only flubbed badly when she said that Banting and Macleod won the Nobel Peace Prize for the discovery of insulin. I noticed her remarkable blue eyes and equally remarkable aged hands. On a Vancouver open-line talk show I tossed off a comment about the silliness of the anti-vivisectionists in opposing the insulin research and was kept on the air for the next ninety minutes fending off enraged animal lovers. In Halifax there was little to do, as the city's most important book show had just been replaced by re-reruns of "Romper Room."

American and British editions of *Insulin* appeared within a few months, and soon there were arrangements for French and Japanese translations. Most foreign reviews were glowing. I particularly enjoyed Sir Peter Medawar's in the *London Review of Books*, in which he mistakenly identified me as holding *the* chair of history at the University of Toronto. Within a year or two, the Canadian edition of *The Discovery of Insulin* had earned out its advance, and I was getting additional royalties, as I have ever since. I gave many talks in and around Ontario and began receiving invitations to speak farther afield.

My talk at Yale, to their Beaumont Medical History Club in January 1983, paid an extra dividend when a physician came up to me afterward and said he had a diabetic patient in Hartford, Connecticut, who claimed he had first received insulin in Toronto from Dr. Banting. "We don't know if there's any truth in this, but you might. His name's Ryder."

"Omigod! I've just shown you his picture."

A second of the original insulin patients was still alive. I was showing before and after shots of little Ted Ryder in 1922 and 1923 as a poster boy for the miracle of insulin. Elizabeth Hughes had told me she had known Ryder and he was dead. Now, sixty years later, it turned out that he was alive and well and living in Hartford. Immediately on returning to Toronto I got in touch with Mr. Ryder, was invited to come down, and flew to Hartford, bringing with me a reporter for the *Toronto Star*. We not only spent the day with Ted Ryder, age sixty-seven and not showing any outward complications from his diabetes, but also were visited in Ted's home by his mother, hale and hearty, and undiabetic at ninety-two.

The Ryders had rich memories about their time in Toronto and their meetings with Fred Banting. Ted mostly remembered being hungry from his starvation diet and pasting pictures of food in his scrapbooks. He also had a vivid memory of Fred Banting appearing at his sixth birthday party in drag. His mother remembered Banting sitting up late at night in their apartment telling her his troubles. When he began complaining about all the Jews who had diabetes, Mrs. Ryder interrupted: "I don't know if you realize Dr. Banting, that we're Jewish." Banting was mortified.

As the Ryders told us these stories more than half a century later, in Ted's small house in Hartford, we noticed signs of uneasiness in their relationship. Ted, a bachelor and librarian, made a point of telling me privately that the happiest times of his life had been when he had gone on long ocean cruises by himself. As Ted was seeing us to our car at the end of our day together, the last we heard from the still over-protective Mrs. Ryder was, "Ted, put your sweater on." Ted's story became a footnote added at the end of later editions of *The Discovery of Insulin*; then I featured him in *Banting: A Biography*.

One of my talks on insulin and Banting was in the Great Hall of the Arts and Letters Club, on Elm Street in downtown Toronto. In its heyday, the club had been an oasis for practically everyone who mattered in the Toronto cultural world. J.J.R. Macleod and Banting, both amateur painters, had been members, as had all the Group of Seven painters and most of their critics. In the 1980s the club was a little raffish, in the tawdry not the rakish sense, its liver and onions luncheon special was not creating lineups of food lovers, its painters were still in thrall to the Group — whose last remaining member, A.J. Casson, still came out for club events — and practically anyone was welcome to join who could afford its quite low fees. Various friends said that Banting's biographer should become a member. I was flattered, already knew several members because of their associations with Tom Thomson, Canoe Lake, and Taylor Statten Camps, and joined the club in 1981.

Liz enjoyed coming to the "Ladies Night" dinners at the still all-male club, and I toyed with writing sketches for the Spring Show, the oldest annual revue in the city. Standards were both high and proper, the Arts and Letters Club's bohemianism being frozen in the genteel radicalism of the age of Walt Whitman, liver and onion lunches, and unlimited rye whisky at members' dinners. My first submissions for the Spring Show were rejected as being much too vulgar. I had better luck later, writing on such subjects as reformed vampires who drink only orange juice, x-rays of dead cats (catscans), and politicians getting pies in the face. Contacts at the club gave me further leads as I began writing the Banting biography.

We seldom had a boring night at the Arts and Letters Club. As a member of its executive in 1984–85 I saw no reason why women should not be admitted as full members. When we opened up what everyone said would be a divisive issue, I moved the resolution that eventually led to the end of male chauvinism. Only a couple of curmudgeons balked as the Arts and Letters Club came closer to joining the modern world.

I tried to keep as many career irons in the fire as possible for as long as possible. If only because of the need for income security, I could not see my way to giving up my professorial appointment. In 1983, I turned down an offer to become editor of a Southam Press trade magazine aimed at chief executives, a prospect that would have turned me into a senior business journalist. But I still had little desire to go back to full-time teaching. I wanted to keep on writing and to keep on experimenting with other possibilities. Joe Clark and Dick Clippingdale hoped I might be the instrument through which the Conservatives' contribution to the constitutional revolution of 1981–82 would be remembered. Clark thought he and the party had done important service to the country in using their parliamentary skills to force Trudeau to refer his constitutional proposals to the Supreme Court rather than proceed unilaterally with a request to England. The Supreme Court's advice had led to the compromise with nine provinces that gave Canada patriation of a new constitution with a Charter of Fundamental Rights and Freedoms. Clark wanted a share of the credit for what many Canadians were now hailing as a great milestone in the country's evolution.

I agreed to do an arm's length history of the Progressive-Conservative Party's role in constitutional reform. I turned down offers of financial support beyond travel expenses. I spent two weeks on Parliament Hill in February 1982, interviewing Conservative MPs, policy advisers, and Clark himself, on the constitutional struggle. Everyone was generous with their time and I had complete access to party files. With one exception, the PCs were proud of their contribution to the process. The exception was Senator Lowell Murray, who had voted against the final package because Quebec had not formally consented to it. No one else shared Murray's concerns, except as a matter of mild regret. At odd intervals in 1982 I expanded my research and began drafting chapters.

But the subtext of many of my conversations, including those with Joe Clark, had to do with his precarious position as party leader. Even at the PC's 1981 Christmas party, which featured Santa dressed in blue, it was evident that many MPs still had not forgiven Clark for the fall of their government in 1979–80. Within caucus there was almost open revolt, and several contenders for Clark's job were not-so-secretly organizing leadership campaigns. By the Conservative convention in Winnipeg in 1983, Clark and his remaining backers were so enervated by party disharmony that they resolved to force the issue. Probably unwisely, the Clarkites declared that 67 percent support was insufficient, and launched a new leadership contest.

I had been impressed by Clark in our interviews, first for *Canadian Business*, then on the constitution, and offered personal support in his fight to keep his leadership. In March 1983, I was approached by some long-time Clark supporters in Ottawa and asked if I would become national chairman of Canadians for Clark, a kind of independent, fellow-travelling fan club for Joe. Without much thought and expecting to be just a figurehead, I agreed. CfC would either be a quick fizzle or a great national movement, probably something in between, I noted in my diary.

It fizzled. The Ottawa organizers completely misled me, and perhaps themselves, about membership and support. When I went to Ottawa in April for a media event, meeting Joe, meeting the press, handing out Canadians for Clark buttons, I claimed we had several thousand members. Privately, I thought that we had probably no more than 500. Actually, I was told later, the figure was closer to 120. In truth, it may have been no more than a dozen, not counting Liz Bliss, who was not interested. Nor were the voting members of our local Don Valley West PC Association interested in sending me to the leadership convention as a Joe Clark delegate. Canadians for Clark had already died a quiet death before Joe was beaten by Brian Mulroney on June 11, 1983.

I had attended a couple of pre-convention policy sessions chaired by Clark before the convention, and met him a few months afterward in Toronto as he was considering his future. In his suite at the Royal York he looked markedly aged and tired, but insisted that he wanted to stay with electoral politics rather than go to the Senate, in part because there was always the possibility of Mulroney being hit by a bus. He thought there might be opportunities to lecture on constitutional matters. I gave him my unfinished chapters, saying I doubted I would ever have time to do the book we had talked about. The bitterness of Clark and friends like Dick Clippingdale toward Mulroney and his sleazy, fairly right-wing friends, was palpable, though I think they always felt that the deepest stabs in Clark's back had come from other members of caucus. The machinations and money provided by Frank Moores, Walter Wolfe, and Karlheinz Schreiber, which achieved national notoriety many years later, were salt poured into Clark's wounds rather than decisive factors in their own right.

During my brief period as an active Clark man, I had thought that if he kept his leadership he was certain to become prime minister again, and I might wind up serving in Ottawa in some kind of capacity. A course never taken, and just as well. A journal entry on August 26, 1983, is an obituary for my fifteen seconds on the political playing field:

> I hadn't believed it possible that Mulroney could beat Joe, and since he has I don't know whether or not I even want to be identified with that party. As I learned in being beaten in the Don Valley delegate stakes, the

hard-faced Tories were all against Joe, and I'm not at all sure I want to support their sense of Canada, which is more for them, or Brian Mulroney's sense, which is power, power, power.

I don't have any regrets about having tried to help Joe Clark (though Canadians for Clark was a cross between a joke and a fiasco), though I do wonder if he wasn't considerably less competent than I had realized — that I, in fact a novice in the world of politics, hadn't been taken in by Joe's people ... I just don't know.

I think I know that public life ... isn't really for me. When I went to Ottawa the one day to promote Canadians for Clark, I had to lie to the press, and no matter how much of a gentle face was put on it, it was the kind of expedient lying I can see politicians doing all the time. No thanks.

I kept my rolls of "Canadians for Clark" stickers and packages of Joe Clark lapel pins in the hope that they might appreciate in value. They did not. I do not think I voted in the 1984 general election — I thought the choice was between a banal Liberal leader and a sleazy Conservative. John Turner, who still pinched women's bums in public, seemed to be the voice of Winston's Restaurant in downtown Toronto and the Granite Club of north Toronto. A Liberal cabinet minister's wife summed up Brian Mulroney to me as "the kind of man my father told me never to get in the back seat of a car with."

The quandary about my future was put off for three years when Manulife, prodded by Linda McKnight, who was then president of McClelland & Stewart, came back to me in early 1983, somewhat apologetically, and renewed their proposal to underwrite a history of Canadian business on exactly the terms I had first proposed. The Banting manuscript would soon be finished, and, except for more writing on Canadian conservatism, I had had few thoughts about what to do next. The idea of pulling together everything I had learned about the history of business in Canada in one synthesis or overview seemed timely — not that I wanted to become a career guru of Canadian business history, but rather to enable me to sum up a period of my academic work before going on something else, perhaps more medical history.

I worried that questions would be raised about my objectivity in accepting a commission from Manulife, so we wrote an airtight clause protecting my independence into the contract. Without fully considering my own interest, I also suggested to Manulife that they could meet the hazard of authorial non-performance by writing time-driven penalty clauses into the contract. Final payment would be contingent on an acceptable manuscript being ready within exactly three years from the September 1, 1983, start of the work.

The university agreed to let me carry a one-third teaching load for the next three years. By then, most of my colleagues in history were not sure that I was coming back or that they wanted me back. The rest of my salary was, in effect, a research grant provided by Manulife. Still bitter about the battles with the Office of Research Administration over ethical review and the thirty-cent stamp, I did not run the grant through the university — which was taking up the insidious habit of counting the amount of other people's money its professors were bringing in, and would have been delighted to crow about a $160,000 grant to a professor in the humanities. I dealt directly with Manulife on a private basis, and we got along splendidly. They also insured my life while I was working on their centennial project.

I finished the manuscript of *Banting: A Biography* in a burst of productivity in May and June 1983. In less than two months I wrote the final five chapters, some fifty-thousand words. We celebrated the end of the big project by taking the kids on a two-week tour of the Maritimes, flying into St. John's so they could see Newfoundland, and ending with a visit to Liz's aged relatives in Prince Edward Island. There was time on the island for riding and golf and playing in the big barn at Hazeldean Farm and taking in "Anne of Green Gables" at the Confederation Centre in Charlottetown, after which Jamie and Laura fought over who would get to read the book first. As we left I noted that we had probably visited PEI for the last time.

I cut back on other commitments to clear the decks for the Manulife project. No sooner would I get out of one obligation than another would crop up, usually a request to give a talk to a diabetes or scientific group about the coming of insulin. Still, I got a start on the research in the autumn of 1983 and on January 4, 1984, began to draft the first chapter of a book I was then calling "Enterprise and Opportunity: A History of Canadian Business."

Later that spring, *Banting* was published, again to good reviews — except from a respected Nova Scotia physician, Chester Stewart, who had briefly known Banting and strongly disagreed with my judgment that Banting's consumption of ten ounces of rye whisky per day amounted to a drinking problem. To a Nova Scotian it certainly did not. I was particularly pleased to notice gender differences in the reaction to *Banting*. Men would say, "That's a fair portrait. Banting wasn't such a bad guy after all." Women would comment, "I'm glad you were so fair to his first wife and showed how crude and offensive he really was." My only regret about having written the book's final chapters so quickly was that I simply forgot to include a number of Banting anecdotes, including Bill Banting's story that his father got drunk on his wedding night and was unable to perform. Given the mess he made of his marriage that was pertinent data.

I was sometimes disappointed that neither *Insulin* nor *Banting* made more than transient appearances on Canadian bestseller lists, let alone becoming the blockbuster sales successes and popular award winners I always vaguely hoped for — not unlike brother Jim hoping each piece of research would win him the Nobel Prize. The accuracy of the lists was extremely suspect, especially when one's books did not appear, and *Banting* did earn out a $20,000 advance and more. Because Fred had achieved so little in life, other than the discovery of insulin, the biography was never published separately in the United States. Concern about that was diluted when word came that I had been awarded the William Welch Medal of the American Association for the History of Medicine, for *The Discovery of Insulin*. The trip with Liz to the AAHM's San Francisco meeting to receive the Welch Medal would have been unalloyedly happy had it not been for the sixty-eight examination papers that had just come in from the one course I was teaching. The grades were due the day after we returned. During every spare moment on my first trip to San Francisco I marked U of T exams, and finished the last paper on the plane home.

It seemed an honour to be elected to fellowship in the Royal Society of Canada, our most prestigious academic organization, which still had fairly rigorous selection criteria. I could then add FRSC to the letters after my name. The induction ceremony at the 1984 meeting of the Learned Societies in Guelph, Ontario, was modestly impressive until, at the celebratory luncheon, one of the fellows at our table began telling off-colour stories, generating uproarious laughter from everyone but me. The Royal Society's president joined in the merriment. I could not believe what I was hearing — some of the supposedly best brains in Canada sitting around at a meeting of its most elite intellectual society telling smutty stories out of a men's locker room. I reflected that George Orwell had told us things would be strange in 1984.

Chapter Ten

On the Road

Cleveland was not much of a city to visit at any time of the year. The Ohio burg was particularly bleak in January 1985. My hosts put me up at the splendid University Club, which owned one of the last of Euclid Avenue's beautiful nineteenth-century mansions, but I was advised not to go walking in the neighbourhood at night. The hostess of a local television interview show variously called me Martin Bliss and Martin Best and, reminiscent of Margaret Trudeau, declared that Dr. Banting had won the Nobel Peace Prize. I was interviewed about the discovery of insulin by the food editor of the Cleveland *Plain Dealer*. The group I was in town to address were the kind of middle-initialled folk after whom Great Lakes freighters are named, as in John G. Fitzgerald. Everyone was apologetic about Cleveland's reputation as a stagnant place whose polluted river, the Cayahoga, had once caught fire. The lead item on local newscasts was of the suicide of the city's school superintendent. I thought my first visit to Cleveland would probably be my last.

On the other hand, these were people whose lives had been touched by the blight of diabetes, and the 180 members of the Greater Cleveland Diabetes Association who came out to hear me were deeply interested in the story of how diabetes had been forever changed by the medical research that produced insulin. I had learned to adjust my talks to the needs of different audiences, showed terrific slides, and found that every run-through of the discovery story, especially insulin's impact on such early patients as Elizabeth Hughes and Ted Ryder, still thrilled and inspired both me and my audiences. I always got a lift from giving these talks. If they took me to some not very inspiring cities — Indianapolis, Indiana, and Timmins, Ontario, were no great improvement on Cleveland; Fort Wayne, Indiana; Bismarck, North Dakota; Lubbock, Texas; and Monroe, Louisiana were worse — well, diabetes was not limited to interesting people who lived in attractive cities.

Most places had their good points. The pervading aroma of chocolate in Hershey, Pennsylvania, especially pungent at the intersection of Chocolate Street and Cocoa Avenue, might not be everyone's piece of cake. But what a good time Liz and I had on a five-day junket to New Orleans to give a talk on insulin at Tulane University, an annual lecture sponsored by Eli Lilly and Company. No fee was attached to the lectureship, but in traditional Louisiana fashion a dean slipped me an envelope containing several crisp $100 bills, which we happily spent on Bourbon Street and at Preservation Hall and on a paddle-wheeler cruise on the Mississippi.

My assumption that interest in *The Discovery of Insulin* and *Banting* would fade after the initial book tours and scattered speaking engagements, the usual author's experience, was wrong. So many people in so many places — millions of them around the world — have had to live with diabetes one way or another, and the stories I had uncovered were of interest on so many levels, that I found I had a practically endless series of audiences. Listeners ranged from Nobel laureates to public-school students. By 1985, I seemed to be in constant demand as a speaker at diabetes meetings, drug company events, scholarly and medical occasions.

Invitations came from across Canada and the United States, from Europe, and eventually South America. Some were for *pro bono* talks, others at set fees or honoraria. Speaking tours might last a week or more, but usually I was in and out of a city as quickly as possible. In the early years I was in and out of Indianapolis most often, speaking to groups at Eli Lilly events. On the first of these, at a downtown hotel, just as I began to speak a rock band started up in the next room. Lilly functionaries scurried out, flexed their corporate muscles, and in about two minutes the music stopped. There was seldom a month without at least one insulin speaking gig; in busy seasons I travelled almost every week.

Being a professional speaker on the road became part of my life. I often reflected on how it had started with that despised schoolboy public speaking. Like a child actor, I had been groomed for a life on a stage, or at least behind a podium. Years of talking to students made me comfortable, or apparently comfortable — I knew how to fake it — in front of crowds.

Thorough preparation was much of the knack. I always had a complete manuscript on the lectern, and had learned how to read a speech without appearing to. Fear of making terrible layman's gaffs while trying to talk knowledgeably to doctors and other health-care workers caused me to be careful in response to questions and cautious in even casual conversations. I was sometimes the first non-physician or non-scientist to address groups like the Physiological Society or the Endocrine Society, and made a point of correcting people who thought my credentials were better than they were. These I never tried to fake. Even being correctly called "Doctor" Bliss was problematic — in real life situations a Ph.D. means less than an M.D. Still, I gained confidence after an insulin talk at a Winnipeg hospital when, nervous after having given Grand Rounds before a medical audience, I asked my sponsors why there had been so few questions. "They're afraid of you," was the answer. "They're afraid of asking a professional historian a question that will appear to be foolish."

Many trips were adventures in the tedium and bad food and sleep-deprivation that comes with modern air travel. Others were special. In 1985, I was invited to address the Scientific Section of the British Diabetic Association, at its annual meeting in Oxford. The six hundred diabetes researchers and clinicians in plenary session in Oxford's

Examination Halls were the largest live audience I had ever had. You don't get intimidated by big audiences — small ones are actually more daunting — you just go ahead and talk. I was nicely launched when the slide projectors the BDA was using jammed on about the fifth of my fifty slides. As distinguished scientists wrestled with elementary equipment failure, I stood speechless on the podium — thinking of jokes about British technological incompetence that I dared not make.

The scientists finally got the projectors working again. That night, Liz and I were dazzled to sit at High Table at a glittering BDA banquet in Christ Church College. I made small talk with Dorothy Hodgkin, a double Nobel laureate for her work on aspects of the insulin molecule. Ms. Hodgkin was no longer young — when she was introduced to the company I had to tactfully prod her awake. Nobody went to sleep a few days later at the BDA-sponsored lecture I gave at the grand old Methodist Central Hall in central London, where I was heckled by anti-vivisectionists. Speakers from the floor claimed my book proved that slaughtering dogs was not an integral part of the discovery process. "I'm in the fortunate position of being the author of the book, you cite," I responded to one questioner. "So I can say with fair certainty that you haven't understood it."

The anti-vivs, who were going through a period of significant activity, continued to spread their gross misreading of *The Discovery of Insulin*, often citing me as an authority who supported their beliefs. I did everything short of going to law to try to stop them. A perfect comeuppance was staged by a scientist in California. Scheduled to debate with one Brandon Raines, America's leading anti-viv, the scientist alerted me in advance and asked if I could help. He later sent me a video of the debate, held before a very large audience at UCLA. When Raines cited me as authority for his views, his opponent interrupted him and told the audience that it was important to know what I really thought. He read out — and put up a slide of — my words, a letter I had sent him declaring that anyone who distorted my views in the way Raines habitually did was either a knave or a fool. Raines was effectively laughed off the stage.

A reference in my Oxford talk to the University of Toronto's collaboration with Eli Lilly in the early days of insulin production got back to someone in the United Kingdom branch of Lilly, who realized that it could be useful to the company to sponsor more of my talks. For several years I was in the U.K. at least annually, speaking at symposia, diabetes education days, and Lilly-organized or supported functions. We brought then-fifteen-year-old daughter Laura on one of the major British trips, introducing her to the sights of London and Cambridge, and then to the highlands of Scotland. In return, she was forced to attend an elegant formal dinner at the Royal College of Physicians of Edinburgh, where she was the youngest member of the party by a margin of about forty years. After that agonizing night of making small talk to distinguished physicians and surgeons and their wives, Laura was never socially intimidated. The security intimidated me during a one-night visit to Ulster during the time of troubles. I was shown the scars of IRA bullets on hospital walls. My evening in Belfast ended with one of the city's leading diabetologists telling me in his cups how the worst decision of his life had been to return to Ireland after a year's study in Canada.

Sally, our French immersion student, had her first visit to Paris largely courtesy of Lilly France. Even in December, Paris was magnificent. By coincidence, we visited the dazzling new Musée d'Orsay on its opening day. Sally would lag behind us during sightseeing walks, pretending that she was seeing Paris on her own. One morning a car picked us up at 5:00 a.m. for a tour of Great War battlefields in Flanders. It happened to be a day when units of the French Army were on training manoeuvres, and it was eerie beyond words to see the dim figures of soldiers moving through the mists of early morning while we were en route to Courcelette, Thiepval, and other sites of the 1916 Somme offensive. The magnificent Canadian monument at Vimy Ridge was bathed in sunshine and perfect blue skies by the time we reached it. Sally pretended that chasing sheep was the best part of her Vimy experience — but back in Canada for three years she built a public speaking career, in both English and French, around that visit to Vimy.

The other great insulin companies, Novo and Nordisk, both head-quartered in Copenhagen, also had their roots in the 1922 events in Toronto that I had described in *The Discovery of Insulin*. So I was a guest of the Danes on several occasions, beginning with two weeks in 1986 at Nordisk's compound in the Copenhagen suburb of Gentofte. At the end of the first day of Nordisk's high-powered Steno Symposium on the molecular biology of diabetes, all of us were given bicycles. Upward of a hundred-strong, we took our collective exercise pedalling several kilometres into the heart of Copenhagen's Royal Deer Park, where we drank and dined in rural splendour while the herds of deer ignored us.

My contribution to the Steno Symposium was an after-dinner talk at the final banquet about Denmark and the coming of insulin. The venue was a chic art gallery in downtown Copenhagen. As we boarded our bus for the dinner, one of my sponsors mentioned that even though Danes were a tolerant people it would be hard not to be offended by the art currently on display. Indeed. I rose to speak at 10:50 p.m. to an audience of renowned scientists thoroughly drugged on alcohol and rich food in a room whose walls were covered with massive acrylic paintings of genitalia and acts of copulation.

An evening with Belgian doctors at the Mona Lisa Restaurant and Music Hall in Florence, greatly enjoying a Lilly junket, was non-strenuous until I had to break it off to be able catch my morning flight home. I had used my free afternoon to sit in a park by the Arno and finish marking another set of U of T exam papers. I occasionally rescheduled classes to facilitate travel, otherwise turned down opportunities where there was a conflict with teaching. Sometimes I went straight from long flights to my Monday-evening Canadian history lectures, and may have been more incoherent than usual.

The conflicts of interest involved when researchers, clinicians, and pharmacists accept drug company largesse have led to disclosure guidelines and tightened regulation. As a historian who had worked independently of drug companies, I had no qualms about being given pleasant opportunities to describe great and inspiring events in the history of medicine. I never sought sponsorship, but was happy to accept support from virtually any source, and never had to consider improperly rigging or distorting my talks. In my standard lecture on the coming of insulin, for example, I would mention both the Lilly and the Danish connections. For in-house presentations, at Lilly or Nordisk (Novo-Nordisk after the Danish firms merged), I would give special lectures telling researchers, sales reps, and other employees about their firm's roots in the early insulin days.

While there was egregious extravagance at some of the drug company events I attended, especially in Europe, most meetings featured fairly high-powered sessions with informed speakers, often world-class scientists. Many of my trips were to give named lectures or rounds at universities and medical schools, or to be a keynote or plenary speaker at professional and academic meetings. Unlike many speakers, I made a point of attending other sessions of meetings, picking up what I could of the content (the science often went over my head), and studying others' platform styles.

Max Perutz, Nobel laureate and a founding father of molecular biology, gave a terrible, disjointed talk at a Lilly seminar in Cambridge, England. I could not decide whether Perutz was just slumming to pick up a high fee, or, more likely, whether he was naturally incomprehensible. I did not get to meet Perutz, but after the meeting was collared by Cambridge's distinguished transplant surgeon, Roy Cahn, who insisted that, having just shown my before and after pictures of the effect of insulin administration, I visit his office to see his before and afters of the effects of pancreas transplants. Don Steiner from Chicago, a great figure in diabetes research, was also a guest at Nordisk's 1986 Steno Symposium. Over a long breakfast in the deserted Domus Hagedorn one Sunday morning, Steiner told me in detail of the research adventure that led to his discovery of pro-insulin, work which at the time many felt was of Nobel calibre.

My first talk in the Netherlands was at a post-graduate symposium in endocrinology. I told the organizers that even the fifty minute slot they gave me was never adequate to do full justice to my subject. They asked me how much time I needed to give my ideal presentation. About three hours, I replied. The next year they had me back, presenting in two ninety-minute evening sessions, with a champagne intermission.

We were all exhausted, or at least drowsy, by the end of the evening. My host for insulin talks at the University of California, San Francisco, was Martin Goldner, another of the grand old men of diabetes research, whose memories went back to his student days in Germany in the early 1920s. He insisted that I stay with him in his beautiful Palo Alto home. On his poolside patio, in the shade of orange and lemon trees, Martin reminisced about the day Oskar Minkowski introduced the first insulin to Germany, and went on to describe his own escape from Nazi Germany to America.

Listening to Goldner's memories was, in effect, research. On these trips I often visited archives to do more research on the insulin story or whatever else I was working on. Talks at the National Library of Medicine, in the Johns Hopkins medical history program, and to researchers at the National Institutes of Health, created important academic connections, and in some cases lifelong friendships. One of the warmest, nicest, most exuberant men I have known, Jesse Roth, then head of diabetes research at NIH, arranged my first visit there — and also arranged that Ted Ryder would be present at my talk. When I told the audience that this original patient was still alive, the lights went on, Ted stood up and took a bow, and later gave autographs to diabetes researchers. Jesse also arranged for me to interview Ted on tape at the National Library of Medicine.

In these years of generous frequent-flyer bonuses, our teenagers were able to see great American cities with their dad. Laura and Jamie had their first visits to Manhattan thanks to insulin. Cleveland was worth a second visit, as Jamie and I bracketed an insulin talk with baseball tickets to see the Indians play the Toronto Blue Jays. After a San Francisco gig we paid a scalper $200 to sit in the highest row of the Oakland Coliseum to watch a World Series game. The Californians were in an egalitarian spasm so extreme that even a fifty-year-old had to show proof of age to buy beer at the ballpark.

In 1988, the private foundation of zillionaire surgical-instrument maker Arnold Beckman threw a special symposium to celebrate the development of the first pharmaceutical product made by recombinant DNA technology, which was Eli Lilly's Humulin brand of synthetic human insulin. About sixty distinguished research leaders, plus three historians, were invited to attend the conference in Irvine, California, all expenses paid. There were five Nobel laureates and several near-Nobels among the speakers, beginning with James Watson on discovering the structure of DNA. The others took the narrative from DNA to Genentech's re-engineering of the insulin molecule in partnership with Lilly.

We were awestruck at the living history on display and the stories being told of the unravelling of the mysteries of life. It seemed as though we were at a meeting of, say, the Spanish Academy in 1520, listening to first-hand reports of the voyages that discovered the new world. "Deciphering the genetic code was from a personal view a fascinating experience ..." Nobel laureate Marshall Nirenberg concluded his talk, "a real scientific adventure ... the real mccoy. I like to think they'll be using this work every day as long as mankind goes on." A few minutes later I found myself chatting with Dr. Nirenberg in a slow-moving cafeteria lineup. We talked about history, Canadian politics, smallpox in Montreal, AIDs, and the National Institutes of Health. Later, I was waylaid by Roger Guillemin, Nobel laureate for work in neuroendocrinology originally inspired by J.B. Collip. Guillemin wanted to reminisce about his Montreal days, and gather advice on how to dispose of his personal papers. I urged him to give them to the U.S. National Library of Medicine. As I was having mountaintop experiences at the conference, daughters Laura and Sally, jet-setting to L.A. at ages seventeen and fifteen, rode roller coasters at Disneyland and took each other's pictures with Goofy and Mickey. After the conference we went sightseeing.

In shorts and T-shirt I jogged over the Golden Gate Bridge on my first visit to San Francisco in 1985, stopping in the middle to drink in the view. In Gentofte, Denmark, after Sunday breakfast with Don Steiner, I had a ten-mile run through the Royal Deer Park. Our endocrinology seminar in Holland was at a seaside resort, otherwise deserted during the late autumn. Late at night in wind, rain, and snow, I ran for an hour along the dimly lit promenade, reminiscent of Eric Ambler scenes from Europe in the 1930s or 1940s. In the Highlands of Scotland I jogged on trails through lonely glens, accompanied by rabbits, quail, and grouse. In Montreal I ran all the way from the old city to the top of Mount Royal; in Quebec I covered the Plains of Abraham. I ran through High Park and Kensington Gardens in London, by the Thames in Oxford, through Central Park in New York, by the Potomac in Washington. On visits to Vancouver I jogged around the sea wall in Stanley Park, in Ottawa by the Rideau Canal. In Toronto, in September 1986, I ran my first marathon.

In my early forties I had shed weight and gone on a fitness kick, returning to athletics by taking up jogging, then long-distance running. It was personally an important transformation, a conscious rejection of the bad habits that had helped kill my father and perhaps my brother. While everyone seems to run these days, at the time I had run across a huge generational/cultural divide. I had broken from the pattern of turning into a couch-jock after college. More on the model of the baby-boom generation, I had chosen a new, healthier, younger lifestyle. Joining the running boom was exhilarating, a kind of rebirth. Except for my colleague, Ned Shorter, who I then knew only casually, and who had become a serious early morning runner, none of my friends shared my interests. When someone at the Arts and Letters Club said that all the joggers he saw on the street looked tired and unhappy, I told him that I always smiled as I ran.

In the 1950s we had thought of marathon runners as freakish super-athletes. By the 1980s, reflecting a revolution in our understanding of human physical potential, tens of thousands of North Americans were running marathons. Through the summer of 1985 I trained systematically for the Toronto marathon, upping my mileage to sixty-plus a week, including twenty-mile runs to approximate the marathon distance. I peaked too early in my training. In about the eighteenth mile of the marathon I felt I was hitting the wall, as runners say, and had to walk. By the time I finished, with Jamie and Sally running with me, Liz, in the near-empty stands at Varsity Stadium, had become convinced that I must be lying dead of a heart attack in the Don Valley. A few weeks later I tore cartilage in a knee, had to cut back my running, had to be arthroscopically cut by surgeons. The several thousand miles I managed in the next fifteen years, on the streets of Leaside and in the Toronto's ravine parks, were all a bonus before the knees gave out entirely — mostly the consequence of having had the soul of a marathoner inside the body of a fullback. There never was a second marathon, but my use of metaphors relating to marathoning and long-distance running probably became tiresome to my students, as it may now be to my readers.

—————————————

Writing the history of Canadian business, on commission from Manulife, was a long run on a tough and tedious course without a map. There were no previous histories of Canadian business and only a few dull syntheses of the history of American business, useful largely as models to avoid. For many years one scholar, Alfred Dupont Chandler, who held the chair in business history at the Harvard Business School, utterly dominated the field. Chandler's major works about the rise of American managerial capitalism, *Strategy and Structure* and *The Visible Hand*, were treated as near-sacred texts. I could have spent a lifetime wandering around the Canadian wilderness, but had committed to having a manuscript ready by September 1, 1986, for publication in Manulife's 1987 centennial year.

Most commissioned histories — most histories of any kind — take longer than their authors originally estimate. Cockily, and perhaps foolishly, I proposed the clause in my contract with Manulife involving a $25,000 penalty if I did not finish on time. The positive side of the relationship was that the Manulife executives never bothered me. I reported progress every six months, we had friendly luncheons, and Liz and I enjoyed a week in the firm's London flat while I did perfunctory work in the Beaverbrook Papers at the House of Lords. There was no attempt to influence anything I wrote. I was on my own to do my own book, but had to get on with it.

The schedule called for me to produce about one chapter every six weeks. Fast pace.

I drew on the archival work I had done for my thesis and for the Flavelle biography, but otherwise relied mostly on published sources. There were more of these than I had realized. A surprising amount had been written about all aspects of Canadian business history, from works on the fur trade through company histories, biographies, studies of industries, and monographs on business-government relations and trade policy. I hired research help to cover a few small topics, but did the rest myself, slogging through books and articles and then reworking a mass of disconnected material into a coherent synthesis. I stayed the course with grim determination and not a lot of enthusiasm. I worried that I either could not meet the deadline or would do it only by producing a second-rate book that would damage my reputation.

It was impossible not to become interested in the evolution of enterprise in the history of the northern half of North America. Taking a cue from Donald Creighton's definition of history as the interplay of character and circumstance — the only time I was ever directly influenced by Creighton — I described business history as the dialogue between enterprise and opportunity (the book's eventual title, *Northern Enterprise: Five Centuries of Canadian Business*, came to me one day in the shower). The territories and peoples that came to make up Canada provided many opportunities for enterprising peoples — initially Europeans, then Americans, and always Canadians — to create wealth and to dissipate wealth, especially when they misread the country's resources and its potential. Inputs of entrepreneurial energy were strikingly ubiquitous throughout Canada's history, and they generated constant, and usually fierce, competition from the days of the fur trade through the breaking of every attempt at monopoly in manufacturing, railways, retailing, and finance.

The power of competitive forces became a distinctive theme of my work, a sharp contrast to Chandler's celebration of the power of the visible hands of corporate managers to control market forces. I realized that even as Chandler wrote, that thesis was being undermined by the inability of great American corporations to withstand competition. Even in Canada, most markets were too dynamic to be controlled by anyone for very long, even if you found ways of capturing the government so you could enlist its taxing and law-making power to advance your interests, a common enough Canadian strategy. The irresistible tides of competition would eventually sweep away every corporate sandcastle and battlement.

The metaphor of history as an intricate dance was also on my mind in those years, as I read Anthony Powell's great extended novel, *A Dance to the Music of Time*. I saw rhythms and harmonies and disharmonies in the dance of Canadian enterprise. I was struck by the canniness of aboriginals as economic bargainers in their fur trade with Europeans, but also surprised by the comparative insignificance of a continent-wide enterprise that amounted to the harvesting of a few shiploads of animal skins a year. The colony of New France was pretty much an economic backwater, not comparable to New England. It was treated by France as little more than Voltaire's "a few acres of snow" — and the snow was usually stained by blood from Indian and imperial wars.

It was not true that the natural lines of commerce in North America followed the east-west pattern of the overrated fur trade. Furs were constantly smuggled south, American capital financed both the Bank of Montreal and the building of the Canadian Pacific Railway, Canada's "National Policy" of protective tariffs encouraged American investors to jump over tariff walls and take control of Canadian manufacturing, and so on. The book ended in the 1980s with Canadians' realization that they could not ignore the reality of continental economic integration, leading to the decision to opt for a free trade agreement with the United States. I was proud of writing the first coherent history of the development of the petroleum resources of Western Canada (proving that I could have done the Pacific Pete history), of my revisionist interpretation of Canada's most renowned public entrepreneurs, especially C.D. Howe, and of my attention to corporate misadventure and political folly. Even in gloomiest moments about the project I hoped good writing would carry me through.

By the home stretch in the summer of 1986 I had long since hit the wall and was exhausted. Interrupting the work to go off and give talks about the discovery of insulin had been both energizing and enervating. In late July, after a one-day return trip to Vancouver to talk at a congress of physiologists, I came down with pneumonia. I spent most of August in my bathrobe, hacking and sniffling at my desk as I tried to revise and polish my manuscript.

Luckily, by then I was working on my first computer. Through the early eighties I had been suspicious of the new-fangled machines — the pioneer computer users among my students were always coming to me with stories of crashes and printer failures and submitting texts that were now visually, as well as intellectually, unintelligible. The photocopier remained my technology of choice — so much so that for the business history project I had bought my own for $2,200, mainly to copy out-of-print material. In January 1986 someone from McClelland & Stewart called to offer me an Apple Macintosh computer, plus printer, as part of a deal they had made with that company to supply Canada's top twenty-five writers with the marvellous new "Macs." I learned that I was not among the top twenty-five (except on the occasion when a drunken Jack McClelland introduced me as the novelist Timothy Findley) but some among the elite, such as Farley Mowat, had refused to give up their goose quill pins, and so I was offered a free computer on reversion. I adapted to it easily and totally and, as Apple undoubtedly had hoped, became a complete loyalist — this is being written on my eighth or ninth Mac. The productivity gains from working on a computer were immediate and very important. As the technology improved the benefits kept on accumulating.

Friday September 5, 1986:

> Well, it's done. The god damn book is done … Tuesday morning I took the manuscript to M&S and Manulife. It was done, and right bang on time. Monday night the Lapkins sent over a bottle of sparkling wine for us to celebrate … Went back to the doctor on Weds a.m. to learn that the pneumonia is back — more anti-biotics.

Magazine feature writing became a casualty of the business history project, as there simply were not enough hours in a day. My relationship with *Saturday Night* had soured a couple of years earlier when I was appalled by its publication of a morally slovenly defence of the FLQ murderer, Paul Rose. I wrote a long critical letter to the editor and resigned as a contributing editor. A few months later I was contacted by Peter Cook of the *Globe and Mail*, the founding editor of its then-new *Report on Business Magazine*. Would I like to do a monthly books column for the new journal? Yes, I could call it "Bliss on Books."

Writing and appraising books was my life. Through the 1970s I had done occasional book reviewing in both scholarly and popular publications. In 1983–84, I wrote several reviews for *Maclean's*, which paid well but also over-edited its writers' prose. Reviewing good or thoughtful books was always stimulating, but when *Maclean's* seemed to be giving me a diet of boring clunkers, I responded by satirizing the books in my reviews. We parted ways when the journal refused to publish a parody I had written of one of former general Richard Rohmer's unbelievably awful pulp novels. At the *ROB*, by contrast, I chose my own books to review, almost never had my prose tinkered with, and at $1,500 a column, I later learned, was paid more than the other regular columnist, Conrad Black. We both appeared in the first *ROB Magazine*, published in March 1985.

A happy connection developed with another magazine in 1985 when I was approached by Bill Nobleman, a Toronto publisher and consultant whom I had met as a fellow Joe Clark Conservative. Bill had been hired by the Hudson's Bay Company to advise on the future of its in-house journal, *The Beaver*, which for some sixty-five years had published stories about the fur trade, life in the north, and other aspects of Canadian history. The HBC was now proposing to kill *The Beaver* as an economy measure. But its corporate secretary, Rolph Huband, believed the journal could be saved, or at least spill a lot less red ink.

He and Nobleman decided to turn *The Beaver* into a general magazine of Canadian history. A new editor, Chris Dafoe, was brought in to make the transformation, with oversight by an editorial advisory board to consist of Huband, Nobleman, HBC archivist Shirlee Smith, and myself.

We met twice a year, mostly to criticize imbalance in Dafoe's selection of articles. *The Beaver* was published in Winnipeg, the editors were Manitobans, and the journal's contents were initially far too Manitoba-centric. The team soon learned how to put out a vastly improved magazine whose circulation more than doubled in a couple of years. *The Beaver* was not only saved, but began to be noticed and subscribed to by history buffs across the country, and in the best years even made a few dollars for the HBC.

Business book reviewing led to my being asked for advice by the accounting firm of Coopers & Lybrand, who wanted to fund an annual prize for the best book published about some aspect of Canadian business. I urged them to make the award a generous one, to have a prestigious jury with real business expertise, and gave advice on how to set up the rules of the competition. In 1986, the National Business Book Award was founded with the highest book prize going in Canada ($10,000), and I was asked to be the member of the jury who would pre-select a long list of eight or ten semi-finalists. I received all the good books published every year about Canadian business — the bad ones too — and an honorarium to boot. John Aird, a public-spirited businessman and former Lieutenant-Governor of Ontario, was the first Chair of the jury, which worked remarkably harmoniously. The first winners, for a book on the adventures of trust companies in Canada, were the young business journalists Pat Best and Ann Shortell. The annual NBBA luncheon, hosted as a public relations event by Coopers, became an instant institution, attracting everyone who was anyone in Canadian business writing plus a number of laconic accountants.

During the three years of work on *Northern Enterprise* I taught one course at U of T, supervised several doctoral students, and otherwise had little to do with the History Department. Professionally, I was functioning almost as an independent scholar, enjoying easy access to the media and what many thought was lucrative private sponsorship of my research and writing. Most years I was too busy to bother to attend annual meetings of the Canadian Historical Association, having found that a majority of the sessions were tedious and irrelevant.* Some of my colleagues wondered if I had sold my academic values and reputation in return for a mess of Manulife's money. "You've sold out to Manulife. You're just writing the books you're paid to write," Ramsay Cook said to me during a heated, intense conversation at a party in December 1985.

My contract with Manulife contained much tougher terms than came with any government grant, and I was aware of many grantees, some of them friends and colleagues, who were not rewarding the public's trust in them with anything like serious productivity or professionalism. The argument that the source of one's funding necessarily colours research works both ways. If privately financed history must be biased toward private enterprise, then publicly financed history must be biased toward public enterprise, and so on. Attributing motives and questioning objectivity *a priori* becomes a mug's game.

The history of business is drenched in lobbying and special pleading by groups claiming that it is in the public interest to advance their private interests. I could not see that the lobbying and special pleading of cultural producers, from artists and writers through to history professors, was significantly different. Trying to feed at the public trough had become a ubiquitous habit in most modern democracies, and academics, including my friends, bellied-up as eagerly and as self-righteously as the best of them. While the Canada Council and other granting agencies

---

* After an early experience of CHA dreariness in the 1970s, and noting that papers were being distributed by mail anyway, I had written its council proposing that, for quality reasons, and to save money, the association should only meet every other year. The proposal was, of course, ignored.

had erected some buffers against blatant back-scratching and the politicization of cultural subsidies, it was not hard for an insider to see both the personal and structural flaws in the system. It always matters who you know in Canada. Even the detached objectivity of peer review at its best falters because peers themselves have an interest in the screening process being porous. The collective interest becomes getting maximum money out of governments and it generates an uncritical sense of entitlement.

Many of the mores of academic life continued to leave me cold and skeptical. Trying to get grants was a begging game. Much academic publishing, of obscure articles and books that no one would pay real money to buy, was a vanity fair. Giving professors tenure was fraught with problems, both practical and philosophic. Sabbaticals were ridiculously unpoliced and abused.

But I had tenure, I published with firms that asked for and took public subsidies, I took advantage of perks such as sabbaticals and the Public Lending Right (payment of Canadian authors for the use of their books in libraries), and every now and then I would try to get research support through a grant or fellowship. My arrangement with Manulife had worked smoothly, but I also knew perfectly well that many private payers of pipers also expect to call the tune. They could not be relied on, a person always had to be wary, and there were many benefits of an academic position. Academic life was fraught with compromise and, a term just coming into vogue, political correctness. Especially in Canada.

The more I studied Canadian history, the more I saw of the Canadian present, the more convinced I was that the country had little hope of fulfilling its potential. The Canadian market is small and often further fragmented by regional chauvinisms. We cannot consistently reward excellence in Canada because we have to reward geography and ethnicity — we have to divvy up pies on a regional and racial basis — so much for the west, so much for the Maritimes, as little as possible for Ontario, and much more than its population warrants for Quebec. Canadians often seem to be a people who are content with this, content with mediocrity, content with the second-rate. In the 1980s the Canadian way seemed increasingly to be to subsidize every interest group in every part of the country. As well, despite the clear intentions of the Fathers of Confederation, the country was far more decentralized than the United States, the provinces were continuing their century-long sabotaging of the dream of domestic free trade, which was supposed to have been established at Confederation, and there seemed no end in sight to provincial premiers' parochial and self-serving lust for more power at the expense of a weak and confused national government.

I did not think that the government was well led under the Progressive-Conservatives. Pierre Trudeau had done more than his share of damage to the country with his economic policies, but at least he had been a person of obvious national stature, a prime minister who commanded respect for his intellect and strength of character, his determination, his commitment to one Canada. Brian Mulroney never seemed to me to be more than a shallow, glib hustler, whose governments after 1984 failed repeatedly to face up to our most pressing national problem, which was to rein in spending and deficits. Ottawa was rife with patronage and sleazy cronyism and blatant hypocrisy under both Liberals and Conservatives, with no party, no group of politicians, willing to talk seriously about reforms to elevate our public life. Except for the progress the government was making toward free trade with the United States, Ottawa was failing woefully to give the Canadian people real leadership.

I had never forgotten an essay by the nineteenth-century Americanized Canadian, Erastus Wiman, in which he spelled out a vision of the opportunities that would be available to talent if the border were erased and Canada and the United States became one great continental society. Each year I would begin my lecture on Canada's Confederation movement by asking the students how they would respond if it were suddenly announced that a practical plan for a complete Canada-U.S. union had been worked out. Ninety percent of the students were always opposed to such a union. I would then accuse them of the same kind of parochial contentment that caused people to oppose the movement toward British North American Union in the 1860s. Why shouldn't we dream of great unions?

I had a strong and healthy sense of being a Canadian — it revolved around being an heir to both British and American cultural traditions and my upbringing in Essex County — but I did not think I had any of my compatriots' stock of anti-American sentiments. Both as a border person, in and out of the U.S. hundreds of times, and in my intellectual ruminations, I admired most of the core values of the United States. I thought the American political system worked at least as well as the Canadian, I respected Americans' profound commitments to democracy and individual liberties, and at times I felt intellectually (as well as genealogically) a child of New England transcendentalism. I often read Walt Whitman in the 1980s and identified with his democratic humanitarianism, and his inclusive vision of human and American possibilities. Compared to the United States of Jefferson, Emerson, Thoreau, Whitman, and Lincoln, also Melville, Poe, Hemingway, and F. Scott Fitzgerald, Canada seemed intellectually and politically confined, a claustrophobia-inducing sort of place. Given the vastness of our natural heritage, it was sad that we hadn't made more of our opportunities. But, in a way, that was the root of the problem: too much geography, too few people, too tiny their vision.

It would have been quixotic and immediately marginalizing to advocate Canadian-American union, but like many supporters of free trade, I hoped that tearing down commercial fences along the border would be a step toward eventually erasing the border. I usually felt perfectly at home on either side of the border, was pleased that books like *The Discovery of Insulin* could be well received in the United States, and, when professionally restless, wondered about the possibility of moving to a good American university.

The professional quandary was gradually resolving itself, though, as I got over my mid-life fling with freelance writing and fantasies of ink-slinging independence. Unless one was independently wealthy, or sold fabulously bestselling books, a senior professorship at Canada's best university was not to be sneezed at, not to be walked away from. I could rant about the featherbedding and hypocrisy of academic life, but deep down was probably a university professor to the core — content with teaching and long summer breaks so I could write books that did not have to be aimed at low common denominators.

A six-year period of doing little undergraduate teaching in the History Department would end in 1986. I decided to turn down our chair's offer of a permanent part-time relationship, and, having gotten through mid-life, agreed to return full-time. The airport was always handy, and there were running shoes in my closet.

Chapter Eleven

Loathsome Diseases

The men's washroom in the History Department corridor in Sidney Smith Hall was originally designated for staff only. As a graduate student in a hurry I had once broken the exclusion, only to be embarrassed when a silent and almost certainly disapproving Donald Creighton came in and used the next urinal.

When I became a member of the history faculty in 1968 I found that the "Staff" designation had been removed in the interests of the new equality. You might find yourself peeing next to any unkempt, vaguely odiferous stranger. A coin-operated condom dispenser was then installed, funded by the Students Administrative Council as a service to its constituents. When I began using the washroom regularly again in 1986, after my years of leave and part-time teaching, I noticed the condoms had disappeared. Now there were posters over the urinals advertising a service offering to teach students how to become entrepreneurs.

By the mid-eighties, student radicalism had vanished from campus like ice and slush after a dismal winter. Students were interested in getting on with their studies, were deferential to a fault, and seemed to be middle-of-the-road in their politics and other attitudes. There were no more disruptions or demonstrations, there was much less disagreement in class, the best undergraduates seemed brighter than ever, and teaching was both easier and less challenging. The bankrupt old Rochdale College had long since been cleared by police of its last drug-addled, drug-dealing residents. A few years later the fumigated and redecorated building was reopened as the David Croll home for senior citizens. I used to conclude my lecture on trends in recent Canadian social history with the suggestion that as a retirement home the Rochdale College building had finally reached the cutting edge of the frontier of social change.

The History Department was having trouble retaining a sense of identity and common purpose. As my generation entered middle age we tended to go our own ways, as scholars, as teachers, and socially. Collegial socializing declined. After 1985, I gave up lunching at the Faculty Club and soon let my membership lapse. Our Kamloops Society with York had withered and died. There were fewer official department parties and receptions. Chairs (the term that came into vogue to replace "chairman") stopped entertaining in their homes. Common room chit-chat fell off or became boring; I decided I didn't have time for it, usually scarfing down a sandwich in a cafeteria or at work in my office. Some colleagues stopped attending department meetings; some appeared on campus only for the six or seven hours a week they had to teach classes; some were wrestling with serious personal problems, often depression. Most of the grey-beard seniors of my early days had now retired, several of them only after losing a court challenge to the university's compulsory retirement regulation, which they took all the way to the Supreme Court of Canada. I was delighted that they lost because I believed that the university ought to have the means to renew itself and that age should know when to move on.

One of our compulsory retirees, Jack Gerson, insisted that he had not retired, maintained office hours to meet non-existent students, and put his name in for sabbatical leave. There was also attrition in the middle ranks, such as a mediaevalist who left academia to run a bicycle shop, and the energetic European historian, Bob Harney, a pioneer of multicultural studies, who died at age fifty after receiving a heart transplant. A colleague of my vintage who was known to be crippled by depression eventually killed himself. Others seemed spiritually beaten. Few thought the History Department, beginning to shrink absolutely in numbers and suffering in other ways from years of financial stringency, was a happy place. Sidney Smith Hall, an architectural excrescence from the day it opened its doors, was poorly maintained and shabby. My spirits often sank as I entered my office as a full professor at Canada's largest and, we hoped but sometimes doubted, still its best university.

Many colleagues had given up active scholarship. Everyone was said to be working on something — how else could sabbaticals be justified? — but some colleagues had been working on the same project for twenty years, with no visible progress. I decided there was a key question to put to professors in the humanities and social sciences: "What's your next book and when will it be done?" A small handful of colleagues, no more than seven in a department of forty-five, could give an immediate and interesting answer to this question. For many of the rest it would be an embarrassment. Better not to ask. The situation was not confined to history or to the University of Toronto. Across academia, a world in which all the faculty members are supposed to be creating new knowledge through research, and for which they are given immense perks in the way of low teaching loads, long summers, and regular sabbaticals, actual productivity as measured by hard criteria (there often seems to be a tacit conspiracy at the very highest level of academia not to measure at all, or to use very low or even meaningless bars, such as monetary input rather than research output) is alarmingly low. I often thought of Ramsay Cook's suggestion that someone should go around to professors' offices every morning at nine o'clock to see who is working.

I was never going to be a model camper or a team player among the professoriate. My colleagues realized this and largely left me alone. I was seldom asked to serve on committees at any level of the university (an early exception was a year's stint on the Honorary Degrees Committee, during which an attempt by an aggressive dean to award honorary degrees in return for financial contributions was summarily rejected; not many years later that policy was effectively reversed). But I had more or less concluded that I would spend the rest of my career as some kind of academic somewhere, so I tried to find ways to invigorate the teaching that would necessarily take up a fair bit of time.

I had always been comfortable lecturing in our big survey courses in Canadian history — a job often dismissed as scut work — and volunteered to give all the lectures in History 262, our one course that covered the whole history of Canada. I also volunteered to schedule it at nights, as we were now required to do with a portion of our offerings (night teaching for extra pay had been abolished). It was considerably time-saving to give the course's two weekly lectures back-to-back on Monday nights — Monday night history I called it, as in Monday night football — and I liked the mix of undergrads, part-timers, old, young, and in-between students who came to a night course. The *quid pro quo* for taking on a heavy lecturing load was not to have to teach tutorials or mark more than a handful of papers and exams.

Lecturing in history had always meant talking to students about the content and themes of history for fifty minutes, interrupted by the occasional question. By most standards of public speaking, talks this long require heroic feats of concentration on the part of both talker and listeners. I never saw any of my professors or my history colleagues supplement a lecture with visual aids before I began showing slides to accompany my Canadian history lectures in 1986. It had occurred to me to show students in my annual lecture on health care the beautiful before-and-after pictures of the impact of the discovery of insulin on diabetic patients. Then I realized that I had access to an excellent visual resource in the archive of the old Canada's Illustrated Heritage project, in storage at McClelland & Stewart. Slides of anything could be made in the Faculty of Medicine's audio-visual shop. So I began having slides made to illustrate everything in Canadian history — pictures of prominent people, illustrations of great events, political cartoons, works of art, anything that might visually enhance a lecture. My History 262 lectures became rich in illustrative materials, each lecture a slide show in its own right. I kept adding to my collection through the 1990s until it reached well over 1,200 slides.

Instead of giving the students a break between the two fifty minute lectures of a Monday evening, I would hold a question period. It was remarkable how questioning and discussion could develop in groups as large as two hundred. Some students complained that the question period became so interesting that they didn't want to leave it to go to the bathroom. Sometimes the teaching assistants would ask questions and join the discussion. History 262 always got very high student ratings. It began attracting noticeably more students than the survey courses in pre-Confederation and post-Confederation Canadian history, taught collaboratively during the daytime.

For a few years my second lecture course, usually one term long, was in the history of Canadian business. I began offering it in 1986–87 when I could use the manuscript of *Northern Enterprise* as the text for my lectures. The next year, after the book was published, I found it difficult to know what to do in class. I had published my lectures. The course did not attract high quality students — most were majors in the undergraduate program in commerce and finance looking for a soft humanities option. Many were smooth operators who attended as few classes as possible and tried to pawn off third-rate work in their assignments. This is charitable — at the time I told my diary that I was teaching "the absolute dregs of the university." I converted the course to a seminar for a year and then ended it.

Having to give seventy-eight formal lectures in a year had not been an unusual load when I first joined the History Department, but was now quite heavy by department standards. I gradually realized that it was four or five times the lecturing that most of my colleagues in physics, chemistry, and the biomedical sciences were required to do. The disparity in teaching loads across our faculty was hard to measure because on this matter the scientists, who normally believe in measurement, simply refused to allow quantification and comparison. The humanists, who were mostly ignorant of anything that happened in the sciences, did not know enough to protest. In terms of teaching load, as well as compensation, the humanities, I began to realize, were in danger of becoming the slums of the university. Would I become stuck in the slums?

Students had been asking to study the history of medicine under my direction. That subject was formally being taught at our Institute for the History and Philosophy of Science, but the appointee there was reputed to be difficult, having, in fact, been dismissed by the Faculty of Medicine as its first Hannah Professor of the History of Medicine. In January 1988, having decided to do more scholarship in the field, I screwed up my courage and founded a half-year seminar on the history of health care in Canada. I think it was the first course on that subject taught in the country; certainly it was unique at the University of Toronto. It attracted a mix of outstanding graduate students and senior undergrads (allowing both graduates and undergraduates into a seminar seemed a way of maximizing one's chances of having a full complement of good students), along with one part-timer, Dr. Charles "Bud" Godfrey, a rheumatologist at the Toronto Wellesley Hospital, who had already written four or five books on aspects of the medical history of Ontario. I was thoroughly intimidated by the high quality of the students on the one hand and Bud Godfrey's presence on the other. However, the students spent so much seminar time attacking the medical profession — and Bud, more than a little shocked, spent so much time trying to defend it — that I had little to do other than referee.

The seminar was an outstanding success, one of the very best I ever had, and a sharp contrast to the listless course in business history. We had our final class over lunch at the Arts and Letters Club. One of the graduate students, Barbara Clow, gave a paper so stunningly good — it was later published — that it brought the students to the edge of applause. They did applaud as we brought the meeting to an end, the first time I had seen that happen in a seminar.

Three of the students who took that first seminar, Barb, Alison Li, and Geoff Reaume, went on to do doctorates in the history of medicine under my supervision. They were the pioneers in the second tranche of my doctoral students. The first group, beginning with Veronica Strong-Boag and Jim Struthers in the 1970s, had worked on mainstream Canadian social and political subjects (actually with an emphasis on social, Nikki being a pioneer in Canadian women's history and Jim doing his thesis on unemployment insurance). Other students found their way to me to do business history, church history, political history, and now the history of medicine. As well as supervising my own students, I had to help examine other students, serve on thesis supervisory committees after we were required to implement a committee system, and occasionally hold comp preparation colloquia or give reading courses at the graduate level. Working with graduate students, a theme I've neglected until now, consumed a huge chunk of my university time.

I found graduate teaching too arduous to enjoy it. There is so much at stake in the highest level of university education. Bright young men and women dedicate what could be the best years of their lives to advanced studies that will, they hope, prepare them for careers as university professors. Work done by a doctoral student at the direction of a supervisor has a major steering effect on the rest of the student's life. Being a supervisor is a huge responsibility.

I did not like having that much responsibility without being able to control the outcomes. Most of my students were good, hard-working, and professional. But, of course, they wanted advice and help; sometimes they needed more help than they were willing to admit or than anyone else had the courage to supply. Supervisors had to tell doctoral students what would and would not work as thesis topics. We had to give advice about field preparation, comprehensive examinations, and thesis research. We had to read and critique drafts of chapters, and do it over again with second drafts and then third drafts. We had to tell the students when we thought their theses were ready for examination, and hope that we were right. We also had to tell them when they were failing to meet our standards and when they should consider cutting their losses, abandoning their dreams, and leaving our program — which happened far more often than it should because of the allure of the graduate student life to a certain (under)class of bright young people not quite ready to grow up. We had to uphold the standards and reputation of our program. We had to do this mostly in one-on-one, face-to-face interviews.

These could be highly emotional. On one occasion, an undergraduate student became so angry and belligerent that I rushed out the door and took refuge in the chairman's office where he could not follow me. One year, one of our female students showed enough signs of being likely to set up somebody for sexual harassment charges that I asked my secretary to be present whenever she came. There was almost the reverse problem with several breathtakingly beautiful, utterly businesslike women students, whose looks had to be coldly, resolutely ignored as we worked our way through complicated issues of bibliography and footnoting. It helped that I was happily married — probably helped the students too. The single most disturbing confrontation I had was as a thesis examiner, when another professor's student came to the door of our home, long-overdue thesis in hand, and said that even though she had recently fought off a rapist she could understand why I might not stretch a point in her favour, and might refuse to read her thesis. I thought that if I did not stretch the point she might try suicide.

I liked most of my students, and usually called them by their first names (which increased the stress on them, not knowing how to respond), and tried to make a point of inviting them to our home, either singly or in small groups. But I also thought the professional relationship was too intense to be allowed to cross the line into the personal. While they were in program my doctoral students were not my buddies. A little distance, a little aloofness, was a useful buffer. Trying to maintain a kind of amiable equanimity, I could come down on them hard when I had to. Harder on some than on others, but hard on almost all of them for their poor and disorganized prose. Inability to write well was the single greatest weakness I saw in history graduate students during my career. Too often it also seemed to reflect a problem with thinking well. The second greatest weakness was graduate students' propensity to dawdle and procrastinate. As their coach I was always pressing them to keep focused and run faster.

We would set the students to work on their projects and not see them for months. In history, unlike the sciences, there has traditionally been minimal collaboration between supervisor and students. The doctoral candidates chose their own thesis topics, wrote their theses under their own names, and then published books and articles under their own names. I almost never collaborated with any of my students (or any of my colleagues, for that matter) on anything. What I did do was always be available for consultation and give the students very fast feedback when they submitted work. "Very fast feedback" I judged to mean a week or less. By academic standards, and in the years before we all became computerized, that was lightning fast. The horror stories students told about supervisors who went off to Europe for a year, sat on work for months, and never responded to calls, were yet another disturbing aspect of academic life. In the late 1980s we adopted supervision by thesis committee partly to serve as a check on colleagues' individual irresponsibility or bad judgment.

Comprehensive field and thesis examinations were an ordeal for everyone involved. By the time a student reached the oral stage of the comprehensives (designed to test general knowledge of broad fields of history), or an oral thesis defence, he or she was often a nervous wreck, sometimes quivering near incoherence. All our instincts as examiners were to be kind — indeed all the pressures on us were to forgive, tolerate, turn a blind eye. It took a cold heart to cast the vote that failed a student at this stage in life, and then explain to the student in kind tones why it had been done. Yet our professional responsibility was to maintain the standards of the university and the program. So we did the best we could, wobbling along on webs of professional tightropes, often coming out of exams berating ourselves for being too kind and letting shoddy work pass.

Although judgment of the quality of students' work was highly subjective, we were expected to supply letters of reference that would enable scholarship committees to award very large scholarships on an apparently objective basis. Writing letters was a frustrating obligation that involved putting the best possible interpretations on a student's performance and potential without exactly lying. None of our students was ever less than brilliant, none was below the top 10 percent in his category, every single one was deserving. Yadda, yadda, yadda. After they finished their doctorates and began applying for jobs, often with faint hope on a flooded market, the writing began all over again and with even more at stake. Give the poor students the best break possible, keep your integrity as best you could, privately wonder whether the whole game is loaded against these poor young players.

Everyone knew certain colleagues whose expressed judgments on students could not be trusted. The trouble was that one was never sure whether one's own judgment was trustworthy. Long-term academic achievement is almost impossible to predict. One of the most productive and most cited of my doctoral students has been the one I once firmly advised to drop out of the program, saying I was certain he had no future in academia. The two doctoral students for whom I wrote the most unqualifiedly enthusiastic letters both dropped out of our program and became high school teachers, never to finish theses or to publish a word of scholarship. A third became a civil servant. They may well have been happier for the decisions they made.

In the years before I joined the department there were so few graduate students that supervision was done as an extra to one's normal teaching load. When that became clearly unfair to some of the professors most in demand as supervisors — I soon became one, as Ramsay Cook had before me — the department instituted a system of partial work-sheet credit, which resulted in some offsetting reduction in one's undergraduate load. These credits never came close to compensating for the time spent with doctoral students, a fact that further widened the gap between the productive scholars in the department and the drones and time-servers. I was the principal supervisor training about forty would-be doctors of philosophy in history, as many as six or seven at any one time. Half of these stayed in the program to break the tape and receive their degrees. By the standards of the humanities, this was a lot of doctoral students. Some colleagues never had one. No wonder we were puzzled at what they did with their time.

Were there greener academic pastures? We liked living in Toronto, liked it a lot, and it would take a fabulous offer to persuade us to leave the city. I did not think, for example, that there was anywhere else in Canada where I could have such access to good students, research libraries, culture, the media, and other urban amenities.

What about the United States? In 1986, word of my restlessness was passed back to Duke University, which had a well-established program in British Commonwealth Studies, including Canada (Jack Granatstein was probably its most distinguished graduate, and I later learned that he had mentioned me to Duke), and which was considering appointing a distinguished professor of Canadian studies. Duke contacted me to see if I was interested in being a candidate for their chair.

They made arrangements for Liz, myself, and one of our children to come to North Carolina for several days of interviews and assessment. Laura, our social sophisticate, volunteered to come as the teenagers' rep. We had an intense, fascinating weekend with the Duke people, discussing every aspect of a move, from the subjects I might teach to the housing situation in Raleigh-Durham and Chapel Hill. We were also given tickets to a Duke basketball game, a sure sign, everyone said, of their seriousness about persuading us to move. Fortunately, none of our Duke hosts was with us to notice Liz Bliss falling fast asleep during the bedlam of the Duke-Oklahoma game.

Things did not quite click with Duke. It was not clear to me that they had a deep interest in studying far-off Canada, as remote to that part of the United States as Chad or Ghana, and I learned that a faction in their history department was still lobbying for Latin American studies as an alternative. It was not clear to anyone, myself included, exactly what I wanted to do as a scholar. Was I a Canadian historian, a business historian, a medical historian? Liz was enamoured neither of the Duke sporting scene nor of much else about the United States, despite — or perhaps because of — having a sister who lived in Tennessee. She loyally indicated that she would stand by me if it came to a move, but the reluctance was palpable. Speaking for the children, Laura claimed that the price of their consent would be a car for every sixteen-year-old forced to live in the North Carolina forest.

A concrete offer from Duke, which had mentioned a possible salary in the six-figure range, would at least have given me a bargaining chip at Toronto. No offer came. Duke never filled a chair of Canadian studies, eventually hiring a Canadianist from McGill to a regular staff post. A mediaeval historian whom they did poach from us a few years later was said not to have been very happy with the move. The Bliss family got its basketball fix down our street at Leaside High School. In 1986–87, I volunteered to serve as coach of the Leaside High Junior Boys team, which would otherwise have folded. Jamie was the star player. The team had a dismal season, probably because of the coaching.

Another American possibility developed in the summer of 1987 when my new friend, Jesse Roth, director of diabetes research at the National Institutes of Health in Bethesda, asked me to consider a two-year appointment to do research in the history of medicine, with a view to the position becoming permanent. This was a fine compliment, and I did think seriously about it for a few days, but realized I could not take the risk. I was not a trained medical historian, I was not sure that Jesse could deliver on permanence, and I had no interest in giving up the almost unlimited security I had at Toronto to take my research in any direction.

Northern Enterprise: Five Centuries of Canadian Business, 640 pages of text, bibliography, and index, was published by McClelland & Stewart in May 1987. On the official publication date no one noticed the existence of the book except daughter Laura, who left a bunch of carnations on my desk with a note "Have a Happy Book!" But a few days later Manulife, sponsor of the project, staged a lavish party for one or two hundred of my closest friends. It was held in executive suites that were elaborately decorated as a native Canadian room, a Victorian Canada room, and a modern Canada room, food and servers appropriate to each décor, champagne a staple in every era. After cocktails we were treated to a special performance by Roger Abbott and Don Ferguson, the principal members of the Royal Canadian Air Farce, making jokes original to the occasion and subject.

My confusions about the occasion are nicely captured in a diary entry:

> It was a wonderful evening, in fact quite astonishing. It was some time into the Air Farce presentation when I realized that this was probably the most sensational book launching I've ever experienced, possibly that there's been in Canada in years. And I dimly realized that it was a tribute to me and to my achievement — thought to myself that if people are going to do this maybe all that agony's been worthwhile.
>
> Did sort of worry about the lavishness of it all. What are the puritanical historians saying? What are they assuming about the research money, etc., I must have had? Isn't it all too much? Met a CBC producer who wasn't there the next day and said I felt vaguely guilty about the lavishness of the launch and he said, "You goddamn typical Canadian, feeling guilty about a tribute to you."
>
> Right. I don't feel guilty for a fucking moment. I earned it all over the years; it's a great book (actually I'm beginning to believe this), and that was a fantastic party.

Northern Enterprise got a lot of media and reviewer attention and McClelland & Stewart sent me on another national promotional tour. Not every event worked, as businesslike organizers who tried to charge admission found that hardly anyone was willing to pay real money to hear Bliss talk about his book. Academics would have known better than to try to charge. Still, I talked about Canadian business history "From the Fur Trade to Free Trade" to groups ranging from the Business Council on National Issues through the Insulating Glass Manufacturers Association of Canada and the West Toronto Kiwanis Club — the Kiwanians meeting was in the basement of Canadian wealth's greatest architectural folly, Casa Loma. The book sold well in both hardcover and paperback, and the royalties came to me, not to Manulife.

The academic reception of *Northern Enterprise* was marginally less enthusiastic. The Marxists, of course, panned it — though I liked the misprint when a reviewer said that I was championing the "tickle-down" theory of Canadian economics — and even some friends had puritanical trouble accepting the bona fides of a project launched with such an extravagant party. Bob Cuff, on the other hand, who had been teaching American business history, told me it was a book that would not be understood or appreciated in Canada where its theoretical framework and the issues it raised, mostly relating to competition and managerial capitalism, were poorly understood. In that regard he was right.

Literate businessmen — not the oxymoron it sometimes seems — did like the book. I had resigned from the National Business Book Award jury to avoid a conflict of interest in the year *Northern Enterprise* was published. The reconstituted jury gave me that year's award.

The overall reception of the book made me reconsider the idea that *Northern Enterprise* would be my personal farewell to business history (I always hated closing off career options and usually tried to keep as many as possible open for as long as possible). The business schools at most Canadian universities were not very aggressive or lively places, but now and then there would be flashes of interest in the business history of their country. I gave a named lecture at the University of Ottawa's business school, and was a keynote speaker at a conference at Western's Ivey School. The University of Toronto's Faculty of Management Studies, a particularly inert place, took no interest in my work, no advantage of my being on the spot in the History Department. York University's Business School, on the other hand, was developing quickly and aggressively. I had come to know its founding dean and sometimes Conservative cabinet minister and NBBA juror, Jim Gillies, who liked my work. So did others at York, most obviously Bob Cuff, but also the dynamic incoming dean, Dezsö Horvath. In March 1988, York offered me an appointment in the Business School with a cross-appointment in their history department. I would have a light teaching load and a much higher salary.

My chair at Toronto, Michael Finlayson, told me he was authorized to match York's offer. The president of York, Harry Arthurs, phoned to hope that I would make the move. Liz was indifferent. I weighed the options as carefully as I could and decided to take my winnings — a big salary increase and a permanent decrease in my teaching load — and stay at the more convenient and more prestigious university. In perfect character with that institution's disarray in those years, it was only after the deadline had passed and I had made my decision that a call came from our president, George Connell, urging me to stay. One of the factors in my decision was the success of my new medical history seminar and the prospect of doing more work in that field at Toronto.

When Finlayson and I settled things in April, a great burden was lifted. After a long period of alienation and complaining I had clawed my way up the salary ladder (from $32,000 in 1980–81 to $85,000 in 1988–89), been guaranteed a relatively light teaching load, and was also promised that every effort would be made to promote me to Toronto's highest rank, that of University Professor. This plus my personal conservatism and my appreciation of the complete freedom I had at Toronto, overrode the greener pastures syndrome. At age forty-seven I knew that I would stay put at U of T until retirement. The later, troubled history of York University made me very glad I had stayed downtown.

———————————————
———————————————
———————————————

Negotiations with York and the University of Toronto exactly coincided with meetings to discuss the possibility of writing a commissioned history of the Reichmann family, at that time one of Canada's best-known business dynasties because of the billions they had made in New York and Toronto real estate. I was approached by senior executives of their principal firm, Olympia & York, in company with lawyers, and given the impression that I could virtually name my terms.

This was the most intriguing of several opportunities flowing from my work in business history. Financier and philanthropist Hal Jackman, a fan of my Flavelle biography, tried several times to interest me in working on some of Flavelle's Methodist associates, and to promote a history of the Gooderham family, who had made their first fortune as distillers. There was also the possibility of doing a biography of Canada's most colourful liquor magnate, Sam Bronfman, patriarch of both the Seagram empire and perhaps the country's most prominent Jewish family. In 1987, Michael Levine, Canada's leading literary and theatrical agent, approached me on behalf of Charles Bronfman, who wanted to commission a biography of his father. I indicated tentative interest — Sam Bronfman had had a magnificent career that had been absurdly distorted in one of Peter C. Newman's sniggering bestsellers, and the sources would be very good — which led to a formal interview with Charles Bronfman at his Montreal mansion that August. It was a surreal experience to be waiting in Bronfman's library studying all his books on baseball (he was the principal owner of the Montreal Expos) hard by an original Van Gogh painting, and then to meet with the amiable billionaire, accompanied by his cultural advisor (Bob Rabinovitch, later president of the CBC), and discuss how misleading it was of Newman and others to see the family saga as just a jazz-age bootlegging story.

My diaries record doubts about the Bronfman project — I didn't want to be seen to be in the pay of the fabulously wealthy — but I was attracted by the idea of writing a fabulous bestseller. The idea was still in play — the family was canvassing several other writers — when the Reichmann people contacted me, leading to wry merriment about being wooed to be the biographer of Jewish billionaires.

The problem with the Reichmanns was the doubts I had about being able to keep my independence. They wanted a family history to counter a view of the origins of the Reichmann fortune that had been popularized by a leading Canadian journalist, Elaine Dewar, in a long article in *Toronto Life* magazine. The family was suing Ms. Dewar for libel. Having read her article closely, I thought this was a preposterous, ominous resort to litigation. "I have to live in this community," I noted, "and I won't be part of what will be perceived as the use of law to suppress an honest journalistic attempt." In intense discussions I told the Reichmann lawyers that I could not consider taking on the project unless the suit was dropped. That ended our negotiations. Several years later an American business journalist published the requisite book, but by that time the Reichmanns had crashed in bankruptcy. Now they are largely forgotten.

The Bronfman biography was eventually given to my colleague and good friend Michael Marrus. Michael, whose expertise was entirely in European history, promptly invited me to collaborate with him. By this time I had decided to carry on with my own projects, mostly medical. Marrus, a consummate professional, settled down to work and wrote a first-class biography of Sam Bronfman that more than justified the family's choice. His best Bronfman story involved a secretary interrupting his own first interview with Charles Bronfman to announce that the prime minister was on the phone, wishing to speak to Mr. Bronfman. "Which prime minister?" Bronfman replied. Even so, the Bronfmans, much of their fortune squandered by members of succeeding generations, have also largely disappeared from prominence.

The final round in my adventures with Jewish entrepreneurial sagas came when Avie Bennett, then head of McClelland & Stewart, told me that the flamboyant theatrical promoter Garth Drabinsky "liked my work" and wanted to commission me to do his biography. I didn't take the suggestion seriously. A journalist wrote the puff-book Drabinsky had in mind. When I wrote the first draft of this memoir, in 2008, Mr. Drabinsky was on trial in Toronto for fraud. By the first revised draft he had been convicted, by the second he had been sentenced, but by my final deadline he was still not in jail. After *Northern Enterprise* I wrote no more serious business history.

This run of roads-not-taken was varied by a pleasant event that I never thought would happen and had very little to do with. In 1986,

McClelland & Stewart told me that a Toronto-based company wanted to take an option on the film rights to *The Discovery of Insulin* and *Banting: A Biography*. It only involved preliminary payments of one or two thousand dollars, and most film options never amount to more than that. But a contract had to be negotiated just in case the option was firmed up. "These are the most complicated deals we make," M&S's rights editor told me, "and we can't really guarantee you that your interests are fully protected. But I can tell you that these people appear to be the first honest film producers we've ever worked with."

That was encouraging, and I was favourably impressed when I had lunch with Gordon Hinch and Joe Greene, principals in Gemstone Incorporated, a company ambitious to make a mark in serious entertainment. They both had considerable experience with the CBC and in other ventures, they seemed anxious to do a good job of turning *Insulin* into a television mini-series, and they seemed confident they could raise several million dollars to finance their project. I doubted they could, but saw nothing to lose in our granting the option. I told Gordon and Joe that I knew I would not have any control over their treatment of my work, would praise them loudly and publicly if they did a good job, would damn them even more loudly if they made a hash of it.

Over the next few months I was pleased, though still skeptical, when Gemstone would call to report progress — a writer working on scripts, actors eager to play Banting and Best, financing falling into place, and so on. Then everything clicked. Gemstone firmed up its offer, a schedule of royalty payments was triggered, and production began on *Glory Enough for All*, a two-part, 3.5-hour television mini-series backed by Thames Television in the U.K. and the CBC in Canada. What a lucky professor I was to have my scholarship dramatized on television. Whether or not it worked I was pocketing some $60,000 in royalty payments.

I had agreed to be available as a consultant on the basic script, written by a professional Canadian screenwriter. From the beginning it was clear that Gemstone aimed at doing an honest job of bringing history alive. There were no Hollywood flourishes, such as making Banting and Best sexually attracted to each other or moving all the research to the U.S.A. I did grumble about the script's early portrayal of Macleod as a villainous figure, and I warned Gemstone that they would almost certainly be sued if they persisted in portraying young Margaret Mahon Best, a prim and proper and still very alive woman, as a gin-drinking, sex-crazed flapper in the insulin years. I suggested alternative wordings for crucial scenes with Macleod.

Gord Hinch, who was producing *Glory*, invited me to spend a day on the set during filming in the summer of 1987. The brilliant Canadian actor R.H. Thomson was perfect as Banting. Indeed, Thomson was Banting to a fault, Hinch claimed, in trying to tell everyone how to do a better job. Warned by Hinch, I tactfully resisted Thomson's suggestions that as author of the books I should support his ideas for inserting new scenes. Hinch observed that it was easier to work with the trained dogs supplied for some of the scenes than with the human actors. When he later invited me to appear as an extra in *Glory*, I was on holiday in Algonquin Park and could not be bothered to drive down to Toronto. I wish I had.

I had also been consulting on the scripts for a major and very expensive CBC series, *Chasing Rainbows*, a historical romance about Montreal enterprise made by the hotshot Montreal producer, Mark Blandford. When *Rainbows* went to air in 1988 it became a major disappointment, a complete flop actually, largely because of miscasting and uneven pacing. I had no illusions that *Glory* would necessarily be any better.

I received my first cassettes in June 1988, and wrote in my diary the next day:

> Oh, Wow … Super acting — by everyone. Terrific professionalism in sets, editing, props, costume, make-up, everything. Makes *Rainbows* look like rank amateurism … My eyes water in half a dozen places. … I love Gordon's symbolism — taking the Christian imagery much further

than I did — into symbols of baptism, washing, purifica-
tion — using swearing as markers. Just beautiful.

Asked to introduce the film at a preview put on by the Canadian
Diabetes Association, I began by saying, "You know I really didn't have
very much to do with the making of this film from my books. And now
that I've seen it I'm glad I didn't." As the audience gasped, I explained that
as a professor I was a rank amateur in everything to do with dramatization
and if I had been involved I would have made a hash of it. Instead, these
professionals had done a magnificent job.

Glory Enough for All was shown in England and in Canada, and eventually in some forty other countries, including China. It won a trunk-
ful of Genie awards for Canadian television excellence, and Thomson's
portrayal of Banting was rightly singled out as outstanding — the best
re-creation of a historical figure I had ever seen. It was another great thrill
when Gordon Hinch called up to say that *Glory* had been sold to PBS
in the United States, where it would be shown on its prestige program,
Masterpiece Theatre. When I congratulated Hinch on the sale, he told me
it was a disaster: they had been very close to a deal with one of the big
three networks that would have made very big money; PBS paid peanuts
by comparison. Still, when I saw my name come across the little screen
in the introductory credits on *Masterpiece Theatre*, it sent chills down my
spine. The Gemstone people lost a bundle of money on their next venture,
bringing a major play to Toronto, and went out of business.

Glory's success did not yield further royalties, but I was delighted to
learn that one of my books would become a (Canadian) mass-market or
drugstore paperback. McClelland & Stewart reissued *The Discovery of
Insulin* in cheap paperback form under the title *Glory Enough for All* with
a scene from the mini-series on the cover. Instead of resetting the book,
however, they simply downsized their full-sized format, which meant
that the print was so small as to be nearly unintelligible. They withdrew
Glory from the market and "pulped" all their copies. *Sic transit*. Copies of
that edition are very rare.

Frustration with the parochialism of the Canadian history beat, what Maurice Careless called the Beaver Patrol, had nagged at me for years. The evidence that *The Discovery of Insulin* was the best thing I had done, the doorways it had opened, all the satisfaction I received from talking about it, kept the idea of doing more work in the history of medicine lurking in the back of my mind. It jostled there with other possible projects — a two-volume general history of Canada, provisionally entitled *Northern Visions*, for which my History 262 lectures could be a basis, or perhaps a biography of the much misunderstood Canadian humourist and social commentator Stephen Leacock. The one Canadian medical biography that was crying out to be written would be of Sir William Osler, one of the patron saints of the coming of modern medicine.

My deepest interests still seemed rooted, as they had been in the 1950s, in the human search for transcendence. Most of my work in Canadian history, outwardly the basis of my serious professional interests, had actually been of limited relevance and interest. The history of medicine, far from representing a narrowing focus, would be a way of broadening out. In a secular world without God, the human quest necessarily centres on finding ways to fend off our physical mortality. It would be a logical development to try to write more about medicine and doctors.

I had always been interested in the New England transcendentalists, and had renewed an interest in Walt Whitman that had first been kindled in Algonquin Park in 1960. Whitman's pantheistic humanism seemed very appealing. I was particularly struck by reading these lines in his preface to *Leaves of Grass*:

> Of physiology from top to toe I sing. Read these leaves
> in the open air each season of every year of your life,
> reexamine all you have been told at school or church or
> in any book, dismiss whatever insults your own soul, and

your very flesh shall be a great poem and have the richest
fluency not only in its words but in the silent lines of its
lips and face and between the lashes of your eyes and in
every motion and joint of your body.

I thought this was a fine personal credo generally, and that it could
also be interpreted as a mandate for immersion in the history of physiology.

I seriously considered doing a new Osler biography, but a reading of
the classic two-volume, 1,400-page *Life of Sir William Osler*, by Harvey
Cushing, published in 1925, discouraged me. Osler's life was so complex,
so deeply engaged with technical medical issues and institutions in three
countries, so very wide-ranging, that I doubted I could master it for
biographical purposes. Even if an Osler project was possible, it would
surely take years to do and require major financial support in released
time alone, not to mention other travel and research costs. Having been
so badly burned in my failed requests for research support, I wanted a
project that I could virtually fund from my own pocket.

Some twenty years earlier a graduate student friend who was doing a
thesis on Canada's mixed-breed rebel leader, Louis Riel, had happened to
mention that he thought a smallpox epidemic in Montreal in 1885 had
done as much to harm English and French relations as Riel's Northwest
Rebellion and subsequent execution that year. My friend never finished
his thesis and dropped out of our program. Now, at the end of August
1987, just after my interview with Charles Bronfman, a light suddenly
clicked on:

On Wednesday we drove to the Schatzkers' cottage in
Haliburton. At Friday breakfast something Valerie said,
perhaps about AIDS, suddenly triggered the thought in
my mind — it hadn't crossed it for years — that the
Montreal smallpox epidemic of 1885 was an event just
waiting for a book. Of course it is. Years ago I'd mentioned

this often, but just had let it slip away. Reminiscent of insulin: a subject I've thought for years there was a good book to be written about. Well, why not go and do it? So many attractions — doable, medical history, a venue for good writing and exact re-creation — even a way of getting into the rebuilding of my French capacity ...

A quick check of obvious sources revealed some of the potential of the topic. In 1885, more than three thousand Montrealers had died of smallpox. It was a nearly unthinkable calamity, even at that time, because practically everywhere else in the developed world vaccination was confining smallpox to short outbreaks, fairly easily contained. Most of Montreal's 1885 smallpox deaths were of unvaccinated French Canadians. Something terrible had gone wrong that this should happen in a Canadian city at the height of the progressive nineteenth century. There was very probably a good book to be written exploring the subject. In the 1987–88 academic year I began learning about smallpox and the great Montreal epidemic in my free time.

Such free time as there was. While I had been canvassing new history projects in that summer of 1987, Canada's politicians had been making the worst kind of history, inflicting what I saw as a loathsome new disease on the country.

Brian Mulroney and our ten provincial premiers had agreed that Canada's 1982 constitutional settlement was profoundly unsatisfactory and had decided to reopen the constitution. Their ostensible purpose was to get the Quebec government's formal acceptance of Canada's new constitution. They falsely argued that this was an urgent problem, ignoring the reality that no province's "signature" on the constitution was required and that separatism and the Parti Québécois were at a low ebb. In fact, most premiers sniffed an opportunity to gain more power at the expense of the central government. As well, an activist mentality had gripped would-be constitution-makers, both in politics and academia. They were like ambitious surgeons — having seen the constitution operated upon in a major way in 1981–82, they were keen to go in again and get some of the glory that had mostly gone to Pierre Trudeau. They did not realize that Canada, their patient, needed a prolonged period of healing after the first operation.

Meeting at the prime minister's Meech Lake retreat on April 30, 1987, the eleven "First Ministers," as they liked to call themselves, announced that they had made a historic deal to amend the constitution in a variety of ways. They proclaimed themselves the proud fathers, or midwives, of a reconfederated country. Quebec would come in out of the cold and sign on. The leaders of the other national parties, in fact almost the whole political leadership of Canada, supported by many pundits and editorial writers, almost immediately endorsed this work.

Recitation of the exact terms of the Meech Lake Accord is probably even more sleep-inducing now than it was then. As constitutional expert Patrick Monaghan commented, "The subject appeared to many to combine the incomprehensible with the arcane." My own interest in Canadian politics was at a low ebb at that time, partly because of my growing private belief that the country would be better off in the long run if economic integration might someday lead to political union with the United States. I thought of myself as an internationalist, deeply suspicious of nation states and nationalism generally, of Canadian parochialism and chauvinism in particular.

I paid attention to the Meech Lake Accord partly out of a sense of citizenship, more strongly as a scholar who lectured constantly to young Canadians about how their country was constituted. The more I thought about the Meech proposals — constitutionalizing Quebec as a "distinct society" within Canada, transferring various powers of appointment and vetoes on constitutional change to the provinces, and much more, the more I saw the package as balkanizing an already weak federation into something approaching ten principalities. At one of my *Northern Enterprise* events I listened to very high-placed Quebec businessmen defend Meech Lake for creating what one of them called a country that resembled a husband with ten brides. They liked the idea of weakening the husband. "I've been thinking about the current constitutional agreement," I wrote in my diary on May 6, "and believe it's absurd if you want to have a real nation — decentralization gone mad."

I drafted a letter to the *Globe and Mail* pointing out some of the implications of the accord. As a check on my judgment I called Ramsay Cook, who I knew was a staunch supporter of the 1982 constitution, and asked if he thought there was a problem with Meech. He told me he had just been on CBC calling the deal a constitutional Munich. On this matter we thought similarly. I did not yet know what former Prime Minister Pierre Trudeau felt about the Accord — I had never met or spoken with Mr. Trudeau — or whether he would take the highly unlikely step of coming out of retirement to comment on his successors' handiwork. In any case, my sometime disdain for the country's future under the 1982 constitution was giving way to a realization that our national political leadership was literally conspiring to make the future for Canadians much worse. In the first draft of my *Globe* letter I wrote:

> Do even the most alienated Maritimers and Westerners and Quebecers really believe that provincial premiers and provincial legislatures are the best guardians of the future of a younger generation that deserves the same national heritage created for us in 1867? Are we going to turn the constitutional future of Canada over to the level of government that gave us Aberhart in Alberta, Duplessis in Quebec, Hepburn in Ontario? Do we not still have a sense that there should be at least the possibility of someone speaking for Canada? Where is Mr. Trudeau now that we really need him?

The issue had immediate urgency because the first ministers had agreed to meet again early in June to solidify their accord, after which they had pledged to rush it through their legislatures without further amendment. A much-abbreviated letter indicating my general view on Meech Lake was published in the *Globe and Mail* on May 16. A few days later I was phoned by a voluble law teacher at the U of T named Deborah Coyne, who said she was organizing opposition to the Meech Lake Accord and wondered if I would help. We began gathering names of academics and others who opposed the accord. Deborah, who seemed to be a human whirlwind, organized an open meeting in Toronto on the issue for the night of June 1, just prior to the first ministers' meeting in the Langevin Block of the Parliament Buildings the next day.

I at first declined Deborah's request that I chair the meeting because I had obligations out of town. Then, on May 26, Mr. Trudeau emerged from retirement to launch a scathing, take-no-prisoners attack on the accord and the men who made it. I not only completely agreed with Mr. Trudeau's views on the destructive impact of the proposed constitutional changes, but was moved by the idealism and patriotism underlying his criticisms. I felt intense resonance when he told the CBC's Peter Gzowski that he was speaking out so he could explain himself to his children. Trudeau seemed like the politician of 1968 all over again, the man of intellect and vision seizing the moral high ground against a gang of cynical and not very bright politicians. "He made me feel proud to have spoken out," I wrote, "and determined to keep on speaking out — so I too can tell my children that I've tried." I truncated my scheduled trip. At noon on May 31, I lectured about the discovery of insulin at a diabetes meeting in Sebasco, Maine, and then drove 1,100 kilometres home, snatched a couple of hours sleep, and threw myself into organizing our anti-Meech meeting and explaining our position in the national media.

The gathering of some four hundred people in the Moot Court chambers at the University of Toronto Law School, housed in Sir Joseph Flavelle's former home, was the first large protest against the Meech Lake Accord. I chaired it, had written a statement for the media, and made myself available for comment. Events proceeded. The gang of eleven first ministers emerged from their Langevin meeting in the early morning of June 3 to announce that they had formalized their deal.

For several days I practically lived at the CBC, always maintaining my civility on the air, but intensely angry at the catastrophe being promulgated on the country by a political and intellectual elite composed about equally of naïve dimwits and cynical opportunists. In my diary I recorded unlimited scorn for Meech cheerleaders like Hugh Segal and William Thorsell (whose off-air conversations about the "real" effect of Meech put them firmly in the cynic camp), and once, in the Green Room at the CBC, I chewed out a semi-articulate Queen's University constitutional "expert" for engaging in social engineering that would have all sorts of unintended consequences. "I despise Meech Lake and all it stands for," I wrote in my journal,

> and want to speak my mind. I want to do what I can to defeat it so it can be said — to our children, for the record, for the history books — that at least we tried. Tried to save Canada, a desperately troubled and weakened country, from the kind of dismemberment by stupid politicians that would lead to more exploitation of ordinary people, more closing off of opportunities, a final end to mobility and the prospect of real achievement in this northern land. Yes, I think it's probably an impossibility, but at least we tried.

The Meech-Langevin package of proposed amendments to the 1982 constitution had to be ratified by Parliament and all the provincial legislatures within three years of the first government's ratification. The rigidity of this amending procedure meant that it would be practically impossible to make any further changes in the deal, no matter what Canadians felt about it. There would be no references to the people of any province, no referenda, no more meaningful debate. Without quite realizing the logic of what they had done, the eleven white, male politicians who had made the Meech Lake accord fell back on the letter of parliamentary practice from an earlier age and maintained that elected majority governments can, in effect, do anything they want to. The people had spoken by electing them, and would not be allowed to speak again. In Toronto some fifteen or so of us, including Deborah Coyne and Ramsay Cook, met to create a Coalition for the Canadian Constitution, aimed at continuing the struggle as best we could. The prospect was not at all encouraging, and we were not very enthusiastic, but it seemed important to keep trying.

Chapter Twelve

The Road to Hazeldean

Being a media professor had become as much a part of life as researching in archives or giving lectures. I had progressed from talking about sex in Canadian history on the radio to supplying historical background on political and business events, then commenting during constitutional debates, and finally being asked for regular political punditry and analysis. Eventually I appeared on every major public affairs show in Canadian radio and television and in every national magazine and newspaper. I worked hard to master the media's demands, made a few dollars in fees, and had bully pulpits for proclaiming my views on current issues.

By the 1990s I was sometimes characterized as a Canadian "public intellectual," or "public historian." This seemed flattering, but I often thought that media appearances were evanescent, their subject matter shallow and forgettable. My serious work was the scholarly books I was publishing every three to five years. All the journalism and broadcasting in between was partly what I thought a professor ought to be doing to popularize his expertise, mostly what the serious writer Margaret Atwood called her "knitting." Still, it led to the creation of piles of intellectual caps, socks, and mittens, not all of which unravelled as quickly as they were made.

On a few occasions media events directly influenced my scholarship. A CBC *Morningside* panel of historians I was on, asked to discuss the time in history each of us would most preferred to have lived, fell flat when we all immediately agreed on the present. We concurred that modern health care, plus affluence, made the present distinctly preferable to any time in the past. I have many times in talks and articles used this panel as evidence that the idea of progress in history is far more defensible than most academics care to admit.

The best interviewers I met in the Canadian media were Barbara Frum, Peter Gzowski, and Steve Paikin. Also, when he feels like it, Michael Enright. A great interviewer is well-prepared, has or appears to have a genuine interest in his subjects, and is often smarter than the people he interviews. The very smartest interviewer I encountered was Don Harron, who preceded Gzowski as host of CBC Radio's *Morningside*. Harron had been a gold medalist in philosophy at the University of Toronto, a serious Shakespearean actor in love with words and language, and, above all, a compulsive and brilliant punsmith — best known to Canadians as the farm hick, Charlie Farquharson, "outstanding in his field." Don was an inveterate scene-stealer. In every interview I had with him, Harron made all the jokes, paid no attention to his script (most interviewers are supplied with lists of carefully prepared questions they should ask), talked about whatever happened to be on his mind, and left me feeling like a klutzy undergraduate failing an oral exam.

I learned to talk back to Harron, and we eventually became good friends as summer stock on Prince Edward Island. I wish there had been time to become better friends with Barbara Frum before her early death from leukemia in 1992. She combined passionate professionalism with a warmth of personality and a curiosity about history, ideas, and people that made me and hundreds of her other friends feel that Barbara was a genuine kindred spirit, the sister one would have liked to have had. Barbara used me often as a guest on her great television public affairs program, *The Journal*, and, as she did with many others, would telephone me from time to time to keep in touch and to chat about Canadian personalities, politics, and ideas. Barbara's private presence was even more impressive than her public face. The CBC never found an adequate replacement for her. They should never have let young Steve Paikin, who soon matured into Canada's finest public affairs interviewer, by far, get away.

The best time I had on *The Journal* was during the 1988 election campaign, when the free trade agreement between Canada and the United States was the dominant issue. Much as I despised the Mulroney government, I just as passionately supported free trade, and was thrilled to be part of a *Journal* debate with my former professor, Ken McNaught, who opposed more truck and trade with the capitalist Yankees. We had the full forty minute time slot to ourselves, an audience in the millions, and later bantered for months about all the people who had contacted us saying how we had each wiped the floor with the other. The best comment of the session was never broadcast: McNaught closed the debate with his view that free trade would mean the importation of American health care and gun violence into Canada, and we went off the air. Barbara, a border person like myself and a closet free-trader, turned to Ken and said with a cold smile, "That was the stupidest thing I've ever heard."

I thought a lot about how to do well as a media commentator. It involved overcoming the stereotype of the academic as long-winded, mumbly, egotistic, and irrelevant. The media have their needs and people who don't meet them don't get asked back. You have to talk clearly, avoid jargon, stick to the point, and, above all, be brief. Radio is an easy medium because nobody cares about appearance, grimaces, or fidgets. On-air radio personalities vie with rock singers as the worst-dressed entertainers in the world. Peter Gzowski was the worst of the worst, and he also stank from the smoking that eventually killed him. On television it is important to dress well, sit still, and appear to be natural and relaxed. Audiences respond differently to the two media: "I heard you on the radio," friends would say, "it was an interesting discussion." "I saw you on television the other night. Can't remember exactly what you were talking about, but you looked good."

Confrontational public affairs debating featuring sharp and occasion-ally angry exchanges by ideologues of left and right had a brief vogue in

Canada in the 1990s. It still survives when panels of political partisans are permitted to behave in character, which is to escape from rules and rationality. I learned to play the debating game when it seemed appropriate — though once discombobulated a CBC "Face-Off" panel by conceding that one of my opponents was right and I was wrong. Normally television guests are expected by both audiences and producers to be well-mannered. Do not interrupt, do not hog airtime, do not insult opponents or hosts. Be cool, be good-humoured, always be sincere. Never, ever lose your temper on air. Never be halting or nervous.

I badly lost my composure only once, in an early *Journal* discussion of the Meech Lake Accord with a gaggle of politicians. Just as we went on the air someone commented that the audience might be more than two million. The thought of all those viewers suddenly made me nervous, the babbling politicos would not let a professor get a quiet word in, and I was reduced to short, increasingly angry interjections. I was comforted by the thought that most viewers dismiss fast-talking politicians as bags of flatulence.

The most important qualification for getting on the air often seemed just being available. I was in Toronto, I answered my own phone and always returned calls, I always made time to give journalists background comments and help with their stories, and I was always on time for appointments. I was patient during the telephone "pre-interviews" that give associate producers a sense of where a guest is coming from and how to prep hosts with questions. I sublimated my outrage the few times I was told I did not "fit" as a guest because of my views or because of geography and gender. On several occasions indiscreet CBC staffers said they would prefer using a woman, a Westerner, virtually anybody but an over-exposed white Toronto male, on such and such a panel — adding that they would call me back if they couldn't find an alternative. Sometimes they would ask me for names of alternatives.

More often than not I would tell callers that I didn't have the expertise they wanted, and would recommend people who might. As with writing projects, it was the broadcasts one did not agree to do that made the difference between becoming a game-show professor (there were a few of these in Canada, one of whom, everyone's favourite silver-tongued French Canadian, eventually became a senator) or remaining a reasonably well-respected authority.

The requirements of print journalism are not wildly different from the other media. No worries about appearance or speaking skill, but you have to think hard about your audience, have to express yourself clearly and forcefully, absolutely have to write to the length editors request, have to be willing to take criticism, and have to meet deadlines. None of this comes naturally to the large numbers of academics with unworldly or prima donna dispositions. The knack develops with experience but requires constant polishing. By the late 1980s I had done enough journalism to be fairly confident of having mastered the game. The prima donna problem never fully went away, but I could write to exact length, was never blocked, was usually so well organized that I could meet any deadline (I sometimes had copy ready so far ahead of time that I held on to it rather than reveal how quickly I worked), and, most important, knew when to say no, when to realize what I couldn't do. Knowing when not to get over your head means you are unlikely to drown.

Book reviewing was the mittens and socks of my literary knitting. "Bliss on Books" migrated from the *Report on Business Magazine* of the *Globe and Mail* over to *Saturday Night* when my friend John Fraser became its editor, then back to the *ROB* and eventually to *Canadian Business*, where it morphed for a few months into a "back-of-the-book" general column. Finding interesting books to review for a business audience was not easy — especially as I was losing interest in the subject — and it became annoying to have to spend time reading bad books. My conscience would not let me review a book I had not completely read. Spending time reading and reviewing books one ordinarily would not read made the pastime gradually less appealing. By the mid-1990s I had stopped regular reviewing. Writing a regular column was not easy either, because it presumed being willing to sound off whether or not there were any serious issues, a sort of literary masturbation. I never did it on more than a bi-weekly basis.

Academics who dabble with journalism are sometimes thought to be whoring or slumming, mainly by colleagues. This never bothered me because I was confident that tut-tuts about my "popularizing" could be more than countered by the range and success of my scholarship. A more pressing question involved getting paid for punditing. Most presentations and publications in academia garner prestige at best; in many disciplines contributors even have to pay to get their papers published. I never liked these conventions, never liked the thought that my work was of so little value that no one would pay for it, never liked the expectation that my expertise could be exploited for nothing. I expected to be compensated for working. Over time, my contributions to non-paying academic publications became fairly infrequent. The exceptions were when I had a particular reason for reaching an academic audience (I did several follow-up pieces on the insulin research, for example, including, shortly after Margaret Best's death, a major account of how her husband had systematically tried to falsify history), had already been paid for material delivered as lectures, or was helping out a friend.

Even in the good years the Canadian broadcast media preferred not to pay their "guests," reasoning that most people are grateful for access to airtime. Fair enough for those advocating causes or promoting books or themselves, and perhaps an expert professor should not mind giving up a few minutes of time to share his knowledge with a wider audience. But few people actually do much work for free. None of the interviewers at the CBC or editors at the *Globe and Mail* was working for nothing, nor would the media expect significant time donations from lawyers or doctors. Drawing a line between paid and *pro bono* commentary is often tricky and no one seems to know where it should be. I developed a working rule that any commitment involving leaving work or home, or taking more than half an hour of my time, should be paid for at professional rates. I swallowed what was probably a naïve distaste for appearing materialistic and always made my fee expectations clear. Media work and money-making by moonlight were not important enough to cause me to incorporate as some media profs did, but for several years I was a card-carrying member of ACTRA, the Canadian performers' union. The affiliation saved a lot of bargaining time.

Speaking fees were another grey area. Many groups expect professors to give talks as part of their public service role. Others, such as business groups, expect to pay appropriate professional compensation. In betweens, such as senior or later life learning clubs, exploit professorial goodwill for honoraria so small that I privately found them insulting. I tried to err on the side of being generous with my time, never used an agent or joined a speakers' bureau, and sometimes found it politic to waive a fee or donate it to a charity. All the activities did add up though — four or five thousand a year from broadcasting, ten to twenty thousand from print journalism, the same again from speaking, along with advances and royalties. In most years my outside income exceeded 50 percent of my university salary, occasionally 100 percent — bringing my total remuneration almost into average doctor or lawyer range. When the Mulroney government brought in the hated Goods and Services Tax (GST), I had to register, collect, and remit.

It was not always clear whether my media appearances were as a disinterested expert or a principled advocate. I usually did nothing to dispel the confusion because it was often useful to be able to work both sides of the street. The media often wanted to use me as a token conservative or Conservative, and that was fine at times. But I would eschew any formal label, even at the cost of losing appearances. I would not be booked as a regular spokesman for any particular viewpoint. I wanted to avoid being pigeonholed in order to preserve my freedom to fly off in any direction.

During the Meech Lake debates and their aftermath I was willing to go anywhere, be an expert or an advocate, work for nothing or pocket a fee, so long as there was an opportunity to say what I thought about the wretched constitutional mess being foisted on the country by a political class who combined knavishness and foolishness in about equal measure.

Nothing in my lifetime soured me more about the quality of political life and political elites in Canada than the constitutional struggles of 1987–92. A constitutional revolution was designed by eleven men, deeply influenced by pathetic macho competitiveness with former Prime Minister Trudeau,* aided by a cadre of unelected but professionally sycophantic advisers. They then tried to foist this, without further amendment, on an ostensibly democratic country of thirty million people.

If the terms of the pact were not bad enough, the almost total intellectual dishonesty of the presentation and defense of it was worse. In Quebec, the accord was billed as the most important change in French Canada's status in North America since the Quebec Act. The "rest of Canada" — an ugly term that entered common usage — was told that nothing in the accord was particularly significant. Meech was presented as minor constitutional surgery in one part of the country, reconfederation in Quebec. If it passed it wouldn't mean much, but if it didn't pass Quebec would justifiably consider separating from Canada. The ghastly logic of the Meech Lake bargain led to a prime minister of Canada threatening Canadians repeatedly with the dissolution of their country — constantly implying that separation would be a legitimate response if he did not get his way. An utterly unnecessary round of constitutional negotiations (the best thing after 1982 would have been to let the constitutional dust settle) had morphed into a nauseating game of political blackmail by Brian Mulroney, ten provincial premiers, and a few hundred law professors, bureaucrats, editors, and other opportunists who presumed to know how to write constitutions in other people's best interests.

The national politicians had closed ranks on Meech within weeks, however, so the debate seemed to be over before it had really begun. Even with the considerable support of Mr. Trudeau, the handful of us who had come out against Meech could only carry on a guerilla campaign in the media and hope for a miracle.

---

* The rivalry with Trudeau is shown in the recreation of the Langevin block debate presented in Patrick Monaghan's *Meech Lake: The Inside Story* (Toronto: University of Toronto Press, 1991), an account that has not been challenged by any of the participants.

The miracle gradually unfolded at the provincial level, as the working of democracy slowly undermined the Meech Lake consensus. The then-new premier of New Brunswick, Frank McKenna, briefly showed a flash of political courage in disagreeing with his predecessor's support for the accord. McKenna was eventually cowed and brought into line, but Clyde Wells, the then-new premier of Newfoundland, had firmer principles, and became the leading spokesman for the political opposition. Quebec's Robert Bourassa was forced to make significant concessions to extreme *pur laine* nationalism on language issues, thus alerting many Canadians to the one-sidedness of what was otherwise being sold as a creative compromise. Opinion in Manitoba, the province that sits in several ways at the vital centre of Canadian life and culture, became increasingly negative.

Aside from criticizing the accord in the media, my only direct involvement in the anti-Meech agitation was to organize a visit to the University of Toronto by Clyde Wells in January 1990. We had a reception and luncheon for him in our departmental common room, and then he spoke to some 500 to 600 very sympathetic people in Convocation Hall, garnering good media coverage. A month later I was involved in a "fireside chat" about Meech Lake at a meeting of young corporate executives at Whistler, BC, where I was challenged from the floor by a pleasant woman in her early forties, who I was told was a minister in the British Columbia government. After some sparring about how to recognize Quebec as a "distinct society" without ruining the country, my diary records that the minister,

> then said "You're being like Trudeau, too Cartesian. Don't be rational; constitutions are about passion."
>
> I said, moderately appalled, that if anything in politics should be about reason it should be the constitution of a country. That we are dealing with the governing structure for our children and grandchildren.
>
> After our session we went out talking together and it became evident that we don't agree at all — we have

different concepts of Canada — hers is really that of a compact of provinces and she's ready to turn it over to the Premiers. I thought how sad to meet such a parochial politician, but perhaps that's what could be expected in the BC cabinet.

Yesterday Kim Campbell, who I mistakenly thought was a BC minister, was promoted from Minister of State for Indian Affairs to Minister of Justice for Canada. Weep for Canada.

Deborah Coyne had become Clyde Wells's constitutional adviser, and other Meech opponents, such as historian Michael Behiels, were active on the spot in Ottawa. During the accord's denouement in June 1990, when the first ministers met for a week in Ottawa, haranguing and cursing one another, lying to the press, bullying Clyde Wells, and further disgracing themselves and their cause, I sat at home, fretting and writing gloomy meditations on whether or not Canada would be better off breaking up than being constitutionally neutered. It was hard to make sense of an abject failure by a political class trading nakedly in hysteria and blackmail. The acid of the process had begun to corrode even the credibility of the CBC, whose on-air anchors seemed to be actively cheerleading for the accord, and whose Ottawa correspondents, led by David Halton, were wallowing in rumour-mongering.

"What a spectacle we're making of ourselves," a sad-voiced Barbara Frum told me when I called to complain about *The Journal*'s lack of objectivity. At CBC Radio, on the Sunday morning when the first ministers thought they had an agreement to go forward, I noticed that off-air the studio crew was cheering on Clyde Wells and making cracks about whether TV news anchors Peter Mansbridge and Wendy Mesley would be asked to sign the constitution too. We have forgotten the brinksmanship and degradation of that wretched time in Canada's political history. As one of the few dissidents with relatively good access to the media, I grimly told a national radio audience that the first ministers were striking at the heart of Canadian values and that night said on television that the first ministers were in danger of destroying the country while trying to save it. Other observers suggested that in many countries citizens would be demonstrating in the streets against a travesty like the Meech Lake process.

And then Canada was saved. At the last moment, a Cree member of the Manitoba legislature, Elijah Harper, was able to block final consideration of the accord by that province, leading to the expiry of the three-year deadline for gaining formal provincial agreement to the package of constitutional amendments.* There was no exultation, only a sense of exhausted relief, as though one had helped fight off thieves who had broken into one's house and done a lot of damage, or, as Jack Granatstein said, fought off a rabid dog who bit you during the battle. When the accord failed, Canada's pygmy politicians immediately had to reverse themselves completely, arguing that a country they had been picturing as fragile and on the verge of dissolution was actually strong and ready to face the future. Prime Minister Mulroney, then as later a disgrace to Canada, did not have the courage or decency to resign. Nor did any of his constitutional advisers.

I joked that for pleasant change from observing Canadian politics I was writing a book about the ravages of smallpox. During the summers of 1988–90 and in spare time during term I was often immersed in the carnival of death Montreal experienced with its smallpox epidemic of 1885. Spiritually, it was a healthier experience than being ringside at the Canadian political circus.

The topic proved unusually easy to research. Coverage of the epidemic in Montreal's nine daily newspapers came at the beginning of a

---

* In 1991, the late Izzy Asper told me that the anti-Meech forces in Manitoba would have killed the accord procedurally whether or not Harper had stood in the breach, but that it had been handy that a Native had done the act. Asper said that standing outside the legislature with Harper, he pointed to the statue of Louis Riel and told Harper that if he held out, some day they'd build a statue to him on these grounds. "Harper said 'I hope I don't have to be hanged first.'"

golden age of municipal reporting, and it was richly detailed. I could make instant, cheap copies of articles from microfilm, and simply organize my material in daily files. These were sufficient for my purpose, as quick trips to Montreal revealed an almost complete lack of supporting archival sources that would have to be waded through. Official city council minutes in the municipal archives, for example, turned out to be clippings from newspaper accounts, so detailed and authoritative because many of the reporters took shorthand.

The only research assistance I needed on the project was supplied by the three Bliss teens, set to work in front of a microfilm reader in Robarts Library with instructions to copy every article mentioning smallpox or "picotte" in the Montreal papers for 1885. Jamie Bliss sometimes lunched in the library cafeteria with some of the history graduate students — he came away convinced that it took a peculiar temperament to devote a lifetime to historical research. Liz Bliss experienced more of her historian's strange temperament when he took her on a walking tour of onetime smallpox-ridden slums of Montreal on a suffocatingly hot, humid summer day.

Was I fluent enough in French to do a book about Montreal? For all of Madame Wilson's discipline problems, I had learned high school French well enough to have a decent reading competency, and had honed it trying to keep up with the scholarship of Fernand Ouellet, Michael Brunet, Marcel Hamelin, Jean-Pierre Wallot, and other Quebec historians writing in French. I never had learned to speak French with any confidence. This was a sometimes embarrassing shortcoming in a Canadian historian and media pundit — I could never appear on French language radio or television — but it did not seem to affect me professionally. Through the 1970s I had considered immersing myself in a Quebec milieu for a few months to try to develop verbal fluency, but always had other priorities. None of my research projects seemed to require French-English bilingualism. I had no serious aspiration for involvement in national governance, could do without journalistic exposure on Radio Canada, and, in any case, believed that English was evolving into the world's *lingua franca*. Science and its history, for example, which had once required knowledge of German, were now being conducted almost universally in English. I concluded I could spend time more profitably learning about the history of medicine than learning how to speak French.

The challenge of the smallpox project, provisionally titled "Death in Montreal" or "Carnival of Death," was to recreate a year in the life of a city attacked by a terrible scourge. I read widely in the literature of plagues and epidemics, from Defoe's *Journal of the Plague Year* and Poe's "Masque of the Red Death" through Mann's *Death in Venice* and Camus's *The Plague*. I was also reading the modern British novelist, Penelope Lively, whose work evokes both a sense of history and an understanding of the problems of re-creating instants in time. Seeing my insulin book come alive in *Glory Enough for All* heightened my interest in visualizing and dramatizing Montreal's ordeal with smallpox. It seemed another natural subject for adaptation to film.

There are literary flourishes and allusions in all my books, most of them seldom noticed by reviewers or, apparently, by readers. For the smallpox book, I would be more explicit in using every literary technique I could to bring history back to life. I thought that Truman Capote's much-publicized notion of the "non-fiction novel" (which we now realize he had corrupted in writing *In Cold Blood*) could be applied to this event in Canadian history. I had agreed to have this book handled by an agent, David Colbert, who sold the concept to the Canadian branch of Harper Collins for an amazing $60,000 advance, the highest I would ever receive. Their hope was that I would write a Berton-like Canadian history best-seller.

After the debacle of Meech, I settled down in the gorgeous summer of 1990 to finish my history of how thousands of innocent children in Canada's greatest city at the height of the Victorian age had been killed by a preventable disease. The source material was superb. As had happened with the discovery of insulin, the event proved more complex and interesting than I had anticipated, raising issues swirling around vaccination, medical quackery, English-French relations, Catholic-Protestant relations, bigotry, law and order, the use and abuse of state power, the uses and abuses of journalism, the limits of public health regulations, smells, sanitation, and more.

The writing went beautifully — a satisfying contrast to the course of political events, which in Quebec became even more bizarre when Canadian troops had to be called in after Mohawk Indians barricaded highways and seized a bridge in a dispute with the Bourassa government. On August 16, 1990, one of the best writing days of my life, I wrote the "Epilogue" to my story, finishing it exultantly at exactly 5:00 p.m. with what I thought was the perfect concluding sentence, "For smallpox, history has come to an end." A week later I submitted the manuscript to my agent and publisher, a few days ahead of schedule, and we went off for another September Camp holiday in Algonquin.

I had begun to wonder about changing fashions in Canadian history at the 1985 Montreal meeting of the Canadian Historical Association. It was personally a splendid occasion, for I was awarded the Association's F-X Garneau Medal for the best history book published by a Canadian in the five-year year period from 1977 to 1982 (the award was for *A Canadian Millionaire*; it should have been for *The Discovery of Insulin*). But the presidential address that year, given by the prominent social historian Susan Mann Trofimenkoff, was about the role of gossip in history. It seemed a trivial subject, unworthy of what had once been a prestigious occasion. But it was *au courant* with fashions in social history, an area starting to be rebranded as part of "cultural studies," in which nothing is unworthy of scholarly attention. The uncovering of the commonplace and the seemingly trivial in history was becoming something of a young historian's cause. Major traditional areas, such as political or constitutional history, were being ignored by some of the brightest minds in the new generation of scholars, many of them female, some alums of the New Left, who set out to explore the everyday gender, class, and racial assumptions they presumed had governed ordinary life in the past.

My own work having largely been in the realm of social history, and as former editor of the Social History of Canada series, at first I was not uncomfortable with these trends. Gradually, I began to worry that they might be fragmenting our responsibility to teach national history. If we called ourselves Canadian historians, surely we had a responsibility to provide a coherent picture of the history of our community, Canada. During the Meech Lake debates I was surprised to realize how few Canadian historians seemed to understand the constitutional history of the country, indeed how disinterested many of them were in political-constitutional issues. The constitutional lawyers and political scientists who dominated the Meech Lake debates had appallingly little historical sense. And that was starting to become true of the historians themselves. I often thought back to a comprehensive examination some years earlier, when one of the pioneering women historians, whose major field was Canadian history, confessed that she had no idea who had opposed Confederation in Quebec or why. We had passed her anyway.

Imperceptibly, I had become a senior Canadian historian, both in the Toronto department and nationally. I never felt like one. I always thought of myself as an outsider, a position that kept being confirmed in sometimes upsetting ways, such as the failure of Chair Finlayson's attempts to get me promoted to the rank of University Professor. On the other hand, I was invited to sit on the board of directors of the newly incorporated University of Toronto Press, and, in 1990, began a strange experience as a director of Toronto's Woman's College Hospital, a once-prestigious and pioneering institution that was fighting to survive in an era of declining hospital stays and merger mania. I turned down several requests from our administration to write the long-overdue history of the university, as well as Michael Finlayson's suggestion that I write the history of the History Department. Those books were eventually written very successfully by Martin Friedland and Bob Bothwell respectively. On the other hand, when I was invited to give our prestigious Donald Creighton Lecture as part of the department's 1991 centennial celebrations, I welcomed the opportunity.

The invitation came during a running discussion I was having with my teaching assistants in History 262, especially the brilliant and outspoken Tina Loo, about how to balance our priorities and responsibilities as teachers of Canadian history. I realized that I could use the occasion to clarify my feelings about the changing state of the discipline and get them off my chest. The ongoing deterioration of our national constitutional debate was also on my mind in the summer of 1991 as I drafted my Creighton Lecture, "Privatizing the Mind: The Sundering of Canadian History, the Sundering of Canada." It became my most important statement on the evolution of the writing of Canadian history.

I argued that Canadian historians, myself included, had taken our legitimate and healthy interest in social history to such extremes that we had begun to lose sight of the public history of the country. Young historians were turning inward, preferring the private to the public, or they were extravagantly assuming that their private interests superseded the traditional public domain. It was a scholarly acting-out of what the American social historian, Christopher Lasch, had identified as the 1970s "culture of narcissism." It was not obvious in the lecture, but I had the growth of neo-conservatism and the loss of faith in public ownership and big government — many of the themes we associate with the age of Ronald Reagan — on my mind as parallel tendencies. The fact that Canadian historians were also turning their backs on writing new general histories of the country, apparently turning their backs on writing any Canadian history that might appeal to the public, was further evidence of a retreat by academic historians into a world papered with navel lint. I argued that we were seeing an unhealthy sundering of our discipline, which also amounted to failing in our responsibility to write and teach the history of Canada.

We were also turning our backs on our responsibility to talk about Canada's past, present, and future. In one of the last important presidential addresses given to the Canadian Historical Association, my colleague and friend, Desmond Morton, had talked about historians' responsibility to contribute to intelligent public debate about Canada. It would be too bad, he argued, if we neglected this responsibility, because "answers will be provided by us — or by default." Morton and I were on opposite sides of the Meech Lake debate, but what most bothered me was how few historians had participated on either side. Mostly the high airwaves and mass media had been dominated, I wrote, by "Dr. Default, a silly and destructive old quack."

"There was and is a remarkable demand on the part of Canadians," I argued, "amounting to a kind of hunger, for help in understanding where we came from, who we are, and where we might be going. In my view we have a duty as scholars, as university teachers, and as citizens to do all that we can to meet that demand." I ended my lecture with

> a plea that we in part return to the Canadian historian's responsibility to write and talk about Canada, that we return to national history, to public history, to trying to write the history of Canadians as a people who are united - not by myths, not by ephemeral institutions or social programs, but through a rich, common history of achievement and failure, unity and diversity, limited identities and the experience of coping with limited identities. Canada is a country that has been sundered by particularisms and by political blundering ... Surely there is a greater than normal responsibility on all of us to at least talk to our fellow Canadians about our history.

I knew I was treading on dangerous ground so I added highly explicit qualifications:

> If I stop with these comments, I will surely be misunderstood. In calling for a return to national history, I am not advocating nationalist history, I am not advocating the development or upholding of historical mythology, I am not advocating the advancement of a Canadian

"identity" which is not there ... We should renew our appreciation of the history of Canada, yes, but we must not do it at the cost of leaving out those Canadians who were excluded from the old history and whose integration into our historical and national conscious-ness is the finest achievement of our history-writing since the 1960s....

We cannot envisage a Canada of the future whose constitution and whose history books do not embrace the multiple identities of our people and the bonds they share.

Criticism of my Creighton lecture had begun the morning before it was delivered, at one of our department's centennial symposia, as some of our new leftish former graduate students tried to stage a pre-emptive strike on what they thought I would say. They misunderstood me before I spoke, and they misunderstood me after the lecture was published. The misunderstanding was widespread. I became reputed to be both hostile to social history and an old-fashioned national-ist historian. As one of my most sympathetic former students writes, I became "something of a pariah in progressive academic circles." Another student notes how often I was dismissed as a "conservative" historian. This was doubly ironic. Intellectually, my Creighton lec-ture had been an attack on a generation of young ideologues, already too hidebound, perhaps too narcissistic, to change with the times. Politically, I was spending an inordinate amount of time in the com-pany of Trudeauite Liberals, trying to stop a national Conservative government from undermining both the country and the new status Trudeau's charter had given to women, new Canadians, aboriginals, and other outsiders. I was becoming a pariah not only among pseudo-progressive left-wing academics, but also in dim-witted Progressive-Conservative circles.

Plague: A Story of Smallpox in Montreal, was published in September 1991. The newspaper reviews were glowing. The academic reviews came in so late — anywhere from six months to three years had become normal in scholarly journals — as to have no effect on sales. The book was short-listed for the Governor-General's award, which, of course, pleased me, but by a quirk of deadlines that announcement came more than a year after publication, again too late to have any effect on sales. Nor did I win the G-G, which would have been at least a *succès d'estime*.

My publisher had worried that national sales could be hurt if the book was seen to be just a book about Montreal. The publisher was right. There was an immediate sale of rights for a French edition, but outside of Montreal and Ottawa there was not a lot of interest in *Plague*. I knew I was in trouble when at Quebec City's only English-language bookstore the proprietor seemed anxious that I autograph one copy only of his considerable supply of the book. He did not want to reduce the volumes' value when he returned them to the publisher.

It was all very well to celebrate the apparent end of the history of smallpox, but we soon realized that, unlike *The Discovery of Insulin*, this book had no "constituency" of people suffering from or interested in the eradicated disease. (One friend, Gail Regan, did tell me that as she was reading the book she found herself getting itchier. She knew she couldn't have smallpox, and marvelled at the psychosomatic power of my prose, only to find that she was coming down with a case of shingles. Could they have been prose-induced?) I was invited to give only four or five talks about *Plague*, nothing at all like the ongoing interest in my insulin presentations. Nor were there feelers from film producers who I thought would be fascinated by the possibilities of recreating a dramatic epidemic that involved rioting, forceful separation of children from families, racial tensions, and sick people rubbing the oozing pustules of their diseased faces against the clean skin of captive innocents. When I asked Gordon Hinch, who had produced *Glory*, why no one wanted to do *Plague*, he said there was a feeling that sickness and disease had been overdone on television, history was out of fashion, the book didn't have a core of strong characters around which a plot could be organized (it did, but it had too many of them), and few Canadian film companies had the resources to fund elaborate historical reproduction, or even do really good makeup.

Plague was published in the same season as my Creighton Lecture, and by any reasonable standard would be considered both a work of social history and a book infused with concern for the under-privileged, mostly helpless children, who died from smallpox. Perversely, the two or three social historians who eventually noticed the book condemned me for being harshly judgmental about the deluded Montrealers who ignorantly opposed vaccination. Never mind that the procedure, by that time accepted everywhere else in the civilized world, would have saved thousands of lives had it been properly implemented in the French population. Scholars whose moral relativism, or fear of judging, amounted in my view to amoral intellectual solipsism, argued that instead of attributing anti-vaccination sentiment to fear, ignorance, and fatalism, I should have worked harder to understand the fundamental rationality of the vaccinophobes and their leaders.

It did not help that I had used the unfashionable word "story" in my title. History was not supposed to be about stories. Had I used the chic word "narrative" to mean the same thing, I would have been much more correct. Being theoretically and politically correct was now essential to being accepted in the new social history community. Still, it was for quite different reasons that sales had lagged. This was the only time I did not even come close to earning out an advance, and copies of *Plague* ended up on the remainder table. One never gives up on one's children, of course, and I always hoped that *Plague* might sometime be rediscovered.

On my fiftieth birthday, in January 1991, I was sunk in gloom about the course of public events. The Canadian economy was in recession, the

United States was about to attack Iraq in retaliation for the seizure of Kuwait, and our constitutional mess was worse than ever since the failure of the Meech Lake Accord. The premier of Quebec was threatening to hold some kind of quasi-separatist referendum and the rest of the country was in a deep funk about how to respond. Talk of the likely breakup of Canada, and its consequences, was common.

Our private satisfactions as we entered middle age were many and rich. In my fifties, approaching the age at which my father had died of overwork, smoking, and sedentary habits, I began losing some of the aggressive, competitive, occasionally mean-spirited edge that had driven me as an ambitious young professor. Most of my overt struggles in the university and History Department had been resolved. Often, I would compare our lifestyle with the destructive habits of my parents' generation. Liz and I had relative financial security. We had thrown a few pebbles at one another, as husbands and wives do, but our marriage had always been rock solid. We never disagreed about anything important. Our health continued to be excellent — at fifty, I was road-racing and running constantly. Liz played tennis, gardened, lunched, and taught when she wanted to. Our children, who had passed through public schools and summer camps, were moving smoothly into years of college, travel, and courtship.

During the beautiful "smallpox" summers in Toronto, Liz and I had begun talking about buying a summer home, perhaps a cottage north of Toronto. We looked at a few properties, but found nothing remotely suitable. In December 1990, over a family dinner at Trapper's restaurant in Toronto, we got to reminiscing about our 1983 visit to Prince Edward Island. The children remembered good times playing in the fields and in the big barn at "Hazeldean Farm," and we all recalled the achingly beautiful setting of Liz's family's ancestral farmhouse. When someone wondered what would happen to Hazeldean after Liz's aged aunts died, one of the children said, "Dad, why don't we buy it?"

Ten months later we closed the agreement to purchase Hazeldean farmhouse from Liz's relatives, and found ourselves owning a historic four-bedroom home in the exact centre of a province exactly a thousand miles from Toronto. Our first summer in Prince Edward Island began in May 1992, when I arrived in a new minivan loaded with washer and dryer, microwave, and a barbecue. The journey to the island in the early years seemed like a trip to the land of Oz. The endless forests of Quebec, Maine, and New Brunswick were the equivalent of a deadly desert that took a day or more to cross. Then the ferry approached a beautiful green and pleasant land — every shade of green, contrasting with red soil (caused by rusting iron oxides), blue water, and clear skies. Tourists on Prince Edward Island often feel they are in a postcard or a movie set. Now we would summer there, live in a place where the neighbours — many of them Liz's distant relatives, who had worked their farms for more than a century — said "welcome home," a place where we never locked our doors, a place where when a rare break-in did occur the getaway vehicle had been a tractor, a place where the most dangerous drivers on the highways were farmers in their hay wagons.

I spent my first hour as proprietor of Hazeldean talking on the phone with the CBC. On my first morning as a summer islander I drove forty kilometres into Charlottetown, found the CBC building, and appeared on CBC Newsworld, talking about the prime minister's (un)popularity. The drive was beautiful, the PEI CBC people a pleasure to work with, and Canada's ongoing constitutional mess was depressing almost beyond belief.

After the Meech Lake Accord had collapsed in June 1990, there had been endless special inquiries, special conferences, special meetings, special debates, most staged by a discredited political-constitutional establishment that was determined to put Humpty Dumpty together again. I begrudged every moment of attention that I gave to the constitution, telling myself that I should be done with "the pettiness of Canadian politics and the cheap thrills of being a TV professor." But like a moth to the flame, or perhaps as a dutiful citizen, I kept writing and commenting.

Mostly, I pleaded for extremists and activists to calm down, slow down, recognize the virtues of accepting the status quo, and let the 1982 constitutional settlement harden as the country healed. It would not be right to give in to Quebec's threats, which were probably mostly bluster and if ever acted upon would mostly harm Quebecers themselves. I was not a part of any of the organized "save Canada" groups, though would often compare notes with like-minded friends including Jack Granatstein, Deborah Coyne, Andrew Coyne, Michael Behiels, David Bercuson, and Ramsay Cook. On March 21, 1991, I was in the audience at Convocation Hall when Pierre Trudeau was given a special honorary degree at the opening of our Bora Laskin Law Library. Mr. Trudeau used the occasion to deliver an erudite criticism of our Supreme Court's reasoning in its key constitutional decision in 1981, which he — and Bora Laskin — had vigorously opposed, and which he thought had sown many of the seeds of the current disaster. Most of the judges responsible for the decision were in the audience. Mr. Trudeau was given a standing ovation, though not by the judges.

As Jim Spence commented, that event reached a level of civic profundity — a former prime minister publicly arguing fine points of constitutional law with the justices of the Supreme Court — that American politics could not hope to match. It happened that I did not think Trudeau made a convincing case on this issue, but I marvelled at his determination to fight on and defend his stewardship of his country. "They are all pygmies by comparison," I told my diary of our other political leaders, "vain, blustering, pompous, absurd." I had urged my students and my children to come to the event because they would tell their grandchildren about having heard Pierre Elliott Trudeau fighting for his view of Canada in 1991.

In Ottawa, the midgets stumbled on, now led by Joe Clark, Mulroney's designated point man for constitutional negotiations. My diary contains frequent references to gloom, despair, the book of Ecclesiastes, Kafka, parallels to the history of parasitology, Ottawa as a constitutional Dogpatch, and God's comment to a constitutional expert who wondered if Canadians would ever resolve their dilemma: "Yes, my son, they certainly will. But not in my lifetime." Here is an unedited journal passage from November 29, 1991:

> To weep for Canada. A truly depressing week on the constitutional front. Joe Clark is blackmailed by the Quebec caucus into backpedalling on the promise of a referendum. I watch Question Period on Wednesday and he appears utterly craven, frightened, exhausted, dishonest. The implications of denying Canada a referendum on its future are amazing. The next day — yesterday — the feds announce $160 million for Quebec — leading to a ghastly round of "what about us" from people all over the country. You can hear the remaining ties of good will snapping.
>
> The government seems utterly adrift. Clark seems near the end of his rope. The Prime Minister is a cardboard, clownish figure. His only contribution to the mess on Wednesday was to answer a question about people's right to say "Yes" to Canada by popping up and saying "You had the chance to say 'yes' to Canada at Meech Lake."
>
> Yesterday I was on a panel with Jack Saywell and Jamie Cameron talking to 400 students at a seminar organized by the Simcoe County Board of Education. In the question period the students' real sympathies came out — in their applause for one who called Quebec a "festering tumour" on Canada, and support for similar positions. The young are idealistic, passionate, angry, and simplistic. They have turned profoundly against Quebec and against this kind of politics. It was what I knew was happening all through the Meech Lake debate, but I hadn't before been exposed to it in quite as blunt, frightening, and depressing a way. All

> three of us on the panel found ourselves pleading for
> tolerance of diversity … At one point a student asked
> us why we weren't more optimistic. I said "Do you want
> us to lie to you"? He said, "Isn't that your job?" I was
> speechless and finally came back with "Look, I'm not a
> politician."

There is no truth in the story a former student has published that Joe Clark personally lobbied me to come onside on constitutional reform. After 1983, I had no communication with Mr. Clark, whose later career seemed to me to be one disaster after another — not that his early career had been much better.

The summer of 1992 on Prince Edward Island was a time of discovering a magical countryside, of walking for miles on deserted white sand beaches, jogging on mossy lanes under green canopies, rocking on the porch of Hazeldean and smelling the lilacs and roses, going to Sunday evening concerts and strawberry socials, and napping in a perfect hammock strung in a perfect birch grove. Our purchase had included the family archive, including volumes of diaries that had been kept by Liz's grandmother, Lucy Palmer Haslam, her sisters, and her children. Lucy's diaries began in 1884, when she was nineteen, and continued to just before her death in 1947. We had a record of every day in the life of Hazeldean from its christening in 1894 until our arrival. I lost myself in Lucy's diaries, made elaborate transcripts, wandered around Prince Edward Island tracing her nineteenth-century footsteps, and eventually published three long articles about her life *before* moving to Hazeldean in *The Island Magazine*. "Sisters on the South Shore," "Party Time in Malpeque," and "A Farmer Takes a Wife," are among the best of my sixty or so historical articles. Outside of Prince Edward Island, they're my least-read work.

Writing at "Hazeldean," PEI.

"The eggheads are coming" was the theme of a local CBC Radio item about the forthcoming conference of the Learned Societies of Canada that June, on the campus of the University of Prince Edward Island. Having come to the island partly to escape academic responsibilities in the city, I found myself welcoming historian friends and attending many more "learned" meetings than I wanted to.

The first talk at a Royal Society symposium, on "The Future of Post-Modernism," was so abstruse and silly that I walked out of the meeting. At the Canadian Historical Association I was the target of a large chunk of the presidential address. It was given by Gail Brandt, a Canadian historian who had become president that year in a feminist/social historian uprising against the official candidate, my friend and colleague Michael Marrus. When Brandt was not attacking my Creighton lecture in her talk, she was pleading for more attention to the role of women in history, such as the women who had served the food and champagne to the Fathers of Confederation at the Charlottetown conference in 1864. Good grief. I left the CHA's annual meeting as the members were debating a resolution worrying that government grants might be reduced. "The level of critical intelligence at the meeting was somewhere below an average Grade 10 class at Jarvis Collegiate," I concluded. A substantial number of colleagues of my generation lost interest in the Canadian Historical Association after the dissing of Marrus, a historian with a global reputation but unfashionably traditional interests (in such subjects as the Jews in Vichy France and the Holocaust!).

The constitutional nightmare worsened as deadlines loomed and high-level negotiations heated up. If I was not driving to the CBC in Charlottetown, I was at my desk writing articles that drew comparisons between our constitutional struggles and the Vietnam War. Journal, Wednesday, July 8, 1992, 7:15 a.m.:

A deal on the constitution! Every province to have a veto. Native self-government. New Senate. Rejigging of powers. Distinct society. Oh dear.

Sinking feeling, esp. when I hear about the universal veto. Meech II, and perhaps worse than Meech.

Now the lying and the manipulation begin again. Nine premiers, the Prime Minister, Joe Clark, lying through their teeth. Devaluing the Canada we have now, disgracing political discourse. Good for Canada, national unity, compromise, a new country, national spirit, blah, blah, blah. The truth is that it's entirely blackmail from Quebec and power-grabbing by provincial barons. Self-interested, cowardly politicians appeasing Quebec by carving up the country.

I hope Quebec rejects it outright. Everyone outside Quebec knows that if B[ourassa] tries to get more, he'll be turned down flat. How much resistance will there be in the rest of Canada? My own first reaction is to succumb to constitutional fatigue. Who will say no? Clyde Wells sold out! The anti-Quebec bigots will all be opposed. So will Reform.

What will the next few days have in store? Everyone else out here in PEI is more interested in how much sunshine we'll get, if any.

Publicly I struggled to keep my constitutional equanimity, feeling a responsibility to weigh the pros and cons of the draft "offer" to Quebec. The final coincidence that summer was the first ministers' decision to firm up their agreement in a formal constitutional conference in Charlottetown. It was an overt attempt by politicians whose egos knew few limits to mimic the 1864 conference that had begun the birth of Canada. I became an accredited press delegate to the 1992 Charlotteown Conference, held at the end of August. With about a hundred other members of the national media, I waited in the lobby of the Prince Edward Hotel as the first ministers mingled and argued behind closed doors in the mezzanine above us, not even bothering with a pretence of openness. I was on several live network panels, and debated on the CBC's good local news show. I told my diary that it might be a historic conference, but if so it was shitty history-making.

Summer drifted to an end in a muddle of self-doubt and self-confusion on my part about the new Charlottetown Accord. Perhaps it would make sense to endorse the deal that the premiers had worked out, deeply flawed as it might be, for the sake of constitutional peace, national unity, and the need to get on with the life of Canada. At the least it was important to fight one's contrarian instincts and not to pass knee-jerk judgments. I wrote two columns about the Charlottetown Accord for the *Toronto Star*, Canada's largest circulation newspaper, which was now asking me for regular contributions. In one column I marshalled every argument I could think of against the accord, in the next every argument in favour. My conclusion was that perhaps the pros had it, by a narrow margin. On reflection, I had that thought deleted, let the columns go forward without reaching a judgment, and went swimming at Cavendish Beach.

In Toronto that September, I continued to fret about the constitutional deal, even as the politicians had to give in, much against their will, to demands for a national referendum. Earlier, I had become involved in a national controversy about a television miniseries, *The Valour and the Horror*, which had come under attack from Canadian veterans' organizations because of the hard questions it asked about such issues as the targeting of German civilians by Bomber Command and double standards involving Canadian soldiers and the murder of prisoners. Seeing the debate as a free speech issue and considering these questions legitimate, I broke with some of my military history friends and agreed to support the producers of the series, Brian and Terrence McKenna, when their work was examined by a Senate committee. Testifying was not a pleasant experience, for the Senators and their supporters were on a witch hunt redolent of McCarthyism. It was appalling to be heckled and shouted at by hostile veterans in a hearing conducted by the Senate of Canada. I had the satisfaction of saying so in my *Toronto Star* column. The Senators succeeded in muffling if not exactly suppressing distribution of *The Valour and the Horror*.

Brian McKenna's next project was to make a television memoir of Pierre Trudeau. Perhaps as thanks for my support, he asked me if, possibly in tandem with Ramsay Cook, I would like to interview Trudeau as part of the program. Cook declined. I leaped at the opportunity, the first I had had to meet Mr. Trudeau. On September 21, at the University of Toronto Faculty Club, I interviewed Trudeau on film for some forty minutes, and chatted with him off camera for another ninety minutes. At seventy-three, the former prime minister seemed surprisingly small and fragile, but he was also slim, fit, and comparatively youthful. He was in a good mood, polite and utterly lacking in arrogance — though when talking to me about his prime ministerial years I noticed that he never admitted to any serious mistakes.

On that morning Trudeau had been the lead item on all the newscasts because *Maclean's* magazine had just published his fierce denunciation of the constitutional negotiations. He told me he was going to speak out further against the Charlottetown Accord, that he had to because it was clearly irreversible and would cripple the government of Canada forever. He knew I had opposed the Meech Lake Accord, regretted that so many of his former friends had succumbed to the lure of power and abandoned his position, and argued that it was necessary to have "nerves of steel" in resisting the separatist impulse in Quebec.

We all thought the formal interview had gone well — several exchanges made it into the televised memoir — and when it was finished, McKenna asked me to join the group for lunch. Then they asked me where to go in Toronto for a quiet luncheon. I suggested the Arts and Letters Club. In the cab on the way over I mentioned to Trudeau a poll indicating that Canadians considered their most honoured symbol to be the Charter of Rights and Freedoms. He had not heard this, and said, "That's what I always wanted to happen."

The regulars on a quiet day at the Arts and Letters Club took my signing in of a most distinguished guest in their stride. But former President Jim Parr wandered in without noticing anything, slid into a vacant seat at our table, and did a classic double take when his dining partner introduced himself as Pierre Trudeau. The lunch conversation ranged through anti-Semitism in Quebec's history, Orson Wells and the Lux Radio Theatre (young Trudeau had attended a performance in New York), Trudeau's memories of Louis St. Laurent, and his appreciation of the Mona Lisa print over the urinal in the club's men's room.

The next day I wrote the column for the *Star* in which I had promised to make up my mind about the Charlottetown pact. Writing with barely controlled anger, I condemned the accord as incomplete and dishonest, and the referendum campaign and question as nauseatingly biased, "ignorant, manipulative demagoguery by people who should know better." While there was a decent case for supporting a deal that might bring peace to a troubled country, my bottom line was that various provisions in the accord would diminish the charter's protection of Canadians' human rights. "I can't agree to a constitution for Canada that allows the fundamental equality of citizens to be further overridden by racial, linguistic, or territorial collectivities ... I will not tell my grandchildren that I voted to diminish human rights in Canada because I was afraid. Nor will I abstain. I'm voting no, and I hope you will too."

The column contained an oblique reference to our once having had a prime minister with "nerves of steel." "I think I would have reached the same conclusion had I not had the fascinating experience of meeting Mr. Trudeau yesterday," I wrote to myself that night. "But there's no doubt that he stiffened my backbone. I'm haunted by that phrase, 'nerves of steel.'"

During the next month I wrote and spoke against the Charlottetown Accord at every opportunity. At the beginning of the referendum campaign the "Yes" forces seemed so overwhelming — the national and every provincial government, all the other political parties except for the then-small Reform Party led by Preston Manning, and virtually the whole of the country's business and educational establishment. Those of us in the "No" campaign formed a loose and fragile coalition, almost completely lacking in resources. It happened that Manitoba's Izzy Asper had the courage to stand out against an unusually solid national business leadership. He put up $50,000 to finance the filming of a few anti-Charlottetown television commercials. Michael Behiels, Jack Granatstein, and I were talking heads in ads that because of fairness regulations were shown again and again across the country. The night before the vote, a CBC program arranged a live debate between myself and the minister of justice, the Honourable Kim Campbell. Realizing the pitfalls of such an occasion, I made a point of being restrained, responsible, civil, and quiet. I had my say and was satisfied with the course of the argument. When my final pitch at the end of the debate left me with a few extra seconds of time, I told the audience that I didn't want them. "I've said all I want to, and I'm tired."

On October 26, 1992, the Canadian people rejected the Charlottetown Accord in six provinces and by a national vote of 54.4 to 44.6 percent. Four words ran through my head, "We beat the bastards." Public opinion studies later showed that Trudeau's intervention had probably been decisive in arousing hostility to the accord outside of Quebec. The Quebecers rejected it for quite different reasons. Some in the media, such as the *Globe and Mail*'s Ottawa man, Jeffrey Simpson, liked to turn up elitist noses at the unholy alliance of wildly disparate groups it had taken to say "no/non" to Charlottetown. I thought that saying this was the equivalent to a gang of thieves stealing our cars, robbing our banks, breaking all the traffic laws, and, when chased down, suddenly turning on us and proclaiming "Hey, you're unholy!" And fifty years earlier Canada had been in a pretty unholy alliance with the U.S.S.R. to defeat Adolf Hitler.

There would be three more years of national uncertainty about Quebec and Canada's future before the matter was settled, for a long time, by the 1995 referendum in that province. The fact that Canada did not break up, that the 1982 constitution has been made to work, and that the dire predictions of Mr. Mulroney and his henchmen and dupes never came true, was a complete vindication of our view that it was possible to reject their handiwork without destroying the country. In retrospect, it now appears that Meech Lake and Charlottetown were two avoidable aftershocks to the constitutional earthquake Trudeau had engineered in 1981–82. They would not have occurred had the country had wiser, more patient political leadership and fewer public-policy wonks lusting to try their hand at constitution-making.

My editor at the *Toronto Star* thought that my columns, especially the pro and con presentations followed by my decision, had created a measurable turnaround of opinion in metropolitan Toronto. Whether or not he was right, I was satisfied that my contributions to the "No" campaign were the best public and media presentations I ever gave. While most of the media work I did during my career was ephemeral, not nearly as important as my books, I think my constitutional articles in 1992 were some of my best pieces. In public, I kept my temper and manners under control, saving my anger for my diaries and this memoir. If I never again had the opportunity to participate in public policy debates I could be satisfied.

One of the vows I made as an alleged media hound was that I would never become so needy for spotlights and applause that I would descend to advertising my availability to comment or write. Someone once told me that in his last years Marshall McLuhan had been given to calling the CBC offering to go on the air with his latest insights. I did not want my sense of self-importance, which always had to be kept in proportion, ever to lead me to hang on past my time. I never forgot an incident during the Charlottetown conference when I told the local CBC that I was simply too tired to get up at 5:00 a.m. and drive in to comment. "Get some other expert," I told them. It happened that I was lying in bed awake, and turned on my radio at six to hear the other expert that the CBC had found. In my stead, they were interviewing the chief bellman at the Prince Edward Hotel, who offered his insights into the travelling and dining and tipping habits of the visiting premiers. Nobody missed hearing what Professor Bliss might have had to say.

Chapter Thirteen

Scholarly Solitude

I had to write a book about Canadian national history. The constitutional debates had been a personal wake-up call. Canadians at every level, including the highest, knew so little about the political history of their country. As I argued in my Creighton Lecture, the vogue for new forms of social history and the history of esoteric topics involved historians' turning away from the national narrative. This included my own failure: I had contributed my share to the history of pork packing, diabetes, investment banking, and smallpox, but had written little about the evolution of Canada. As unfinished business from the constitution wars, I felt that part of my obligation as a Canadian historian and as a citizen was to get on with telling Canadians about their history.

I had been teaching the national history of the country for years in our big survey course, History 262, and had it constantly at my fingertips. There was a market for good books on Canadian politics, especially political biography, and I was comfortable with the idea of illuminating history through biography. As an undergrad, I had learned a lot about American politics and government from Richard Hofstadter's classic, *The American Political Tradition and the Men Who Made It*, and had often thought someone should do a similar book for Canada. In lectures I had devoted an increasing amount of time to assessing prime ministers. Now I would draw on my knowledge, assuage my guilt, and, I hoped, contribute to our political historiography by writing a "prime ministers" book.

The idea was enthusiastically received by a superb editor at Harper Collins, Phyllis Bruce, who had been a colleague at Lawrence Park Collegiate many years earlier. On the day the Charlottetown Accord failed in 1992 I was offered a $40,000 advance for the prime ministers project, the book to be ready in about a year. I began work on the manuscript on January 1, 1993, and finished it that August, in a blaze of Prince Edward Island productivity. For several weeks in the autumn of 1994, *Right Honourable Men: The Descent of Canadian Politics from Macdonald to Mulroney* was the bestselling non-fiction book in Canada; before Christmas it had earned out its advance and been reprinted.

Right Honourable Men succeeded in part because I was the first to assess prime ministerial performance, what soon became a cottage industry for historians and journalists. The use of "descent" in my title probably also appealed to a jaded audience who believed that Canadian political history had just reached a new low of degradation in the Mulroney years. Whether or not that was exactly true, the strongest theme in the book was of the gradual descent of power in Canada from the grip of autocratic prime ministers and tight political elites to the will of voters in an age of mass democracy, the Charter of Rights and Freedoms, and referenda on constitutional change.

The Fathers of Confederation, especially Sir John A. Macdonald and Sir George-Etienne Cartier, had not believed in democracy. They thought of it as an American political perversion that gave power to the ignorant masses. In the kingdom of Canada, as in mother Britain, it was deemed appropriate that the powers of the Crown be wielded by Parliament, one house of which was elected. Parliament consulted the people from time to time. But normally the political elites led and the people followed, their loyalties secured by favours from above — patronage in the form of jobs, grants, subsidies, and other government programs. It was a top-down system, almost proudly anti-democratic, and remarkably resilient.

With his constitutional revolution, Pierre Trudeau had led Canada in the direction of a new democracy, emphasizing true popular sovereignty. But Brian Mulroney's Progressive-Conservative government seemed to me to have been a reversion to the old days of Macdonaldian

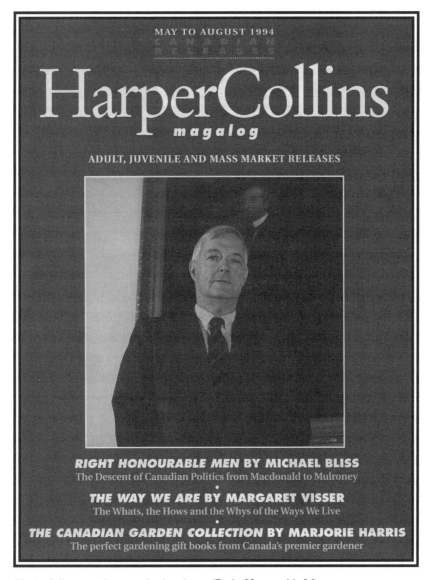

HarperCollins magalog cover for the release of Right Honourable Men.

elitism. The attempt by Mulroney and the Canadian establishment to ram through the constitutional accords without popular consent had reeked of nineteenth-century contempt of democracy. Thanks to the referendum on the Charlottetown Accord that era seemed to have ended.

The more I had thought about politics and government, the more I favoured unconventional, apparently unCanadian approaches to democracy and the limits of power. I believed that in modern democracies sovereignty has to visibly and effectively rest with the people. I had no regard for the retention of the monarchy in Canada. Apart from the pathetic antics of Canada's royal family, the British house of Windsor, the symbolism of the monarchy in a democratic age is all wrong. The American tradition of town meetings and direct democracy, as expressed in plebiscites, referenda, civic activism, the recall of legislators, term limits, and other devices, seems clearly preferable. Politically conservative Canadians, who thought of me as one of their own, were shocked when I would attack the monarchy and suggest that our political model should be California. Direct democracy would give us a check on politicians' tendency to abuse power by bribing individuals and groups into becoming their clients. The two, four, and six fundamental words no one should ever forget about government are power corrupts, power corrupts, power corrupts.

Walt Whitman had characterized old-world government as permeated by "the smells of princes' favours," and that still seemed true in Canada. As I was working that idea into my manuscript I happened to meet socially the Secretary of State in the government of Canada, a pleasant fellow who asked me what my next book was about and thought it appropriate to comment, "And I'll be making it possible for you to publish it." I said nothing, but was inwardly furious that some goddamned politician should think he could take credit for the existence of any of my books. My publisher was not, at that time, relying on any of the subsidy programs run by the Secretary of State. I was always proud that all but one of my speaking engagements outside of Canada had been outside the subsidized "Cancult" circuit.

I built *Right Honourable Men* — its working title was "Princes' Favours"— mostly from the rich body of writing that had accumulated about Canadian politics and politicians. I had read most of it in preparation for teaching. I now reread Canadian political history and reworked it into a new synthesis. Some of the themes and nuances that emerged surprised me, such as the staid Victorianism of Sir John A. Macdonald in his later years, Sir Robert Borden's unflinching moral dedication as a wartime prime minister, the mediocrity of the Arthur Meighens and Joe Clarks of Canadian politics (men who, as was said of a British politician, always played the game and always lost), the camouflaged mediocrity of Louis St. Laurent, the concern by many who knew him about John Diefenbaker's mental stability, and Lester Pearson's unhealthy relationship with a truly dangerous mediocrity, Walter Gordon.

The more I reflected on Mackenzie King, prime minister off and on from 1921 to 1949, whom it had become fashionable to ridicule for his strange ideas about spiritualism, his sexual anxieties, and his total lack of charisma, the more I admired his intelligence, his understanding of the country, and his effectiveness. He was the only prime minister to merit two chapters in my book. I judged him Canada's best. But I also rated Pierre Trudeau, a completely different personality, almost as highly as King. From his ascent to leadership in the 1960s to the constitutional fights of the 1980s and 1990s, Trudeau compensated for many mistakes with personal intelligence, tough-mindedness, cultural sensitivity, and commitment to our country.

He was the last Canadian politician so personally admired that people might name a child after him, the way Americans honour Washington, Jefferson, Lincoln, Roosevelt (and possibly Obama?). I mentioned this in lectures and twice had students come up to me and offer their birth years, 1968, and their given names, "Elliot" in one case, "Pierrette" in the other, as supporting evidence. I told our children that Trudeau would be a pretty good role model for them to follow. Not unreasonably, they replied that perhaps I could finance years of study at Harvard, the Sorbonne, and the London School of Economics, plus sports cars all round.

Brian Mulroney was in almost every way a throwback to an older, fairly common North American tradition of social climbing through politics and patronage. Mulroney was an Irish Catholic, not without skills and smarts, who would have made a good minister in a Macdonald government or a good mayor of Boston in the 1940s. But when it came to charting a course for the future of Canada and holding the highest office in a modern democracy, Mulroney had been hugely out of his depth. Mulroney was notoriously intellectually shallow, "shallow as a birdbath" I wrote (and Liz named our birdbath the Mulroney), and in that respect comparable to the genial, street-smart character of Sam Malone in the popular television series *Cheers*. The exact extent of the moral compromises Mulroney had been willing to make to achieve power and personal wealth was always hard to evaluate, but journalists and others had made a strong case for concluding that his governments were contaminated with a layer of political sleaze and sewage that sometimes rose to the top. I did not know whether, as prime minister of Canada, Brian Mulroney had been personally "on the take," to use writer Stevie Cameron's loaded phrase. I thought he was too careful to do anything really sleazy. As it unfolded after Mulroney left office, episode by episode, year after year, the story of Mulroney's acceptance of substantial cash payments from the really sleazy German lobbyist, Karl-Heinz Schreiber, and his absurd explanations of his mendacity, showed that I had been naïve.

The first edition of *Right Honourable Men* ended on the hopeful note that in the 1990s Canadian politics were beginning to come to terms with the coming of modern democracy. A reform spirit, I thought, was in the air. There was literally a Reform Party, the public seemed to be holding politicians to higher ethical standards, and the fiascos of Meech and Charlottetown had surely shown the limits of the political scientists' ugly phrase, "elite accommodation." From 1992 through 1994 I made these and similar points often, on broadcasts and in articles for the *Toronto Star*. After Meech and Charlottetown I was in steady demand as an academic pundit.

I hoped that the Progressive-Conservative party might reform itself after Mulroney — Preston Manning's break with Mulroney to create a separate Reform Party in 1986 should surely have been a major wake-up call — but was less than impressed by the choice of Kim Campbell as his successor. If Mulroney was Sam Malone, Ms. Campbell seemed to have much in common with his barmaid, Diane Chambers. She had not impressed me in our constitutional debates and she did not impress me or anyone else as prime minister, particularly during the 1993 election campaign. September 28, 1993:

> Prime Minister is on "Morningside," absolutely pathetic. Completely out of her depth. No understanding of economics whatever. Outrageous contradictions.
>
> An archetypal naïve politician. Trying to play the old game, and doing that badly. Just a hamburger for real pros like Chrétien and Manning. At best a backbencher, junior minister.

I planned to vote for our Reform candidate in 1993, but at the last moment concluded that "too many right wingers are unpleasantly sour and selfish," and voted Liberal. Perhaps the Liberals would bring about reform. Certainly the Canadian people had had enough of the Progressive-Conservative Party. Brian Mulroney and Kim Campbell left it in complete ruin, reduced to two seats in the House of Commons. The self-immolation of a Canadian political tradition.

My profile in public policy debates led to more speaking engagements, more conferences and panels, and more speculation by friends and others that I was ambitious to go to Ottawa. It was natural to assume that someone who had so much to say about public life wanted a larger role in public life. I was occasionally consulted by senior civil servants, sometimes by a cabinet minister, but only for casual background input. I never had significant access to any corridors of power and distrusted people drawn to politics so they could wield power. Years earlier, when approached by a former student, Tony Clement, I had turned down an opportunity to be in on the ground floor of the rebuilding of the Ontario Progressive-Conservatives under Mike Harris's leadership. In February 1994, the Liberal backroom "rainmaker," Senator Keith Davey, invited me to lunch and asked about my ambitions. I told him that all I wanted to do was write and be an academic, and never heard from him again.

The more I wrote about public life, the more I realized that my greatest satisfactions in life, family excepted, came as a writer working alone in my study. I did not find writing pleasant or easy in any conventional sense. For me it was always intense intellectual work. The metaphors I used to describe a day at the desk ranged from "slogging"— usually when piecing history together from documents — to "skating on thin ice" — doing journalism and lectures at a very fast pace. Writing was often frustrating and exhausting, and the exhaustion became physical when hyperactive thoughts led to insomnia. But it was also deeply satisfying to literally be writing history; to be writing informed, effective journalism; to work through intellectual tangles; to polish sentences and paragraphs until they shone. I was more alive intellectually in long hours in my study than anywhere else or with anyone else. When I was not regularly writing I feared that my skills and my mind were rusting, decaying. Most of the time I realized that writing was the essence of my vocation.

I had mixed feelings about many social situations. I could go through the motions easily enough, but seldom enjoyed public events, less so as the years passed. It was often strenuous to seem effortless, unnatural to seem sincere, contrived to be charming. Socializing could be energizing after a period of solitude, but in more than small doses its stresses included the peculiar anxiety that comes from painful boredom. I knew some writers who seemed to glory in conversation. In 1995, we spent a memorable evening, for example, with three great Canadian popularizers, Pierre Berton, Charles Templeton, and Arthur Hailey; their table talk was endless, rich, and easy. Closer to home, Liz Bliss had changed from a shy Harrow girl, ill at ease with academics, into a far more natural conversationalist than her husband. She genuinely liked people and enjoyed their company. When we were first married she had had to drag me away from parties; now I was usually the one who wanted to go home first.

My unease was less obvious but perhaps closer in spirit to that of four creative writers I occasionally saw at public events. Haunted by his genius, my friend Hugh Hood had trouble containing his ego in conversation, or listening. Robertson Davies was a shy man, bereft of small talk, hiding behind a façade of ritual and high culture. Margaret Atwood probably tried hard, but obviously had trouble suffering the social and intellectual foolishness generated by other people. Mordecai Richler was warm and funny in one-on-one conversation about family and values, but in formal social situations, such as interviews or talks about his work, froze up and took visible refuge in tobacco and alcohol. I didn't like the number of social situations in which I found it easy to choose the lubrication of another drink. After a few days of even moderately heavy socializing, I had to recharge my batteries with solitude.

The corollary of being a temperamental outsider, walking and running by myself, was that I felt little loyalty to or fulfillment in the work of organizations. I could play on a team when I had to, but, Bartleby-like, preferred not to. I was not a natural joiner, and was seldom content to submerge my views for the sake of getting along. Compromising never came naturally, and too often seemed to mean standing down morally. Every time I joined a political party I left it within a few months. It was even hard being an employee of a university, one of society's most tolerant organizations. Governance and administration were intellectually undemanding, but the thought of being responsible for the decisions they took, or for organizing events, almost frightened me. What if things went wrong? Deep personal insecurity and fear of failure lurked just below the surface through most of my life.

The best way of containing these anxieties, maybe the easiest or laziest way, seemed to be to turn inwards, not to have to rely on others. At my typewriter or computer I had total control of what went down on paper. Time was not wasted. Productivity was real and measurable. When all else failed click on Word Count. There were few working days when I could not create three thousand new and publishable words, three times John Kenneth Galbraith's guideline. And I loved the creative process.

If writing provided my best intellectual experiences, researching in archives was a close second. A person who is excited by documentary research and the ambience of scholarly settings — an austere carrel, a seat at a table in a book-lined reading room, the slow, sleepy buzz of researchers at work — perhaps has a claim to be a genuine scholar. I had felt that way during the Flavelle and insulin research. By the early 1990s, however, it might have seemed that I preferred to be on camera, chattering to audiences, or passing through an airport. Not much sustained archival research had gone into my last several books.

In my early fifties I felt I was at another crossroads. I could follow most of my colleagues into administration or some other form of scholarly inactivity, or I could muster the energy for another engagement in the historical trenches. Between 1992 and 1995 I gradually reoriented my career. I withdrew from many of my outside commitments, turned inward intellectually and at the university, and tried to become a serious historian of medicine.

The annual meeting of the Canadian Historical Association was always held in the late spring at the end of the university year. That was just when I would be anxious to get started on summer writing or research, the quality of presentations was never particularly high, and the social networking was unusually tedious. So I did not make time for the CHA or most other learned scholarly societies. By some standards, sometimes even my own, this was a lapse in professional commitment. Whenever guilt overcame me and I re-tested the waters, they seemed as cold and lifeless as ever.

Some of the ideas in my Creighton lecture became part of the intellectual underpinning of a new society, the Organization for the Study of the National History of Canada, which a number of my friends, especially Jack Granatstein, created in 1995. At its founding convention in Ottawa, I spoke to an audience of about 150 on a panel on the future of federalism. In the discussion I had a pointed disagreement with one of the young Quebec delegates, Stéphane Dion, who wanted English Canada to make far more concessions to Quebec nationalism than I thought possible. At this meeting I found I was losing my taste for all academic conferences. "Saturday night at the noisy pre-banquet cocktail party at the Chateau, I realized the last thing I wanted to do was sit down for three more hours with fellow academics. So I just left, bought a *Globe*, had a lovely quiet dinner by myself at a pub, then to the hotel and bed." Too many of the organization's members were like me for it to become important in the long run.

The Beaver had become a first-class magazine of Canadian history. By the early 1990s, Hudson's Bay Company Secretary Rolph Huband had developed a plan formally to donate the HBC's remarkable archive to the Province of Manitoba and use the ensuing tax credits to set up a foundation to support *The Beaver* and other historical projects. Rolph carried this out adroitly, leading to the folding of *The Beaver* into a new organization, Canada's National History Society. The *Beaver* advisory board became the core of the CNHS Board of Directors.

When we discussed possible activities for the new society I suggested that we fund a prize for a significant contribution to popularizing Canadian history, that we called it the Pierre Berton Award, and that we make Pierre Berton the first recipient. We did and he was and the Berton Award has become one of the most prestigious in a now-crowded field. I stayed on the new board for a year or two, thought it was time to move on, and left in 1994. My replacement on the board was, of all people, Joe Clark. Joe soon left the board to write more chapters in a career of constant political failure.

I had enjoyed the association with Toronto's Arts and Letters Club, but never being a club man at heart found it hard to fit A&L activities into my schedule. In 1993, I turned down the prospect of a term as president and instead let my membership lapse. A year or so later I also abandoned all interest in supporting the Writers Union of Canada, which I had joined, left, rejoined, and now re-left as it seemed have become a club dominated by whining literary politicians.

I had been asked to rejoin the National Business Book Awards jury and particularly enjoyed the opportunity to get to know its new chairman, former Ontario Premier William Davis. Bill liked to chat with me about politics, and informally I bounced off him many of the judgments that went into *Right Honourable Men*. Broadly speaking, and always off the record, he endorsed my views of all the prime ministers from Diefenbaker through Mulroney.

In 1994, our jury was sharply divided about Conrad Black's memoir, *A Life in Progress*. After our one encounter at the CBC in the 1970s I had seen Black at a couple of Bob Bothwell's parties, and at one or two *Report on Business Magazine* functions. His adventures as he transited from the Argus Corporation into becoming the baron of the Hollinger media empire had been mostly beyond my purview until I dipped into this latest book, which I thought easily the best-written of the year. But the businessmen on our jury, and Davis too, were flatly opposed to honouring a man whose ethics they considered suspect. That year's prize went to Professor Duncan McDowall of Carleton University for his good commissioned history of the Royal Bank of Canada. Which was fine, except that Duncan was a close friend of mine, I had given his publisher an enthusiastic blurb for the dust jacket of his book, and, ironically, the award led to criticism of me for having had an obvious conflict of interest. I decided it was time to move on.

I had joined the Board of Woman's College Hospital in 1989 under bizarre circumstances — at the request of a former college girlfriend, Gail Phelan Regan, heiress to the Cara Industries empire, who was leading a revolt to prevent the historic women's hospital from being swallowed up by the Toronto General Hospital. Gail and her friends carried out a dramatic legal coup and took control of the WCH corporation. Our new board kept the hospital open, our new managers got its finances into the black, and our feminist legal team fiercely fended off aggressive threats by the university's Faculty of Medicine.

It seemed to me that WCH, for many years the best place in Toronto for mothers to give birth (our children had all been born there), could have a bright future now that skilled women graduates were beginning to pour out of the medical schools. After the revolution, however, WCH still found itself being squeezed by a province that objected to the extra spending that had made our birthing experience special. In the Canadian system of the state as a monopoly insurer, we were forbidden to charge extra fees to cover a premium product. So we had to water it down, and become like every other hospital, moving the mothers and their babies out as fast as possible.

Woman's survived and ran a financial surplus only by gradually closing beds. At an early board meeting, I pointed out that we were heading toward becoming a profitable hospital by eliminating our patients. Seeing not much of a future in this, I left the board in 1993 as part of the rearrangement of my priorities. A few years later, Woman's entered into what became a stormy marriage with Sunnybrook, soon insisted on a divorce, and then carried on as an ambulatory facility, effectively without patient beds. It even gave up obstetrics. The women graduates in medicine, of course, are taking over all the hospitals.

A more natural professional connection was with the University of Toronto Press, one of North America's largest academic publishing houses, also a major printing firm and owner of Canada's largest university bookstore. Beginning with my work on the Social History Series of Canada in the 1970s, I had been close to the senior editors at the Press, frequently vetted manuscripts, and was involved in sometimes barbed discussions of such issues as the future of subsidized publishing, the fine line between genuine academic contributions and vanity publication, and the Press's obligations to the university.

A financial crisis in the late 1980s led to the creation of a Management Advisory Board, to which I was appointed. At first it seemed as though I had boarded another sinking ship, as we took large losses and considered selling assets. But one of our consultants, George

Meadows, who had extensive experience in commercial publishing, agreed to take over as CEO. In the early 1990s, George wrought an amazing revolution. He cut staff, cut wages, initiated performance reviews, incorporated the Press as a body separate from the university, and totally re-energized what had been a sleepy academic backwater. Meadows liked to regale us with stories of astonishing incompetence he had uncovered, such as the print division's having forgotten to fulfill a major contract for the Alzheimer's Association.

After a year or two of considerable turmoil, the Press not only broke even, but began making money. At our increasingly pleasant Board of Directors meetings we had to curb George's exuberance, reminding him that "profit" was not a politically or legally correct word to use in a not-for-profit organization. Soon, the Press was contributing substantial "surpluses" to the university to further academic study of the book.

The university's then-new president, Rob Prichard, former dean of the law school, was delighted by the turnaround at the Press. Many of us were delighted by Prichard's energy and priorities. At first he was not much of a public speaker, but he said the right things: at his first reception for U of T Fellows of the Royal Society, Prichard gave us a terrific pep talk on the importance of high-achieving faculty to an institution whose central value was the pursuit of excellence. It was fresh air after decades of retrenchment, denigration of faculty as just another lobbying special interest, and demoralization. Under Prichard's leadership in a new climate of liberalization and expansion, the University of Toronto began to flourish as it had not since the 1960s. Rob became our greatest president since Claude Bissell, perhaps since Sir Robert Falconer at the beginning of the century.

Rob had a highly developed sense of public relations. He liked to see faculty engaged in the media and in public debate. We did not always agree, and sometimes our sparring could get testy. A column I wrote in the *Star* attacking tenure as an unnecessary anachronism that only encouraged featherbedding, seriously raised his hackles:

It's not every day that you get publicly dressed down by your president, before a crowd, and in his house. Last night we went to the reception for new FRSC's, and we enjoyed ourselves, chatting with lots of old friends and university people. On the way out Rob shook my hand and then said, "I don't like your piece very much; I understand what you were saying, but others don't; they think it's an invitation to intervene; I can't tell you how much I've heard about it." I muttered something about the need to set our house in order — he said we are in order — we can't abolish tenure because of the North American university situation — none of the leading US universities has done it — I said that the leading ones have so restricted it that they've taken away much of its stigma. He repeated himself. I repeated myself. He said I wasn't making his job much easier. I did not say that that wasn't part of my job.

Various people in the exit line listened to this with great interest, and probably surprise. ... Liz followed along and said "I'll say something nice; our daughter loves the law program."

In 1993–94 I spent hundreds of hours chairing a hearing that adjudicated an attempt by the university to fire a tenured professor in the Faculty of Education, allegedly for having offended female students. Under archaic procedures, about to be abandoned, the entire process, including our judgment, was confidential. In a closely reasoned report, which I wrote, our panel concluded that the students had a legitimate grievance, but that the administration had not given the professor due process. Having spent hundreds of thousands of dollars trying to fire the man, the university had to buy him out. Prichard was quite annoyed and one day, as we were coming out of a meeting, told me that I would never have dared write such a judgment if it were to be a public document.

"Mr. President," I said, "if it were a public document I wouldn't change a single word." I was distressed that one of my best pieces of writing and an important contribution to the debate about tenure in universities would be forever sealed.

(Prichard caused me a mildly embarrassing, ultimately amusing moment one night at a small dinner party he threw at 93 Highland for a distinguished visiting expert in international affairs. As he introduced the table and came to me he said, "Bliss, what are you doing here? You're not supposed to be here." He had meant to invite Michael Marrus.)

The History Department seemed unaffected by Prichard's winds of change. We staged a splendid centennial celebration in 1991 — Barbara Frum's reminiscences of student days in Honours History were the highlight of a memorable dinner in Hart House — but we had little capacity to look forward. Entrepreneurialism, such as fundraising, or even acknowledging donations, did not come naturally to historians. Lost in the sprawling Faculty of Arts and Science, the department did not know how to counter demoralizing austerity. Even as the cost of long-distance telephoning was dropping toward zero, senior profes-sors of history at the University of Toronto were told it was necessary to submit chits detailing telephone use. Our offices were shabby, our support staff unhelpful. The department no longer had much collective *esprit*, high or low. It happened that Barbara Frum died tragically a year after our centenary, and her family, remembering her joy at our banquet, asked that memorial donations be made to the History Department. For several years we had annual Barbara Frum Lectures by world-famous historians, a glittering event. The Frum Lectures helped mask another chapter in the department's long decline, until they too died of neglect. Almost congenitally restless and unhappy in my shabby office, I was not going to leave the university, but I wondered if there were greener pastures somewhere else on campus.

(Some of my colleagues who have read these paragraphs consider the judgments too harsh. The History Department was struggling to renew itself and was able to appoint a new cohort of promising young historians, with more varied interests and ethnic backgrounds than in former years, and continued to do well in both internal and external appraisals. It's true that I was drifting out of touch with younger colleagues, perhaps behaving toward them more like a Creighton than a Stacey, and I've added these cavils because I don't want to be unfair. There does seem to be general agreement about the decline of departmental collegiality and historians' public profile both within and without the university.)

<hr>

I first saw high-powered medics in political action in 1989, when I served on an International Peer Review Committee to advise the government of Canada on how to distribute some $250 million in start-up grants to what it called Networks of Centres of Excellence in Research. I was one of two humanist members of a twenty-person panel, chaired by former Ontario Liberal leader Stuart Smith, that was charged with appraising and rating applications from networks of researchers from across the whole spectrum of academic disciplines. It was the biggest one-shot grant competition yet held in Canada. I never knew how or why I had come to be asked to serve on the IPRC, as I was mostly a non-person to Ottawa granting agencies, having refused to play the game of appraising Canada Council and Social Sciences and Humanities Research Council applications out of the goodness of my heart and/or in expectation that my own turn would come as supplicant.

In several day-long meetings in the winter and spring of 1989 we assessed grant applications for hundreds of millions of dollars from groups of Canada's best researchers, in fields ranging from artificial intelligence and robotics through cardiology, molecular biology, nanotechnology, psychology, and much more. The medical research community, I found, dominated the competition by virtue of its proven excellence and its leaders' shameless and ruthless appetite for success. Humanists and social scientists were utterly out their depth. Despite embarrassingly naked lobbying by SSHRC and the Canada Council, it was simply impossible to give more than token support to one or two proposals in the social sciences. At one point I told the committee that I felt like a restaurant reviewer assigned to cover the slum district, a remark that infuriated the SSHRC bureaucrats. It was a token of my own naïveté about the world of big money grants that I did not realize that most of the applications in the competition, even in those years, had been ghostwritten by professional grant-application writers. At the end of our deliberations the medical researchers had walked off with much of the money, possibly deservedly. It was typical of Ottawa that I never heard another word about how the centres we had funded performed and never sat on another jury.

But I became a high-powered ghostwriter for the Medical Research Council of Canada. Its president, Henry Friesen, a distinguished researcher from the University of Manitoba who liked *The Discovery of Insulin*, hired me in 1992 to help make sense of a stew of policy recommendations that had accumulated at a strategy conference and that a hapless consulting firm was unable to shape into a coherent document. I put in a few long days running the material through my computer and thus became the author of the Medical Research Council of Canada's first Strategic Plan. Doctor Friesen came back to me on several occasions to help with speeches and documents, and I saw a lot of academic research medicine.

Would I do any more academic research myself? "What are you working on? What's your next book?" was the constant question from friends and strangers alike. It was possible to consider doing nothing. Why not just rest now and coast to the finish? The thought had been on my mind in September 1991, when Liz and I spent a long weekend in Baltimore at a convention of diabetes educators. A visit to the beautiful, ornate, and musty Peabody Library in Mount Vernon reminded me that libraries were my favourite haunts, and that I wanted to spend more time in them. A visit to the home of one of my literary heroes, the Baltimore journalist and social critic H.L. Mencken, underlined for me his complete professionalism, his total devotion to books and writing. "Between his home and the Peabody," I noted, "I was powerfully reminded how much I want to focus my life on the production of good books, or at least good writing." I couldn't stop now.

Writing *Right Honourable Men* both assuaged my guilt about not having contributed enough to Canadian national history and convinced me that I had done enough in that field. I did not much care for the moral messiness of politics and its history. There was no more Canadian national history that I wanted to present, except in knitting sessions for the media. The idea of turning my lectures into a general history of Canada kept lingering, but I never became enthusiastic enough to make a commitment, perhaps because it seemed to verge on textbook writing or hack work. I thought I still wanted to contribute to original scholarship, still wanted to work in archives, and, above all, wanted to see if I could do more serious work in the history of medicine.

The problem was that my list of interesting and important Canadian topics in medical history was very short. Most of the time it consisted of one name: Osler.

Sir William Osler (1849–1919) was by far the most influential physician Canada ever produced. Even the bad biographies we had of him — there was no doubt that Harvey Cushing's 1,400-page "magnum Osler" had become out-of-date and virtually unreadable — were clear enough in describing the tremendous breadth of his work, first at McGill, then in the United States at Pennsylvania and Johns Hopkins, and finally as Regius Professor of Medicine at Oxford. Osler had not made significant discoveries, but as an educator and clinician had had almost incalculable influence on the course of twentieth century medicine in the North Atlantic world. His life was crying out for biographical re-examination.

I had not thought it was a project I could handle. Osler's life seemed so multi-faceted and so embedded in a rich and complicated medical times stretching over seventy years and at least three countries, and the archival sources were so massive and so scattered, that I did not think I could possibly muster either the expertise or the time to make sense of it. The only alternative project in medical history that appealed to me, a history of diabetes after the discovery of insulin, would probably be just as complicated as an Osler biography, and possibly less interesting. It would only be viable if I set a team of researchers to work, but I had neither students who were keen on such work nor any enthusiasm for supervising surrogate scholars.

The alternatives seemed to be Osler or middle-aged academic desuetude. In December 1993, having put *Right Honourable Men* to bed, I retreated for a week to Hazeldean with my copy of Cushing's *Life of Sir William Osler*. The aim was to decide once and for all whether to attempt a new Osler biography.

In the decade since I had first considered Osler after doing insulin and Banting, I had written three significant books, two of which were fairly wide-ranging. Writing Osler's life, I now realized, would be about as challenging as a presidential or prime ministerial biography. The sources were nothing if not rich. The Cushing biography's strengths and weaknesses were a good rough guide to some of the dimensions of the problem. The research could centre on the resources of the Osler Library at McGill, which lay conveniently on the path I was regularly beating between Toronto and Prince Edward Island. Necessary visits to other medical archives in the United States and England might not be unpleasant.

I could do most of the research myself, and the advent of laptop computers seemed to portend a major productivity improvement in translating archival work into manuscript. After hog marketing, pancreatic secretions, and the epidemiology of smallpox, I felt fairly confident in my ability to present technical material clearly. If the project took the rest of my academic life to complete, as I thought it might, that hardly mattered. I no longer had anything to prove to anyone. Osler would be pure bonus. If the project dragged on I might finish it in retirement. Or it might be the unfinished pile of papers my executors might donate to an archive. I could probably finance the research costs of the project out of my pocket, as I had my two most recent books, but if necessary I was surely well positioned to return to the grant-seeking game. So with nothing to lose and no competitors anywhere on the horizon I decided to give Osler a try. At least I would be able to tell friends that I was working on a respectable next book even if I had to admit having no idea when it would be finished.

My inward-turning, deck-clearing activities and the decision to tackle Osler were not a pure withdrawal to scholarly solitude. In my determination to keep options opened, I usually tried to balance intense scholarship with more public activities. In 1994, I was invited to become a senior fellow of Massey College. Massey had opened in the mid-1960s as a quasi-independent haven for graduate students at Toronto under the mastership of the anglophilic Canadian writer Robertson Davies. In the early years, I was repelled by the college's forbidding exterior and the musty, vaguely unpleasant odour of Oxbridge snobbishness that hung over the place. Like other mere mortals, I also found Robertson Davies intimidating.*

Outside Massey's walls, and outside of the university, there was ongoing interest in both my scholarship and my thoughts on public issues. In Canada, I was asked to talk about the discovery of insulin, business history, prime ministers, health care, national and even provincial politics. Opportunities to speak outside of Canada about the coming of insulin kept coming almost like clockwork, though venues and audiences could never be predicted.

In 1987, I had had my only excursion behind the old Iron Curtain, speaking to a group of doctors in Warsaw, Poland, with sponsorship from Eli Lilly's Eastern European division. At the firm's dinner, in a fine hard-currency restaurant, the local Eli Lilly representative ate the good and scarce food ravenously until his chair collapsed under him. In my few spare hours in the city I saw the empty stores of Communism, the shoddy plastic raincoats and boots worn by beautiful women in decaying

---

* And not professionally easy to deal with. A thesis examination of a student in our Drama Centre became seriously embarrassing when, as the outside examiner on a study of the history of Canadian playwriting, I was asked to approve a shabby, hastily assembled piece of work that argued that the Canadian dramatic tradition had reached fruition in the work of none other than Robertson Davies. After a tense, difficult oral examination of a clearly inadequate student, I voted against acceptance of the thesis. All the other votes being favourable, the student passed. It did not occur to Robertson Davies, who had been one of his supervisors and examiners, that anything in the situation might cause him a conflict of interest, and I did not have the courage to raise the matter. On the other hand, a few years later, when I asked Mr. Davies to give a named university lecture on the subject of "Magic and the Novelist," he was obliging and genial and gave a virtuoso performance.

public squares. Liz and I saw huge extremes of wealth and poverty during two weeks of insulin talks in Chile in 1990. My translator in Santiago was an elderly German woman, Eva Saxl, who was legendary in diabetic circles for her Second World War experiences in Shanghai. When the Japanese cut off insulin supplies to the civilian population, Eva's husband organized an effort to make insulin from water buffalo pancreas that kept five hundred diabetics, including Eva, alive for more than three years. Eva's Spanish translations were sometimes ten times longer than my English sentences, as my stories reminded her of various adventures and people she had met.

Driving home from a conference in the United States in 1995, I stopped to explore Chautauqua, New York, a Christian resort town frozen in time from the nineteenth century when it made legendary contributions to the popular culture of middle America. A few days later I was lecturing on the discovery of insulin in the ruins of an eleventh-century hospital in Cappadocia at a meeting of the Turkish Diabetes Federation. Beyond the expressway and the ultra-modern hotel where our symposium was held, peasants trudged behind donkey carts much as they had eight hundred years earlier.

In Nashville, Tennessee, our waitress at dinner in a downtown restaurant overheard us talking about "diabetes" and asked if any of us knew anything about Sir Frederick Banting. She turned out to be a niece of Banting's second wife, and it made her day when we told her what the paintings she had by Uncle Fred were worth. I didn't have the courage to ask her what she was doing waiting on tables in Nashville. While I was waiting to speak in Monroe, Louisiana, the friendly nurse-educator in charge of the diabetes day gave me a monologue on the need to discipline children, as she disciplined hers, by "whupping" them every now and then, whether they deserved it or not.

The Louisianans, like most audiences, responded enthusiastically to the story of the discovery of insulin, even though it had only one whupping. The hardest audiences to reach were Midwesterners, especially Hoosiers, who seemed genetically determined to sit on their hands at public occasions. However, the response in Indianapolis the morning I was to be interviewed for a video at Eli Lilly headquarters was dramatic enough: As we entered the Lilly corporate archives, where bright lighting for the interview had been set up and turned on, we were met with a sudden wall of water. The lights had activated a sprinkling system. After a few minutes of pandemonium — archivists scurrying around trying to save boxes of precious documents — the downpour ended, and teams with powervacs appeared like summer sunshine. I was later told that the water had only seriously damaged one portrait held in the archives, and that was of a lesser Lilly. We even got the video done, in a different studio. Perhaps it was only coincidently that the diabetes staff at Lilly headquarters, where corporate memory is always a problem, then got it in their heads that I was no longer available as a speaker because I was either seriously ill or dead.

The most lavish junketing we ever experienced, almost obscene in combining luxury and conspicuous consumption with *Reader's Digest* intellectual content, was at Young Presidents Organization (YPO) conferences at Whistler, BC, in 1990 and 1991. Billed as working holidays for busy CEOs and their families, and obviously crafted to maximize tax deductibility, the YPO conventions and "university" could charitably be described as Chautauqua for the yuppie rich. The beautiful attendees took it all in their stride — special trains, special banquets, special souvenirs, a special air show, and all the other special activities after the ritual two hours of daily lectures. Everyone was polite and positive. Keynote speakers like Stephen Lewis collected what must have been the largest speaking fees of their careers; lesser talkers such as Robert Fulford, Alan Fotheringham, and Professor and Mrs. Bliss, were along for free holidays and gawking.

The three worst functions I was ever involved in were trying to be a master of ceremonies at a giant, raucous Taylor Statten Camp reunion in Toronto in 1993 (what could have possessed me to try to make jokes about Kim Campbell?), trying to talk Canadian business history to two hundred chartered accountants who responded, I noted, "like a school of dead fish" (most of them probably had family roots in Indiana), and trying to give an after-dinner talk to five hundred parents and their diabetic children at a Disney resort in Orlando. On that occasion I had assured Liz that Disney technology would make the talk a piece of cake. My visuals of children ravaged by diabetes before insulin scared many of the little children I had not been told would be in the audience; then the vaunted Disney technology broke down completely and I never got to show my "after" pictures. At least the speaking engagement from hell had given me the opportunity to share a platform with Mickey and Goofy, as opposed some of their impersonators on academic stages. To vent the stress I went to "The Magic Kingdom" and, regressing to age ten, went on every ride.

I became tour guide as well as speaker when Eli Lilly U.K. brought parties of physicians and endocrinologists to Toronto, en route to annual American Diabetes Association conventions. The groups would land in Toronto, hear lectures about insulin past and present, then follow me around taking pictures as I showed off our insulin sites and our university. We would finish at the Fisher Rare Book Library for a special display of the original notebooks and other documents. This was always the highlight of the tour. To receive an honorarium from Lilly, paid at my suggestion, was a rare and welcome occurrence at the library. The jet-lagged doctors' day would conclude with a lavish dinner at the top of the CN Tower, capped with Canadian ice wine, and they would fly off — one year some of them bicycled off toward Boston — even more tired, the next morning.

The university and the Faculty of Medicine were very proud of our insulin legacy, but I had the damnedest time trying to interest anyone in doing anything to preserve and display our historical artifacts, let alone rectify the injustice of having buildings and departments and chairs named after Fred Banting and Charley Best while completely neglecting J.J.R. Macleod and Bert Collip. In 1990, a progressive dean of medicine, John Dirks, agreed to name our medical sciences auditorium, built on the site of the old medical building, after J.J.R. Macleod, and to put up a permanent historical display in the auditorium's foyer. The guest of honour at the naming/opening ceremony was Ted Ryder, the last of the original insulin patients, still going strong at seventy-four — in fact, he brought his girlfriend to Toronto with him. Even the case-hardened doctors were thrilled to meet Ted. When he came to dinner at our home, we ordered Jamie, Laura, and Sally to be present, as they would tell their grandchildren about having met one of the patients who had received insulin in 1922.

In July 1992, Ted became the first human to survive seventy years on insulin. He went rapidly downhill and died in the spring of 1993, mostly of old age, complicated by his diabetes. A few years later, I had a call from the Faculty of Medicine to tell me that they had just received word that the residue of Mr. Ryder's estate, some $56,000, had been willed to the University of Toronto to support research. His family also sent to the Fisher Library the scrapbooks he had kept while on his starvation diet in 1921–22, the ones in which he pasted so many pictures of food.

Toronto celebrated the seventy-fifth anniversary of the discovery of insulin in 1996, with a grand symposium that attracted all the top people in the world diabetes community. At the opening ceremony I gave a special talk, "A Field of Medical Dreams," in which I described the growth of clinical and research capacities at Toronto in the early years of the twentieth century, drawing a parallel with the command, "Build it and they will come," in the popular movie *Field of Dreams*. The big insulin companies, Novo-Nordisk and Eli Lilly, hosted gala receptions at the Royal Ontario Museum and Casa Loma. The Fisher Library put on a spectacular display of the insulin documents, framed by a catalogue/book that I had written. The university held a special convocation to honour two world-class diabetes researchers; I was the beadle carrying the mace at the head of the academic procession. The only sour notes in the festivities were caused by ubiquitous Romanians, who would corner me or anyone else they could find to talk about the great injustice done to their man Paulesco. Proving that chauvinism and pettiness were not exclusive to Romania, Charles Best's son Henry had written President Prichard, complaining about the way glory was being given to all four members of the insulin team, rather than to Banting and Best.

In Copenhagen, Novo-Nordisk marked the seventy-fifth anniversary with a special Steno Symposium, to which spouses were also invited. The spouses joined us for the ritual cycle to the Royal Deer Park, the libation of Tuborg ale in the Royal Pavilion, and the wobble on to a lavish dinner at the restaurant in the park. The next day we all took the train to Denmark's landmark contemporary art gallery, Louisiana, where, after a tour and champagne, the crowd packed the auditorium to hear me lecture on "The Discovery of Insulin: The Danish Connection." I still was not impressed by the art in Danish galleries, but it was a wonderful week for both of us, even if Liz needed to work on her cycling style. I wondered if we would still be pedaling in 2021–22 at the celebrations of insulin's centenary.

I was trying to cut back on media work in order to free time for Osler, but the next chapter in Canada's endless unity crisis, the Quebec referendum of October 30, 1995, interfered. Like many Canadians, including Prime Minister Chrétien and his cabinet, I had completely underestimated the strength of separatist sentiment when aroused by the passionate and demagogic oratory of Lucien Bouchard. October 19, 1995:

> I told Laura on the way to the campus this morning that for the first time I'm worried that the Yes might win the referendum. Bouchard ... has brought them a long way and the polls show a very close race. It should self-correct, but it may be a near thing. If we lose it will be because the volk have found a fuhrer — but the consequences will be ghastly. It really will be the end of the Canadian dream ... Nothing to do but to watch and wait. I turned down a request from Quebec's provincial television channel to come to Montreal, at their expense, to be part of a group discussing, with simultaneous translation, what the negotiations would look like. I told the kid on the phone that it was a fantasy to believe there would be negotiations.

I pundited in a minor way, but mostly wrote private confessions of dismay and despair ("I have trouble facing up to the possibility that everything I've been saying for years about Quebec is wrong … I had no idea at all how powerful the appeal of utopianism 1960s style can be") until the votes came in on October 30 and the separatists were narrowly defeated. It had been another low point in our attempts to make a country work, and left many of us feeling jaded and apolitical, if not exactly ready to stop chattering. November 13, 1995:

> Saturday noon I spoke on the post-Referendum situation to a luncheon of the Periodical Marketers of Canada, a trade association of periodical wholesalers. Hadn't thought it would be more than routine, but it was lifted out of the ordinary by the sponsorship of the luncheon: Montcalm Publishing, whose principal, perhaps only product is *Gallery Magazine* — "Home of the Girl Next Door" — fairly raw masturbatory porn. The organizer explains to me that they distribute all kinds of magazines and this is the way the sponsorship schedule happens to fall. Okay.
>
> At luncheon cocktails a *Gallery* centrefold, tastefully if tightly dressed, is on hand to meet people and autograph a (clothed) poster. *Gallery* gives a little presentation at the beginning of the luncheon, stressing their mainstream articles and how profitable it is to sell their mag. They give us all complimentary t-shirts and copies of the magazine.
>
> I give an intellectual talk on Quebec, lightened by suggestions that we could all cool off by reading *Gallery* and that the article on "Politicians with their Pants Down" may help us see their problems — though with Jacques Parizeau [drinking heavily and talking indiscreetly on referendum night] it might be "Bottoms Up." Talk

seems to go okay — no significant questions, though, but I think this is an audience only once removed from a mafia-dominated industry. Pocket my cheque for $750 and enjoy the rest of the day at home.

The unity issue settled down after the Quebec referendum. In its aftermath, our little group of concerned Toronto intellectuals held a memorable meeting one morning in April 1996, at the home of Deborah Coyne, who several years earlier had given birth to a baby fathered by Pierre Trudeau. Mr. Trudeau was in town to visit his daughter, and had agreed to talk about a dozen of us informally about the unity issue. At seventy-seven, looking fit and trim and tanned — he was just back from a ski holiday — the former prime minister presided over what turned into a seminar on the Quebec question. He had no new ideas to offer he said, only the need to keep promoting bilingualism, strengthen Ottawa's presence in Quebec, and try to keep the country strong. After about two hours, Deborah mentioned that Sara had finished her nap and was ready to go out. Mr. Trudeau waved goodbye to us and went off for the afternoon hand-in-hand with his little daughter, a beautiful sight.

I saw him again a few months later, at a conference on the public good held to honour his former colleague, Allan J. McEachen, at St. Francis Xavier University in Antigonish, Nova Scotia. The conference was a serious look back at the Trudeau years of Liberal governance, and I had been asked to give a keynote address on concepts of the public good during the postwar era. As I delivered a carefully argued presentation, mostly about the discovery of the limits of government during the Trudeau years, I was almost overcome by the realization that most of Trudeau's cabinet, and the former prime minister himself, were in the audience listening intently. They were very kind in their comments afterwards. Over drinks a couple of partisans did say that I had made three references to John Diefenbaker and only one to Pierre Trudeau. Liz observed, though, that a reference to Diefenbaker preceded by the phrase "crazy old coot" ought not to be considered a compliment.

Mr. Trudeau said little at the conference, other than to pay gracious tribute to Allan McEachen. In small talk at social events we discussed our children and the fact that both generations of Trudeaus and Blisses had gone to the Taylor Statten Camps. When I checked out of our motel on the final morning, Mr. Trudeau was also at the desk paying his bill with his credit card. I only saw him once more, briefly, before his death in 2000. On every one of these occasions I was left with a sense of having been privileged to have met a very great Canadian, an extraordinarily fine human being.

A sense of having been privileged to meet so many fine human beings — from great medical researchers at world-class conferences to ordinary souls wrestling daily with the curse of diabetes — sometimes haunted me. It was an antidote to the tendency to retreat to privacy and self-interest. It reminded me, perhaps not as often as it should have, of the responsibilities of citizenship and good fortune.

Chapter Fourteen

Osler

On June 15, 1995, I realized I had a problem with the Osler biography. Working at Osler's own desk in the shrine-like Osler Library at McGill, fighting the boredom and fatigue that often accompany archival research, I came across the letters and notes and poems young doctor Osler wrote in the mid-1880s to the three children of one of his first cousins, Marion Francis. Here is one sample, to little Bea Francis:

> ... I love you a thousand pounds ... I would give half my mustache to hear you laugh this minute ... My heart bleeds for you in three places ... You are the apple of my other eye. The left one. Gwen is the apple of the right ... I love you 1000000000000 pounds and don't you forget it ... Why did I go away and leave you? I have been homesick all the week and wished very often to fly away to the Island. I sing to myself. Who will take her on their knee? & who is smoking my meerschaum pipe? ... I am so glad you are better. Is your nose very sharp? Can you use it as a Knife to cut bread & butter? Glad you liked the ice cream — was it cooked enough?

There are about two hundred more postcards and letters in the file, all in the same vein, and they amount to a wonderful outpouring of love, imagination, wit, and verbal play. Never meant to be saved, the correspondence was a display of sensibility and skill reminiscent of Lewis Carroll. No wonder the Francis children worshipped their "Doccie O" all their lives. Perhaps there really was substance to Harvey Cushing's claim that the subject of his adulatory biography had been "one of the most beloved physicians of all time," and to the innumerable testimonials of friends and colleagues to the same effect. Everyone had loved Osler, I realized. And now me too? "This was the day I found myself falling under his spell," I noted.

This was not supposed to happen to an objective modern biographer. Part of the attractiveness of my project was being free to write a warts-and-all biography of Osler, one that drew attention to the man's peccadilloes, prejudices, limits, conceits. I had certainly done that in my biography of Fred Banting, with his almost unlimited capacity to be a horse's ass. Some of my biographical profiles of Canadian prime ministers, notably Brian Mulroney, achieved a level of frankness that incurred significant personal cost. The active former prime minister of Canada considered me to be an "arch-enemy" and I was *persona non grata* in traditional Progressive-Conservative circles. No matter. I did not think that as a biographer I was a muckraking "pathographer," to use Joyce Carol Oates's term, but I did have a professional obligation to tell the truth about my subjects.

What if the truth about Osler was almost entirely positive? What if he really had been a delightful, magical, nearly flawless person, and a near-perfect physician to boot? This would make him, I realized, something of a biographer's nightmare. It would be extremely difficult to present a credible and true portrait of Osler without being accused of hagiography, of having fallen under his spell and lost my objectivity. What to do?

I had decided to get serious about the project in 1994. As soon as I got going I began to see the biography's potential. There could be a fine and important book here, as good as anything I had done. There was no point in starting the project at a half-assed walk, expecting to spend the rest of my scholarly life on it. I began mapping the course and estimating how long it would take.

I was going to need help. The costs of research assistance and travel for a biography this complex, while much less than most scholars would estimate, would not be trivial. While continuing to rant to myself, and sometimes to others, about academics with their hands out seeking princes' favours, I decided to again swallow my scruples and apply for grants. Associated Medical Services, through its Hannah Institute, was the logical angel and they responded generously with assistance totalling about $35,000 — notwithstanding one of their appraiser's grumbles that I wasn't using enough Freudian or Marxian theory and should not work so quickly.

Unbeknownst to me, AMS was also funding a scheme dreamed up by my friend and colleague Ned Shorter to induce me to migrate and join him on the medical side of the campus. Ned, who had become our Hannah professor of the history of medicine, had his office in an old church at College and Elizabeth Streets, in the centre of Toronto's medical education and hospital complex. After sounding me out about my future interests — I told him they were entirely Osler-centred — Ned persuaded AMS to finance the conversion of the unused balcony of the church — we had to use a big ladder to climb up to see it — into one of the largest and most beautiful offices on campus. With major support from our entrepreneurial dean of medicine, Arnie Aberman, he was also able to promise me the services of half a secretary. I would have a nominal cross-appointment in the Faculty of Medicine and a vague title in the History of Medicine program, but continue with my normal history teaching responsibilities.

In my dreary quarters at rundown Sidney Smith Hall, with the department telling us to write our own letters, refurnish our offices ourselves, and submit chits for long-distance calls, I could hardly believe such good fortune. I left Sidney Smith with something like elation. My new quarters were an academic fantasy come true. What a delight to walk through the reception area at the church, walk into the supply room, and, Harry Potter-like, ascend a hidden winding staircase to my private little kingdom — all the bookshelves and filing cabinets I could possibly need, beautiful desk and credenza, work table, storage area, personal computer, personal stationery, windows on the great hall of the church, and the services of our secretary, the wonderfully helpful and efficient Andrea Clark. Moving to the Faculty of Medicine was like moving uptown. It helped give me a career second wind, helped make me feel that my excursions into the history of medicine were valued. In fact, the dean of medicine gave the History Department $10,000 a year transitionally as compensation for not having me in its corridors. Liz pointed out that it was now worth more to History to get rid of me, which we thought appropriately symbolic.

As icing on the cake I liked to think that when I parked my car at the Banting Institute adjacent to the church it was in Fred Banting's spot. The relics that eventually found their way to my office included one of Banting's desks, two of his pipes, and a piece of the parachute he was wearing when his plane crashed.

I used some of my AMS grant to employ Elsbeth Heaman, one of my most energetic doctoral students, who had just finished a thesis in Canadian intellectual history, to do preliminary research on Osler. In the spring and summer of 1995, Elsbeth almost overwhelmed me with the work she did photocopying, filing, and cataloguing Osler's output of some fifteen hundred articles, mostly in ancient medical journals. Elsbeth was one of the hardest working and most enthusiastic students I had ever seen. I found her thoroughness and enthusiasm for the Osler project another breath of fresh air, another challenge to rise to the excitement of the opportunity. I had sometimes felt tired and jaded and old. Elsbeth's good cheer, her discipline, her eagerness, helped get me going again — it was as though she had run with me on the first circuit of the course, a genuine and, in my career, a rare example of how youthful students can inspire flagging professors.

(Elsbeth herself was fighting professional and personal despair, as her attempts to find employment on the flooded Canadian history job market were leading nowhere. After she finished her work for me she went home to Victoria, BC, revised her thesis for publication, and then gave up on Canada and moved to England, looking for any kind of work. She was serving as a barmaid in Brixton when I urged her to answer an advertisement by a committee at St. Mary's Hospital, London, for a trained researcher to write the institution's history. Of course, I wrote a glowing letter for Elsbeth, but we were both a bit surprised when she got the very good assignment. Exactly on schedule, she produced a splendid full-length history of Mary's. She won a job competition back in Canada at Queen's University, and then moved to McGill where she holds a Canada Research Chair.)

I had thought it might be possible to have a manuscript ready by 2000. The precondition would be to secure released time from teaching. While I had a sabbatical scheduled for 1998–99, perhaps I could free up more time with a Killam Fellowship. Having been a three-time loser in Killam competitions, I crafted a careful, detailed, and humble grant application. I eschewed Freud and Marx and most social theory, but was careful to set my project in the context of the literature, explain its possibilities, and, of course, show its relationship to the work I had done. If nothing else, my track record was hard to deny, and in the autumn of 1995 I learned that in 1996–97 and 1997–98 Killam funds would pay the university to hire a junior professor to teach my courses. With the sabbatical, I would have three years as a research professor to get on with Osler.

Harvey Cushing had shown the way seventy-five years earlier, as he compiled the first Osler biography. Cushing had kept his every footprint, as it were, saving every document, note, and draft used in his project, as well as extensive correspondence with people who knew Osler and with readers of his book. Most of Cushing's Osler material was on microfilm, and became my first point of orientation at each stage in the project. It was delightful to be able to use borrowed or bought reels of Cushing microfilm in my office in Toronto.

I accumulated many weeks at the Osler Library in Montreal while coming and going to Prince Edward Island for summers. I also had to visit the Johns Hopkins medical archives in Baltimore, the splendid Huntington Library in Pasadena, the Countway Library in Boston, Yale's Medical Historical Library, and half-a-dozen repositories in Philadelphia. These trips were all strenuous because I was determined to minimize time outside of Toronto. I would be at an archive first thing in the morning — earlier than the formal opening time if I could persuade the staff to let me in — and would work until closing, taking the briefest possible coffee breaks and half an hour for lunch. Sightseeing was done on the fly.

Some days were particularly fruitful. Philadelphia, December 1996:

> Wednesday one of the busiest archival days I've ever had. At 8.35 I'm at the Philadelphia City Archive at 401 Broad St. N., a rundown area, an old forties type office building, the archive not changed much since the forties. But friendly enough and it takes only 5 minutes before I'm looking at the Blockley Minutes for Osler's years (actually the Board of Guardians). Not a lot there, but useful, very useful in some ways.

> At 10.30 a cab to Franklin Field, the Upenn football stadium, which also houses the Upenn archives. Very friendly, and also some useful material — Minutes of Medical Faculty, Weir Mitchell's nb letter recommending Osler, realization of the importance of the theme of gentle-manliness — discovery of the pathologist who gets left out — quick lunch at the student food court. Finish there at 3 and over to the main Upenn library, where they have Wm. Pepper papers.

> Do the paperwork to see Pepper, dash through the finding aid, check out letters in six boxes, all by their 4.30 closing time. There it is — three key archives in

one day ... Very fruitful for the project, but I wish I were home....

Won't have many memories of my first visit to Phil. Didn't see the historical area. City hall quite a glorious baroque structure. The Coll. of Physicians itself in a neat area, next to First Unitarian Church, one of the first in the US, now 200 years old, which was having a Christmas tree sale, and listed the Andy Warhol Foundation as one of the sponsors of its renovations. Next door to the Sidney Hillman medical centre for workers in the garment trade. Etc. Saw a bit of the Rittenhouse Square district, but was just not going to take the time. I want to be home. It's been a four day sprint.

The most memorable sight in Philadelphia had actually been Osler's brain, which had been preserved for later study after his death, and could be viewed by appointment at the Müttart Museum. In 1996, the brain was no longer an impressive specimen: "Some tissue cloaked largely in cotton in a jar. Sad pathological specimen — the part of his body that goes on, and is an ultimate symbol of something or other." Later, I found that I could squeeze more interest out of Osler's brain, not least because his own early work had been in the dead house, detaching, preserving, and studying organs. What a fine true story: that Osler had put on a special display of diseased brains at the Canadian Medical Association's 1880 meeting in Canada's Parliament Buildings.

Nobody else was working on an Osler biography. Unlike science, historical research is seldom very competitive. But early in the work I learned about the existence of something called the American Osler Society, and, of course, wanted to join it. I was told that I had to attend one of its meetings and give a paper before being vetted for membership. Charles Rolland, the Hannah Professor at McMaster University and an "Oslerian" of long standing, arranged for me to give a paper at the AOS's

1995 conference in Pittsburgh. I described my project and some of my early discoveries and met the Osler buffs — a fascinating group then about sixty strong, mostly distinguished physicians but with a sprinkling of historians and medical librarians, all in agreement that Osler's legacy must be passed on to future generations. The AOS had been founded in the early 1970s as a kind of learned society *cum* fan club, and was now evolving into a senior counterpart to the larger, more academic American Association for the History of Medicine.

Members had presented and published papers on aspects of Osler's life and medical times; some, including Rolland, had done bibliographical and antiquarian work that was very helpful in my research. I was welcomed into the club, found it useful to check my knowledge against the collective insights of the Oslerians, formed good friendships and connections, and made a point of not missing the annual meetings. If archival trips were mostly lonely and strenuous, Osler conferences were rich in socializing, medical tourism, and opportunities to see great American cities. Liz often came.

Lecturing to the American Osler Society.

The highlight of our Osler travels was several weeks in Great Britain in September 1996. I did archival research in London and at Oxford's glorious and comically stuffy Bodleian Library (there was much to-do about my not having come with a letter of reference; I offered to ring up an Oslerian peer, Lord Walton, who liked my work), visited the grand old Victorian pile at 13 Norham Gardens that had been William and Grace Osler's "Open Arms" during their Oxford years, toured the old Radcliffe Infirmary in Oxford and the hospitals and the museums of medical London, and visited the bucolic almhouse in the village of Ewelme of which Osler, as Regius Professor, had been Master. We saw the seaport of Falmouth, where it was instantly clear why Osler's father had made a first career in the navy, and we tried to imagine the rhythms and sights and sounds of the Osler's holidays in seaside towns like Land's End, Swanage, and Bute. Insulin lecturing helped cover the cost of the trip, which we concluded with a few days at our favourite spot in Scotland, Kildrummy Castle Hotel in the Highlands outside of Aberdeen.

Following in a subject's footsteps, soaking in the places that shape personality and career, is a common part of biographical research. Many Osler sites were close at hand around Toronto. The Toronto Medical Historical Club, to which I belonged, had erected the cairn in Bond Head on the site of the rectory where he had been born; our presidential gavel was made from a piece of Osler parsonage wood. McGill still owned many of the pathological specimens Osler had preserved in the 1880s, along with other relics ranging from desks to topcoats. Visiting the daughter of one of Osler's cousins, I was invited to spend the night in a bed Osler had used, which had been brought back from Oxford after his death. I declined.

Where I really wanted to follow Osler was into the dead house, the morgues where he had carved out his early career as a pathologist by doing hundreds of autopsies on stinking, decaying cadavers. It happened that the secretary of the Toronto Medical Historical Club, Arthur Gryfe, was a pathologist who still did the occasional autopsy. He invited me to see one. Wearing apron and boots, I stood for several hours in the stainless steel and white-tile morgue of the Queensway General Hospital while Arthur demonstrated techniques of incision, organ removal, and dissection. I felt no queasiness, only immense interest and curiosity. I immediately understood the detachment a pathologist develops — the cadaver was just a dead body, no longer human. Still, most of the pictures I took that afternoon cannot be shown, even to students. And I teased Arthur for years about how for all his skill he had been unable to find the cause of the patient's death.

Among the living, there were many Osler relatives in and around Toronto and Montreal. They were invariably interested and helpful, not proprietary, but could not supply me with more than a few new documents. I met just three people who had actually met Osler. Two had the dimmest of childhood memories. The third, Betty Harty, had been Osler's five-year-old chum at Oxford in 1918, a year before his death. Eighty years later, she told me vivid stories of sitting on Osler's feet to keep them warm on cold days, setting out with him to dig to China in their garden, how he removed black magic spells by eating the centres of cakes sent from Canada, how he led the children in rain dances, told them ghost stories, did card tricks, gave them maple sugar, and promised her that when she left England she could have the rabbit from the Peter Pan statue in Kensington Gardens. All her life, Betty Harty Osler Nelles (she married a relative) remembered the magic of Osler, and her eyes filled with tears when she told me of hearing about his death and how they tried to do his rain dance and rain chants but nothing happened.

Osler had been a great teacher of clinical medicine. I asked to be allowed to follow some of our faculty's finest teachers on their hospital rounds, and immediately realized that teaching skills are not specialty specific, but are mostly a function of personality and commitment. The Osler literature contained dozens of articles by former students and colleagues who marvelled at the man's knowledge, grace, commitment, tolerance, friendliness, equanimity, and cheerfulness. There was no evidence of Osler warts anywhere in the literature — except for his real "cadaver warts," small tubercular growths on his hands from handling bodies in the dead house (he would not have worn gloves). Student attitudes to Osler had been summed up by an intern at Johns Hopkins: "We all worship him and if it would give Dr. Osler any pleasure to walk over me, I would lie on the ground and let him do it." An obituarist wrote that those who had known Osler would remember "the privilege of having seen and felt power without evil — a transcendently beautiful life." Another friend had told Harvey Cushing that the problem for a biographer would be to capture "the shimmer of Osler's wings."

The attempt to do this gradually took shape in our personal paradise on Prince Edward Island. My writing always went unusually well there. We spent two or three months of every summer at Hazeldean, and sometimes in the shoulder seasons I would hide there for a week or two of solitude and writing. We formed good friendships on the island and cherished the refuge from the big city. I wrote the first words of the Osler biography in Toronto in October 1995 — the first sentence is homage to Cushing, a close paraphrase of the first sentence of his book

At Hazeldean Farm.

— but soon got distracted by the Quebec referendum and did not return to writing until the summer of 1996.

> Monday, July 15: Started writing Chapter One this morning. Sat down at 8.27, worked till 4.40 with about 45 minutes off for lunch and another 20 minutes when Phillip Gallant came by with a painter to do the touch-up job on the house. Very pleased with the progress, which amounted to well over 2,000 words. Much too soon to say this, but I may be able to write this book faster than I have planned — all my estimates of the work and research are probably pretty conservative — which would be wonderful. It was pleasant to be at the computer all day — none of the fatigue and frustration with writing that I've experienced often enough in the past and all my noting and filing systems appearing to work well....
>
> Friday, July 26: Yesterday was a perfect day. I didn't want to work but sat down at 8.30 saying to myself, "Well, if you take the day off you'll spend it thinking about fiddling with this chapter — no pressure, go ahead and fiddle" — so I started writing, moved outside in the sun at 10.00, and by 4.00 p.m. had finished the basic first draft, 11,000 words, and subject to one more revision, pretty good stuff I think. Certainly makes me happy about all the work so far — as though the new plane has passed its first test flight, or the first story of the building has been put up on the foundation and hasn't fallen down.

I was back on the island in early May 1997, writing even longer hours and taking time to capture my delight at the way the material came together. "The sources are disclosing so much. WO hasn't yet appeared in my dreams, but the other day during my afternoon nap I dreamed that

I got out of a bathtub and there was a severed head someone was using as a specimen … This is a writer's dream come true — as though all my powers and energy have returned. When I haven't been writing I've been running.…"

The end of that month saw an epochal event in the history of Prince Edward Island, the opening of the remarkable Confederation Bridge to the mainland. It had been several years in the building, more than a hundred years in the talking. As part of "Bridgefest" opening weekend, some two thousand of us took one final ferry ride and gathered on the New Brunswick shore for the start of "Bridgerace," a 13.5 kilometre fun run over the bridge. The runners included a piper, a pig, and several Annes of Green Gables. It was a grand event, though all the cheering, photo ops, helicopters, and congestion made it hard to concentrate on running. To participate I had had to pass up the opportunity to be a political panelist on Peter Gzowski's last broadcast of his great cross-Canada radio show, *Morningside*. I told myself it would be more fun to be present at a christening than a wake.

The summer of 1997 on Prince Edward Island was perfect. Everyone found that the Confederation Bridge was a vast improvement on the slow, erratic, albeit romantic ferry service. A huge increase in visitors to PEI was easily absorbed in a frenetic summer-long party atmosphere — "every possible fiddler fiddling and step-dancer stepping; restaurants on every corner, half a dozen festivals every weekend." The weather was perfect, day after day of sunshine, blue skies, green fields. Liz joined me on the island toward the end of June, and presided over a busy social time at Hazeldean while I filled days and nights with what I thought was the best historical work I had ever done. Often I wrote outside, setting up my computer on a table in our birch grove or in the shade of our pighouse. Week after week I recorded better progress on this difficult project than I had dreamed possible. Everything kept falling into place and becoming clear. One Monday morning, for example, I set out to read Osler's 1892 textbook, *The Principles and Practice of Medicine*, worrying that I was over my head technically and would never be able to say anything learned about the book. I finished it on Thursday, knowing how I would write about it.

Research and writing days have often turned out to be more productive than seems possible when, half-asleep, I sit down with my coffee to start writing in the morning. But nothing was like this magical summer with Osler:

> July 27, 1997: This week's work was the most exciting of my life as an historian. I spent five days fully engaged with WO, getting ready to write about Hopkins, and had discovery after discovery as I studied the sources … None is at all earth-shaking, but combined they add up to a wonderfully exciting engagement with my material — in an environment splendidly enriched by day after day of warm sunshine, so that most of the week I spent outside, looking up at the greens and blues of this place whenever I left the page or screen….
>
> I was with O and company from about 8.15 each morning until 4.30. The experience was so rich that I found myself saying that this will do: I've been standing on the academic mountain-top, breathing that magnificent air — week after week of it actually — and if I never have the opportunity or perhaps energy to attain such heights again, it's okay … whether anyone else appreciates these experiences or not can't tarnish them in my memory.

The golden summer drifted to an end in a haze of harvesting, the festivities of Old Home Week, visits from adult children suddenly showing impressive judgment in possible life partners, and long runs on the Confederation Trail and swims at Cavendish Beach. On Labour Day weekend Liz flew back to Toronto. I drove to Montreal for another week in the Osler Library. My first afternoon there, I was sitting at Osler's desk studying his old daybooks when I noticed that a student had just placed something at the foot of the inner "shrine" of the library, where editions of Osler's writing bracket a plaque behind which his and his wife's ashes sit. A freshman biochemistry student had left a bouquet of flowers and a card asking for Osler's blessing on his student life at McGill. Osler-worship was ongoing.

The writing continued in Toronto. It was not as difficult as I had feared to deal with the problem of Osler's nearly flawless personality. If the evidence of something close to perfection in the art of living was compelling, the serious job was to describe that life in its multiple dimensions. I had to delineate for my readers Osler's family inheritance; his cultural background; his interests in medicine; his medical times; his research contributions; his relations with colleagues, students, patients, women; changes in his views, his humour, quirks, and idiosyncracies; the impact on him of the Great War and his son's death on the Western front; his own illnesses and attitudes to doctors; and much more.

Important issues came up at every stage of his life. How had he gotten along with his clergyman father? Cushing had misled everyone on this. Had young Doctor Osler had an affair with cousin Marion, in fact, becoming the father of several of her children? The story was an embellishment by leering, Freud-influenced descendents, not supported by a shred of serious evidence. Was Osler a male chauvinist, discouraging women from entering medicine? Yes, but the Smith College Archives disclosed that the subject/author of the most quoted anecdote about Osler's misogyny actually worshipped him. Why was he so interested in Stokes-Adams disease, sometimes called slow pulse? Because he thought that he and his family were prone to it — a connection all the Oslerian physicians who had studied his articles had missed. Did Osler really believe in euthanizing sexagenarians as he proposed in his farewell address to Johns Hopkins? No, but his views on aging sparked the first major debate about retirement in America. Did Revere Osler's death at Passchendaele destroy his father's will to live? No. No one knew better than Doctor Osler how to grieve for the dead and get on with life. Did he realize that he would not recover from the bout of Spanish influenza, with complications, that finally killed him in 1919? No. Osler was a typical patient — gloomy when feeling particularly sick, optimistic on the good days. Beware the peril of selective quotation.

Every sentence historians write begs issues about the use of evidence and contains judgments about relative importance. During the writing of the Osler biography I felt more at home with my material, more confident in my ability to judge objectively — fairly, in context, verifiably — than with any previous project. Perhaps it had been important not to have tackled Osler earlier. Maybe maturity helped. Maybe the thought of the Oslerians, and their critics, looking over my shoulder, ready to second-guess every phrase, was a stimulus. Time and again I recorded determination to make the biography as good as it possibly could be; a master work. I wove important themes through the chapters — the clergyman's son who becomes attached to medicine as a secular religion; the Canadian who exemplified the best of British and American values (an aunt commented that the Osler boys were "English gentlemen with American energy"); the mentor and role model so impressive that he spawned a worshipful cult, including some of my friends in the American Osler Society; a running meditation on concepts of salvation, death, and immortality. I tried to set all the issues about his reputation (and immortality) in context in an unusual final chapter, "Osler's Afterlife" — that ends with a quasi-whimsical account of the survival of his brain. The last words of the last sentence are "the art of biography."

After showing a prospectus and draft chapter to several of the publishers I had worked with, I signed contracts in early 1997 with the University of Toronto Press in Canada and Oxford University Press in the United States. I resigned from the board of UTP before negotiating. They offered me a $25,000 advance against royalties, Oxford a further $15,000. Harvard had not been interested, and the Johns Hopkins University Press, a logical publisher for an Osler biography, had been unenterprising and cheese-paring. Oxford was logical too, because it had published Cushing's

Osler sixty years earlier. Unlike Cushing, I always intended that my biography would be a single volume because few modern readers have any appetite for a multi-volume life and times. I could now write to length almost unconsciously and could estimate productivity fairly accurately. With the idea of pushing myself to the finish, I contracted to deliver the manuscript by January 1, 1999.

The first draft was mostly finished by the spring of 1998. At Hazeldean that summer I revised and polished, intending, I wrote, to make the prose "sparkle like diamonds." Whether or not that happened, the summer's work went beautifully, only interrupted by concerts, runs, swims, and immersion in Prince Edward Island's almost transcendent beauty. There was no one time when I broke the tape with Osler. As with most books, there was a series of finishing experiences — the day of Willie's death in our birch grove, the day I finished the epilogue, the days I finished the footnoting, acknowledgements, minor revisions, further minor revisions, final corrections, incorporation of new material, and so on. It was like sprinting to break tape after tape. Almost the final finish line was reached in Toronto on October 7:

> It was eerie yesterday. By 2 p.m. I had everything done — the Note on Sources, the covering letters, phone calls. Suddenly there was nothing to do on Osler. Nothing — for the first time in almost five years. It had stopped, I had stopped. Just like stopping after a long run. What to do? — limp around in circles — I played some solitaire on the computer, read the newspaper, stretched out on the office floor and had a nap, went for a walk in the rain, tried to buy flowers for Liz but all the flower-sellers had quit for the day, went over to Massey early for a meeting and read a bit in the Upper Library. At home in the evening I stretched out in front of the tv, read the paper, walked, enjoyed.

There were a few more small changes to make, but the Osler manuscript went to the publishers more than a month ahead of schedule. I returned several thousand unspent research dollars to AMS/Hannah.

—————————————
—————————————

I became more involved in history of medicine activities while I worked on Osler in my church-balcony eyrie at 88 College Street. I overcame self-doubt and began considering myself a real historian of medicine. My history of medicine seminar was almost always the most stimulating course I taught. Most of my last group of graduate students were doing theses related to the history of medicine in Canada. Regardless of my leaves or travels, they had first priority in relationships that were always intense, sometimes trying, usually satisfying. Eventually six students earned doctorates in history of medicine under my supervision — Alison Li, Chris Rutty, Barb Clow, Geoff Reaume, Shelley McKellar, and Sasha Mullally — in addition to Renaissance woman Elsbeth Heaman. All but one of their theses has been published and the missing one should be. I learned more history of medicine from my students than they learned from me.

The Faculty of Medicine was pleased to support energetically publishing historians of medicine, but Toronto's tradition was not to incorporate history in its medical curriculum. We helped when we were asked — for some years I gave the first two lectures in a course for public health students — but Ned Shorter and I were left mostly alone by the faculty and its students. We taught history courses mainly to history students. We had an uneasy ongoing relationship with the university's Institute for the History and Philosophy of Science and Technology. Practically every contact I had as a result of my cross-appointment at IHPST, and the frequent requests I got for help from its students, became frustrating or worse. I made no secret of my belief that IHPST was too small and inbred to work as an independent institute within the university. Of course, IHPST outlasted me.

To raise our profile, Shorter and I organized a visiting speaker program, our Hannah Seminar, which became a well-attended and agreeable way of bringing four or five high-profile medical historians and their work to the attention of our community each term. After a presentation and discussion we would serve beer and sherry, then host a dinner for the speaker. The only problem with our Hannah Seminar dinners was Ned's strange schedule. Shorter had voluntarily enslaved himself to a routine of rising at 4:30 and running five miles to start the day. By eight or nine in the evening he would be tired and would become noticeably impatient for our dinners to end. When a speaker did not particularly interest him, which was at least half the time, the festivities would be cut off embarrassingly abruptly — though not on the night when the severely good-looking American academic presented to us on the rise of sadomasochism as sexual style.

I functioned as decorative and sometimes useful Canadian content in Shorter's kingdom. It was usually left to me to show the Toronto flag at meetings of the American Association for the History of Medicine or the Canadian Society for the History of Medicine. Graduate students came to me or to Pauline Mazumdar at IHPST, leaving Ned free to put in his miles, give a few seminars, consult in defence of tobacco companies and the Alberta government's former policy of having sterilized the feeble-minded, and write one scholarly book after another. He was easily the most productive and internationally best-known historian on the campus, perhaps in all of Canada. Ned always accommodated me and was helpful to my students, whether or not he genuinely believed they were doing anything significant. Dec. 3, 1998: "Shelley McKellar's thesis exam this afternoon — piece of cake. She is very impressive in her presentation and handling of herself. Pauline Mazumdar a bit of a problem, wanting to force the conclusions being rewritten, but we outvote her. Ned came into the exam wearing sunglasses and eating a big hot dog."

Massey College was my safety valve, my ongoing involvement with a wider academic world. I did not get off to a happy start as a new senior fellow — at a meeting of Corporation in 1994 we were asked to authorize naming the college's dining hall after a potential donor, Christopher Ondaatje. I thought it wrong to suck up to donors by putting their names on academic institutions, and I knew that in earlier years the University of Toronto had a policy against this. Buildings were named after distinguished scholars, not fat cats seeking ersatz immortality. Meetings of the Massey Corporation were almost always pleasant and non-contentious. Not this one. When we got to the naming question,

> I remark that this raises many more issues than I could possibly go into but that in general I find it offensive to my sense of academic values.
>
> This sets the cat among the pigeons, and the other members of corporation, one by one, led by president Prichard, disagree — saying that everyone sells names, that it's consistent with university policy, that there's nothing wrong with honouring donors this way, citing (quite incorrectly) Burwash Hall, citing Leland Stanford and Stanford U., various American examples, the middle ages, *etcetera*.
>
> I make one interjection after this, suggesting that we could sell fellowships next, and then … degrees, and perhaps we could, on the Stanford model, put the name of the university up for sale.
>
> There were more disagreements with me — not a single expression of support — and a vote to accept the report with one abstention, mine. I restrained myself and did not utter the word "prostitution," nor observe that the concept of being *On the Take* [a recent book on Canadian scandals] struck much closer to home than I had realized.

Upset by such dissent and division, the Masseyites were further alarmed because I appeared to be criticizing the college's first successful fundraiser, John Fraser. In fact, John had been a good friend for many years as the husband of my dearest former student, Liz MacCallum, and we had worked together professionally when he edited *Saturday Night*. I was the first person to tell John what I had said at the corporation meeting. He laughed off my concerns, saying fundraising was a swamp. I took comfort in the thought that many people in academia would assume that Ondaatje Hall honoured the creative writer Michael Ondaatje, Christopher's brother.

Its bare exterior can still be off-putting, but Massey College is an architectural masterpiece. To sit in the (still unnamed) common room and observe the tranquil life of its perfectly proportioned quadrangle lifts the spirit. And usually the people at Massey were even better than the bricks. Its senior and associate fellows were among the finest minds in the university, its junior fellows slightly smarter. Luncheon conversations at the college were almost always stimulating (the exception was the day nobody could stop talking about Bill Clinton and Monica Lewinsky), far better than the talk I had experienced at any other college high table or common room. Grand old men of the university, such as Claude Bissell or Douglas Le Pan, might put in an appearance; your tablemate could be a refugee journalist from Zimbabwe, a law student from Australia, a shy physicist from Manitoba. Someone from the CBC might be visiting to discuss upcoming Massey Lectures. The scientists would be entertaining a Nobel laureate — if not, we had our homegrown Nobel, chemist and polymath John Polanyi. Preston Manning, Bob Rae, any number of politicians and judges might turn up in the cafeteria line. Formal high table dinners in the college, held about eight times a year, were particularly elegant, glittering occasions, a special blend of ritual, good food and wine, shameless academic back-scratching, and the best kind of respect for civility, the life of the mind, and the quest for excellence. In my early years at Massey I went to all of them, and I never had a boring evening, which is the best testimonial I can give.

In 1995, John Fraser succeeded Anne Saddlemyer to become the college's fourth master. Fraser was born to be master of Massey College. His first stroke of genius was to fix the sagging leather seats in the dining hall without offending our heritage vigilantes. Having saved our butts, as it were, he went from strength to strength, perfectly blending respect for the college and its traditions — John was a pure Church of England Red Tory — with a determination to reach out to, welcome, and tap the broader community. His enthusiasm for his college, his friendliness and generosity of spirit, his commitment, the sense he conveyed that everything in Massey and in life should be taken both seriously and with several grains of salt, made him an enormous success.

Certainly there were odours of privilege in the air at Massey, plummy whiffs of steak, scotch, strawberries, and social concern. John collected people, he dropped names, he gossiped. He exulted in social coups — the day the Duke of Edinburgh, who had laid our corner-stone in 1962, returned to Massey, the visit from the Queen of Sweden, collegial contacts with governors-general, lieutenant-governors, all the high and mighty. But there were also big bursaries at Massey for junior fellows, a haven for refugee journalists, and hearings for advocates of every good cause. When I asked John's wife, Liz MacCallum, what she thought of a *Toronto Life* profile of John that stressed his love of establishment types, she said that was true but the author had failed to emphasize that John is a truly good person. Most of us at Massey in the Fraser years understood this, just as we also understood that John's Liz probably outshone him in goodness, common sense, and toughness.

I did not share John's religious beliefs, his devotion to the monarchy, or many of his other enthusiasms. My inclination was to be a monkish, reclusive, gradgrind scholar and iconoclast. But time and innate conser-vatism were having their effect, seniority and productivity were opening doors. I had entré to several establishments in Canada — the highest levels of academe, good friends in literate business circles, friends and acquaintances in politics and journalism, and contacts I'd made in medicine. These all generated more opportunities for work, occasions where I felt privileged to be involved, and, at times, led to unexpected honours.

There was usually a low buzz from people bending my ear about books I should write — an attack on the monarchy, a biography of a famous criminal lawyer, a history of the Law Society of Upper Canada, the story of the discovery of vitamin Q, a revision or abridgement of *Northern Enterprise*. I seriously considered the latter, but found that the business scene was changing too quickly for a revision to work (I would have had to rewrite half the book), and, in any case, my heart was not in it. I gave much more consideration to the opportunity to follow the Osler biography by writing the official history of the University of Toronto. It was a project that had been conceived, nurtured, aborted, resurrected, and generally kicked around, often at high cost, from about the time I had joined the faculty in the 1960s. I came close to buckling under pressure from Rob Prichard, but finally decided that committing to another big project immediately after Osler would be too strenuous, like starting a new marathon the next day.

The chronology is a little vague, but I believe I played a crucial role in suggesting to Prichard that his friend and colleague in the law school, Martin Friedland, should be sounded out about the project. At high table at Massey one night, I raised the idea with Friedland, arguing that he was ideally qualified. Prichard was keen, Marty was keen, and in 2002 some thirty-five years of false starts and confusion ended with the publication of Friedland's magisterial *The University of Toronto: A History*.

In the late 1990s, Henry Friesen at the Medical Research Council hired me to help them update the strategic plan I had written a few years earlier. We spun our wheels at first because there was confusion about where an austerity-ravaged council wanted to go. I was an amanuensis at meetings of Friesen's inner circle of advisers, doing all I could to help steer discussions toward a developing vision of turning the MRC into a Canadian Institutes of Health Research (CIHR) on the model of the National Institutes of Health in the United States. I watched, ghosted, and eventually wrote preliminary histories of the transition as Henry mastered the art of lobbying, played to Liberal Ottawa's interest in bold initiatives in the funding of research, and, under the sexy umbrella of the new CIHR, helped double the annual budget for medical research in Canada.

My medical friends' intense belief that their work served humanity made them convincing and powerful advocates. I had private doubts about whether it could be shown that investments in medical research generated the results the researchers confidently anticipated, but how could you argue with the search to save lives, especially if you were the historian of the discovery of insulin? Less privately, I also questioned the conventional wisdom that Canada's single-payer system of state health insurance gave Canadians anything like optimal health care. The belief that state planners could figure out how to match supply and demand in health care better than markets that were sensitive to incentives and price signals struck me as highly questionable. Apologists' praise for a system beginning to bog down in queues, bed shortages, and everyday cruelty to sick Canadians, seemed increasingly wrong, sometimes deliberately dishonest. I wrote a number of op-ed pieces in the *Star*, the *Globe and Mail*, and the then-new *National Post*, questioning the government's monopoly of health care and the straight-jacket of the Canada Health Act. These won me friends at the Ontario Medical Association and other doctors' organizations, raised eyebrows in left-liberal circles, and may have helped lay the foundation for the growing realization that our system was unsustainable.

Sometimes I balked at what I noted was "the endless round of festive dining occasions" that came our way. We were intrigued, though, when invitations arrived to events at the home of Mr. and Mrs. Conrad Black — once to dinner, several years to their Christmas Open House at the Black mansion in the Bridle Path neighbourhood of north Toronto. After his early adventures in Canada, Conrad had struck it rich in Britain as proprietor of the *Daily Telegraph* and then built his newspaper holdings into a great empire. He and his glamorous wife, Barbara Amiel, had become a force in conservative politics in several countries, and they tried fully to live up to a role as patrons of political discourse and the arts, in Canada as well as the United Kingdom.

On our visits to Black functions we were struck by the opulence of the occasions — the best of everything, servants everywhere — and by the grandeur of the house, its circular library, Conrad's collection of letters from Napoleon, Churchill, Lincoln, and many others, as well as the opportunities for people watching. Everyone seemed to turn up at Barbara and Conrad's Christmas parties — premiers and prelates, half-plastered former prime ministers, society models pasted into low-cut gowns on the arms of tired-looking bank presidents, tweedy university presidents, John Fraser, Rosie Abella, and even Conrad's old arch-enemy Ramsay Cook. In the ritual few seconds of social chatter, Conrad and I would always ask about each other's writing. He surprised me when he said he was doing a biography of Franklin D. Roosevelt, disappointed me with the conventionality of his interpretation. I had the courage to tell him that he had no hope of winning a lawsuit against Prime Minister Chrétien for blocking the plan to give him a British title, but realized that Conrad used the law like some people use guns — he was trigger happy and shot wildly. Eventually, he abandoned his Canadian citizenship, and the lawsuit, to become Lord Black. Privately, I also wondered about his judgment in thinking the Canadian market could absorb a second national newspaper. Surely the *National Post* would be Conrad's folly.

Increasingly, at social functions one noticed distinguished people wearing the pretty snowflake rosette that signifies membership in the Order of Canada, the honours system Canada had put in place in the 1960s in lieu of the old British titles. From time to time, I had wondered if I had a shot at receiving the Order of Canada, but doubted it. I thought I had made too many enemies. I thought it *gauche* to aspire to honours and would usually push such thoughts out of my mind. When my friend Jack Granatstein, who had been recently inducted into the Order, offered to organize my nomination I was flattered and agreeable, though not hopeful. But what could the downside be?

There was none. It was an unalloyed pleasure when I was offered membership in the Order of Canada in 1998, and formally invested, along with fifty-seven others, in February 1999 by Governor-General Roméo LeBlanc at Rideau Hall in Ottawa. I bought my first tuxedo for the occasion. Liz and I enjoyed every minute of the ceremonies, from Micmac prayers through the reading of citations and bestowing of medals, the national anthem, cocktails, a dinner buffet — I was at the chief justice's table, Liz the governor-general's — and partying at the Château Laurier with fellow inductee Sally Armstrong and her family.

Other inductees with whom we chatted that day included the poet P.K. Page (who was giving Chief Justice Antonio Lamer a hard time about the Supreme Court's recent liberalization of child pornography laws), Normie Kwong, famous as the "China clipper" of the Edmonton Eskimos in the 1950s, Major Brasseur, the first woman in the Canadian Forces to fly jet planes for Canada, and the always-rumpled, desperately-in-need-of-a-cigarette Peter Gzowski. Gzowski eventually got his cigarette outside with the governor-general's wife. Before the investiture there had been a special reception at the Château by the Medical Research Council for health care achievers joining the Order, our members of Parliament all in attendance. "How can I complain about anything to anyone ever again in my life?" I asked my diary, resolving to be a better person. "I so wish I had a parent alive to see this — I know what Osler felt when he thought of his family and of the climb from Tecumseth — above all you're sitting on your family's shoulders."

Two months later, I noted in my diary the development of "very disturbing international events." Canada was joining in air strikes against Serbia as part of a mission by the countries of the North Atlantic Treaty Organization to force it to stop taking action against the secessionist Albanian majority in the province of Kosovo.

> I don't usually pay much attention to international affairs, especially the tangle of the Balkans, but have gradually tried to understand the situation, and have become increasingly upset at what we are doing. The Americans

have dragged NATO into taking sides against the Serbs for their treatment of a minority — there isn't a shred of legality in NATO's action; indeed it's clearly illegal. Canada has never done something like this before. While I understand the humanitarian argument, it isn't generalized for other countries by the Americans — notably the Turkish treatment of Kurds — and if used sets the conditions for international anarchy.

I had seldom commented on foreign policy issues because I thought they were usually too remote and complicated for armchair pundits to understand. But as the Kosovo war escalated I began writing and speaking out against it, and filling my diary with reflections on why it was wrong for us to be complicit in the evil unleashed by reckless idealists. During that time I was everywhere in the Canadian media and at anti-war events in Toronto and Winnipeg, trying to explain why the cause was wrong and how serious the long-term consequences might become. I was part of a strange coalition of foreign policy realists, left-wing anti-Americans, and Serbs and their sympathizers. We had little success.

My stand on the war caused establishment pundits in the media to wonder what had come over me, and made me a momentary favourite of expatriate Serbs and anti-war New Democrats. I was also briefly first-named by Brian Mulroney, who came out against the war, possibly influenced by his Serbian wife, Mila. When I left a message of support at Mulroney's office his secretary asked for my telephone number and the next day Mr. Mulroney spent thirty minutes on the line telling me how completely he supported my position, how Jean Chrétien was making Canada an even more insignificant country with this involvement, and how it was all the fault of U.S. Secretary of State Madeleine Albright. "I told him I hoped he would use his behind-the-scenes influence. He said of course it's limited. He concluded by saying that one thing that would wake people up would be an op-ed piece in the

Globe written by both of us. I said I'd go along if he would. He said we'd see how things develop."

The war ended after three months, with Serbia's defeat, NATO occupation of Kosovo, and the beginning of Albanians' ethnic cleansing of Serbs from what, nine years later, breaking all sorts of commitments, they turned into an independent country. Disillusioned about many things, remembering why I had opposed the Vietnam War, and unrepentant about what I had written and said (perhaps I did go too far in calling the military "hired killers"), I gradually turned my attention to other issues. Involvement in public life was so often disappointing, disillusioning, demoralizing. As the aftermath of Kosovo gradually made clear, the establishment consensus could be wrong and dangerous and stupid.

Our children had grown into adulthood, earned a handful of degrees, and, after a few false starts, left the family nest. Laura and Jamie were lawyers, apparently intending to be British Columbia based, Sally headed for high school teaching in Toronto. Along with Massey College and history of medicine events, we still went to a few dinner and cocktail parties composed mostly of historians, other academics, and old friends like Jim and Kathie Spence. We were starting to enter the years of renewing old acquaintances at funerals. I started to lose touch with the rhythms of Toronto social and intellectual life outside the university. It was infinitely more important to go canoe tripping with Sally in Algonquin Park.

We left Prince Edward Island a week before Labour Day in 1999 and flew to Vancouver to attend Laura's call to the bar. While we were there my publisher couriered out my first copy of *William Osler: A Life in Medicine*. I examined and coddled and cradled my latest, and hoped it would have a long and happy life. *Osler* came with us to Laura's celebration dinner, where it had its own seat at the table.

Chapter Fifteen

Cushing

Osler was both a critical and a reasonably popular success. It earned out its advances in its first year and continued to sell nicely. It received universally glowing reviews, including a seven-page rave by Sherwin Nuland in *The New Republic*, and in Canada rose as high as number two on *Maclean's* magazine's national bestseller list — the first time a University of Toronto Press book had stood that high. First-year American and Canadian sales were about eight thousand copies in each country. While *Osler* never rose higher than about six hundredth place on Amazon's list of U.S. bestsellers — I soon realized that tracking its course was a mug's game — it did rank number one at Johns Hopkins.

The book market was evolving to favour shorter, simpler works of non-fiction — in the *National Post*'s bestseller list, *Osler* was summarized as "a big fat book about a doctor" — and I soon abandoned unrealistic hope that the book would sell like hotcakes. I was pleased that I was again a finalist for the Governor-General's Award, and not surprised when my big fat book was beaten out by a forgettable slim volume about water. When John Fraser announced that I had won that year's meaningless Massey College literary competition he said it was as consolation for not getting the Governor-General's Award.

It was actually for a submission featuring a pun on "acetylsalicylic" (aesthetes'll sell a silly kid). Osler would have approved.*

My friends in the American Osler Society generously praised and promoted my book, although I did overhear the odd grumble about how it still hadn't replaced Cushing's biography. The many living Oslers in Canada also seemed approving — I signed dozens of copies at a family reunion at Bond Head to celebrate Willie's 150th birthday. One distant Osler cousin did tell me to my face that she found it a dense read; on her evidence the read seemed to require substantial liquid accompaniment.

After the years off to do Osler, I returned to full-time teaching in the autumn of 1999 at a university beginning to be visibly transformed by changing demographics, prosperity, and a new spirit. Our student body had become culturally very diverse, while still reflecting high intellectual abilities, with a remarkable breadth of experience and opportunities. Walking into Massey College one day, I overheard a student telling another about a cousin who had just sold his internet company for $100 million.

Kids who hadn't been raised in protestant Canada had trouble getting their minds around some of the intricacies of Canadian history that we had assumed everyone understood. For Confucian, Hindu, Muslim, and many other students not bred by a lifetime in the Canadian public school curriculum, the distinctions and conflicts between Anglicans, Presbyterians, and Methodists in, say, Upper Canada after the War of 1812, now took quite a bit more explaining in our survey courses. Some of our once-required readings, such as T.C. Haliburton's classic *The Clockmaker*, were virtually incomprehensible to this student generation and had to be dropped. In general, we found ourselves having to simplify (the euphemism is "recontextualize") our Canadian history

---

* *Osler* also won the Canadian Historical Association's prize for the best book of the year on a non-Canadian topic and simultaneously got honourable mention in the CHA's competition for the best book of the year on a Canadian topic.

survey courses, a necessity not much to my liking. In the spring of 2000, I stopped giving my big Monday-night Canadian history course, and from then on taught only senior seminars.

We also noticed that enrollments in Canadian history at Toronto were beginning to decline, reflecting a trend at many Canadian universities. "National" history had been out of fashion in the historical profession for almost a generation. Social or cultural history, transcending national boundaries, was said to be the future of the past. Canadian history was additionally handicapped, particularly at Toronto, by its reputation, both deserved and undeserved, for parochialism. Colleagues in the History Department had always tended to look down their noses at Canadian history; now their hiring priorities included practically everything but Canadian, a bias that extended to the admission of graduate students. Ostensibly opting for recruiting the highest quality of students in the international marketplace, deliberately cutting doctoral enrollment — as well as their own not terribly strenuous workloads — my colleagues had turned their backs on Toronto's traditional role as the centre for training future historians of Canada. "Nobody cares," I noted after raising the issue at a department meeting in 2001. As fellow Canadianists retired they were not replaced. The Canadian "area," once numerically and academically the strongest in the department, shrank and then disappeared into North American history.

The brighter side of this coin was the opening of the university to market-like forces. In the 1990s achievement in the academic marketplace began to matter more than in the decades of stuffy, conservative, pseudo-egalitarianism, the years when quarter-hour differentials in work-sheet credit or hundred dollar a year salary differences could cause Pecksniffian expressions of discontent in endless department and committee meetings. Rob Prichard's presidency set a dynamic standard for the campus. Public scholarly achievement was noticed and valued. Academic stars were encouraged to shine, and their lustre rewarded. Public and private money was beginning to pour into the universities to support research, endow chairs, and attract talent. Salary and workload "inequalities" were disregarded in the competitive struggle to upgrade our best faculties and departments. The Faculty of Law, which had given the university Prichard and half a dozen other dynamic administrators, thrust itself to the absolute front rank in global legal education. The Rotman Faculty of Management tried to do the same. The Faculty of Medicine went from strength to strength as its researchers brought in hundreds of millions in "soft" but very real grants. If Rob had tried hard he might even have been able to reform tenure.

Sadly, the humanities and social sciences, traditionally weak sisters in the university, fell farther behind. A number of disciplines, notably sociology and English, tended to implode ideologically. Many others, such as political science and economics, seemed to turn inwards. There were exceptions, especially when dynamic individuals saw opportunities to transcend departmental boundaries. Thanks mainly to political scientist Janice Stein, who spent more time in television studios than any professor I ever knew — and she was good at everything she did — our Munk Centre for International Relations, at first just a tarted-up old residence building, became one of the university's most highly regarded intellectual loci. It was directly across the street from Massey College, which John Fraser continued to take from strength to strength — though what he hoped might be his ultimate coup, a visit from the Pope, proved beyond even his networking skill. Even in the History Department, a new chair, Ron Pruessen, simply stopped kowtowing to the forces of mediocrity and common-room politics. Meetings were minimized, the formal worksheet disappeared, salaries diverged more sharply, course loads were negotiable, and named chairs made their appearance.

I benefitted from many of these changes. Pruessen encouraged me to teach less, my salary increases were always satisfactory, my committee burdens minimal. In my church balcony at 88 College, I felt I had the best possible combination of Faculty of Medicine perks and History Department freedom. The deans of medicine and arts indicated that they were hoping to raise money for an endowed chair that I might hold — we hoped it could be the world's first chair in medical biography. Nothing came of that (it might have been a hard sell to donors anyway, even if Fred Eaton, an acquaintance from Flavelle days, had not been distracted from fundraising by far more serious problems with the historic family firm), but in the spring of 2001 I was given Toronto's ultimate promotion, to the elite rank of University Professor. With it came a further lightening of my teaching load plus $50,000 in research funding over the five years remaining until my scheduled retirement.

The Osler biography had gone so surprisingly well that in 1999 I found myself with no major scholarly project on my plate. Did I have an appetite for one more? What to do between now and retirement? Basking in seniority and the good academic life would be too much like vegetating. But there was nothing in the cupboard to turn to. I had thought Osler would be my last significant book, academic icing. I had not thought beyond it.

Osler had whetted my appetite for doing more medical history, ideally biography, but I could not think of another Canadian subject. After tackling the highest peak, it's not very interesting to trudge up wilderness foothills. I privately reflected that the only Canadian project that would interest me would be to do a full-scale life of Pierre Trudeau, the most fascinating public citizen of Canada in my lifetime. That was never a possibility, partly because of my lack of French fluency, partly because I had no Liberal connections. Shortly after Trudeau's death in 2000, it was announced that John English, who had done an excellent biography of Lester Pearson, would do the official biography. John proved a good choice.*

The most interesting figure I had come across while doing the Osler book was Harvey Cushing (1869–1939), Osler's protégé and

---

* The best short tribute to Trudeau in the days immediately after his death was Peter Gzowski's reuse of a remark originally made about the hockey player, Bobby Orr: "He should have played in a better league."

    I also heard this Trudeau story over lunch at Massey College: David Silcox, who had been at the funeral, said everyone felt limp afterwards. He had canoe-tripped with PET and told me of an incident on one of their trips when they had no option but to cross a very windy lake, knowing that anyone who dumped could not be rescued. When someone asked what they would do if the worst happened, Trudeau replied, "Paddle harder and sing stronger." I emailed that story to daughter Sally, who was on a canoe trip on the Churchill River in Labrador.

first biographer. I had known almost nothing about Cushing, but while working on Osler I gradually realized that Cushing was not only a towering figure in the history of neurosurgery — arguably the founder of effective brain surgery in the first decade of the twentieth century — but that he had left one of the best collections of personal papers I had ever seen. Looking for Osler tidbits, I had necessarily immersed myself in Cushing's correspondence and could not help realizing what a splendid entré it was into the life of a very high-achieving, very important figure in the history of medicine.

With Osler at the press in the winter of 1999, I reread John Fulton's fifty-year-old authorized biography of Cushing with a view to considering the need for a new one. Fulton's was a massive and murky book, but not quite as dated as Cushing's *Osler* had been. As well, I thought that the technical challenges of understanding Cushing's contributions to the evolution of brain surgery and other medical specialties (he was no mean endocrinologist, though he liked to call that field "endocriminology") would probably overwhelm me. Further, Cushing's was purely an American life. Did I have the background and ability to master and convey his embedment in American history? My Canadian background might be a handicap with Cushing rather than the asset it had been with Osler.

By summer I had fully recovered from the Osler project and was beginning to chafe about the need "to be saying something about something. I just can't be lazy and self-indulgent very long." *Faute de mieux*, I was beginning more work on Liz's grandmother's diaries with a view to writing more articles and then a book about this Prince Edward Island farmer's wife — "Lucy of Hazeldean." It would at least prove that I could capture the uniqueness of an obscure, ordinary woman's life.

On Thursday, June 17, 1999, I had a startlingly clear intellectual epiphany. I recorded it in detail:

> A big decision day. Last night I finished Ian MacEwan's
> *Amsterdam*, which I thought was very very slight

— little more than a good short story. This morning after finishing Kershaw's *Hitler* I spent a desultory hour with Lucy's diaries, thinking that while I could write about the rhythms of a farmer's wife's life, it was kind of unexciting — indeed. Then I went for a very long run along the Confed. Trail (12ks) that finished the morning and seemed to finish me, or at least my legs. When I recovered from it around 2 o'clock I settled in with Thornton Wilder's *Theophilus North*, rereading it with the haunting images I have in my mind of beautiful life in times past ... Once again I was struck on coming across the passage I quote in the Flavelle bio, when North says: "My idea was that somehow I might penetrate that magic world (my father used to call it 'plain living and high thinking') and glimpse those enchanted late afternoons in Newport when professors played croquet with their children until fireflies hovered over the wickets and a voice called, 'Come in children, and wash your hands before supper.'"

Not many minutes or pages after reading that I suddenly realized that my next book really must be the Harvey Cushing biography. It's the one project that would take me into that magical American world, but in all sorts of dimensions, including the interesting history of neurosurgery, including too the torments of HC himself, who was clearly a man of more emotional and personal complexity, I think, than WO, but with amazing talents and an immense appetite for life. There is also, of course, the Cushing family ... It's very much an American epic story, in all sorts of ways — the great universities in their golden age, the country's coming of age, the glamour of surgery, the glamour of Brookline and high society — also the fact that HC's career is the turning point — he's the first American [medic] the world flocks to see, setting the model for the future. One thinks of it as Harvey Cushing and the Promise of American Life.

As I mulled it over I realized that I need and want to put an end to the aimlessness I've been having — I don't want to go through the summer that way — that I need to start organizing and declaring another project — and also that all the Canadian projects I've been mulling over haven't amounted to anything significant that I really want to do — or that can't wait until retirement. If I'm going to do more medical history, which everyone thinks I should, this seems clearly the way to go — Osler not having led to any other follow-up projects. The market for the book should be good, and it's not going to shrink ...

This all came to me very quickly, almost as an epiphany ... This is very satisfying — I really think it's the day the future course is charted — and, in a way, is exactly what should result from this period of ostensibly aimless solitude and solipsism. It's like suddenly trying on a new piece of clothing and having an exact fit.

Or it was like the decision to enter another ultra-marathon.

All the second thoughts were positive. I had absolutely nothing to lose. Cushing would be an extra, a bonus, and it would not matter if it were never completed. The problems of writing about neurosurgery and doing an American life suddenly seemed like challenges to be embraced. I had always wanted to write about the United States and had thought Canadians are positioned as the outsiders most capable of insight into American life. I had read American history and literature all my life, I did not believe the border should be taken unduly seriously (Kingsville was only thirty miles across Lake Erie from Cushing's home city of Cleveland), and I had cut fairly deeply and successfully into American medical history with Osler. After mastering earlier technical projects, the successful puzzling out of Osler's complex medical life convinced me that I could eventually find my way through neurosurgery. Neurosurgeons would surely be available to help. One of my graduate students, Shelley McKellar, was finishing a thesis on a Toronto surgeon, Gordon Murray, and I found her deft handling of the history of surgery an example of how it could be done by a layperson.

There was also the joke writers make: when people who are barely literate suggest they'll take up writing in retirement, as though anyone can do it, writers respond that our retirement project will be to take up neurosurgery. What fun it would be almost to come close! There is a mystique about neurosurgery as one of the most difficult and exotic of all medical specialties. While it might or might not be a medical Everest, comparable only to rocket science, I thought neurosurgery was certainly a high peak, a challenging vicarious climb.

The clinching thought was the realization that I could spend the months it would take to scour Cushing's papers without having to leave Toronto or Prince Edward Island. The massive Cushing collection at Yale's Sterling Library had been photographed onto microfilm in an excellent pilot project during the heyday of enthusiasm for that technology. There were 157 reels of Cushing microfilm, each containing about 1,250 pages of correspondence and manuscript, and all were available for purchase and/or as a loan from Yale's Medical Historical Library — itself a special and friendly place that would be a pleasure to work in when direct visits proved necessary. I had read about a dozen reels of Cushing microfilm while doing Osler; now I could study the rest of the collection at my own pace and in the comfort of my own work space. I would do the research myself — time didn't matter — and knew I could either scrounge small grants or draw on my Osler royalties to cover travel and other expenses. It turned out that the research money accompanying my University Professorship more than covered the costs of doing the Cushing biography.

In early November 1999, the day after a splendid launch party for *Osler* at Massey College, and conscious of the symbolism, I began work on new reels of Cushing microfilm. Hoping to plunge instantly into the inner secrets of Harvey Cushing's family, I had chosen a reel that the collection's finding aid indicated contained intimate family correspondence. "To my surprise, consternation, and a host of other feelings," I wrote in my diary, "I find the files are full of letters to Kate Cushing from Willie and Grace Osler — the master collection of such material. Shit. Day after the launch party, day after publication of the U.S. edition, and I discover documents I could have/should have had and completely missed!" Luckily, the new letters only added more detail to the understanding I had already reached of the Oslers' lives, and would not have materially changed the biography. At the next meeting of the American Osler Society I explained what had happened and gave an update paper, "New News from Norham Gardens: Grace Osler's Letters to Kate Cushing." which was soon published. My later Cushing research also served to reinforce the judgments of the Osler biography, particularly in the evidence I kept finding of unqualified love and admiration for Osler.

It was hard to get going on Cushing because of the press of university and media obligations. The conflict between teaching and the activities of a public intellectual on the one hand, and my desire to become a "hermit scholar of neurosurgery" on the other, never did end. But my light teaching load and relative lack of outside commitments (except to give talks on Osler, insulin, sometimes Osler and insulin), gradually made it possible to hit my stride with Cushing in 2001. Teach a seminar, lunch at Massey, talk to a journalist, three hours at the microfilm reader.

I was well enough into Harvey's life via his own papers to begin broadening the research by checking subsidary collections at Yale. In several weeks of intense archival work in New Haven that spring I struck pure gold. Both Cushing's personal secretary, a literate Smith College graduate named Madeline Stanton, and his protégé and first biographer, the neurophysiologist John Fulton, had also kept their personal papers, including massive diaries. These were available and completely unmined at Yale. And what rich and fascinating collections they were — not only Stanton's personal diaries of daily life with "the Chief" and his "harem" of support staff, not only Fulton's notes and correspondence about Cushing, but also a remarkable story of Fulton's seduction of Miss Stanton, his personal descent into alcoholism, and her survival after all the men had died to become the much-beloved custodian of Yale's great Medical Historical Library. By his own admission, John Fulton, the fair-haired golden boy of American medical research at Yale in the 1930s, had written Harvey Cushing's first biography in something like an alcoholic haze. Stanton and other Cushing secretaries had virtually held his pen. Then Fulton had finished his self-destruction.

The image that occurred to me of John Fulton as a kind of F. Scott Fitzgerald of American medicine was beautifully buttressed by the fact that Fulton had come from the same city, St. Paul, Minnesota, as Fitzgerald, that his father had been the Fitzgerald family's physician, and that, for a time, the two families had lived on the same street. Small circles: at Yale in the 1930s one of Fulton's neighbours and friends had been Thornton Wilder — who might well have seen the retired brain surgeon, Harvey Cushing, playing croquet on Fulton's lawn while fireflies lit the night air and his children urged him to come home for dinner.

The Stanton and Fulton papers supplied the raw data for a true jazz-age story of clashing ambitions, tough and lonely women, tough and fragile men, operating room dramas, and barrels and barrels of booze (some of it brought to New Haven in 1929 by one of Cushing's former students, Ken McKenzie, the first Canadian neurosurgeon; Miss Stanton noted that the gin he brought down for Cushing's sixtieth birthday party took the finish off furniture). There were layers of tragedy: nothing had ever been written of the circumstances surrounding the death of Cushing's first-born son, William Harvey Cushing, in a car accident in 1926. An hour's search of the New Haven newspapers in the

Sterling Library gave me all the details of a sensational tragedy — Bill Cushing's joyride with local floozies to celebrate the end of exams at Yale, the missed curve on the Boston Post Road, the wreck of the borrowed Willis Ste. Clair roadster, four bodies reeking of alcohol. Miss Stanton's papers described how completely the nearly broken Cushing family closed ranks and kept on going.

As with Osler and my other biographies, I only approached descendents after having committed to the project. A friend from the American Osler Society and president of the New York Academy of Medicine, Jerome Barondess, introduced me to Kate Whitney, the granddaughter of Harvey Cushing who was most interested in the family's history. Kate's mother had been Betsy Cushing, her father Jimmy Roosevelt, the eldest son of Franklin D. Roosevelt. When Betsy divorced the philandering Jimmy and remarried Jock Whitney, Kate and her sister Sara had been adopted as Whitneys. Kate had inherited the Cushing family papers from her mother, along with a great personal fortune.

I did not know what to expect when I first met this granddaughter of Harvey Cushing and FDR for lunch at an Upper East Side deli. Kate was gracious and friendly, unpretentious but curious about the family history, her soft voice infused with lilting good humour. A relatively private person, at least compared with her mother and her aunts Mary and Barbara (Mary had married Vincent Astor, Barbara had been better known as best-dressed socialite Babe Paley), Kate decided I was fair-minded and that she would make available to me her mother's and grandmother's papers.

In the autumn of 2001, I had one of the best weeks of research ever, going through boxes of intimate Cushing family correspondence in Kate Cushing's spare Manhattan apartment above her office. Kate's only conditions for the use of her material were that I must tell her if I found anything really scandalous in the collection and that I tell her my food preferences so she could stock the apartment's kitchen for my meals. I duly showed her the viciously anti-Semitic comment in a letter written by her great-grandmother, Sara Delano Roosevelt (who had never been a Cushing family favourite, having remarked to Betsy, "I understand your father is a surgeon. Surgeons always remind me of my butcher"), and I spent every minute of my time with the documents except for an hour's visit to Ground Zero, the wreckage of the World Trade Center. There was also a memorable dinner with Kate and her sister, Sara Wilford, as they reminisced about their two sets of grandparents — was it at the inauguration in 1936 or 1940 that they had such fun sliding down banisters in the White House?

If the Stanton, Fulton, and Whitney-Cushing papers put beautifully marbled flesh on the bones of Harvey Cushing's life, the heart of the matter, as it were, remained his achievements as the founder of effective brain surgery and a pioneer of endocrinology. My first and greatest challenge was to understand and then explain and assess in intelligible prose Harvey Cushing's role in the history of medicine. I knew there would be months of slogging through his hundreds of publications about his work (beautifully organized on the microfilm), but more than with any other of my projects I also knew that I needed to see the real thing. I had no idea what a neurosurgical operating room even looked like, let alone what happened during an operation.

So they showed me. Mark Bernstein, chief of neurosurgery at our University Health Network, invited me to come in early one morning in March 2001 to observe him operate on a seventy-one-year-old patient suffering from a very large tumour, a meningioma that had thrust itself from the brain's lining deep into the brain itself. It was exactly the kind of tumour Harvey Cushing had doggedly pursued — indeed Cushing had coined the word "meningioma."

Everything about the experience — from putting on operating room greens, to cleanliness protocol (no need to scrub so long as I did not touch anything blue, i.e., sterile), to figuring out where to stand — was strange and a little intimidating. A neurosurgical operating room is just a big room full of equipment, with a patient on an operating table at the centre, and nurses, anaesthetists, technicians, and surgeons bustling around. The technology is magnificent — monitors display images of the patient's brain, clearly outlining the tumour. Ironically, the most significant trouble of this whole day came as the team had to apply itself to correcting a malfunction of the operating table. It was like a car full of surgeons having to fix a flat tire.

As the only observer, I could stand very close to the action as the unconscious patient's head was shaved, his skin washed with antiseptic fluid, his face covered, and the instrument table swung over his body. For now he was just a few square inches of exposed flesh. Using a high-lighter, the surgeons outlined where they intended to cut, then stapled blue paper covering over the rest of the scalp. They made an incision with a hot knife, peeled back the scalp, sucking up blood as they went, and applied clamps, sutures, and retractors to keep the skull exposed. From my notes: "Then comes the power drill — and it's exactly that — with Mark complaining about lack of power — as they drill three holes, about ¾" in diameter, creating a triangle along which they then use a power saw to cut out the whole piece of clean yellow bone. It had never occurred to me that there would be bone-dust spilling down the side of the action, just like sawdust."

After removing much more bone, Mark, who is Jewish, and his Arab resident, Mubarrick, cut into the brain's lining, the dura, "and Mark makes a production for me out of finally exposing the great organ, the brain." They retracted the dura and began probing into the brain tissue for the tumour, checking their progress against a surgical navigation guide hooked to a monitor. When they finally reached the tumour — the journey had taken about three hours — they swung a powerful magnifying lens over the operating field for better visibility during the next stage. A built-in television camera showed the scene on a monitor.

The surgeons then began to dissect the tumour away from the brain — a delicate process of teasing their way through or around blood vessels, nerves, healthy tissue, tumour tissue, cutting, severing, sopping, sucking, and cauterizing as they went. It took several hours, during which another resident spelled Mark off while he kept an appointment with another patient. One of the O.R. nurses took me to the cafeteria for a lunch break. When the surgeons had finally cut away most of the blood supply from the tumourous tissue they began removing pieces of it with their "tumour grabber," a set of flat-plated forceps. More hours of careful, painstaking work. Bernstein kept up a running commentary on how Cushing would have proceeded eighty years earlier. He would have had no diagnostic or navigational imaging, no magnification, and only primitive suction devices to combat bleeding.

"From the first I've been thinking that what I'm doing is having my first flight preparatory to writing about flying — except that I'm on a jet plane and will be writing about the Wright Brothers — or in Cushing's case perhaps the Wrights to Lindbergh." I gradually realized that the image was wrong, because modern pilots can put the plane on auto and take naps. These surgeons were still using all the old skills. When I commented on the aviation analogy, Mark thought the better metaphor was mountain climbing — even with vastly improved technology, the surgeon still couldn't afford to make one slip.

Mark had thought that after a few hours I might have seen enough and would want to call it a day. "I decided to stay to the end," I wrote a few hours later, "to achieve 'closure' on the day, as Mark puts it." Once the tumour was gone, the problem was to back out — remove sponges and pledgets, cauterize bleeding points, irrigate at every step. It was a bloodier business than I had expected, and even the floor got messy as the hours went by. When they were finally ready to exit, the surgeons stitched the dura closed, and went to work replacing the bone they had removed. "This is astonishing — they take the pieces of skull and some tiny plates and drill holes and plate the bones back in using screws — almost like a Meccano set. The scalp is rolled back down and stitched back together using first deep sutures à la Cushing and then using a lot of stainless steel staples with their staple guns. The whole operation is the oddest mix of drilling and screwing and stapling with the most delicate artistic deep brain dissecting."

It had taken nine hours. Bernstein, who I later learned was impressed that I had stayed through it all, commented that I must have found it a fatiguing day. "What about you?" I asked. "Aren't you drained?" "Yes, of course. You spend nine hours concentrating on procedures that could kill a person if you slip once and you're bound to be drained." Bernstein, an intense, hard-driving man, thought he worked as long as or longer in a week than Harvey Cushing did, perhaps ninety to a hundred hours, but doubted he could stand operating more than two days a week. He was astonished to learn that Cushing did an operation a day, six days out of seven.

Some months later, I was back in the O.R. to watch two surgeons do a "tag-team" procedure to locate and remove an acoustic tumour (arising from the acoustic nerve, toward the rear of the brain), another of the growths Cushing had been the first to attack. Again, I took extensive notes, marvelling at the use of "fat grafts" to fill the literal hole made in the patient's head, at the use of bone wax, the use of bits of muscle and flesh to staunch bleeding, reliance on the modern-day electric scalpel or "Blue Wazoo," and the smell of burnt flesh it sometimes creates.

During these long operations — this one took nine-and-a-half hours — some neurosurgeons have music playing in the background and some of them chatter constantly about wine tastings, motorcycles, family. They made a point of introducing me to O.R. lore — stories from the bad old days when high-strung surgeons threw instruments, kicked residents, reduced nurses to tears with their profanity and sarcasm. Nobody gets away with this anymore and most surgeons make a point of handling stress carefully. I only saw a few quietly tense periods when no one spoke — much like the atmosphere when Cushing operated. One of the surgeons told me as he worked that the old mystique of brain surgery was passé; he treated his job as a trade, something like plumbing. I could understand this intellectually, but came away from these operations — and several more that I was privileged to observe — awestruck at having seen wonders of modern surgery. They were mountaintop experiences, recorded in great detail in my diaries (I also kept my anti-bone dust goggles as a souvenir), and they had the effect of redoubling my determination to make the Cushing biography the best book I could possibly write.

So did most of my other contacts with neurosurgeons, an intimidating group in the abstract, in real life immensely friendly and interesting. I told everyone about my project, made contact with the neurosurgeons interested in the history of their specialty, and in the spring of 2001 was invited to speak at the annual dinner of the History of Neurosurgery Section of the American Association of Neurological Surgeons, which had originated as the Harvey Cushing Society. The event was in Toronto. Liz came with me, and on the way listened to my anxieties about describing my project to an audience like this. There was no need to worry. Most had read and liked my *Osler*; most were delighted that a professional historian cared enough about their specialty to write about its founder. The group gave me a standing ovation before I had said a single word, and a second standing ovation when I had finished. I wasn't drinking that night, but Liz wondered if I was flying too high to drive home.

As with Osler, the early months of dogged slogging through what seemed like endless files of correspondence gradually gave way to a realization that I had covered a lot of ground and could begin to step up the pace. My raw material was wonderfully rich; I had the old *Insulin* feeling that if this project failed the fault would only be mine.

I began drafting the first chapter of the Cushing biography at Hazeldean in July 2001. The first half of it was mostly written on peaceful summer days on the island — nocturnal tranquility marred by dreams of Harvey Cushing drilling into my skull, taking out tumours, doing subtemporal decompressions. Every chapter of the Cushing biography was as intricate and complex as anything I had done. Many days I would notice that the coffee on my desk was going untouched, a sign of total immersion and ingestion of real intellectual caffeine. At Yale the archival research had been so exciting that I almost scalded myself trying to shorten my coffee breaks.

Often I had to be researching as I wrote. The magic of microfilm made it possible for me to access the whole of the Harvey Cushing papers in my dormer alcove in an old farmhouse on Prince Edward Island. This led to a startling archival adventure on a lazy Saturday afternoon in July:

> Around 4, despite being depressed and vaguely anxious about nothing, I tried a couple of hours on Harvey, just

to get in a bit on a weekend. Cruising along desultorily through the mfm of his Collected Reprints, and articles of no lasting importance, when I realize that I'm looking at a strange drawing of a man's backside, a view up the anus as it were, and notice that it's signed by Max Brödel, and said to be a view of HC's backside!

Gradually realize I've stumbled across one of the more remarkable illustrations in the history of modern biography — it appears that HC decided in writing an article on an appearance of herpes zoster, that he needed an adult equivalent of the embryonic position to show parallels in nerve development, and to show Brödel what he wanted he posed for him. Then he stashed away B's original in his reprint of the article … and never looked at it again. But there it is — "the other side of Harvey Cushing," as it were, something much more than a warts and all view of my man.

Tomorrow I'll call Yale and see if they can find the original [it only took them ten minutes] — and begin to get it photoed … What fun I'll have in my talks.

Still mulling over that discovery when the Deacons arrived for our dinner party, followed by the Dirks. Liz had gone all out to put on an elegant country evening at Hazeldean....

The fact that I was writing a book about the United States paralleled and then undoubtedly interacted with and reinforced discontent I was once again feeling about the condition of Canada.

With a reduced teaching load, I continued to write about the state of the country and the national political scene, in fact, had something of a punditing second wind in the new *National Post*. The end of the twentieth century seemed a dreary time in Canadian history. The Liberal government of Jean Chrétien drifted along without effective opposition, buying the support of client groups with grants, subsidies, and other kinds of favours. Our health-care system, the darling of nationalists and leftist ideologues, was visibly deteriorating and most politicians were simply lying about it, often while trading in witless anti-Americanism. Aside from disliking Americans, Canadians seemed to have no national vision. Quebec carried on with its game of sulking and blackmail, the west felt estranged, the Maritime provinces — especially Prince Edward Island, where I had a ringside seat — shamelessly milked Ottawa for every cent they could get.

No politician on the national scene had come close to taking up the mantle of Trudeau. The Reform party had fizzled. Cynicism and corruption continued to be endemic in Ottawa. My commentary on political developments gradually became more critical and pessimistic as I realized how far short we fell of democratic ideals. Privately, I began meditating, somewhat as I had in the 1980s, on whether Canada was a hopelessly minor-league country, especially compared to the wonderfully dynamic republic where *Cushing* was set, that my family had come from, that gave the world modern democracy, and whose culture I had absorbed since early days in Kingsville. Like many business leaders and some intellectuals, I had hoped that Canada–U.S. free trade might lead to more integration of the two countries. This was not happening either.

At the beginning of the new millennium, in the summer of 2000, I fretted that the Canada I had grown up in and had high hopes for — right from my first public speech in 1951 — was passing away. Pierre Trudeau was dying, as were some of my most respected Canadian friends, the writer Hugh Hood, and our university's great humanist president, Claude Bissell. A certain kind of "Canadian style," never more than partly actualized, seemed to be passing away. My private thoughts were more confused than my usually confident journalism, and more gloomy. I thought that my Canada, a lovely marriage of the best of British and American cultures, was largely disappearing.

On the morning of September 11, 2001, I was reading in my study when Liz phoned from her mother's house to tell me that the media were reporting a terrorist attack on the United States. Like everyone else, I was glued to the television for several days, mourning thousands of innocent people murdered by barbaric fanatics, wondering if our world had changed forever (in the *National Post* I dissented from orthodoxy in suggesting that it had not, that these terrorists were incredibly lucky and that repetition was unlikely). In the aftermath of 9/11 I became more convinced of the need for continental integration, more pessimistic about Canada's destiny as anything but a northern suburb of the United States. Increasingly, in my journalism and in talks about Canada's future, I began to wonder if our best course would not lie in the closest possible relationship with the United States, not ruling out political union.

Almost immediately, I began having second thoughts. While I supported George Bush's war on terrorism, and hoped that Canada would do its bit, the build-up of American hostility to Saddam Hussein's dictatorship in Iraq seemed fraught with peril. I could see a mess like Vietnam developing all over again. The spirit of moral crusading that was being mobilized to mask the invasion of an independent country reminded me of the cover stories for NATO's attacks on Serbia over Kosovo. Righteous idealists, I thought, should never be trusted with guns. On the other hand, that applied in spades to Islamic fundamentalists, and the prospect of Iraq developing weapons of mass destruction seemed to be almost convincing justification for taking out Hussein. In my diary, I wrote in February 2003, that about 35 percent of the time I thought the Bush people were right, about 65 percent of the time I thought they were insane in their policies. Almost paralyzed by conflicting concerns, I wrote almost nothing about the Iraq war except a letter in the *National Post* in which I worried that the Americans might not understand what a mess they were creating.

When invading Iraq proved to be an essential part of the neo-conservative agenda, I realized it was not for me. Nor were many other elements of the new conservatism, which at close scrutiny seemed to cloak limitless economic selfishness as surely as the left's moral libertarianism rationalized hedonism. The certainties and company of the rich and doctrinairely conservative, who often turned out to be surprisingly sour and selfish people, no more appealed to me than the certainties and company of doctrinaire Liberals or New Democrats. Writing about Harvey Cushing's neo-Puritanism heightened my sense of being also in that tradition (the New England Blisses had been Puritans, like the Cushings) and fostered estrangement from the crassness of American materialism and the crudity of popular culture.

There was also the possibility that my gloominess and pessimism partly reflected growing old. I worried that I might be changing into a grumpy old man, ranting against the present while imagining that things had been much better in my youth. Aging minds are prone to that bad habit, as are aging historians. As our lives drift toward inevitable calamity we tend to project our physical and mental decline on the world around us. I did not want to seem disaffected or embittered. Jack Granatstein and I often talked about not wanting to become lugubrious Cassandras like Donald Creighton in his old age. While always able to hold my own in bitching sessions, I was actually very happy with life in Toronto and Canada at the beginning of the new millennium. We might be a minor-league Mickey Mouse sort of a country in some respects. In many others, ranging from the tolerant pluralism of the new Canada through almost all aspects of a senior professor's personal situation, life was good and rich and rewarding.

As I entered my sixties, it more often began to occur to me that perhaps it was time to leave the "Canada watch" to next generation public intellectuals like Andrew Coyne, Rudyard Griffith, and Bill Robson, who had fresh ideas and a fresh outlook and razor-sharp minds to grind newer axes. Perhaps it was time to begin thinking about moving to the pleasures of retirement.

At times life seemed to be just one speech after another — Osler, insulin, Canada, politics, Cushing-in-progress, and the wonderful privilege of saying whatever I wanted to graduates of McMaster, McGill, and the University of British Columbia. The Osler biography and a sense of responsibility as a University Professor and all-purpose public intellectual (not the same, surely as intellectual dilettante, though sometimes hard to differentiate) meant many more invitations to speak to alumni and other local groups.

Requests for talks about the coming of insulin had never completely dried up, so I could still keep a watching brief on the changing world of diabetes. The giant drug company, Pfizer, used me as a speaker on two occasions at launches of clinical trials of what they hoped would be a revolutionary new way to deliver insulin, by inhalation into the lungs. If it worked this would be the first breakthrough in insulin delivery since 1922. Pfizer finally got regulatory approval for their inhaled insulin. In October 2005, I spoke in Montreal at the Canadian launch of Pfizer-Aventis's Exubera. I noticed the product managers were warning the sales force that the American experience was proving it a hard sell. Three weeks later the Americans pulled Exubera from the market; the Canadian product lasted only days longer. Unsalable and then found to be unsafe, inhaled insulin goes down in medical history as a kind of Edsel drug, a cautionary tale of therapeutic misjudgment costing hundreds of millions — including a few speaking fees for Professor Bliss.

The diabetes world became suddenly agog in the early twenty-first century with news that a team at the University of Alberta in Edmonton had apparently perfected transplanting of healthy pancreatic islet cells. Human diabetics, it seemed, could have their body's ability to produce insulin restored, and could throw away their needles and insulin pumps. I was invited to speak to the Shapiro-Rajotte team in Edmonton and inscribe copies of my books with the hope that they were writing a final chapter in the history of diabetes. Then I spoke at the National Institutes of Health in Bethesda, where transplant surgeons bent my ear with explanations of the problems of the "Edmonton protocol," particularly the danger of being overly optimistic about short-term favourable results. In the years since I had published *The Discovery of Insulin* the hope for a cure for diabetes continued to prove as elusive as the sign in bars offering "Free Beer Tomorrow."

In 2002, the diabetes unit at Eli Lilly and Company in Indianapolis discovered that I was still alive and available to give talks. Soon I was in as much demand as ever, often sponsored by Lilly, often speaking to groups I had addressed ten or fifteen years earlier. Novo-Nordisk also occasionally asked me to speak, most spectacularly in Vienna in 2005, at the conclusion of a big endocrine symposium they sponsored. The venue was a cavernous ballroom festooned with nymphs and cherubs and gilt in the Hofburg Palace. Liz said I was more nervous before the speech than she had seen me in twenty years. Immediately after I spoke the meeting was brought to a conclusion with a concert by the Vienna Boys Choir.

There were other opportunities. In 2002, I joined the Board of Associated Medical Services, the foundation that had supported history of medicine activities through the Hannah Institute and other programs.

Just before his death, the larger-than-life businessman Izzy Asper ran into me at a conference and decided I should sit on the jury choosing the design for the Canadian Human Rights Museum that his family was pushing to have built in Winnipeg. In several intense meetings in 2004, a group of distinguished architects and experts, plus Robert Fulford and Michael Bliss, finally settled on a spectacular proposal by the American architect Antoine Predock — which then had to be put on ice while the Asper children learned more about the black arts of political lobbying. The Paul Martin government refused to honour Jean Chrétien's verbal promise to Izzy of a seventy million dollar subsidy for the project. The project inched ahead as the Aspers gradually found new political and philanthropic friends.

Because of my media visibility — radio and TV appearances were beginning to fall off, but the *National Post* often gave my commentaries front page space — it was assumed that I shared the obsessions of the political chattering class. In fact, I did not much like the endless yadda-yadda of political talk, especially the inanities spouted by political partisans. I disliked the way that friends and colleagues assumed that politics was my default conversation topic, and only occasionally gave talks about Canadian politics to meetings and conferences. I had no interest, for example, in being on the circuits catered to by speakers' bureaus.

Still, I kept a hand in and in 2003 was happy to accept an invitation to participate in the Rolls-Royce of political conferences, an international Ditchley Foundation gathering at the great Ditchley Park estate in Oxfordshire, England. I went through all the motions of being a good participant, but privately thought the level of discussion, mostly monopolized by British Labour Party policy wonks, was not particularly impressive. The most interesting attendee at the conference, who had actually done something about the democratic deficit by creating a new and important political party, was another Canadian, Preston Manning. The insular Brits paid little attention to him. Preston was my candidate for the best prime minister Canada never had.

On campus, although I had stopped taking new doctoral students I tried to contribute during what would probably be my last years as a member of the History Department. Sometimes the dreariness of our procedures could be interesting — as when we tried to hire the high-flying public intellectual Michael Ignatieff for one of the super-chairs endowed by Hal Jackman, a great patron of the University of Toronto. I had mixed feelings about our wooing Ignatieff — in November 2000 I told my diary that "I think he's a shallow, superficial star, possibly burning out after early flaming, but there are hardly any others around — right now, like it or not, Ignatieff is about the only game in town — so we should go for it." Negotiations with Ignatieff were weird, we were told, because he was the only academic anyone had ever seen who bargained for a university appointment through an agent, the prominent entertainment lawyer Michael Levine. Ignatieff finally turned us down. A few years later he came back to Canada and then fell into the leadership of the Liberal Party, after which he found the University of Toronto not so unattractive.

The history profession and Toronto's History Department had changed so drastically over the years that no amount of effort made me feel at home in the corridors of Sidney Smith Hall. I did not know many of my younger colleagues. Old friends like Paul Rutherford and Bob Bothwell had largely withdrawn into different academic worlds and social circles. Many of the best historians of my generation, such as Michael Marrus, had developed other loyalties within the university. Ned

Shorter, arguably still the most distinguished historian at the University of Toronto, now lived in LaCrosse, Wisconsin. Ned commuted to Toronto to give his classes at the church. He had not physically set foot in the History Department for about twenty-five years.

By the winter of 2002–03 the idea of fading completely from the university was high on my agenda. At sixty-two, and forty years since I had first begun teaching high school students, I realized I had lost interest in teaching either graduates or undergraduates. I could still do it easily enough, the students were pleasant and sometimes quite interesting, but I found myself dreading every class. The very short periods of intellectual fatigue and emotional depression I had sometimes felt became more common and I began to feel qualms of non-confidence. It became a chore to attend other academic events, even at Massey.

The exception was a series of University Professors' luncheons that President Robert Birgeneau held, and at which I felt dazzled and more than a little out of my depth in the company of the very best minds in the university. Most were scientists. Birgenau, a Canadian-born physicist who had come back to us from M.I.T. and would soon leave for Berkeley, seemed to enjoy their company. Perhaps it distracted him from the endless friction his presidency was generating, including much gossip about shouting matches and ultimata at the highest levels of the university. At our sedate luncheons, however, academic harmony was only jarred by distinguished scientists' complaints about having to retire too early on too small pensions. "I think I'm the only person in this room," I said at one luncheon, "who is looking forward to retirement and will be satisfied with my pension. Of course I don't need lab space or research grants."

My one remaining goal was to finish the Cushing biography. At about the halfway point in the writing I had drawn up a prospectus, which I gave to my Osler publishers, Oxford and the University of Toronto Press. In March 2003, we signed contracts for the Cushing biography, with about the same advances I had had for Osler. On the day I signed the Cushing contracts I also won an auction on eBay to buy a slide of William Osler's brain tissue. If was offered by a second-hand book dealer I had mentioned in the Osler biography in my discussion of the fate of the brain. I paid about $1,400 for my little bit of Osler's brain and promptly made most of that back by writing a feature story about it for the *National Post*. I knew that my relic, better than anything the Vatican had, would be a highlight of many talks on Osler and Cushing. It rests inconspicuously on a shelf in my study in a little Glenfiddich tin.

As I began the Cushing backstretch, I still had an appetite for long days at the computer, though even they were beginning to become fatiguing. In the first six months of 2004 I wrote the final 80,000 words of the first draft of the Cushing biography. My diaries record day after day of intensely hard grinding, punctuated by exclamations of delight when problems were worked out, relationships fell into place, and Cushing, an egotistical son of a bitch, lived up to his reputation as a surgical genius. March 3, 2004:

> This morning I come into the study at 8.30 in my bathrobe and carry on slogging through Cushing's papers, *seriatim*. At one point I sit back and reflect on this marathon grind — it's long and tiresome and I hope it's worth it. Then, with a kind of mental sigh, I dive into something entitled "Experiences with Orbito-Ethmoidal Osteomata Having Intracranial Complications: With the Report of Four Cases" — have to look up the terms right away, and am rather surprised that he would use this as his presidential address to the American Surgical Association. Then I get into it and am gradually fascinated to realize that I'm reading an absolute masterpiece of a surgeon delineating a new procedure and how he came to understand and do it, after losing two patients. It reads like a detective or an

adventure story, and I found myself caught up in it, and caught up in the wonder of doing medical history — to come across this masterpiece from 1927, this example of my subject at his absolutely best and most characteristic. One of those mountain-top moments for an historian, that turned a dreary morning into something like intellectual adventuring.

A few days later, as I read correspondence describing a desperate attempt to save a patient's life in Cushing's operating room in 1911, I was so engaged that cold shivers went up and down my spine — chills of historical time travelling. The notion of the historian as time traveller, while not an image I have stressed in these pages, often occurred to me, for reasons both profound — the idea of the present as unintelligible without an understanding of how it is made by and contains the past, a view I shared with Hugh Hood — and emotional — a sense I often had of actually being able to move through time, witness people and events of other eras, get to know these friends and their lives as though I lived with them. It's a wonderful sense of liberation and freedom, which many historians feel. We're privileged to live much longer lives that way.

With only one chapter left to draft I spent most of the summer of 2004 correcting, revising, and polishing the manuscript. There was still mop-up research to be done in Baltimore, Cleveland, and Boston. My visit to the Johns Hopkins Archives proved extremely disconcerting when, despite being William Osler's biographer, and having been welcomed there before, I was made to feel like an intruder, forced to jump through hurdle after hurdle, including supplying a letter of reference. The Hopkins archivists had been spooked by recent U.S. patient privacy legislation. Yale archivists, by contrast, paid no attention to it. The compensation in Baltimore was being invited to give neurosurgical grand rounds at Johns Hopkins to about sixty of Harvey Cushing's direct professional descendents. The brain surgeons are informal and start early — I presented at 7:00 a.m., an hour when neither the Owl of Minerva nor historians' muse Cleo is ever awake.

In Boston there was still a sense of embarrassment that Harvey Cushing, founding chief surgeon at the Peter Bent Brigham hospital, had not gotten on well with Harvard and had exited for Yale on his retirement. I was not asked to present at the Brigham until several years later. The special delight of visiting Cleveland, Cushing's hometown, came when the archivist at the Allen Medical Library said he fully understood my need to see whatever I wanted in the stacks, and that I could spent as long as I needed working in them. As a security precaution, however, he had to lock me *into* the stacks! Hopkins would have preferred to lock everyone out. The next day, at the archive of Ohio's Western Reserve Historical Society, I was charged a visitor user fee. It was the first I had ever had to pay, a new form of impediment to the archival freedom that had facilitated my research over almost forty years but may never be experienced again by historians.

The last chapter of the Cushing biography was finished in September 2004. On September 19, I exulted about his death in my study and the immediate flood of relief it generated. Two days later, when I opened the file of that chapter on my computer I found it completely blank. Somehow I had accidently erased all that I had written. After the desire to break down in tears and despair had passed, I found an earlier version of a draft of the first two-thirds of the chapter, then put in a twelve-hour day recreating the final four thousand words. "It's as though I had broken the tape after the marathon, collapsed, and been told that there was a mistake and I have to run another lap. You have to get up and do it, but the pain is excruciating and now there is no joy."

In fact there was joy, and the analogy was wrong. As with my other books, I broke one tape after another — when finishing touches were added, readers reported, editors edited, corrections were made, and the last new material was added. The manuscript was delivered to the publishers a month early.

The page proofs were being read for final corrections in March 2005, when Ian McEwan's novel, *Saturday*, a fictional recreation of a day in the life of brain surgeon Henry Perowne, appeared to great fanfare. I bought a copy right away, read it, and was not impressed. McEwan had done his homework in O.R.s, but I thought his technical descriptions were stilted. More significant, he had plotting problems. "McEwan's effort seems to me to fall apart in the last half, as it becomes melodramatic, fantastic, almost silly — certainly losing believability. At the end of the book I had an immense sense of an opportunity missed, of a failure. Very disappointing, though I suppose it means that it isn't going to be the classic of neurosurgery. I had considered adding a kind of homage to McEwan in the final corrections — mention Henry Perowne's operating room music in my last paragraph, but I don't think I'll do it, for I think my book will outlive his."

Liz Bliss found this judgment a telling comment on the egotism of writers. From time to time during the project she had warned me that I was in danger of becoming too much like Cushing, a driven workaholic. As I made the really good and detailed index for the book, a job that almost all authors now leave their publishers to organize (who then do it badly), I thought that I did relate to Harvey Cushing's perfectionism and attention to detail. Only one editor ever noticed, and did not comprehend, how I had paid homage to surgery by giving the book an "Opening" and a "Closing" rather than an Introduction and Conclusion.

My first copy of *Harvey Cushing: A Life in Surgery* came to me at Hazeldean that August. I examined and hugged my new child, decided that its contents and design were both excellent, and thought about how my mother had instilled a tremendous need to prove ourselves in her sons. Perhaps I didn't need to prove myself any more times. I particularly liked the last sentence of the book, Harvey Cushing's comment in homage to his predecessors, "What has been accomplished does not die."

Launch parties were becoming rare occurrences in Canadian publishing. *Cushing* never had a Canadian launch. But that September it was doubly launched at a meeting of the Oxford University Medical Alumnae, celebrating the centenary of Osler's coming to Oxford, and then at a

Cushing family reunion hosted by Yale's Department of Neurosurgery to publicize its plans to display the Harvey Cushing Brain Tumor Registry (Cushing's magnificent collection of specimens and photographs that had been hidden for years in basement storage). Both events were beautifully organized. Liz was with me as I signed piles of books, as we dined with the Oxford doctors in the splendour of Christ Church College, as at Yale we met beautiful Cushing women and men who were young, middle-aged, and sexagenarian incarnations of Harvey himself. At the Oxford reunion I talked about Osler's humanism, and at the Yale reunion I talked to the Cushings about how their grandfather/great-grandfather/ great-great-grandfather had thought his work was more important than his family, and how that had caused heartbreak and estrangement.

At Oxford, we met for the first time a Toronto neurosurgeon, Harley Smyth, one of whose specialties was attacking the basophilic tumours of the pituitary gland that Cushing, in another stroke of genius just at the end of his career, had identified as a sometimes cause of a syndrome that immediately came to be named after him. When we were back in Toronto, Harley called me up to wonder if I would like to see him operate to remove the tumour in a case suspected to be Cushing's disease. Because the pituitary gland sits at the bottom of the brain, Cushing had pioneered an approach to it from the front of the face, entering just below the upper lip. I had long wanted to see a transsphenoidal operation for a pituitary tumour, but the opportunity had not arisen while the book was being written.

Harley Smyth's approach was just slightly different from Cushing's. In a four-hour procedure he worked entirely through an entrance in one of the patient's nostrils, made an opening in the sphenoid bone at the bottom of the brain, found and removed tumourous tissue, then backed out and closed. He took me with him to chat with his patient in the recovery room. She was a thirty-five-year-old woman, number 239 in Smyth's series of cases of Cushing's disease. She had given permission for me to observe the operation; later she asked for an inscribed copy of *Harvey Cushing*.

After coffee and a cookie, Smyth had to go back into the operating room and assist another surgeon who was attacking a large pituitary tumour. As I sat and watched the surgeons perform another long and painstaking medical miracle, I could not keep my eyes open. There was truth in the remark a surgeon had made to me that watching them at work would surely be as tedious as their watching me write. I snapped awake when Harley said they were finished. After a while you take these things for granted.

Chapter Sixteen

Retiring

In 2005, the University of Toronto abolished its long-standing policy of requiring that faculty members retire at age sixty-five. From the time I had been hired in 1968 I had assumed I would retire on June 30, 2006. Now I did not have to. I was on my own when it came to one of life's biggest decisions.

Most of my friends thought I would stay on as a respected, productive elder at the University of Toronto. With nothing to push me but my own will, I decided to retire as planned.

After so many years of work I was tired. Tired of teaching; I liked the students as individuals, but found I could no longer muster enthusiasm for the effort involved in running and appraising classes. Tired of research; the fatigue after finishing the Cushing marathon did not lift. I could not imagine finding energy, particularly for out-of-town archival research, to sustain another big project. I was bone-tired of the trivia of academic life — it seemed unthinkable to continue to be involved in grading undergraduate term papers, reading thesis chapters, marking exams, attending stupid meetings, pretending to take long-winded colleagues seriously, being an employee. When I reminded myself how ridiculously minimal my duties had, in fact, become, I realized that if I stayed on I would also feel guilty at being so well compensated for doing very little.

The public intellectual side of life was also of fading interest. It was a bother when journalists interrupted me to ask for background on the trivia of Canadian politics. Why bother with the hard work of writing ephemeral political commentary to tight deadlines? Why give up an afternoon or evening to fight through traffic to a television studio for a few minutes of on-air chatter that no one would remember the next day? Why spend two hours working with CBC or CTV reporters to be given ten seconds of airtime on the news?

I had no serious fear of the transition involved in suddenly having no employer, no job to go to, no phones ringing. Most of the time, I looked forward to switching from public to private intellectual. I rather desperately wanted rest, wanted to be able to take time to smell the roses — which have been particularly abundant at Hazeldean — read new books, linger over lunches, and go to more concerts and plays. I had taken my career very seriously and had found great fulfillment in it, but it had always been work. I always knew there were other attractive and important ways to spend time.

I had largely lost interest in much of the popular culture of the young — either because I was old or because it was meretricious or for both reasons. Our children were long gone and doing well. Lawyers Laura and Jamie had each married lawyers, and were living in Vancouver and Nelson, BC, respectively. Sally was a high school teacher in Toronto, married to a social worker. We had not given much thought or anticipation to becoming grandparents, so when our first two grandchildren arrived, in British Columbia in 2003, both of us were taken a bit by surprise — I suspect many others are — by the intense delight of having children in the family all over again.

I will not pass over grandparenting in a sentence. Having grand-children instantly became one of the most thrilling experiences of our lives. Suddenly there was an exception to the rule that we can't relive the past. Suddenly we could re-experience the delights of parent-ing, the life-fulfilling satisfaction of being involved in helping a new

Grampa, with Kate Bliss.

human being unfold through infancy and childhood. We could have kids again — we could be kids again (the culture of the very young is wonderful) — we could experience those special bonds of unconditional love all over again. Grandparenting is the perfect incarnation of nostalgia, the best of the parenting experience without the sleep deprivation and responsibility. You could go home again, you could replay that championship season. A bonus at the end of life. Cool! At the end of his life William Osler had decided that children were "the only people in life worth talking to." In the presence of an Oxford don he added, "Except an occasional College fellow," but I don't believe he meant it.

Although I had spent my academic life at the University of Toronto, I had never stood still. I had moved on from project to project, subject to subject, and whenever a term of service had expired. I believed that people normally should move on. The thought was sometimes difficult to swallow, but I had not changed my youthful view that oldsters have an obligation to accept their limits, act their age, and turn the stage over to the next generation of players. Osler had said just this when he retired from Johns Hopkins at fifty-six, making jokes about being worn out and useless, but actually moving into another rich and productive stage of life. If Osler could give up the finest job in American medicine to be Regius Professor at Oxford, I thought I could walk away from the University of Toronto to be emeritus historian and grandfather on Bessborough Drive in Leaside and at Hazeldean, Prince Edward Island.

In the spring of 2005 I confirmed my decision to retire the next year. I confirmed my view that it should be a clean break — no hanging around counting cobwebs in an empty office. I began making plans to pack up my books and papers and move home when the clock struck. I stopped writing for the *National Post* and began turning down other work in the media. My final teaching responsibilities would be two seminars in the autumn of 2005, my formal departure would be six months later. I was particularly satisfied that I would be publishing another major academic book in my final year at the university. I like athletes who quit before their skills are gone.

The Cushing launch, plus a host of speaking commitments, on campus and off, made the 2005 fall term as hectic as any I could remember. I managed to fit in the Oxford and Yale events for Cushing, a second trip to Yale to give neurosurgical grand rounds, three public lectures on our campus, one extra classroom appearance (at our business school, the first invitation I had had to speak to students there in thirty-eight years, and twenty years since I had lost interest in business history), a convocation address, and a final out-of-town trip, all without missing a class. I taught two seminars of about fifteen students each, one on modern Canadian political history, the other on the history of health care in Canada. I had taken that teaching mode to what seemed an ideal form, one in which the students were expected to do all the work while the professor, as daughter Laura once put it, sat at the back of the room and looked mean. Students were now sometimes giving PowerPoint presentations in class, and would applaud each other's work (a practice I meanly banned as inhibiting frank feedback). Discussions were lively and collegial, perhaps not as intense as they had been in the 1960s and 1970s.

> December 5, 2005: Last politics seminar. Very weak presentation on Mulroney and free trade, but impossible not to have a good discussion this close to the present. We also had a mock ballot and I found that the 17 students were almost all Liberals and all but one believed the Liberals would win the [upcoming] election. The young women undergrads found Harper scary and sinister. I tried to suggest that he was a paragon of innocence and integrity compared with Martin. I told them, though, that in our family there were 2 Conservative votes and 5 or 6 Liberal, because the Conservatives had let a generational gap grow up. Turning the discussion back to history, we agreed that

411

Mulroney had let Humpty-Dumpty fall off the wall and no one had been able to put it together again — the students agreed that no one on the right seemed to them a credible leader.

Liz came to my final class, a health care seminar discussion of the evolution of Canada's system of health insurance. I introduced her to the students as a special guest, the Ontario minister of health. They saw through it, though by the end of a very lively discussion even Liz had joined in. After both seminars we all walked across Queen's Park to Massey College for lunch. When one of the students asked me why I was retiring if I didn't have to, I said that we did not want to be tied down with teaching obligations when we wanted to see our grandchildren.

My first university lecture had been given at Harvard in 1968. It was a perfect coincidence that after my last class at Toronto I flew to Boston to be a visiting speaker at Harvard's Canada seminar. I gave a carefully prepared paper on failed Canadian dreams to an overflow crowd. "A good feeling to have given this, my omega lecture at Harvard following the alpha lecture in 1968." Just before Christmas I marked thirty undergraduate essays, handed in the grades for my courses, and cancelled my parking permit.

I had vaguely hoped that *Cushing*, arguably my best book, might break out of the mostly medical readership *Osler* had garnered and be recognized as the definitive account of a great American saga. That did not happen. The book received glowing reviews in medical journals, plus extravagant praise from Sherwin Nuland in *The New York Review of Books*, but was not noticed by *The New York Times* or other popular journals. Its constituency was neurosurgical and surgical, plus a substantial sprinkling of medical history buffs, medical students, Osler enthusiasts, and others. It sold better in the United States — where it quickly earned out its advance — than in Canada where there were fewer than two hundred neurosurgeons.

The spring term of 2006 was a kind of phantom retirement, much of it spent cleaning out my office in melancholy solitude. I had a problem with the books I had accumulated over the years, fairly good working libraries in three or four areas of history. With about three thousand books at home clogging every inch of shelf space, I could not possibly add three thousand more books from my office. So I gave about four thousand books away. My old Canadian business history library went to our Rotman School of Management. My library of Canadian history was donated for an Ontario Historical Society Book sale. I kept a basic library of Canadian history as well as most of my medical history, Osler, and Cushing books. A career's accumulation of photocopies, offprints, unclaimed essays, and other detrita were tossed out. I carefully organized and indexed thirty boxes of my correspondence, plus eight boxes of important research notes, that were to join previous donations I had made of personal papers to the University Archives and our Fisher Rare Books Library.

As it became known that I was slipping into retirement, there were a few feelers about other work. I was not interested in new academic responsibilities. When I was asked if I might be interested in being the Conservative candidate in my riding (Don Valley West) in the 2006 Canadian general election (the outcome of which my students proved wrong about), there was no hesitation. I told my diary that after sitting in the press box writing about football for many years, I knew far too much about the game to agree to go down on the field and try to play it. In fact, I was suffering the physical consequences of having played real football years before and of having run so many miles for recreation in the years since. The cartilage in both my knees was so worn out that walking and even standing at lecterns had become very painful. Mainstreeting would have been a double agony, physical and spiritual.

The most lucrative consulting work in medical history in North America has been generated by lawsuits against tobacco companies. Shorter had worked for years for big tobacco. I was approached by lawyers in both the United States and Canada about my willingness to consult and do research on behalf of the companies. I could name my fee. A figure like $400 an hour, for hundreds of hours of my time, would not have raised eyebrows. I had no trouble making up my mind. Intellectually, I fully understood the legitimacy of making expertise available to either side in these lawsuits. As a practical and moral matter, I refused to have anything to do with that work.

Colleagues and former students held several retirement parties for me that June. They were being nicer to me than I deserved, or they were glad to see me go, or both. In my speeches I talked about not wanting to exit from life the way one of my historian friends had — he died in the act of marking an undergraduate essay. I also told the story of the CBC and the expert bellman at the Charlottetown hotel as evidence that neither I nor anyone else is indispensable. When someone commented that I'd soon get angry about some public issue and start writing again, I said that my retirement goal was to become warm and cuddly and content. I talked about Claude Bissell's advice to us in 1958 to become "angular," about Jules the Maoist disrupting my classes, about being the only two-f "Proffessor" in the university according to my Governing Council gavel. The most important things I said at my retirement parties, the hardest to phrase and to get out, were tributes to Liz. I ended my last retirement talk by mentioning how my nervous seminar students, not knowing how to conclude their presentations elegantly and forcefully, would just fizzle out with "I guess that's all I have to say."

After the celebrations, after the last academic duties at the university, after turning in the keys to my office, I had two more talks to give before formally retiring from the staff of the University of Toronto on June 30. Both talks were about the coming of insulin at our university some eighty-five years earlier. The first was to the Board of Directors and senior executives of Eli Lilly and Company, meeting in Toronto. I then flew to Chicago and, on June 27, gave the same talk to nine hundred enthusiastic members of Lilly's insulin sales force. Feeling very tired, I declined invitations to dinner afterward, and had a quiet meal in my hotel room watching *Cinderella Man,* a movie about the life of boxer James J. Braddock.

———————————

We left Toronto on the morning of June 29, 2006, our forty-third wedding anniversary, to drive to Prince Edward Island. We planned to reach the island about midday on the 30th, my last day as an employee of the University of Toronto. We had booked a dinner reservation at one of the island's best restaurants to celebrate our anniversary and retirement. At about 9:30 a.m. on the 30th we were just pulling into Fredericton, New Brunswick, when our cellphone rang. "There's been a fire in your house," a neighbour told us. "And it's serious."

We drove 1,300 kilometres back to Toronto that day, checked into a hotel, and began retirement on July 1, Canada Day, by inspecting charred stinking wreckage inside and outside our Leaside home. During a fierce electrical storm on the 29th, lightning had hit old telephone wires running into the house, causing a surge of electricity that had ignited a plastic fitting, which had smouldered for several hours and then burst into flame. At 5:30 on the morning of the 30th the neighbour who helped look after our house when we are away had noticed flames in an upper bedroom. A handicapped woman with a mental age of about six, she had called her sister, who told her to call the fire department.

Another twenty minutes delay, the fire chief told us, and our whole house would have been destroyed, along with our next-door neighbour's. As it was, we had effectively lost the upper story of our house, and there was water and smoke damage in practically every other room, my study being the lucky exception. It was a sickening experience. Jokes about having been given a message regarding retirement and now being really burnt-out were not comforting.

The good news was that we were fully insured, and, thanks to daughter Sally, an adjuster had been on the scene before the firemen had left. We had lost none of our good furniture, nothing from my study, and only about five hundred books from upstairs bedrooms, mostly our collection of second-rate fiction. After five months of house-sitting for generous friends we were able to move back into a fully restored home without the slightest sign or whiff of fire damage. In fact, we had taken advantage of the opportunity to have improvements made. I considered trying to interest *Toronto Life* magazine in an article about what it's like to have a fire in north Toronto — it's not supposed to happen to the well-to-do — but by the time we moved in again I was mentally and physically exhausted.

The last tradesmen were still doing after-fire repairs when I entered hospital, after a year on a waiting list, to have both of my knees replaced with titanium joints. The operation is another of the great miracles modern health care offers us. As I write this, my artificial knees are completely painless and my mobility is almost unlimited. I cross-country ski in winter and I can even run a few steps to catch a bus. At the time of surgery there were complications, and the recovery was very slow. Liz, who had retired from teaching several years earlier, had also had temporary health problems. The years 2006–07 was our "annus horribilis."

We gradually recovered, regained our balance — in my case literally — and settled into retirement. We had too many roots in Toronto to think seriously about leaving the city, and our rebuilt Leaside home was more attractive to us than any condo. I abandoned my fantasy retirement plan of living in a rambling clapboard house with wraparound porches in a small town in upstate New York, rereading the novels of Richard Russo and Joyce Carol Oates.

We had unlimited time for grandchildren Kate, Michael, Jasmin, and Joseph, who gave us boundless delight. Flying between Toronto and British Columbia and Charlottetown, the Bliss families kept Air Canada in business. Neurosurgeons and diabetics and other medical groups kept me travelling and doing as much speaking as I wanted, with Liz coming to the better venues. There would always be interesting activities in Canadian history — a Beaverbrook colloquium in Fredericton, debates to organize at the ROM, (the "History Wars" series Jack Granatstein and I conceived had remarkable success in reaching a new market for intelligent discussion of historical and public issues), interviews to be done of distinguished Canadian physicians and researchers, prime ministerial reputations to evaluate on TV. In Toronto we had the quiet rhythms of our interests — organizations, the theatre, ladies who lunch and historians who lunch, and whatever else struck our fancy. We soured on the National Ballet when it was captive to James Kudelka's post-modernist solipsisms, and instead became avid supporters of the marvellous Indian River Festival of concerts in St. Mary's Church on Prince Edward Island, a few miles from Hazeldean. Reluctantly, however, we began making plans to prepare for mortality by giving up our little piece of paradise on PEI, and become renters there instead.

I did rest and I did slow down. I got to my desk later in the morning and I no longer felt guilty if I didn't put in an hour or two's work at night or on a sixth day of each week. I indulged my lifelong interest in sports. "What are my three brilliant senior fellows conversing so enthusiastically about?" Master Fraser asked John Dirks, Peter Russell, and myself at Massey College lunch. "Last night's terrific Super Bowl." "Oh."

Unlike colleagues Dirks and Russell, who were whirlwinds of energy on campus and off, I seldom went down to the university, preferring the serenity of my study. An invitation to give the 2008 Joanne Goodman Lectures at the University of Western Ontario became my excuse to write a small book with a grandiose title, *The Making of Modern Medicine*, summarizing my work and thoughts about the modern history of medicine. In some talks, I tried to explore methodological parallels between doing medical history and physicians taking histories or doing post-mortems. We got out a twenty-fifth anniversary edition of *The Discovery of Insulin*, and Montreal film producers made a television documentary based on *Plague*. Whenever there was nothing else to do I worked on this memoir.

I had enough writing projects in mind to keep me at my desk indefinitely doing what I liked best, but had little enthusiasm for the archival research required to do another big scholarly book. I waived the last $10,000 entitlement I had to research funds, which went back to the university. When friends asked me what I was working on I liked to joke about self-plagiarism and the literary menopause. I was shamelessly proud of the scholarship, organization, and goodwill that went into the publication by the University of Toronto Press of a scholarly festschrift, *Essays in Honour of Michael Bliss: Figuring the Social*. Fifteen of my former doctoral students contributed chapters to the book. The three editors, Elsbeth Heaman, Alison Li, and Shelley McKellar, conceived and carried it to publication while all starting families of their own. John Fraser hosted a launch party at Massey College.

I worked hard at becoming mellow and cuddly, and on most days easily sublimated the urge to write letters and columns attacking the wrongs of the world. I stayed active in the American Osler Society, even serving a term as its president. What had been a reasonably pleasant seven years as a director of Associated Medical Services ended badly in 2009, when AMS lost its bearings and decided its new initiatives would be in anything but the field of medical history it had done so much to cultivate in Canada. One result was my abrupt resignation from the board.

It was sometimes difficult to adjust to being off the public stage, and on a few occasions I became angry enough to come out of retirement — to denounce the Harper government's recognition of Quebec as a "nation," to denounce the absurd proposal for a governor-general-induced coup d'état to undo the results of the 2008 election, and to try to warn about the seriousness of the financial collapse. I looked forward to adding Stephen Harper, whom I had met on several occasions (he had been born just up the street from us in Leaside) and always liked, to my prime ministerial profiles in the next new edition of *Right Honourable Men*.

When the University of Toronto made me an honorary doctor of laws in June 2009, a more generous gesture than I deserved and a deeply moving experience, literally the thrill of a lifetime, I used the commencement pulpit to offer moderately controversial remarks about the need for academics to temper their sense of entitlement with

Algonquin Park, September 2009.

greater responsibility in accounting for research grants, the use of sabbaticals, and the granting of tenure. Otherwise, I had little to say that was not occurring to other commentators. As our economic horizons darkened I was more conscious than ever of our ridiculous vanity in thinking we could predict our future. My views about present problems and issues and the future of Canada tended to become less certain and more nuanced, perhaps more concerned about social justice and reform. I could not categorize myself politically. When as an undergraduate looking for reassurance I had tried to explain my confusions to one of my philosophy professors, he had confessed that he too found most issues extremely complicated.

I had trouble sorting out my feeling that we were at the end of an era in public life — a great economic bubble had collapsed, the United States and Europe were on a collision course with financial disaster, the Canadian Liberal Party had collapsed, and the NDP was enjoying hothouse success — with my personal sense of being at or near the end of a career. The future would be shaped by other people, younger people, and that was as it should be. As I suggested to a colleague, we all had a long time to try to change the world before we retired. Maybe after we retired we had a right to just enjoy being in the world.

I felt privileged to have lived in Canada and at a peaceful and prosperous time in the history of the world. I was thankful to have benefited from a lucky roll of genetic dice that seemed to have been loaded against the other members of my family, satisfied that I had gone the distance in a good profession, and more grateful than I could ever say to Liz Bliss for agreeing to unite our lives in marriage. As we have set a new balance in our lives in retirement, I find that I intend to keep on writing, mostly about the past, present, and future of health care — none of which is particularly well understood — and perhaps a little more about the history of my country. When the worst begins to happen, like Osler I will try to be content with having had a good inning.

I guess that's all I have to say.

Index